COSMOPOLITAN THEOLOGY

For *Dean Sunghyun* and *James Jihyun*,
my more than me

I love you and I am smiling at you wherever I may be.
–Jacques Derrida

COSMOPOLITAN THEOLOGY

Reconstituting Planetary Hospitality, Neighbor-Love, and Solidarity in an Uneven World

Namsoon Kang

CHALICE PRESS
ST. LOUIS, MISSOURI

Cover art: Shutterstock
Cover design: Scribe, Inc.

Visit www.chalicepress.com

Print: 9780827205345 EPUB: 9780827205352 EPDF: 9780827205369

**Library of Congress Cataloging in Publication Data
available upon request.**

Printed in the United States of America

Contents

Acknowledgments

To begin at the beginning is to invite oneself to the world of gratitude, interconnectedness, and memory of events and people from the past, present, and future. I realize, however, there is a *double bind* in acknowledgments: *necessity* and *impossibility*. I owe a big "thank you" to so many people around the world. However, it is impossible in this genre called *acknowledgments* for me to list all the names of those countless people in my life journey who kindled and rekindled my passion for this cosmopolitan project. It is frustrating to realize the *impossibility* of showing the gratitude that I owe.

I would like to thank Brad Lyons at Chalice Press for embracing this book project with enthusiasm. I also thank my editor, Gail Stobaugh, for her infinite patience and great advice. I owe a great debt of gratitude to Steven Sherwood at TCU for his astute and meticulous assistance in the preparation of the manuscript; he clarified the content throughout. I would like to express my profound gratitude for the many exchanges that I have had over the years with my students at Brite Divinity School, Texas Christian University. My conversations and seminars with them inspired, motivated, and developed ideas and insights in this work. I must express my deep gratitude to my tireless research assistants—Adam DJ Brett, Sam Castleberry, and especially Robert Kyle Warren for his tremendous work for indexing.

My intellectual-academic debts constitute an indescribable world. I thank the colleagues-friends in different regions of the world whom I have known and worked with through WOCATI (World Conference of Associations of Theological Institutions) since 2002, and who have challenged, motivated, encouraged, and affirmed me in what I think, theorize, act, and judge. The countless encounters with them have helped me see the significance of human *faces* regardless of our differences in theopolitical-philosophical positionalities, doctrinal beliefs, value systems, cultural codes, or sociobiological attributes and orientations. I am deeply grateful to Catherine Keller for her ongoing companionship with me throughout my personal, intellectual, academic journey. My debts to her constitutes an unmappable domain.

Although I finished the manuscript of this book with the current waves of cosmopolitan discourse in mind, I have been thinking and reflecting on these issues for a long time. I revised and expanded bits and pieces of the material here from earlier publications and presentations. In particular, portions of the presentation that I gave at the Transdisciplinary Conference at Drew University in 2007 appeared as "Toward a Cosmopolitan Theology: Constructing Public Theology from the Future" in a Fordham University Press volume edited by Stephen D. Moore and Mayra Rivera, titled *Planetary Loves: Gayatri Spivak, Postcoloniality, and Theology* (2010). I also explored other ideas in my presentation at the annual meeting of the American Academy of Religion in 2010.

In the end, the issues of human identity, our curiosity about one another, our care for one another, and our endless responsibility to one another might matter the most to us all, which one cannot fully comprehend through self-enclosed academic languages.

Namsoon Kang
Fort Worth, Texas, U.S.A., 2013

Preface

This book began as a presentation for the Transdisciplinary Conference in 2007 at Drew University, Madison, New Jersey, USA. It was both a privilege and a joy for me to spend unique time and space with Gayatri Chakravorty Spivak and other wonderful theologians during the conference.[1] I had originally intended to publish only the presentation as one of the chapters in the book from the conference. However, as I began to revise the presentation, I found myself increasingly convinced that I needed to expand the presentation paper into something like the current form.

This book is the result of my conviction that theology is not just a professionalized discourse that offers intellectual insights and pleasure in academia only, although such intellectual joy is also an important part of human life. I believe theology should be about one's way of life, a kind of gaze into oneself and others, and a mode of one's profound existence in the world. Cosmopolitan discourse has deeply intrigued me, primarily because it provides one with a *public gaze* with which one can relate oneself to others in a different way. If we begin to regard all people we meet simply as fellow-humans, fellow-citizens-of-the-cosmos, regardless of their gender, skin color, physical/mental ability, sexual orientation, social class, or citizenship and nationality, it is not hard to imagine what the world would look like. A world in which every individual human being becomes an equal fellow citizen of the *cosmos* may seem impossible to envision. However, I believe that dreaming an *impossible* dream, envisioning a seemingly *impossible* world, is itself the task of theologies and that the disparity between *the world-as-it-is* (reality) and *the world-as-it-ought-to-be* (ideality) is where a *prophetic call* comes in. Acknowledging and trying to narrow down the disparity between reality and ideality requires a passionate commitment to transformation and betterment of the world and the humanity in it.

The primary readers I have in my mind for this book are students—both close and distant students. I wrote this book as if I were talking to my students, who have been the source of my inspiration, insights, passion, and love for the world. They have also served as significant interlocutors who have shaped my sense of responsibility for myself, others, the world, and the Divine. *Amor mundi*—the love for the world—is the greatest lesson that I have learned from teaching and engaging with students in various regions of the world. In this sense, teaching has been a significant redeeming act in my life journey. Through teaching, I have been able to maintain my desire and passion for moving beyond a sense of hopelessness, despair, indifference, or disappointment, and to constantly affirm and rekindle my faith in human beauty and goodness, *in spite of* and *regardless* of who/what one is.

Jacques Derrida (1930-2004) has been one of my significant interlocutors throughout my journey of writing this book. His passion for the *impossibility*, the *unconditionality* of hospitality, friendship, law, and justice has greatly inspired and sustained my work. Derrida, a person of tears and prayers,[2] a compassionate mourner who says, "I mourn therefore I am,"[3] taught me that religion is about radical affirmation of the others and unconditional responsibility for the others.

Every piece of writing, including this one, is always *incomplete* and in the process of birthing another beginning. I completely concur with Roland Barthes, who says, "[T]he author enters into his [*sic*] own death. . .[I]t is languages which speak, not the authors."[4] Like you, I will be a reader of my book, as no one can claim an absolute *authorship* of one's writing. The languages, not the author, speak in the book. As Derrida would say, I *survive* and *live*, and will *survive* and *live* my death in writing.

1

Dreaming *the Impossible:* Thinking, Judging, Acting *Otherwise*

> *Only write here what is impossible, that ought to be the impossible rule.*
>
> —JACQUES DERRIDA[1]

> *"Nothing will be impossible with God."*
>
> —LUKE 1:37

From Metanarratives to Glocalized Narratives

Jean-Francois Lyotard characterizes postmodernity as "incredulity toward metanarratives,"[2] and it is a general condition of the contemporary world. Metanarratives of legitimation and representation are no longer plausible. Where, then, can we find a discourse of legitimation in this postmodern era? According to Lyotard, legitimation becomes plural and local, and an overarching theory for justice comes to lose its political relevance. What he proposes is a "justice of multiplicities."[3] In this postmodern context, what we hold together, according to Lyotard, is the *social bond,* an interwoven thread of discursive practices, but not a single overarching theory that runs throughout the whole.

In this postmodern context, general social categories such as gender, race, class, or sexuality can be too reductive of the complexity of social identities to be effective. Instead of attending to the *localized narrative,* as postmodernists such as Lyotard suggest, I would like to fashion a *glocalized narrative* that vindicates the intersected and interconnected nature between the grand narrative and the small narrative, between the global and the local, while it questions and resists totalizing power and theories that have institutionalized, normativized, and naturalized various forms of social inequality. One of the significant contributions that postmodern discourse has made is its complex, sophisticated, and influential criticisms of foundationalism and essentialism. It is, however, important to maintain a place for *transversally* based relations of imperialistic dominance, oppression, and injustice along the analytical axes of gender, race, class, sexuality, ability, or citizenship, etc. The binary approach to the grand versus small, the universal versus the particular, or the global versus the local makes one incapable of dealing with the complex reality of human life in this contemporary world. The question is not, therefore, *whether* a theory is grand or small, or whether it is universal/global or particular/local, but *what function* a theory plays and *whose interest* it serves. Here, theory/discourse such as cosmopolitanism is not about an abstract world but about the very *worldliness* in Edward Said's sense, a way to engage the public world. Said says about his worldliness: "[W]hat moves me mostly is anger at injustice, an intolerance of oppression, and some fairly unoriginal ideas about freedom and knowledge."[4] In this context, the theories Said produces, for instance, are ways of engaging the public world and movements for transforming the world. Through this book, I want to affirm that thinking and living, knowing and doing, theory and practice intersect. I also want to commit to the theological task of reconciling the binary clash between the two poles that have always existed in human life. Gilles Deleuze articulates theory as *practice* and further contends:

> A theory is exactly like a box of tools. It has nothing to do with the signifier. It must be useful. It must function. And not for itself. If no one uses it...then the theory is worthless or the moment is inappropriate. We don't revise a theory, but construct new ones; we have no choice but to make others....A theory does not totalize; it is an instrument for multiplication and it also multiplies itself. It is in the nature of power to totalize....[5]

Deleuze employs Nietzsche as a *tool* to challenge a dominant philosophical voice today, and Jacque Derrida also uses Nietzsche to deconstruct the logocentrism of Western metaphysics. I find cosmopolitan discourse to be an effective *tool* for theologizing, since it offers a possibility of thinking, judging, and acting *otherwise* in the contemporary world, where neo-imperialism and globalization permeate every sector of life on the globe. A discourse as a *tool* can effectively *function* only if it elaborates the *utopian* urge to think, judge, and act *otherwise*.

One's judgments on the existing reality always come from a utopian reality. Here *utopia* signifies the viewpoint of the ideal but fundamentally realizable, running against a general perception of a utopia as merely an unrealizable dream. Paul Ricoeur rightly illustrates in his engagement with Karl Mannheim's notion of utopia that "a utopia shatters a given order; and it is only when it starts shattering order that it is a utopia. A utopia is then always in the process of being realized."[6] In this sense, the absence of utopia is the death of society because "it would no longer have any project, any prospective goals."[7] A discourse cannot be a mere acceptance of or compliance with the *status quo,* where one experiences a "deep sense of marginality" because one "knows what it is to suffer absolute emotional and intellectual devaluation, to die unfulfilled and still isolated from the world's centre."[8] A *utopian* discourse such as cosmopolitanism can earn its legitimacy only if it provokes and invokes the passion and longing for *the impossible,* the impossibility of ever-enlarging the *decentered center* so that everybody can be the center but no one claims an absolute ownership of the center. Such a *utopian* discourse opens up a new space for transformation by confronting the problem of power and offering an alternative view of the reality that is in between the *world-as-it-is* and the *world-as-it-ought-to-be,* between the *world-of-already* and the *world-of-not-yet.* Ernst Bloch talks about human utopic longing and the function of utopia that "each and every criticism of imperfection, incompleteness, intolerance, and impatience already without a doubt presupposes the conception of, and longing for, a possible perfection."[9] Cosmopolitan discourse involves dreaming of the world that fulfills what is missing or lacking in our reality: It provokes us to dream *the impossible.*

If a discourse can effectively function as a *tool,* it should be neither trapped in the *world-as-it-is* (reality) nor indulged in the naive vision of the *world-as-it-ought-to-be* (ideality). Cosmopolitan discourse provokes us to think about what Derrida calls the "question of a justice to come,"[10] offering the cosmic scope of conviviality, justice, peace, and equality among/between all beings, including both humans and nonhumans. As a reemerging discourse, cosmopolitanism resituates, refashions, and relocates who one is in the world and how one is to be in relation to the other. Therefore, as Gayatri Chakravorty Spivak says, "[T]he production of theory is in fact a very important practice that is *worlding the world* in a certain way."[11] Spivak goes on to say:

> Who speaks and acts? It is always multiplicity, even within the person who speaks and acts....Representation no longer exists; there's only action—theoretical action and practical action which serve as relays and form networks.[12]

Cosmopolitan discourse that captures the spirit of *planetary conviviality* is what we need in our uneven world of power-differential and multiple forms of oppression, *worlding* the world in an altogether different way. One's gender, class, race, age, ability, nationality, sexuality, or religion has been affecting humans' lives in the world in a serious way. The question one comes to ponder in an uneven world follows: Is there a hierarchy among different forms of social oppression in terms of their significance and urgency? How would one's *victim experience* function in one's life? I have learned from my life experience in various regions of the world—i.e., South Korea, Germany, the United Kingdom, and the United States—that all forms of oppression and discrimination play out in different ways and on different levels of reality, and that it is dangerous to establish a *hierarchy of oppressions* among the different forms of oppression. However, people often think that there *is* a *hierarchy of oppressions.* People in advocacy movements for different causes, for instance, often work against each other, claiming the more urgency and significance of their cause over others. They offer different readings of *the signs of our times*. The discursive emergence of cosmopolitanism has led me to encounter deep sociohistorical ironies about what it means to live *our times*.

Reading the *signs of our times* is one of the most significant tasks of theologians. However, the questions of who constitutes *we* and who/what defines *times* in *our times* are complicated to answer. The answers to these questions vary depending on one's *geocultural* location and *socio-politico-ethico-theological* position. The *we* in *our time* has mostly consisted of Euro-U.S., white, middle-class, male, heterosexual Christians with able bodies. I believe decentering this centered *we* is a precondition for, and urgent task of, offering a reading of the *signs of our times*. People ground a desire for *purity* in the process of constructing *we* in the antagonistic dualism of we-they, civilized-primitive, Christian-nonChristian, male-female, abled-disabled, heterosexual-homosexual, Black-White, West-nonWest, and so forth—a process that does not allow the space for in-betweenness, *mestizaje,* hybridity, many-ness, heterogeneity, or beyond-ness. The construction and universalization of the monolithic *we* is the product of modernity in Europe. Given the critical awareness of the role of both Christianity and Enlightenment philosophy in relation to colonialism/imperialism, it may sound odd for me to claim that cosmopolitanism is an effective discourse for constructing contemporary theology today, especially when the genealogy of cosmopolitanism ordinarily lists Immanuel Kant as a key figure for articulating and popularizing it, and scholars have criticized Kant for his Eurocentric, white suprematism and androcentrism.

I do not, however, have a desire for *purity* in any kind of form. After all, humans and their institutions, whether religious or socio-political, do not possess *purity* whatsoever. As Spivak argues, "[I]nvoking any of the so-called great religions of the world" for reaching the internationality of justice might be impossible "because the history of their greatness is too deeply imbricated in the narrative of the ebb and flow of power."[13] Desire for *purity* has resulted in holocaust, crusades, witch burnings, excommunication, and acts of violence in the name of *purifying* and *cleansing* the *impurity*, whether it is racial, ethnic, religious, or sexual. Even seeking a *theoretical purity* sometimes results in picking up "the universal that will give you the power to fight against the other side, and what you are throwing away by doing that is your theoretical purity, while they keep themselves clean by not committing themselves to anything."[14] One of the great lessons of the *history of sin* is the plain truth that virtues and vices are inextricably intertwined, whether in humans or institutions. What I would like to seek for, therefore, is not *purity* but the *possibility* for an alternatively liberative way of perceiving the world and humans in it. Retrieving the cosmopolitan spirit from Immanuel Kant, for instance, does not mean that he is immune to scrutiny for his blind racism, white superiorism, androcentrism, or inherent Eurocentrism. I do not wish to totally abandon a philosophy or a religion simply because it is *polluted* or *impure*. If one looks for a thinker or a theory that is *pure* in the sense that one cannot find any limit, flaw, ignorance, or epistemological blind spot, such a *desire for purity* would leave us with nothing to spare. In this sense, a *blanket judgment* that encourages either a total rejection or a total acceptance of a theory or figure is too naïve and pointless. My desire is to scrutinize the possible *vices* in thinker(s) or discourse(s) and, at the same time, retrieve the *virtues* that may have possibilities to help us widen our perception of the world and get out of our comfort zone so that we can enlarge and complexify our understanding of who we are, what we are capable of, what we ought to envision, or how we are to perceive and to be in solidarity with *others*.

As Michel Foucault claims in his articulation of the "author-function,"[15] one could in fact circulate a discourse such as cosmopolitanism without any need for an *original author*, and the *author* will disappear at the moment it begins to affect one's thinking and acting in one's own context. Cosmopolitanism has offered me an ethical perspective and a conceptual framework with which to read the *signs of our times* as a theologian and intellectual who has a public responsibility for constantly offering a way to engage in this rapidly changing public world. In order to concretize the very spirit of cosmopolitanism as theological norms and practices of global justice, one must start with *provincialization* and *vernacularization* of the universalized monolithic West-centered *we* in *signs of our times,* because cosmopolitanism is to reveal the greatness of *all* humanity, with their differences and similarities. Cosmopolitanism is a defense for a simple commonsensical notion that all beings are equal and therefore deserve rights and dignity in their full sense—both in the private and public, and in the political and religious world.

There is no discourse or utterance that is not *context specific*. One should locate and interpret even a single word that one uses in its own specific context. One day I wrote a quote from Michel Foucault on the board in my class: "Do not ask who I am and do not ask me to remain the same."[16] Without providing my students with the specific context of this quote, I asked them to interpret this line. The responses from students were interesting. Some interpreted the line as if it came from a robber, or from an unfaithful person in an intimate relationship, or from a schizophrenic person. Students could hardly make a connection of this line to the context of a counter-essentialist position in the politics of identity. Without providing my students any context of this single quote, what I was trying to do was to invite them to rethink the significance of the specific context of every utterance and the deferment of our perception of the utterance.

Needless to say, a deferral of the signified and the signifier always exists in human reality, and our attempts to understand something are an endless journey of knowing and understanding the meaning of the signified. If we keep reminding ourselves of the *deferment* of human perception, we can lessen the distortion, misunderstanding, or misinterpretation of the discourse that we engage in. Every adoption of a certain discourse in one's writing would be relevant only when one locates it in a *context-specific* space. My initial interest in cosmopolitan discourse has grown out of my personal and academic struggle with a politics of identity and its theological significance and public relevance. The cosmopolitanism that has interested me is neither about a fancy, disengaged, floating cosmopolitan lifestyle, as many people often perceive, nor about a cosmopolitan culture or politics that mixes everything and makes it ahistorical or apolitical without challenging the normative space of the production of the cosmopolitan culture. The absence of the normative from the scene of the so-called *cosmopolitan culture* is another way of maintaining and reproducing the invisible center that colonizes people's mind.

Beyond Tyranny of Binarism: Theory *Is* Practice

Christian theological discourses have been sources of oppression *and* of liberation or solidarity in the public world. The role of theological discourse in the West is particularly of importance, especially because Christianity has played the role of a *globalizing* oppressor of women, Jews, Moors, pagans, infidels, and heathens. Since the Constantine era, Christianity has played the role of powerful oppressor of *others* through crusades, inquisitions, witch burnings, and holocausts. In order to justify acts of oppression and exclusion, Christianity has produced theological discourses that would offer a sanctioned rationale for such oppression and exclusion. When some people regard the phrase *Christian Europe* as "terrifying,"[17] Christianity as an institutionalized religion needs to undo and move beyond its history of sin by institutionally repenting and theologically amending its great fallacy and wrongdoing. In this sense, we should recognize the significance of theological discourse as public discourse that affects the lives of people in a concrete way. People's participation in the theological discourse can distort or transform their identities and understandings of self, the world, and the Divine. Therefore, theological discourse is neither merely a matter of interpretation of the tradition, the scripture, or doctrines, nor a matter of transmitting inherited religious identities. Theological discourse can be, in and of itself, a form of identity and solidarity. Feminist theological discourse, for example, has transformed identities and established solidarities especially among women. It did not just present the interests of women whose identities they fixed in advance. Feminist theological discourse created both an arena of discourse among women and a stronger voice for women in discourses that were male dominated. The solidarity formed among women and men of conscience had to do with the capacity of this theological discourse to bridge the concerns of personal life and the public institutions and culture.

Theological discourses function in various ways as sites of contestation and resistance, of forming new religious and personal identities, and of building solidarities. Theological discourses that theologians produce, disseminate, and teach in academia are not simply objective interpretations and neutral reflections on the world and the church in it. Instead, theological discourses are productions of and for the world and the church that we live in. Stereotyping theologians and academics as those residing only inside *ivory towers*; bipolarizing theology-ministry, theory-praxis, knowing-doing; or differentiating academism from activism overlooks the significant functions that theological institutions and their theological discourses play for their constituencies, the students they educate, the church in which they interact, and the larger society to which they communicate. Theological discourses are the epistemological ground for educating students of theology who work and will work for the world and the church in it. Theological discourse contributes to the deconstruction of the old and the constant reconstitution of the new religious identities; to new understandings of the self, the world, and the divine; and to a new vision for an alternative world and one's commitment to a more just world. In this context, constructing a new theological discourse such as cosmopolitan theology is not a mere act of producing abstract work for the sake of academism *per se.* Instead, it is a passionate and compassionate way of engaging in the world, of revising the vision for an alternative world, of trying to narrow down the disparity between the *abstract* theory and *concrete* reality. Theological discourses could be the grounds upon which religious practitioners, believers, students, activists, or academics center their practice of belief and their love for the world. Gilles Deleuze says:

> The relationships between theory and practice are far more partial and fragmentary. On one side, a theory is always local and related to a limited field, and it is applied in another sphere, more or less distant from it. The relationship which holds in the application of a theory is never one of resemblance. Moreover, from the moment a theory moves into its proper domain, it begins to encounter obstacles, walls, and blockages which require its relay by another type of discourse....Practice is a set of relays from one theoretical point to another, and theory is a relay from one practice to another. No theory can develop without eventually encountering a wall, and practice is necessary for piercing this wall.[18]

In this context, Foucault rightly points out that "theory does not express, translate, or serve to apply practice: it is practice," though "local and regional."[19] However, neither Deleuze nor Foucault talk about the space in between theory and practice. I entirely agree with Foucault that theory *is* practice and believe that a good theory *is* a good movement that brings about transformation of the world. However, what will happen when theory and its *producer* lack *compassion* and it becomes impersonal? I would argue, therefore, that cosmopolitanism is in a way about the interstice between theory and practice because it offers us a *poetic imagination,* which helps us cultivate the capability of "entering imaginatively into the lives of distant others."[20] Theology/theory/discourse can help us see and build connections and conviviality where they seem hardly plausible. The *poetic imagination* that is in between theory and practice would function by lessening the possibility and danger that theory might reduce others/neighbors to numbers, data, or categories in its practice and implementation. The starting point of the way one can enter into the lives of *distant others* would be cultivating one's view of others as one's own *family,* kin, siblings, or neighbors, which requires a *poetic imagination* that radically connects oneself with *distant others*. We are living in a world of capitalism, technology, and economic globalization, a world that fundamentally repudiates a *poetic imagination* that sees others with great empathy and compassion. But what can a philosophical discourse such as cosmopolitanism offer to the world where people *classify others* merely as numbers and categories and regard the *poetic imagination* as useless? Derrida would respond to these questions as follows:

> All political experimentation....has in it a philosophical dimension. It requires us to interrogate the essence and the history of the state. All political innovation touches on philosophy. The "true" political action always engages with a philosophy. All action, all political decision making, must invent its norm or rule. Such a gesture traverses or implies philosophy.[21]

When *others* become mere numbers within a classification marked by such social traits as citizenship, nationality, skin color, language, religion, sexuality, gender, race, etc., what a philosophical discourse such as cosmopolitanism can do is to transform the perception of others, moving beyond the cruelty of *impersonalization* of others. This transformation of one's perception of the *others* would impact on one's way of voting, of choosing a newspaper, of supporting a radio station, or of electing politicians, for example. To turn one's compassionate gaze onto others as fellow-citizens of the cosmos will allow one to fundamentally refuse reducing neighbors into numbers and to see them as *somebodies,* not as *nobodies*.

The influx of the refugees, the stateless people, the *Heimatlosen,* can be an appropriate example of how *neighbors* can turn into numbers as being *classified* under the sociopolitical category based on the possession of one's citizenship. Hannah Arendt points out that people created the term *displaced persons* during the war to eliminate the issue of the *stateless*. Whereas the term *stateless* recognizes the urgent situation of the persons who lost the protection of the state and the pressing need of preserving their legal status, the term *displaced persons* does not indicate such an urgent need for protection. This nonrecognition of one's *statelessness* mostly means "repatriation, i.e., deportation to a country of origin, which either refuses to recognize the prospective repatriate as a citizen, or on the contrary, urgently wants him [*sic*] back for punishment."[22] Becoming *stateless* persons, the *Heimatlosen,* in a country other than their own would simply mean they have no right to residence or right to work, and always live under threat of deportation. Unless they become a "famous refugee," people reduce them to "anonymous numbers." Therefore,

> [T]he loss of citizenship deprived people not only of protection, but also of all clearly established, officially recognized identity, a

> fact for which their eternal feverish efforts to obtain at least birth certificates from the country that denationalized them was a very exact symbol; one of their problems was solved when they achieved the degree of distinction that will rescue a man [*sic*] from the huge and nameless crowd. Only fame will eventually answer the repeated complaint of refugees of all social strata that "nobody here knows who I am"; and it is true that the chances of the famous refugee are improved just as a dog with a name has a better chance to survive than a stray dog who is just a dog in general.[23]

A discourse such as cosmopolitanism can counter the current systems and policies that often reduce those refugees to anonymous numbers, and reclaim the proper name of those nameless who experience the reality of nobody-knows-who-I-am, regarding them as fellow humans who hold the cosmic citizenship. Certainly, as Jean-Francois Lyotard rightly contends, one's "proper name is a designator of reality," and reality is "a question of the future."[24] It is not surprising that people use numbers, not one's proper name, to identify an inmate of a prison or Nazi concentration camp, which fundamentally denies him or her the human right to freedom. Cosmopolitanism can offer a notion of humanity that goes beyond sociopolitical structures, which provides a ground to reconsider impersonal laws and policies that reduce neighbors to numbers. As a philosophical discourse, cosmopolitanism invites us to rethink our "facile reverence for ontology," and calls upon us to "become responsible for what philosophy essentially is, by welcoming ....the idea of the Other."[25] Cosmopolitanism can therefore be both touchstones and source of inspiration when one uses it to evaluate current policies and gives new sociopolitical and theological shape to planetary hospitality, human rights, justice, neighbor-love, and ecumenism.

Dreaming *the Impossible:* A Prophetic Call

Working on cosmopolitanism was, in a way, too ambitious a project to accomplish—not only because of the range of works that I needed to go through, but more because of the *impossibility* of the utopic idea of *cosmic citizenship*. However, Derrida's *passion for the impossibility* greatly encourages me to write, when he poetically says: "*[O]nly write here what is impossible, that* ought *to be the impossible-rule*."[26] He also emphasizes:

> Go there where you cannot go, to the impossible,
> It is indeed the only way of going or coming.
> To go there where it is possible is not to surrender, rather,
> it is to be already there and to paralyze oneself in the in-decision of the non-event.[27]

The cosmopolitan dream is not just an unrealizable, illusionary dream because it is a *daydream* that one wants to realize in a concrete reality. The intention of such an *impossible* dream is to put into question what currently exists and to transform the current configuration of systems and practices of hospitality, neighbor-love, and justice. In this sense, cosmopolitanism is an *imaginative refashioning* of the nature of religion, the family, citizenship, power, borders, and so on. Cosmopolitanism in our current configuration of the world will remain a constant ideal that we humans will never acquire in its full sense. However, such an *impossible* dream, a view of the ideal, is important because it confronts the problem of power itself, offers an alternative kind of power, and becomes a constant reference for the concrete practices and works toward the ideals of unconditional hospitality, absolute neighbor-love, and planetary ecumenism. The time and space in which I have been working on this cosmopolitan project have convinced me that the disparity between the ideal of cosmopolitan theology and the current sociopolitical configuration of hospitality, welcoming others, unconditional forgiveness, is itself a *prophetic call* to which we all have to respond—as humans, as persons of faith. The *real* is always about calculation and conditionality, whereas the *ideal* of cosmopolitan theology is about incalculability, unconditionality, and planetarity of the *world-as-it-ought-to-be*. Therefore, the disparity between the reality and the ideality is not a space of despair but a space where one's sense of *prophetic call* and passion for *the impossible* must come in.

2

Cosmopolitanism as a Mobilizing Discourse for *Doing* Theology

The globe is in our computer. No one lives there…

The planet is in the species of alterity, belonging to another system and yet we inhabit it, on loan… I propose the planet to overwrite the globe.

—Gayatri Chakravorty Spivak[1]

Let us take hold of the fact that there are two communities—the one, which is truly great and common, embracing gods and men [sic], in which we look neither to this corner not to that, but measure the boundaries of our state by the sun; the other, the one to which we have been assigned by our birth.

—Seneca[2]

It makes no difference whether a person lives here or there, provided that, wherever he [sic] lives, he lives as a citizen of the world.

—Marcus Aurelius[3]

Envisioning *Planetary Love*

Cosmopolitan discourse has recently emerged, especially in the areas of political and social philosophies. People often confuse *cosmopolitanism* with the *universalism* that postmodernism challenges. In the modern sense, universalism can be what Cornel West calls "faceless universalism."[4] Cosmopolitanism starts from the *singular* individual rather than the *faceless* collective. Cosmopolitanism is not, however, simply giving universalism a *face,* because cosmopolitanism emphasizes and is grounded in a *singular relationality* between and among people. Cosmopolitan discourses help one change one's epistemology to move beyond one's boundaries in terms of religion, nationality, ability, gender, class, race, ethnicity, sexuality, and so forth. It also maintains principles of justice and compassion that move beyond nationality, citizenship, and various boundaries, and calls for application of justice to all *individuals* of the cosmos as a whole. Cosmopolitanism, along with discourses of *empire* and *globalization,* has become one of the catchwords of our times. It is no exaggeration to say that cosmopolitanism has become one of the prominent political, philosophical, sociocultural movements and discourses of the turn of the twenty-first century. The list of those who have worked on cosmopolitanism comes from various disciplinary areas. Yet, I would like to recognize some names of those whose works have been helpful for me to engage with: Mitchell Aboulafia, Sharon Anderson-Gold, Kwame Anthony Appiah, Homi Bhabha, Ulrich Beck, Seyla Benhabib, Pheng Cheah, Jacques Derrida, Camilla Fojas, Amy Gutmann, David Harvey, David Held, Otfried Höffe, David A. Hollinger, Walter D. Mignolo, Martha Nussbaum, Sheldon Pollock, Bruce Robbins, Salman Rushdie, Amartya Sen, and Jeremy Waldron. Although "cosmopolitanism is back"[5] in various disciplines and areas such as philosophy, literary and cultural studies, or social and political sciences, there are, thus far, no substantial works on cosmopolitanism in the areas of theology and religion.

If reading the *signs of our times* is one of the significant tasks of theologians, dealing with these keywords that capture the pressing issues of our time could be a significant theological endeavor. Cosmopolitanism invites us to enlarge our horizon of concern from our *fellow nationals* to our *fellow human beings*, and urges us to have a primary allegiance to the universal community of human beings in the entire cosmos. As a set of projects toward *planetary conviviality,* cosmopolitanism emphasizes the duty to understand and care for those who are on this planet with ourselves as fellow human beings. This primary concern for the *universal* community of human beings does not mean to preclude the concern for the *particular* community. There are of course times that the universal concerns and the particular attachment to a country or community may clash. However, this *clash* comes, not out of the fundamental problem of cosmopolitan ideas, but out of the interlocking complexities of human reality.

The cosmopolitan idea of universal community or the *oneness* of all humanity is reflected in Paul's statement, "There is no longer Jew or Greek, there is no longer slave or free, there is no longer male and female; for all of you are one in Christ Jesus" (Gal. 3:28). I would say that adoption of cosmopolitanism is a theological response to the issues of global inequality and discriminations that people have vigorously discussed in social and political discourses. I also view the *impartiality* of the scope of justice and concern on which cosmopolitanism is grounded as the very nature of Jesus' teaching of neighbor/enemy-love, and that such *impartiality* does not necessarily rule out the *partiality* of one's local attachments and particular commitments. The spirit of cosmopolitanism leads us to the mandate of the radical extension of the category of one's *neighbor,* which requires crossing and transcending various borders and embracing every individual human person, and nature as well, as one's neighbor. Unless one can deconstruct the rigid borderline between self, neighbor, and enemy, one cannot love one's neighbor/enemy as oneself.

In this sense, cosmopolitanism can be a theological discourse of resistance, liberation, and solidarity in our times in which various forms of social oppression and discrimination intersect in a complex way. I affirm that all forms of oppression based on gender, race, class, ethnicity, sexuality, nationality, age, ability, religion, and so forth are not just discriminations against specific groups of people but also *discriminations against humanity*. Cosmopolitan discourse helps one see humanity not just as *members* of particular bounded communities but also as singular *individuals*. My theological rationale for defending the spirit of cosmopolitanism is the core Christian message of neighbor-love-as-self-love. Jesus' greatest command, "Love your *neighbor/enemy* as yourself," is by no means just a personal, emotional matter. The act of neighbor/enemy-love is a political act in the sense that it involves not only one's private sector but also one's public sector where one and one's neighbors/enemies experience the multiple intersecting oppression, discrimination, or exclusion. Furthermore, neighbor/enemy-love not only requires a radical border crossing and resistance, but also an attitude of solidarity with the neighbor/enemy, whose full humanity and rights people deny based on the *social markers* that they bear. In the process of refining the notion of neighbor-love in our social context, we must recast, redefine, revise, and rearticulate the Christian notion of hospitality and justice, and its sociopolitical implication in today's context.

My initial interest in cosmopolitan discourse arose from the identity question: How does one distinguish between I/we and you/they? The question of who one is, the question of one's identity, has been a contested and recurring issue in various discourses and movements. The *who-am-I* question was once for me only existential, meaning that I was not fully aware of my multiple "locationalities" in the world.

Recognizing one's location is significant because it affects one's construction of knowledge and worldview. Awareness of one's location, as Walter Mignolo points out, "clarifies the theorizing of colonial experiences as non-neutral with respect to where the act of theorizing is (ethically and politically, not necessarily geographically) located or performed… [I]t inserts the personal signs of the understanding subject (her or his ability 'to be from' and 'to be at') into an imaginary construction."[6] Although I do not adopt an essentialized location of my *being-from,* I found myself, ever since I left the place of my birth, carrying the *locational* label as *being-from-Asia* regardless of my intention or desire. The exclusively existential nature of my *who-am-I* question began to take a new form especially after feminism touched my life.

The awareness of my gender and race in a non-Asian culture extended the *who-am-I* question from a mere existential question to a social, cultural, and geopolitical one. In contemporary identity politics, identity usually refers to the axes of class, race, ethnicity, gender, religion, and sexual orientation. One forms the collective dimension of this kind of identity based on the unique difference of one's particular group from the other groups. In order to claim a collective identity, one needs to create one's own *categories* that make one distinct from other *categories*. Once society labels a group of people as feminist, gay, African American, or Asian, for instance, ideas and categories about the people come to imply social, political, cultural, psychological, spiritual, and theological effects. These labels and categories shape the ways people perceive themselves and their actions and advocacy. In this process of constructing collective identity, one begins to shape one's agency in the public sphere. One has no control over some criteria for establishing one's identity, such as gender, race, ethnicity, ability, or sexuality. However, *choice* determines other criteria, such as feminist, Marxist, postcolonialist, philosopher, theologian, atheist, Muslim, Buddhist, Christian, and so on.

Here identity politics faces a serious question: What is "the stronger mobilizing discourse,"[7] not merely for a particular group but for the globe? Gayatri Chakravorty Spivak offers an answer to this question: *love*. This *mind-changing love* wins "the attention of the subaltern without coercion or crisis" and is "the possibility of an unascertainable ethical singularity."[8] The *mind-changing love* is more essential to move the world than "the collective efforts to change laws, relations of production, systems of education, and health care" because "without the mind-changing one-on-one responsible contact, nothing will stick."[9] Spivak goes on to say: "We all know that when we engage profoundly with *one* person, the responses—the answers—come from both sides. Let us call this responsibility, as well as 'answer'ability or accountability ....In this sense, ethical singularity can be called a secret encounter."[10]

How can *we*, who dream of a planetary love but have ties to different identities and locationalities, form a profoundly radical coalition and solidarity? Is *solidarity in multiplicity* possible? What kind of epistemology can guide such a radical coalition across the dividing line of identity, which a term such as planetary love expresses? One cannot appeal to some transparently universal ground of being, but rather must negotiate the meaning of one's collective identity in relation to structures of language, gender, class, ethnicity, ability, sexual orientation, religion, and so forth. As Friedrich Nietzsche eloquently puts it:

> [F]or the enrichment of knowledge it may be of more value not to reduce oneself to uniformity in this way, but to listen instead to the gentle voice of each of life's different situations; these will suggest the attitude of mind appropriate to them. Through thus ceasing to treat oneself as a single rigid and unchanging individuum one takes an intelligent interest in the life and being of many others.[11]

Historically marginalized groups, based on gender, race, religion, class, or sexuality, insist on their unique identity to avoid reducing themselves to universal uniformity. However, one eventually confronts the dilemma that one can no longer take whiteness, the middle class, Christianity, maleness, or heterosexuality, for example, as the ubiquitous, paradigmatic agent of oppression and marginalization. A simple classification of one's ontological and geopolitical location based on this axis of identities does not reflect the complex reality of the center and the margin or the need for the *planetary love* that listens "to the gentle voice of each of life's different situations" (Nietzsche), and which is possible through an act of "ethical singularity" (Spivak). This planetary love can be an expression of a *deterritorialization* through which one creates one's own identity out of the twisted skeins of one's backgrounds and locality, recognizes differences among/between people without seizing them as levers in a struggle for power, and moves toward a space of *radical planetary love* across all forms of boundaries.

People have perceived, adopted, or used the term "cosmopolitanism" in contemporary discourse in at least two ways: first, a kind of cultural sensibility; and second, a principle for global justice, law, and geopolitical morality. I am more interested in the latter use of cosmopolitanism and will attempt to bridge the cosmopolitan ideal with the core of Christian teaching—neighbor-love, hospitality, and solidarity. I believe *cosmopolitanism* can be an effective discourse with which to advocate a politics of *trans-identity* of overlapping interests and heterogeneous or hybrid subjects in order to challenge conventional notions of exclusive belonging, identity, and citizenship. Cosmopolitanism can help one envision a planetary love through an ethical singularity aimed at a more peaceful and just world. In this sense, I regard cosmopolitanism as a *stronger mobilizing discourse* that captures Spivak's call for a *mind-changing love* for the planet. This book is my effort to illuminate cosmopolitanism as a discourse that calls simultaneously for a *planetary love* through *ethical singularity* in accordance with Spivak's notion, and for a radical neighbor-love in accordance with Jesus' teaching. As such, it is also an effort to articulate a cosmopolitan theological discourse, which I believe can be a mobilizing discourse for a more just and egalitarian world regardless of who/what one is.

Cosmopolitanism is a radical affirmation of the idea of neighbor/enemy-love-as self-love. In other words, cosmopolitanism is about a cosmic scope of justice and hospitality—another name for *love*. It is about finding a place for Jesus' message of neighbor/enemy-love in the world by fundamentally reshaping one's view of others, of the immigration law, of international politics, of the disparity between the rich and the poor from a radically egalitarian way. When a religious teaching such as neighbor-love-as-self-love becomes *de*politicized by locating its implication outside the human reality, it loses its public relevance and ends up being just a romanticized cliché-statement. Religion is about hospitality and responsibility, and about neighbor/enemy-love-as-self-love in a Christian term that requires one to turn a new *gaze* onto others—what I call a *cosmopolitan gaze*. The *cosmopolitan gaze* implies the sheer truth that others are simply *fellow-citizens-of-the-cosmos* equal to me, which has theological, philosophical, spiritual, and political implications and ramifications. In this sense, cosmopolitan theology affirms and radicalizes the belief that the Divine creates each and every human being as equal to every one else as a *citizen-of-the-cosmos* and that no one is either superior or inferior to the other. In order to implement the radical notion of human equality in human reality, separating theology and religion from the realm of politics and economics makes theology/religion impotent in the world. The cosmopolitan theology that I propose is one of the ways to find a place for religion in the world out of my two-fold theological position: religion is about searching for meaning in one's life *and* about practicing an *unconditional, planetary hospitality* in the world.

Cosmopolitanism: Major Aspects and Characteristics

What Cosmopolitanism Is Not

Using the formula *A is not B* is to make distinctions between what one is trying to say and what people usually perceive. I follow this practice in order to set out to make clear what kind of cosmopolitanism I adopt.

- Cosmopolitanism is *not* an overarching, universalizing, totalizing meta-narrative.
- Cosmopolitanism is *not* abstract, *faceless* universalism nor universalism simply with a *face*.
- Cosmopolitanism is *not* a discourse of dismissal of particularity.
- Cosmopolitanism is *not* a Westcentric global design of the world.
- Cosmopolitanism is *not* cultural relativism.
- Cosmopolitanism is *not* a detachment from sociopolitical commitments.
- Cosmopolitanism is *not* a concept complicit with the interests of the powerful.
- Cosmopolitanism is *not* a discourse linked to the ills of *globalization from above.*
- Cosmopolitanism is *not* a liberal multiculturalism that uncritically celebrates cultural/ethnic difference but without commitments to making changes in sociopolitical power-disparities between differences.
- Cosmopolitanism is *not* a discourse on homogeneous unity/uniformity.
- Cosmopolitanism *is* about a cosmic, macro-scope of justice.
- Cosmopolitanism *is* about planetary conviviality.
- Cosmopolitanism *is* about *singular plurality* of human beings.
- Cosmopolitanism *is* about a decolonizing/decentering coloniality of power and domination.
- Cosmopolitanism *is* about *unconditional* hospitality, planetary solidarity and responsibility, welcoming the other, and cosmic neighbor-love.
- Cosmopolitanism *is* about com/passion for *the impossible.*

Three Major Aspects of Cosmopolitanism

Cosmopolitanism has three major aspects. First, cosmopolitanism sheds new light on the politics of identity.[12] People have used the term cosmopolitanism in two ways: negative and positive. People negatively labeled Jews and Bolsheviks, for instance, as *cosmopolitans* in the sense that they were to be excluded as foreigners.[13] This negative use of cosmopolitan is an identity imposed by others, rather than self-claimed. People also have used the term *cosmopolitan* to positively indicate those who are world travelers and are not provincially narrow-minded. In this case, whether ascribed or achieved, one's identity as *cosmopolitan* entails a positive connotation as an indicator of one's affluent economic and sociocultural status that can afford such world travels and multicultural lifestyles. Cosmopolitanism as a kind of politics of identity is twofold: self-identity and the identity of others. When one identifies oneself as *cosmopolitan* in the sense of a *citizen of the cosmos,* the self-identity should extend itself to the realm of the others as also citizens of the cosmos, which makes it possible to grant the others an equal citizenship with oneself. Only when one can see others as equal citizens of the cosmos can one exercise the neighbor-love-as-self-love.

Second, cosmopolitanism posits a fundamental question as to who the neighbors are. The question of whom one regards as *neighbors* is not as simple as people usually perceive. People set their criteria for neighbors on various grounds, such as nationality and citizenship, religious affiliations, sexuality, physical and mental ability, social status, racial and cultural affinity, political positions, educational and professional background, and so forth. Once people set the criteria for *neighbors*, they also construct a different scope of the rights of, hospitality toward, responsibilities to, or justice for *neighbors* and *non-neighbors*. Cosmopolitanism emphasizes that one should regard every other individual human being as one's neighbor, regardless whether one *knows* the other or not. Cosmopolitanism expands the criteria for neighbors from *knowing others* to the *non-knowing others*. Regarding one's others as fellow cosmic citizens regardless of their nationality and state citizenship, legal status, religious affiliation, sexuality, cultural affinity, etc., is a radical sense of *planetary ecumenism* that seeks an oneness of humanity. In this sense, the fundamental claim of cosmopolitanism that one is the citizen of the cosmos is another word for the religious view that regards every individual human being as the child/creature of God.

Third, cosmopolitanism entails the issue of responsibility to the others, hospitality to the others, and the macro-scope of justice. When one views every other as a fellow citizen of the cosmos, as one's neighbor, it is necessary to expand the scope of responsibility, hospitality, and justice that one once applied only to the close neighbors, friends, or relatives—the knowing others—to the non-knowing, distant others. Cosmopolitanism highlights the importance of responsibility and hospitality to those one does not know, although the precise nature of responsibility is of course always context-specific. However, cosmopolitanism does not dispute and preclude the significance of the local tie and particular responsibility that one has to one's intimate, close family, relatives, or friends. The cosmopolitan emphasis lies in expanding the scope of responsibility, obligations, and hospitality to others whom one does not know, but whose lives are inextricably interdependent with one's own—knowingly and unknowingly—as fellow citizens of the cosmos. The nature, scope, and content of the responsibility can be not only personal/private but also societal, collective, national, state, and public. Therefore, there is always a disparity between the *ethics* of cosmopolitanism and the *politics* of cosmopolitanism, because the ethics of cosmopolitanism is unconditional, whereas the politics of cosmopolitanism is always conditional. The disparity between these two poles is where theological and prophetic call comes in. Cosmopolitan theology is a *prophetic call* for an ethics of cosmopolitanism so that the politics of cosmopolitanism can be more embracing, expanding, and transforming toward an unconditionality of cosmopolitanism, although one may never reach the perfect fulfillment of the ultimate unconditionality of the cosmopolitan ethos in one's concrete reality. In this regard, constructing a cosmopolitan theology is an attempt to narrow the disparity between the unconditionality and the conditionality of cosmopolitanism.

Four Characteristics of Cosmopolitanism

Cosmopolitanism as Macro-Interdependencies

Cosmopolitanism is a longstanding concept that wide-ranging scholars have recently revisited. The term dates back to the Cynics, who first began to use the term cosmopolitan to denote *citizen of the cosmos*. When asked where he came from, Diogenes the Cynic replied, "I am a citizen of the world/I am a *kosmopolites*,"[14] which meant he refused to be confined by his local origins and wanted to move beyond local group memberships. Diogenes meant to assert that local affiliations were of lesser importance than a primary affiliation with humanity. Some suggest that Socrates predates Diogenes as the first thinker to regard himself as a "world citizen."[15] When asked where he was from, he also replied, not "Athens," but "the world," thereby embracing the universe as his city.[16] Marcus Aurelius also made a cosmopolitan claim by saying, "It makes no difference whether a person lives here or there, provided that, wherever he [*sic*] lives, he lives as a citizen of the world."[17] Scholars have used this idea of "world-citizen" (*kosmopolites),* strongly related to contemporary human rights issues, as the ground for cosmopolitanism. An identity as *kosmopolites* obviously transcends a specific national boundary, and thereby moves beyond a community-bounded identity.

Communitarianism regards *community* as "a significant source of ethical value," whereas cosmopolitanism sees "individuals as the origin of moral worth."[18] In this sense, communitarianism reduces the application and demand of justice, rights, and hospitality to those bounded by specific community, but cosmopolitanism concerns the rights of and justice for *singular individuals* across the specific communities bounded by gender, nation-state, race, ethnicity, sexual orientation, and so forth. This idea of *world citizen* regards individual markers, based on nationality, gender, class, ethnicity, sexual orientation, and so forth, as accidental and secondary. The recognition of the contingency of *where* and *how* one is born and the attitude of *cosmic citizen* give rise to the concept of a "moral community made up by the community of all human beings."[19] In this context, cosmopolitanism reflects a critically skeptical attitude toward a conventional concept and tradition of society, a refusal to confine one's sense of belonging exclusively to a particular *polis* and instead a claim to belong to a wider human community, the universe—the cosmos. Social and political theorists, especially, tend to use the term cosmopolitanism to argue that individuals and nations have obligations to ensure justice across national borderlines. Cosmopolitanism emerges by way of a proposed new politics, embodying an alternative perspective between "ethnocentric nationalism" and "particularistic multiculturalism."[20]

Ulrich Beck illustrates interconnected principles of the cosmopolitan outlook. These principles reveal an awareness of the interdependence of the global community, which requires overcoming "the boundaries between internal and external, us and them, the national and the international." He contends, "Cosmopolitanism without provincialism is empty, provincialism without cosmopolitanism is blind."[21] Cosmopolitanism favors voluntary affiliations, embraces the intersecting character of many groups, and engages the complexity of one's multiple identities, moving beyond provincial enclosures. Embodying the fundamental ethos of cosmopolitan, a citizen of the cosmos, is, therefore, "the person whose allegiance is to the worldwide community of human beings."[22] In this sense, the spirit of "macro-interdependencies"[23] of all individual beings is at the heart of the cosmopolitanism that I adopt. However, *micro-interdependencies* and *macro-interdependencies* are not necessarily in contradiction. Although we humans have a desire to attach ourselves to local identities and belonging, it is also important for us to construct universal, cosmic identities and belonging because both the micro- and macro-interdependencies of all living beings are double-edges of life. Maintaining the balance of these two types of ethos is not easy, but is important to promoting and enhancing the interest and well-being of humanity as a whole.

Cosmopolitanism as Planetary Hospitality and Responsibility

People usually take Diogenes as the originator of cosmopolitanism with his idea of *kosmopolites*. However, Stoicism strengthens the notion of cosmopolitanism in the sense that it endorses *cosmic community*, which transcends one's national boundary especially in terms of the scope of justice, peace, and equality. Diogenes' idea of *kosmopolites* triggered a significant notion that we should not confine one's belonging only to a national/geographical boundary but should extend it to a larger community—the *cosmos*. In this sense, Stoicism strengthened a theoretical ground and promoted the idea of cosmopolitanism. Stoic cosmopolitanism is significant because it offers an ideal of *cosmic citizen*, which is valuable in social life. However, one should not regard Stoic cosmopolitanism as a "proposal for a world-state."[24] Thomas Aquinas rearticulates this Stoic cosmopolitan ideal in his notion of natural law that is accessible to all human beings as an expression of God's creation. For Aquinas, natural law is a creation of divine will, and a form of moral law. In principle, people could include even non-Christians in the application of natural law.[25] Cosmopolitanism in modern usage is based upon the inherent human dignity and equality of all human beings, and therefore people often use cosmopolitanism in association with the concept of universal human rights. Kant's notion of *perpetual peace* argues for cosmopolitan values that defend the equal claim of every individual person to the recognition, protection, and universal obligations of justice that cross borders of nationality and provincial community.[26] For Kant, cosmopolitanism is about the *principles of universal hospitality* that would ensure *perpetual peace* in the world. Although there is a fundamental contradiction in Kant's own thinking between his Eurocentric hierarchical theory of race and his cosmopolitan ideal, which reveals a fundamental problem in the modern notion of *universality*, his utopian ideal of cosmopolitanism has influenced scholars who envision an ideal world of justice and peace beyond national boundaries.

Emmanuel Levinas calls for a concept of humanity that transcends the economic and political realms. If there is no notion of humanity that transcends sociopolitical structures, on what grounds can theology or philosophy reconsider who/what we humans are? Levinas's approach to hospitality, to humanity, offers an important ethico-theological aspect to sociopolitical issues. Although those who work for justice focus on the power relations between different social groups, they often overlook the significance of individual responsibility in the legitimating of justice itself. The fundamental question of Being, the whole philosophical and theological tradition of the West, remains. Levinas contends:

> Each one, as an "I," is separate from all the others to whom the moral duty is due....From then on, there is no moral awareness that is not an awareness of this exceptional position, an awareness

> of being chosen. Reciprocity is a structure founded on an original inequality. For equality to make its entry into the world, beings must be able to demand more of themselves than of the Other, feel responsibilities on which the fate of humanity hangs, and in this sense pose themselves problems outside humanity....It is a particularism that conditions universality, and it is a moral category rather than an historical fact.[27]

Levinas calls on us never to lose sight of the others, our fellow humans, our *neighbors*. Unless we acknowledge individual humans as our neighbors, and their rights as universal rights, we will likely reduce them to impersonal numbers. Regarding one's neighbors as oneself is the core of cosmopolitan rights and hospitality. Cosmopolitanism advances ethics as fundamental welcoming, unconditional receptivity for the other, and a notion of responsibility for the other, our neighbor. Some scholars associate cosmopolitanism primarily with *global governance*. The danger that I see in this view that associates cosmopolitanism primarily with global governance is its tendency to homogenize the differences and to seek a *unified* regulation between nation-states. My association with cosmopolitanism has something to do with hospitality and responsibility both on a personal and public level, which may require a sense of *transnational* actions, movements, solidarities, and commitments in reality. As Derrida contends, "[R]eligion is responsibility or it is nothing at all."[28] It is another way of saying: Religion is about hospitality, solidarity, and responsibility or it is nothing at all.

Cosmopolitanism as Trans-Boundaryness

There is no discourse without problems, weaknesses, or dilemmas. One of the dilemmas that cosmopolitanism carries is "its perceived inability to acknowledge and properly account for the special ties and commitments that characterize the lives of ordinary men and women."[29] National identity, religious identity, racial/ethnic identity, gender identity, or sexual identity, for instance, creates those special ties and particular attachments for most people. Cosmopolitanism may seem to rule out these particular attachments and advocacies of the marginalized group and therefore seems to be out of touch with what is of value to many people. Yet the universalistic implications of cosmopolitanism and the particularistic commitments that every identity politics entails do not have to conflict. They can be mutually enhancing and complementary.

Here I would like to make a double differentiation between cosmopolitanism as an *ideal* and as an *institutional claim,* on the one hand, and between cosmopolitanism as a claim about justice and as a claim about culture and identity, on the other. First, cosmopolitanism, as a moral ideal and a set of moral commitments, views *individuals* as entitled to equal consideration of justice regardless of their nationality or race/ethnicity,[30] whereas people commonly associate cosmopolitanism as an institutional claim with a world state, which is often the basis of objection to cosmopolitanism in general.[31] Second, there are two kinds of cosmopolitanism: One is a claim about culture or identity and the other is a claim about justice. The former denies that membership in a particular cultural community is constitutive of a person's social identity, whereas the latter concerns the scope of justice and holds that social boundaries do not impose limits on justice.[32] The cosmopolitanism that I adopt from this political philosophical discourse is cosmopolitanism as a moral claim and as a claim about the scope of justice. One can use cosmopolitanism both in negative and positive ways. In a positive sense, cosmopolitanism is a *moral perspective* that is "impartial, universal, individualist, and egalitarian," and its fundamental idea is that "every human being has a right to have her or his vital interests met, regardless of nationality or citizenship."[33]

Despite the contradictory uses of and dilemmas of cosmopolitanism, I find it more enabling, empowering, and liberating than disempowering and confining, especially when the issue of global inequality has become a more and more serious issue in our time, one that requires theological reflection and commitment. The discourse of cosmopolitanism enables one to break out of self-centered, balkanized, collective identity and national/patriotic narcissism and to expand the application of justice and solidarity across and beyond national, regional, and group-based boundaries and confinements. Cosmopolitanism is a standpoint that vindicates impartial, planetary, and egalitarian justice and solidarities across all the different forms of boundaries that divide people. For Jacques Derrida, the concept of cosmopolitanism signifies an "undeconstructable concern for justice."[34] Cosmopolitanism for me maintains principles of justice and compassion that transcend nationality, citizenship, and other boundaries and defends the application of justice to all individuals of the cosmos as a whole.

Paul reflects the *oneness of humanity,* a *planetary ecumenism,* in his statement, "There is no longer Jew or Greek, there is no longer slave or free, there is no longer male and female; for all of you are one in Christ Jesus" (Gal. 3:28). Another text also conveys this idea of oneness of humanity of cosmopolitanism: "So then you are no longer strangers and aliens, but you are citizens with the saints and also members of the household of God" (Eph. 2:19). Cosmopolitanism and its theological adoption is, in this context, a theological response to the issues of global inequality that we are facing. I view the *impartiality* of the scope of justice and concern in cosmopolitanism as the very essence of the Christian teaching of *neighbor-love,* and it does not necessarily rule out the *partiality* of one's local attachments and commitments. The spirit of cosmopolitanism also requires us to radically extend the category of *neighbors,* to cross and transcend various borders, and to embrace every human person and, furthermore, nature itself, as our *neighbors*.

Cosmopolitanism as Politics of Trans-Identity

Questions of identity have increasingly become interlaced with issues of power and representation. The battle to grant rights and justice to new social groups dominates the current political, cultural, and ideological landscape. There seems to be a deep conflict between the diverse identities and the politics of representation. Articulating the relationship among identities along the axes of gender, race, class, ethnicity, sexual orientation, ability, and so forth is not easy. People have taken up identities in the struggle to construct counter-narratives and practices. Identity politics covers complex and diverse theoretical positions, and discourses have evolved around the questions of subjectivity, representation, culture, difference, struggle, and liberation. Identity politics has become one of the more powerful commonsense constructions developed by marginalized groups. Therefore, "[T]he complex, even contradictory character of identity politics must be accounted for in efforts to develop a politically effective critical perspective" and "will remain a persistent feature of our political landscape in part because it produces limited but real empowerment for its participants."[35]

Identity politics since the 1960s has played a central role in politicizing marginalized groups, challenging the mainstream hegemonic power, and providing spaces for the marginalized groups to claim their voices and experiences as legitimate. However, it has often failed to move beyond an unproblematized notion of difference and has thereby clung to the polarized *we-they* binarism. In doing so, identity politics has appealed uncritically to a discourse of essentialized *authenticity*. As a result, identity politics becomes a *politics of heterogeneity* in attempting to construct *identity-in-differential.* Here, we need to make a distinction between "heterogeneity as bohemianism, anarchism, and political indifference and heterogeneity as political destiny." Furthermore, it is significant to acknowledge the distinction between "a categorical heterogeneity, that is, a heterogeneity construed by the homogeneous logic of the 'category' and an acategorical heterogeneity that finds its 'self-expression' through the break-down of the 'categorical.'"[36] What we often experience in identity politics is its fall into a "categorical heterogeneity" where "[d]ifference is transformed into that which must be specified within a concept, without overstepping its bounds," and the "swarming of individualities."[37] For instance, Orientalist and Neo-Orientalist concerns have shaped much of the scholarship on Asian subjects by presenting the Asian other as the product of a timeless, unchanging culture. Here people still confine *being Asian* to the static images of *authentic* Asianness.[38] An essentializing notion of Asian-ness continues to dog Asian theological discourse, and the homogenization and singularization of this vast ethnic group, Asian, continue to lurk in the field of theology. People continue to homogenize *Asians* culturally, ethnically, and ontologically. Furthermore, Asian scholars themselves selectively participate in and produce/reproduce Orientalist discourses. Homogenization of Asian by Asians themselves in claiming their own identity-in-differential from the West is an example of a *politics of categorical heterogeneity*, and the politics of Asian identity thereby turn into a politics of *swarming individualities*.

Identity politics has enabled formerly voiceless groups to claim their own power and to establish their own identities and experiences. Nevertheless, one of the dilemmas that the current identity politics carries is its tendency to invoke a politics of separatism. Identity politics also makes people overlook the differences and power disparities within their own *group*, because that group becomes a homogeneously categorized community of *swarming individualities*. Ellen Willis writes:

> The appeal of "identity politics" is that it arises from a radical insight—that domination is systematically structured into the relations between social groups. The problem is that it gives rise to a logic that chokes off radicalism and ends up by supporting domination. If the present obsession with group identity as the basis of politics has made it hard to imagine, much less build, a broad-based radical collectivity, it has even more tellingly stood in the way of a principled commitment to the freedom and happiness of individuals, without which no genuine radicalism is possible.[39]

The reality of oppression and marginalization is complicated and often paradoxical. A person can belong to a socially privileged category but at the same time to an unprivileged category. For instance, a middle-class, Asian, heterosexual, female, Christian professor such as myself may blind herself to issues of sexual orientation, class, and religious *othering*, and her experience of racial/ethnic discrimination and gender inequality may have made her assume that her experience of oppression based on her gender and race automatically guarantees her understanding of other forms of oppression and privilege. Identity politics often contributes to establishing another form of *interest group*, rather than offering a claim for fundamental transformation of human relationship and its institutional implementation. *Identity politics* is necessary and legitimate only when its claim is to dismantle the discriminatory view of human beings, to claim dignity for the otherwise degraded group, and to enlarge the possibility of human liberation. But I am skeptical about identity politics when it is only for attaining and possessing more power for the formerly marginalized group without changing the fundamental nature of human relationships. Although I believe identity politics "produces limited but real empowerment for its participants,"[40] it is important to note that it contains significant problems: first, its essentialist tendency; second, its fixed *we-they* binary position; third, its homogenization of diverse social oppression; fourth, its simplification of the complexity and paradox of being privileged and unprivileged; and fifth, its ruling out of the intersectional space of diverse form of oppression in reality.

Cosmopolitanism in contemporary use mainly revolves around issues of identity, scope of justice, hospitality, and responsibility. A cosmopolitan claim that one is a *citizen of the cosmos* invites one to revisit and reexamine the current politics of identity, which emphasizes one's unique *difference from*, rather than one's similarity to, other people with a different category of identity based on gender, race, class, sexuality, nationality, state, ethnicity, citizenship, and so on. The primary thesis of cosmopolitan identity is not, however, to deny the particular ties, affiliation, or obligations toward family or relatives, ethnic or national group, or any particular group based on a certain attribute, but to focus on the responsibility beyond national, ethnic, state, or other boundaries. Marcus Aurelius Antoninus Augustus eloquently illustrates the particularity and universality of one's identity: "Now my nature is that of a rational and political being. As Antoninus, my city and fatherland is Rome; As a human being, it is the universe; So what brings benefits to these is the sole good for me."[41] Marcus Aurelius's articulation indicates no need to abandon one's local identity in order to defend a cosmopolitan identity. Juxtaposing the particularity and universality of one's identity in an antagonistic way hinders one from grasping the profound meaning of cosmopolitan "subjecthood" and its practical implications. Seneca makes the possibility of double-identity and double-allegiance clearer. He argues that double belonging is what we humans are because humans belong both to a commonwealth assigned by one's birth and another commonwealth assigned by the path of the sun—the cosmic belonging. Therefore, "[T]here are two commonwealths—the one, a vast and truly common state, which embraces alike gods and men [*sic*], in which we look neither to this corner of earth nor to that, but measure the bounds of our citizenship by the path of the sun; the other, the one to which we have been assigned by the accident of birth."[42] In this sense, both one's *territorial, particular belonging/identity* and *cosmic belonging/identity* do not have to be in contradiction. The idea of cosmic belonging reveals the complex and profound nature of one's identity.

There is a strong pretention to homogeneity of experience covered by the word that signifies one's identity. *As-discourses,* such as *as-woman, as-Asian, as-Black, as-Jews, as-gay,* and so forth, tend to assume that such identity exists in isolation from other identity. Scholars have criticized feminist theories and movements, for instance, for their false assumption and pretention that *all women* are like white and middle-class women, and their experiences under *universal* patriarchy make them *sisters*. In their claim for universal sisterhood, gender exists in isolation from race, ethnicity, sexuality, or class. This pretention to homogeneity of one's collective identity also happens in other forms of identity discourse and movements.[43] All kinds of identity politics and advocacy movements have a strong tendency toward homogenization, ghettoization, and essentialization. Once people fix one's collective identity as such, whether self-claimed or socially imposed, the first act is to draw a new set of *we-they* boundaries. In this collective identity discourse, people genderize, ethnicize, racialize, or sexualize the other, as if one is just *one thing*—woman, Asian, Jew, Black, or homosexual.

As soon as one declares the manyness, multiplicity, and heterogeneity in one's collective identity, other members of the collective regard one as disturbing and threatening the advocacy cause, or compromising with the *conspiracy* of the dominant power. In this regard, a *politics of identity* encourages one to remain as just one thing: *just-woman, just-Asian, just-Black, just-Latina/o,* or *just-gay/lesbian*. This pretention to homogeneity and desire for *purity* are the paradoxes at the heart of identity politics. Since the identity politics tends to fail to identify one with the complexity and multiplicity of human experience, it is important to note that the single, monolithic identity is more constraining than liberating. Edward Said warns about the danger of the monolithic identity claim, whether it is imposed or self-claimed:

> No one today is purely *one* thing. Labels like Indian, or woman, or Muslim, or American are not more than starting-points .... Imperialism consolidated the mixture of cultures and identities on a global scale. But its worst and most paradoxical gift was to allow people to believe that they were only, mainly, exclusively, white, or Black, or Western, or Oriental....No one can deny the persisting continuities of long traditions, sustained habitations, national languages, and cultural geographies, but there seems no reason except fear and prejudice to keep insisting on their separation and

distinctiveness, as if that was all human life was about. Survival in fact is about the connections between things....[44]

When one talks about the heterogeneity of one's identity and intersectionality of various forms of social oppression, people often regard it as undermining advocacy work. Is it possible to give the things women/ Blacks/Latina/o/Asian/gay have in common their full significance without implying that the differences/intersections among them are less important? How can we construct a discourse that moves us beyond a single, homogeneous boundary so that we can work together for justice and solidarity without eclipsing what *we*—as-women, as-Black, as-Asian, as-gay, and so forth—share in common? How can one see various forms of oppression as not in isolation from but in relation to *our* oppression, and any form of oppression as not just oppression against *them* but oppression against *us* the entire humanity? These questions lead us to the fundamental questions about identity, responsibility, and solidarity. Cosmopolitan thinking and ideals capture these aspects of identity, responsibility, and solidarity. Adopting cosmopolitanism discourse is in a way an attempt to overcome the problems and dilemmas of *monolithic* identity politics. Central to my adoption of cosmopolitanism is the need to provide one with the vision to deconstruct the mythic notion of one's *frozen* identity, to address complex relations of representation, and to create liberative principles that make possible solidarity and coalition across different identities and borders. Cosmopolitanism is not, therefore, about *boundary-making* but about *boundary-embracing-and-transcending*.

Identity politics should be provisional, temporal, and partial and move toward a larger community of radical equality and boundary-less inclusion, without undervaluing the significant meaning of *particular* engagement and commitment for implementation of justice and equality for all living beings. I ground the politics of *trans-identity* in an understanding of the complexity of all forms of domination by extending it from merely one form of oppression—such as classism—to gender, sexual orientation, racial, or ethnic injustices. Oppression is a multilayered, complex process that affects different groups and different individuals in different ways and at different times across the various borders that structure our reality. We need to recognize, extend, and transform the ways power and knowledge operate because people now produce knowledge under the conditions of a globalizing neoliberal capitalism and emerging global public sphere. A single-issue movement, based on a singular group identity, cannot address the intersectional complexity of different forms of oppression. Despite its strength and significant contribution, monolithic *identity politics* or *politics of difference* cannot afford to have its connection to wider material relations occulted by a focus on theoretical issues often divorced from the lived experiences of oppressed, marginalized, and deprivileged groups. Here, it is significant to note that being marginal or oppressed is not about one's *essence* based on race, gender, ethnicity, or sexual orientation, but about one's *position* and *location* in a material world. The material conditions include "widespread homelessness, joblessness, illiteracy, crime, disease (including AIDS), hunger, poverty, drug addiction, alcoholism as well as the various habits of ill health, and the destruction of the environment," and these are "the myriad social effects of the late multinational capitalism."[45] If one needs to claim one's identity as such, others can value it only when it can bring a transformative function to challenge the stereotype, to contest a dominating power, or to transvalue the existing oppressive values, but not as a permanent maker of one's essence, as if there is an *essence* in who one is.

In this regard, the politics of *trans-identity* that I propose does not deny one's particular identity, but primarily claims that one's identity is neither fixed, eternalized, nor essentialized. The politics of trans-identity presupposes that one's singular or monolithic identity based on gender, race, class, ethnicity, ability, or sexuality can be a point of departure, but should not be a fixed permanent point of arrival. If one must begin somewhere, one can begin with one's singular identity as such. However, one is more than just *one thing*, such as just woman or man, just black or white, just heterosexual or homosexual. If one fixes one's identity only on one factor, such a single identity is more confining than liberating. Therefore, one can and should have multiple points of arrival, depending on one's context, that one is engaged with. One of the serious dilemmas in a fixed identity politics is that once one uses a label for who one is, it fixes, confines, and controls the point of arrival for one's discursive and political engagements. It does not allow one to see the complex and intersecting dimension of multiple forms of power and privilege, oppression, domination, and subjugation. The politics of *trans-identity* relates personal identity to the struggle for justice and against the institutionalization of asymmetrical relations of various forms of hegemonic power and privilege. Therefore, the politics of trans-identity seeks to move from the *politics of singular identity* to the *politics of multiple solidarities* across various identities without abandoning one's personal attachments and commitments to the group that one finds significant. Here one should take up the issue of *difference* in ways that do not replay mono-cultural essentialism, such as Euro-U.S.-centrism, Anglocentrism, phallocentrism, androcentrism, gynocentrism, Christiancentrism, Asiancentrism, Blackcentrism, Whitecentrism, and the like. What we need is not to reverse and replay the *centrisms* but to create a politics of solidarity and alliance building, of dreaming together toward the *reign of God* on earth that moves beyond a homogenized, ghettoized, naturalized, idealized, romanticized, and essentialized identity politics, which actually serves to keep forms of institutionalized racism, sexism, classism, ethnocentrism, and homophobism intact.

Types of Contemporary Cosmopolitanisms

Skeptical Views of Cosmopolitanism: Eurocentric, Detached, Rootless, and Elite

There is no *cosmopolitanism-in-general*. Every discourse on cosmopolitanism is *cosmopolitanism-in-particular*. Since *cosmopolitanism* or *cosmopolitan* is the older term that people began using from Antiquity, and people have applied the usage in extremely different ways, the significant transformation of the last few decades is the move toward rearticulating cosmopolitanisms in plural. Rapid and major changes in cosmopolitanisms as discourses and practices have both responded to and reciprocally shaped in the impulse to reconfigure, revisit, and reassess various forms and functions of cosmopolitanisms and to attribute new meanings and values to them. As discursive and contextual changes have rapidly occurred in the past several decades, the range and diversity of the new domain that the term *cosmopolitanism* inhabits become increased. Scholars have raised both skeptical and affirmative voices about cosmopolitanism, and these various, often contradictory assessments have offered diverse angles through which one can examine the purpose and function of cosmopolitanism as discourse and sociopolitical, cultural, economic, or theological practice in specific contexts. It is important to note that assessing cosmopolitanism as discourse and practice requires one to exercise critical and complex questioning concerning: *whose interest* the claim for cosmopolitanism serves and *what functionality* it plays in a specific historical and material context. As *cosmopolitanisms* have reemerged in scholarly and intellectual discourse, one can find skeptical views of cosmopolitanism as follows: Eurocentric universalizing discourse, disembodied, unworldly discourse, a discourse wallowing in a privileged and irresponsible detachment, a discourse incapable of participating in the making of history, or a discourse doomed to mere aesthetic spectatorship. People also perceive cosmopolitanism, in a sarcastic way, as a kind of "long-distance nationalism," which signifies "a rapidly spreading phenomenon whereby well-off immigrants to the rich, advanced countries are becoming key sources of money, guns, and extremist propaganda in their distant, putative countries of origin."[46]

It is also significant to note that people have misused the term *cosmopolitan* in an extremely distorted way. Nazis, for instance, used *cosmopolitan* as a synonym for a death sentence, categorizing "all victims of the planned mass murder as cosmopolitans" and identified Jews as *cosmopolitans,* and the Stalinists also used the word *cosmopolitan* to mean "Jew."[47] People also once used *cosmopolitan* to refer to "Christians, aristocrats, merchants, Jews, homosexuals, and intellectuals (while changing its meaning)."[48] People often criticize cosmopolitanism as elitist when it means a *lifestyle* that requires sufficient financial means to afford world travels and an ability to embrace multiculturalism, when the majority of people simply do not have the option to participate in such a lifestyle. People also attribute cosmopolitanism to "North Atlantic merchant sailors, Caribbean au pairs in the United States, Egyptian guest workers in Iraq, or Japanese women who take *gaijin* lovers."[49] These diverse perceptions, understandings, and use/misuse of cosmopolitanism add to the complexity and reach of the discussion about cosmopolitanism. Cosmopolitanism has become the subject of growing disciplines, and the reasons for the resurgence of cosmopolitan discourse are complicated. Scholars have constructed cosmopolitanism from a variety of perspectives that arise from within different academic disciplines. Some scholars deal with cosmopolitanism in terms of ethical imperatives and normative principles, cultural hybridity and critical multiculturalism, or the international/transnational/postnational rule of law and systems and regulations of worldly governance.

Antonio Gramsci, for instance, contests cosmopolitanism. Amanda Anderson describes Gramsci's view of cosmopolitanism as a "culturally conditioned, disastrous detachment, which is specifically linked to imperialism, the false universal ecumenism of the Catholic Church, and the development of a rootless, intellectualized, managerial class."[50] Here, the term *cosmopolitan* signifies, as Tim Brennan points out, "Third World metropolitan intellectuals" who would share "a harsh questioning of radical decolonization theory; a dismissive or parodic attitude towards the project of national culture; a manipulation of imperial imaginary and local legend as a means of politicizing 'current events'; and a declaration of cultural 'hybridity'—a hybridity claimed to offer certain advantages in negotiating the collisions of language, race and art in a world of disparate peoples comprising a single, if not exactly unified, world."[51] In this sense, Gramsci's skeptical view of cosmopolitanism refers to "a lifeless imperial disengagement,"[52] a free-floating intellectual. The term cosmopolitans, in the narrow sense that people adopt here, refers to those who had "the experience of living in several countries, who were educationally privileged, who wrote about general trends and global connections rather than the sentient details of indigenous village life."[53]

Another skeptical view of cosmopolitanism comes from Frantz Fanon. Fanon argues that national weakness arises from the "result of the intellectual laziness of the national middle class, of its spiritual penury, and of the profoundly cosmopolitan mold that its mind is set in," and such a cosmopolitan mold hinders national middle class from fulfilling its national vocation "to make the totality of the nation a reality to each citizen .... to make the history of the nation part of the personal experience of each of its citizens."[54] Fanon seems to perceive cosmopolitanism as a kind of luxurious cultural lifestyle, in which the *national middle class* people detach themselves from their own historical-political reality and, therefore, become apolitical, ahistorical, and indifferent to the daily lives of people. In a colonial context, the primary concern that the colonized people have is the national independence from the colonial power.

Overemphasizing *nationalism* and locating it in opposition to *cosmopolitanism* are understandable actions in such an extremely colonial context. However, both nationalism and cosmopolitanism in their broad and complex senses do not have to be an issue of exclusive *either-or*. It is possible to maintain the seemingly impossible perspectives of *both* nationalism *and* cosmopolitanism, as one can see in W.E.B. Du Bois. Du Bois, a Pan-Africanist, identified himself as a cosmopolitan and did not see a contradiction between his being Pan-Africanist and cosmopolitan. He developed the notions of world citizenship and was thinking of "our planet as one place, of understanding the radical relationality of developments."[55] Therefore, Du Bois had a "global vision, a cosmopolitan vision, a vision of community that's transnational ....and of the responsibilities of the world citizen,"[56] although he dreamt about the Pan-African nation-states. Yet if one adopts nationalism in an exclusive way, there is an ongoing tension between nationalism and cosmopolitanism because nationalism is primarily about *boundary-making*, whereas cosmopolitanism is about *boundary-embracing/transcending*.[57]

One of the harsh criticisms of cosmopolitanism is its danger of *rootlessness*. Since the old ideal of cosmopolitanism overemphasizes allegiance to the worldwide community of human beings, those who hold patriotism, national identity, and local attachments as fundamental values view cosmopolitanism in a skeptical way due to its seeming connotation of *rootlessness* and *detachment* from the local. In his "Starbucks and Rootless Cosmopolitanism," Benjamin Aldes Wurgaft takes Starbucks in his neighborhood hometown as a representative space of *rootless cosmopolitanism* that rejects local culture and *hometown*. The traditional coffee house is, according to Wurgaft, where "everybody knows your name" and a space for "stable neighborhoods and the preservation of a sense of locality." Starbucks takes the place of the traditional local coffee house and serves a "'rootless cosmopolitan' urban culture."[58] Those who have a dire longing for an *unpolluted, pure* local culture tend to perceive cosmopolitan ethos as a fundamental threat to the preservation of locality and particular attachment to their community of belonging. However, one does not need to insist on a homogeneous culture in order to have a *hometown*. Yet Salman Rushdie offers a strikingly different view of cultural/ local *purity*. He enjoys *mongrelization,* but distrusts the "absolutism of the Pure," while celebrating "hybridity, impurity, intermingling, the transformation that comes of new and unexpected combinations of human beings, cultures, ideas, politics, movies, songs."[59] Although I am sympathetic to people's longing and desire for *purity,* for *unpolluted* past, we have to admit that cultural purity or local purity is an oxymoron,[60] as Anthony Appiah points out, because we already live a *cosmopolitan* life, where different cultures, arts, music, films, foods and religions from many places in the world intersect and mutually influence one another—wittingly or unwittingly. In this context, we can imagine the world as "our shared hometown,"[61] and this imagination will feed our hope for a better world as a place where everyone treats everyone else as kin, friend, and neighbor.

Varieties of Contemporary Cosmopolitanisms

A large number of scholars attempt to map cosmopolitanism, both as descriptive and normative discourse and practice, with different emphasis and positions in their works. Cosmopolitanism is *descriptive* in the sense that cosmopolitanism is "stimulated by the postmodern mix of boundaries between cultures and identities, accelerated by the dynamics of capital and consumption, empowered by capitalism undermining national borders, excited by the global audience of transnational social movements, and guided and encouraged by the evidence of world-wide communication (often just another word for misunderstanding) on central themes such as science, law, art, fashion, entertainment, and, not least, politics."[62] At the same time, contemporary cosmopolitanism is *normative* because the Kantian cosmopolitanism of human rights, for instance, takes precedence over national sovereignty. Here, one should see human rights not only in individualized terms but also in a transnationalized context, which "grants these rights to all individuals, independent of status, class, gender, nationality, religion....positing a *legally binding world society of individuals*."[63] Therefore, for this normative cosmopolitan democracy "with all the available human creativity and political-institutional imagination," establishing and testing the idea of "transnational institutions, transnational conflict recognition and resolution" is necessary and "a new political subject needs to be legitimated and founded: movements and parties of world citizens."[64] Cosmopolitanism refers to a *reality of multiple attachments,* or a ground discourse for cosmopolitics, "a name for the genuine striving toward common norms and mutual translatability."[65] One can understand cosmopolitanism in three ways: first, as a conceptual reference to a transnational or international legal and institutional order and governance; second, as cultural hybridities and critiques of liberal multiculturalism; and third, as ethical imperatives for responsibility and principles. Furthermore, the cosmopolitan discourse and exercise are also religious and theological frameworks that help people view self, others, the world, and the Divine in a new mode of understanding. The act of *categorizing* and *labeling* various types of cosmopolitanism is for me provisional, partial, and strategic. It is *provisional* and *partial* because it is impossible to draw a rigid line between different types of cosmopolitanism due to its overlapping and entangling aspects. Yet the reason for my introducing various types of cosmopolitanism here is *strategic:* to offer a clear idea about the differences in emphasis, claims, primary engagement and commitments, or disciplinary areas. There are various types of cosmopolitanism with different labels: Abject, Actually-existing, Comparative, Critical, Cultural, Dialogic, Discrepant, Market, Moral, Organic, Political cosmopolitanism, Postcolonial, Rooted, Rootless, Situated, Subaltern, Working-class, or Vernacular cosmopolitanism. Political and moral cosmopolitanism are the types of cosmopolitanism that I mostly engage, and, therefore, the major aspects of political and moral cosmopolitanism will appear throughout the book. However, whatever label one uses for cosmopolitanism, one must ask the following questions in order to avoid a false universalization and totalizing grand-narrativization: *For what ends* does one claim cosmopolitanism? *Whose interest* does it serve? I will examine several types of cosmopolitanism that might offer new angles through which one can examine and utilize cosmopolitanism as mobilizing discourse and practice in specific contexts. What follows is not to offer a comprehensive list of cosmopolitanisms but a glimpse of endless varieties of cosmopolitanism in terms of its angles, emphasis, and application in different contexts.

Cultural Cosmopolitanism: Cosmopolitanism as Postethnicity

In his *Postethnic America,* David Hollinger argues multiculturalism has its limits when it comes to dealing with the issues of *cultural diversity,* and, therefore, one needs to "take a step beyond multiculturalism,"[66] toward a *postethnic* perspective. Interpreting traditional cosmopolitanism as *proudly rootless,* Hollinger tries to construct *postethnicity* as the "critical renewal of cosmopolitanism"[67] with a sensitivity to *roots*, which means to appreciate the *ethnos* for a variety of ethnic connectedness/rootedness. In this sense, his *postethnicity* is a form of *rooted cosmopolitanism*. His cosmopolitanism, what he calls *postethnicity*, does not rule out particular ties to ethnic and other communities, but he wants to practice *postethnicity* in light of wider commitment to civic-democratic culture at the national level. Hollinger grounds his postethnic perspective in cosmopolitan elements salient in multiculturalism as discourse and movement, while curtailing the *pluralist* elements. He contends that cosmopolitanism is a significant intellectual and political tradition in the United States, and points to two noticeable tendencies within current discourse on ethnicity: cosmopolitanism and pluralism. Multiculturalism has reached its limit because it "is rent by an increasingly acute but rarely acknowledged tension between cosmopolitan and pluralist programs for the defense of cultural diversity."[68] Although both pluralism and cosmopolitanism promote tolerance and diversity, these two differ in various aspects:

> Pluralism differs from cosmopolitanism in the degree to which it endows with privilege particular groups, especially the communities that are well established at whatever time the ideal of pluralism is invoked. While cosmopolitanism is willing to put the future of every culture at risk through the sympathetic but critical scrutiny of other cultures, pluralism is more concerned to protect and perpetuate particular, existing cultures....If cosmopolitanism can be casual about community building and community maintenance and tends to seek voluntary affiliations of wide compass, pluralism promotes affiliations on the narrower grounds of shared history and is more quick to see reasons for drawing boundaries between communities. Cosmopolitanism is more oriented to *the individual*, whom it is likely to understand as a member of a number of different communities simultaneously. Pluralism is more oriented to *the group*, and is likely to identify each individual with reference to a single, primary community....This tension between pluralism and cosmopolitanism is not novel to the multiculturalist debates.[69]

He also distinguishes cosmopolitanism from universalism. Whereas universalism tries to find common ground, cosmopolitanism engages human diversity. In this sense, universalism is *unity-seeking*, while cosmopolitanism is *diversity-seeking*.[70] Hollinger's cosmopolitanism—*postethnicity* is his term—advocates cultural self-reflexivity, multiple attachments and identities, voluntary affiliation, respect for cultural differences and their richness, and affirmation of diversity. Hollinger acknowledges human need for *boundaries*. Yet, with his call for a *postethnic* cosmopolitan perspective, he invites us to an encounter with the questions of boundary-drawing: "*Which* boundaries, and *where*? We are all left with the responsibility for deciding *where* to try to draw *what* circles *with whom,* and *around what*."[71] Cultural cosmopolitanism highlights intercultural linkages, transnational mobility, and respecting cultural hybridities. The cultural hybridities and their richness are prevalent in the contemporary life of transnational travels and exchanges through mass media and social media. Those who simply travel around the world are not cosmopolitans, according to Ulf Hannerz, because they do not have "a willingness to engage with the Other," as "tourists are not participants; tourism is largely a spectator sport."[72] He continues, "[N]ow and then exiles can be cosmopolitans; but most of them are not," and also, "Most ordinary labour migrants do not become cosmopolitans either," because the cosmopolitan perspective "must entail relationships to a plurality of cultures understood as distinct entities."[73] Cosmopolitans, Hannerz contends, are those "who have chosen to live abroad" and "can go home when it suits them."[74] People often criticize cultural cosmopolitanism as a form of elitist cosmopolitanism.

Market Cosmopolitanism: Cosmopolitanizing Free Global Market

Market cosmopolitanism is used to highlight the role of the economic market, while lessening the role of politics of the nation-state. Market cosmopolitans believe in a free global market that would maximize the profit of the free market system and rules. Although market cosmopolitans may sound as if they respect the individual person's singularity, the function of respecting the singularity is to pursue their material benefit. The market cosmopolitanism can arise from the process of economic globalization, where the function of the nation-state gets diminished after the new system of free market gets completely established. It underscores the "free movement of labor" and argues, "[I]ndividuals should have the freedom to migrate, the freedom to choose their occupation."[75] Although market cosmopolitanism may have its virtue in taking all human beings as equal trading partners, market cosmopolitanism has a danger that could fundamentally distort cosmopolitan ethos that regards the individual human being as the ultimate unit of ethico-political concern, not of market concern.

Cosmopolitan magazine, one of the most popular magazines in the U.S. and throughout the world, is an interesting example for how people can misconceive, misuse, and distort the profound meaning of the word *cosmopolitan*. The *cosmopolitan women* that the magazine portrays, for instance, are those whose primary concern is to please men with their sex, make-up, and fashion, perpetuating heterosexism and homophobism. If one takes a look at the magazine, one instantly realizes that all the portrayals of the *cosmopolitan women* look so exotic, sexy, and slender, with dazzling smiles.[76] Market cosmopolitans misdirect the ethos of the *cosmic citizenship* in cosmopolitanism into a capitalized form of *cosmic citizenship* that crosses any type of *border* for the sake of material profit, not for taking a responsibility for the other, for defending the rights of the others, and expanding the circles of inclusion and hospitality.

Critical Cosmopolitanism: Reconceiving Cosmopolitanism for Diversality from a Subaltern Perspective

Walter Mignolo terms and articulates *critical cosmopolitanism,* juxtaposing it with globalization, which is a process of "the homogeneity of the planet from above—economically, politically, and culturally."[77] Although *globalization from below* is to counter *globalization from above* from the experience and perspective of those who suffer from the consequences of *globalization from above,* cosmopolitanism differs, according to Mignolo, from these two types of globalization. Mignolo defines globalization as a "a set of designs to manage the world," and cosmopolitanism as "a set of projects toward planetary conviviality."[78] Mignolo takes globalization and cosmopolitanism to illustrate the complexity of a configuration of modernity, arguing that one cannot separate the development of modernity from the development of coloniality, which Mignolo contends started from the sixteenth century, not from the eighteenth century, as many perceive.[79] Mignolo calls the process of construction of modern world system *global design*. Two global designs in the European Enlightenment and modernity exist: *Christianity's global design* and *the civilizing global design*.[80] Francisco de Vitoria at the University of Salamanca articulated the *Christianity's global design*—a part of the European Renaissance—whereas Immanuel Kant constructed the *civilizing global design*. *Cosmopolitan projects,* which Mignolo contrasts with *global design,* began working with both moments of modernity: Christianity's global design and civilizing global design. Global designs are "to control and homogenize," whereas cosmopolitan projects by Vitoria, Kant, and Marx challenge the global designs, although ambiguously and incompletely. Mignolo points out that coloniality is "the hidden face of modernity and its very condition of possibility." He goes on to argue, "The colonization of the Americas in the sixteenth and the seventeenth centuries, and of Africa and Asia in the nineteenth and the early twentieth centuries, consolidated an idea of the

West: a geopolitical image that exhibits chronological movement."[81]

Mignolo locates *cosmopolitan projects* within the modern/colonial world in the 1500s and argues that the cosmopolitan projects can be *managerial*, as in global designs in Christianity, nineteenth-century imperialism, or late-twentieth-century neoliberal globalization, or can be *emancipatory*, as in the views of Vitoria, Kant, or Marx.[82] *Critical cosmopolitanism* emerges from the awareness of the shortcomings of both cosmopolitan projects and global designs, which are still constitutive of modernity with its coloniality. Here Mignolo distinguishes *cosmopolitanism from global designs* from *critical cosmopolitanism*. *Cosmopolitanism from global designs* still implies "the will to control and homogenize (either from the right or from the left, as in the Christian and civilizing mission or in the planetary revolution of the proletariat)."[83] Mignolo illustrates the ironic and contradictory function of *cosmopolitanism from global designs* as follows:

> In the sixteenth century, the Christian mission embraced both global designs of conversion and the justification of war, on the one hand, and a dissenting position that recognized the "rights of the people" that were being suppressed and erased by Christian global designs, on the other. A similar argument could be made with respect to the global design articulated by the civilizing mission as a colonial project and the "rights of man and of the citizen"—this argument opens up a critical perspective on global designs, although global designs were historically contradictory.... The civilizing and Christian missions shared colonization as their final orientation, while cosmopolitan projects such as Vitoria's and Kant's were attentive to the dangers and the excesses of global designs.[84]

Mignolo points out that *cosmopolitanism from global designs* failed to dismantle the ideological frame captured by global designs. Mignolo does not dismiss but retrieves the critical dimensions in cosmopolitanism from global designs and reconceives them with the name *critical cosmopolitanism*. Two issues are significant in critical cosmopolitanism: human rights and global citizenship. Critical cosmopolitanism calls for the need to reconceptualize the issues of human rights and global citizenship, of which concepts historically emerged in the Eurocentric colonial horizon of modernity. Mignolo warns about the danger in articulating cosmopolitanism today without carefully examining the hidden connection of *cosmopolitan projects from global designs* with Eurocentrism. Following Enrique Dussel's analysis of modernity by linking modernity with Eurocentrism, Mignolo reiterates that modernity includes both a "rational concept of emancipation" and, at the same time, "an irrational myth, a justification for genocidal violence."[85] Kant's cosmopolitanism, with his notion of *perpetual peace* and *cosmopolitan rights*, is an example for the limit of *cosmopolitanism from global designs* that Mignolo points out, especially, I would say, in terms of Kant's view of race. Critical cosmopolitanism involves reconceptualizing the universality of human rights and citizenship that embraces not only the Western but also the non-Western people that modern *cosmopolitanism from global designs* does not have in its horizon. Mignolo proposes a new cosmopolitanism, what he terms critical and dialogical cosmopolitanism:

> Critical and dialogic cosmopolitanism as a regulative principle demands yielding generously ("convivially" said Vitoria; "friendly" said Kant) toward diversity as a universal and cosmopolitan project in which everyone participates instead of "being participated." Such a regulative principle shall replace and displace the abstract universal cosmopolitan ideals (Christian, liberal, socialist, neoliberal) that had helped (and continue to help) to hold together the modern/colonial world system and to preserve the managerial role of the North Atlantic.[86]

Contemporary cosmopolitanism should be critical and dialogic, and an exercise of border thinking from the perspective of particular local histories that a sense of the abstract universality overlooks. In this sense, *diversality*, not universality, "should be the relentless practice of critical and dialogical cosmopolitanism rather than a blueprint of a future and ideal society projected from a single point of view."[87] Mignolo argues that his critical cosmopolitanism is a way for globalization from below, and also a way for geopolitical diversality. The critical and dialogic cosmopolitanism that Mignolo proposes from a subaltern perspective, which "implies not inferiority but awareness of a subaltern position in a current geopolitical distribution of epistemic power,"[88] helps one radically reexamine and reconceptualize the existing notions of human rights, democracy, citizenship, and justice.

Rooted Cosmopolitanism: Significance of One's Rooted Locationality

Anthony Appiah proposes what he calls *rooted cosmopolitanism*. According to Appiah, rooted cosmopolitanism arises from awareness of the significance of one's location, nationality, or cultural differences and is not "the name for a dialogue among static closed cultures, each of which is internally homogeneous and different from all the others; not a celebration of the beauty of a collection of closed boxes." On the contrary, the rooted cosmopolitanism is "a form of universalism that is sensitive to the ways in which historical context may shape the significance of a practice."[89] In this sense, Appiah stands in line with Martha Nussbaum's universalist cosmopolitanism. Nussbaum contends that we humans need to regard ourselves as surrounded by a *series of concentric circles*. She illustrates:

> The first one encircles the self, the next takes in the immediate family, then follows the extended family, then, in order, neighbors or local groups, fellow city-dwellers, and fellow countrymen [*sic*]—and we can easily add to this list groupings based on ethnic, linguistic, historical, professional, gender, or sexual identities. Outside all these circles is the largest one, humanity as a whole. Our task as citizens of the world will be to "draw the circles of somehow toward the center,...making all human beings more like our fellow city-dwellers.[90]

For Nussbaum, like Appiah, local affiliations and attachments are the most sensible way of doing the *universal* way because human beings live best on a rooted, small scale. The cosmopolitan experience is possible not by shared "beliefs and values because of our common capacity for reason," but by a "different human capacity that grounds our sharing.... the grasp of a narrative logic that allows us to construct the world to which our imaginations respond." In this context of rooted cosmopolitanism, the "role of the narrative imagination" is significant because it is "our response to a sequence of particulars."[91] Nussbaum's concept of a *series of concentric circles,* which acknowledges the significance of one's rootedness in the local, raises a skeptical question especially in terms of locating the self at the heart of her cosmopolitan *concentric circles*. Locating the self at the center of cosmopolitan concentric circles presupposes "universal liberal values privileged above family, ethnic group or nation" and such a notion seems "inadequate in relation to the millions of refugees and migrants fleeing violence and poverty." [92]Alfredo Gonzalez-Ruibal harshly criticizes the cosmopolitanism presented by Appiah and Nussbaum. He contends that Appiah's cosmopolitanism is a typical example of "the elite-centered, self-satisfied streak of cosmopolitanism" and cosmopolitanism of "a member of a privileged Westernized upper class."[93] The cosmopolitanism suggested by Appiah is, Gonzalez-Ruibal argues, "a kind of comfortable cosmopolitanism that allows Western(ized) elites to keep their lifestyles and worldviews, while at the same time it appeases their consciences." He goes on to point out that such cosmopolitanism by Appiah and Nussbaum tends to leave "the question of the other largely unproblematized," to have "romantic vision of difference," and to overlook "global structural inequalities, long-term processes of oppression, and the real and traumatic impact that Western culture and politics exercise over the third world."[94] Identifying himself as cosmopolitan archaeologist, Gonzalez-Ruibal defends for *vernacular cosmopolitanism,* which he draws primarily from Homi Bhabha.

***Subaltern Cosmopolitanism:* The Subaltern Can Speak**

Jamil Khader articulates *subaltern cosmopolitanism* primarily based on Caribbean experiences of diaspora, especially through Puerto Rican women's writings, with contexts in the experiences of imperialism, patriarchal nationalism, and circular migrancy between two countries—Puerto Rico and the U.S. Her articulation of subaltern cosmopolitism begins not from a privileged social location but with the extremely marginalized experience of homelessness of the subaltern. She firmly believes: "The Subaltern can speak, but the ignorant and paternalistic colonial experts cannot hear her."[95]

The primary engagement of subaltern cosmopolitanism is in the people of the *circular migrancy* in the metropolitan cities of the United States—the contemporary subaltern whose homelessness continues at the bottom of socioeconomic hierarchy both *home* and *away*. Those whose roots are in Puerto Rico and live in the U.S., for instance, are "more or less permanently in transit"[96] between Puerto Rico and the U.S. Instead of asking *where-are-you-from* to those on permanent transit, James Clifford comes up with a new formula for an "intercultural identity question": "[W]here are you between?"[97] They experience multidirectional displacement as second-class citizens in the U.S. due to their racial, language, and economic status, but remain extending the borders of such multidirectional displacement. Whether they are in their *homeland,* Puerto Rico, or in the U.S., they find themselves *homeless, non-belonging*. For them, therefore, remapping and refashioning *home* in diasporic imaginary is significant in articulating their subaltern cosmopolitanism:

> Home. I'm going home, I thought, and the happiness bubbled in me and spilled over. Home to the broad split leaves of the plantain and banana, the gawky palm, the feathery tree fern, to the red bell of the hibiscus and the yellow trumpets of the canarion, to the warm moist sweet smell of the air....But this was never home! We're staying at Samuel's apartment in the heart of the city, and I bounce around Santurce like a tourist....It's a foreign city for me for all I lived eleven years in Puerto Rico.[98]

After such a longing for home, they realize they cannot find home anywhere and they are permanently in transit. By rewriting, remapping, refashioning home through tropes of homelessness, multilocational displacement, and transnational networks, those women writers reinvent a new sense of agency and articulate new sociopolitical and cultural agendas, not residing in a sense of victimhood.

In her work on subaltern cosmopolitanism, Khader contends that writings by Puerto Rican women such as Aurora Levins Morales, Rosario Morales, and Esmeralda Santiago carry the following four strategies for constructing subaltern cosmopolitanism: First, those women writers rearticulate and extend their experience and condition of homelessness to provincial and metropolitan/cosmopolitan terrains concurrently; second, they take their experience of homelessness into the multidirectional movements within the multiple spaces—insular and metropolitan— linking them to the international groups; third, they present a postcolonial criticism of the United States' imperial practice in Puerto Rico and show their serious concerns about their nation and its well-being; and fourth, they refashion a new sense of home, belonging, and agent-hood as subaltern cosmopolitans, and make a commitment to "communities of struggle everywhere" and foster a "transnational and transethnic politics of solidarity."[99] Subaltern cosmopolitanism is to articulate the subaltern's ability to decenter imperialism and to act in "solidarity with oppressed minorities against the legacies of segregation and identity politics within the borders of the United States and with oppressed communities of refugees, forced exiles, and revolutionaries across the globe."[100] Proponents try to deessentialize the fixed identity, home, and culture and harshly criticize the hegemonic practice of U.S. imperialism, racism, and ecocide, and connect them to "the aggressive masculine desire to control nature and all those who are different, especially women and racial others."[101]

It seems clear that scholars and writers of subaltern cosmopolitanism adopt the term *subaltern* in a different way from Gayatri Chakravorty Spivak. In her controversial work, "Can Subaltern Speak," Spivak concludes, "The subaltern cannot speak."[102] In Khader the opposite is true: subaltern can and do speak as agents for change, while embracing being second-class citizens and permanently homeless. The dilemma of the name, *subaltern* cosmopolitanism, lies in the fact that at the moment the subaltern realize their victimhood, analyze, and speak out about their victimization experience and context, they are no longer the *absolute victim,* the bearer of the name, *the subaltern.* For, according to Spivak, "[i]f the subaltern can speak then, thank God, the subaltern is not a subaltern any more."[103] If one follows the definition of the *subaltern* as those "structurally and systemically written out or excluded from any hegemonic ideology, official history, developed economic structure, or political system of representation,"[104] *subalterns* are the *absolute victims* who cannot even identify themselves as victims and therefore are unable to present themselves as *subalterns*. The subaltern cannot be the *speaking-subject* but only be the *spoken-subject,* and therefore can be present only in absence, not in presence. Accordingly, those *subaltern cosmopolitans* can speak *about/of/for* the subaltern but cannot be subalterns themselves because when they can identify themselves as victims and relocate themselves as the agents, they cease to be, according to the definition of the tem, subalterns. Spivak's formula of *can-question, can-subaltern-speak,* may have to take a different formula, *can-I/you/we-listen-subaltern-speaking*.

Despite its linguistically ironic aspect in *subaltern cosmopolitanism,* subaltern cosmopolitanism presents new cosmopolitan consciousness with transnational subjectivities among those who are at the bottom of the economic hierarchy in a world of globalization. Subaltern cosmopolitanism confirms that cosmopolitanism does not have to be a discourse and practice of the elites, as many perceive. Subaltern cosmopolitanism further invites us to revisit the *travel* discourse from a different angle. In a world of globalization, *traveling* between national/regional borders becomes a daily reality and a significant experience for constructing cosmopolitan subjectivities and transnational identities. However, not all travels have equal function and purpose.

Here it is important to note that not all *transnationals* automatically become *cosmopolitans,* because it is possible for one to be a transnational without being a cosmopolitan in terms of one's willingness to engage with the others, openness to the others, and awareness of the macro-interdependency of the others. Ulf Hannerz makes a distinction between *cosmopolitans* and *transnationals*. Cosmopolitans are "willing to engage with the Other, an intellectual and aesthetic stance of openness toward divergent cultural experience,"[105] whereas transnationals tend to be simply frequent travellers, usually occupational, who hold "structures of meaning carried by social networks."[106] Hannerz runs the risk of being Eurocentric and class biased, due to his separation of "professional-occupational transnational cultures" from "migrant or refugee transnational cultures," as he excludes the possibility of the cosmopolitan subjectivity and identities of working class migrant workers, for instance.[107]

Vernacular Cosmopolitanism: Cultural Translation as an Act of Survival

Vernacular cosmopolitanism, coined by Homi Bhabha, is one of the most important parts of contemporary debates on cosmopolitanism. It raises controversial questions such as whether the local, rooted, specific can exist side by side with translocal, transnational, postnational, transhistorical, universalist, or modernist cosmopolitanism, and whether current cosmopolitanism is only for the elite or if cosmopolitanism for the powerless, the non-elite is possible. Vernacular cosmopolitanism is, in a way, a *non-elite* form of cosmopolitanism in a postcolonial world. Alfredo Gonzalez-Ruibal, a cosmopolitan archaeologist, argues for two kinds of cosmopolitans: "the powerful and the disempowered."[108] The *powerful* cosmopolitans are those who have the power to choose to live in different countries, whereas the *disempowered* cosmopolitans are those migrant workers and refugees who are forced to live in countries other than their own. Gonzalez-Ruibal affirmatively views Homi Bhabha's *vernacular cosmopolitanism* as a sort of redeemable cosmopolitanism, saving cosmopolitanism from its flaw and danger of becoming a practice solely of the privileged Westernized upper class.

Vernacular cosmopolitanism may sound like an oxymoron because *vernacular* primarily concerns the local while cosmopolitanism pertains to the global/planetary. However, the local and the planetary, global, international, transnational, postnational are not necessarily in opposition. These two dimensions—the vernacular and the planetary—reveal the equally significant dimensions of human lives. Rigidifying the traditional boundaries of the local and the planetary does not work any longer when the mobility of the world populations by migrations, refugees, and migrant workers becomes the daily reality of people. Homi Bhabha bases his *vernacular* or *marginal* cosmopolitanism upon three points: First, vernacular cosmopolitanism offers an ethical entitlement to the sense of community without being trapped in the transcendent human universal claim; second, vernacular cosmopolitanism is conscious of the insufficiency of the self and the imperative of openness to the needs of others; and third, vernacular cosmopolitanism finds the significant promise for ethical advancement in the subaltern—the absolute victim.

Homi Bhabha begins his work on vernacular cosmopolitanism with his personal life story, in which he divides his life between two countries, Britain and America, realizing that he cannot go back to perpetually live in India, his own home country. He admits, "I cannot imagine what it would be like to live without that unresolved tension between cultures and countries that has become the narrative of my life, and the defining characteristic of my work."[109] People could regard his life as "a betrayal in itself: a hybrid, a half-breed, a foot in each camp and groundless for all that."[110] However, he has experienced in his daily life a "rich cultural mix of languages and lifestyles that most cosmopolitan Indian cities celebrate and perpetuate."[111] Homi Bhabha builds his cosmopolitanism on the mobility of people, especially the subaltern populations. According to Bhabha, vernacular cosmopolitanism is a kind of *cultural translation* and "cultural translation is not simply appropriation or adaptation; it is a process through which cultures are required to revise their own systems of reference, norms and values, by departing from their habitual or 'inbred' rules of transformation."[112]

In vernacular cosmopolitanism, one delves into cultural differences and their richness, without setting hierarchy among different cultural values or homogenizing their differences in a unilateral way. In a community of vernacular cosmopolitanism, the ethic of proximity remains the essential quality of the community, "where foreigners are warmly invited into the fold, even fetishized for their 'foreignness.'"[113] Here vernacular cosmopolitanism is not an elite's universalist cosmopolitanism that seeks to establish a unity, because vernacular cosmopolitanism as a cultural translation is an *act of survival* of the grassroots people with exile experiences, who encounter marginalization, exclusion as their everyday experiences in the wretched condition. However, they are vernacular cosmopolitans who reveal "in the midst of loss, poverty and defeat, the chances for creativity, humor and the virtues of a common life enshrined in the everyday experience of social marginality—a common life that is not in the least commonplace."[114] Bhabha closes his work on vernacular cosmopolitanism with a deeply moving personal narrative:

> No name is yours until you speak it; somebody returns your call and suddenly, the circuit of signs, gestures, gesticulations, is established. You are part of a dialogue that may not be heard or heralded at first, but your person cannot be denied. The voices of the crossing, once drawn by the siren's song, may lead you astray, but strangely you find yourself the long way around. In another's country that is also your own, your person divides, and in following the forked path, you encounter yourself in a double movement…once as stranger, and then as friend.[115]

One's exile experience, whether it is physical or epistemological, can empower one to create one's own world in between space of *home* and *away*, to adopt life-affirming principles for one's own survival, and to move beyond the rigid boundaries of the mind. It is important, however, to acknowledge that the *vernacular* culture and knowledge, without an awareness of global historical processes and sociopolitical contexts and the interlinkedness between the *vernacular/local* and the *planetary/global*, would lose its relevance in the contemporary world. It is possible for a *vernacular cosmopolitan* to get committed to the specific vernacular experiences and events and, at the same time, to get connected to *transhistorical, translocal* contexts, events, memories, and solidarities. Vernacular cosmopolitanism is to be "on the border, *in between,* introducing the global-cosmopolitan 'action at a distance' into the very grounds—now displaced—of the domestic."[116]

A vernacular cosmopolitan works "on the border—the marginality groups in third world countries,"[117] and transports the border to one's own homeland. As Slavoj Zizek urges one to resist the temptation of the "ethical 'gentrification' of the neighbor,"[118] vernacular cosmopolitanism adopts the radical claim for the responsibility toward others that does not hierarchicalize the others by their national belonging but only by the urgency of the need. It seems to me that the binary of *elites versus non-elites* or *the powerful versus disempowered* of the conceptual framework in vernacular cosmopolitanism is too simplistic to capture the complexity of human sociocultural locations. However, vernacular cosmopolitanism offers an important site of self-criticality about the possible danger of romanticized cosmopolitanism by those who have sufficient material, institutional, and sociopolitical power to freely *cross* the borders, but without making any specific commitments for change in a given context.

3

Cosmopolitanism

Philosophical and Political Discourses

Love the world as your own self;
then you can truly care for all things.

—LAO TZU[1]

[Hu]man is a yes that vibrates to cosmic harmonies.

—FRANTZ FANON[2]

I support universe.

—EMMANUEL LEVINAS[3]

Thought is no longer theoretical. As soon as it functions it offends or reconciles, attracts or repels, breaks, dissociates, unites or reunites; it cannot help but liberate and enslave.... thought, at the level of its existence, in its very dawning, is in itself an action—a perilous act.

—MICHEL FOUCAULT[4]

Diversifying the Genealogy of Cosmopolitanism

The term *cosmopolitan* used by Diogenes of Sinope captures the ideal of *cosmic belonging* and enlarges the space of an individual's belonging from the polis to the cosmos. It is not surprising to learn that Diogenes was the first one who used the term *cosmopolitan,* as he was an exile, an outsider, and a homeless person living on the street. Being in exile helps one see the inessential nature of the narrowly defined sense of one's belonging only to a national or geographical confinement. The use of the term *cosmopolitan* denotes primarily the enlarged notion of one's belonging rather than a citizenship in the polis: *cosmic citizenship*. The meaning of the term *cosmopolitan* extends one's sense of belonging to a more public realm than just a matter of individual belonging, especially in the era of Enlightenment in the West. The cosmopolitan idea is to claim that every individual human being is entitled to human rights and membership in the universal community as *Welt-bürger* (world-citizen). The contemporary use of cosmopolitan or cosmopolitanism that I employ encompasses three aspects: First, an *ethics of singularity* that denotes an unconditional equality of every individual as a singular person; second, a mutual recognition and affirmation not only in private but also in public realms such as politics; and third, a scope of justice and human rights.

Some people perceive cosmopolitanism as denying the importance of local affiliation. Although there is always an innate tension between the particularity and universality of human belonging, the tension should not necessarily mean to reject one over the other. Cosmopolitanism invites one to radically rethink the relationship between particularity and universality. Cosmopolitanism does not aim to reverse the hierarchy between particularity and universality, and to privilege universality over particularity, or to privilege cosmic citizenship over national citizenship. What cosmopolitan discourse offers is a new configuration of the seemingly binary position as a whole. Only when one moves beyond the idea of *binary oppositionality* between particularity and universality, locality and globality, and nationalism and cosmopolitanism, can one acknowledge that cosmopolitanism offers significant universal principles and tools for ethics, politics, philosophies, and theologies for today's world.

Scholars in the West usually consider three or four historical moments of cosmopolitanism: the ancient world (Zeno/Stoicism), the Enlightenment (Kant's moment), post-totalitarian thought (Arendt's moment), and late North American thought (Nussbaum's moment).[5] It is interesting to see how scholars construct a *genealogy* of cosmopolitanism differently depending on the location of the author(s). German scholar Ulrich Beck, for instance, neither includes Nussbaum in the genealogy nor uses her works on cosmopolitanism in his book. Her work is simply absent from the bibliography even though Beck refers to the book *Conceiving Cosmopolitanism,* in which Fine and Cohen illustrate four cosmopolitan moments that include Nussbaum. For Ulrich, there are three historical moments of emancipatory cosmopolitanism, omitting a contemporary moment from North America.[6]

My concern here is not a question about whether or not we should include the *Nussbaum moment,* or how many historical moments are in the genealogy of cosmopolitanism. Instead, my question is about the West-centric nature in constructing a *universal* genealogy of cosmopolitanism and also about the *inequality of ignorance* not only within the West but also between the West and *the Rest*. Here, I use *the Rest* in italics to denote the fundamental problem in the way we categorize the world into two: the *West* and the *Non-West/the Rest.* As Albert Memmi rightly points out, the colonizer always distinguishes the colonized from the colonizer as *Not,* as being deficient in the qualities the colonizer has.[7] In this context, the term *the Rest,* as the *Not-West,* exemplifies the way one's perception places the West at the discursive and political center in the world while placing *the Rest/Non-West* on the periphery. As I do not have an alternative term that solves the dilemma of categorization that undoes the asymmetrical power-differential in languages, my use of *the Rest* in italic is a minimalist act of contestation to reveal the Westcentric view of the world. Dipesh Chakrabarty rightly points out:

> "They" produce their work in relative ignorance of non-Western histories, and this does not seem to affect the quality of their work....We cannot even afford an equality or symmetry of ignorance at this level without taking the risk of appearing old-fashioned or outdated.... The problem is not particular to historian. An unselfconscious but blatant example of this "inequality of ignorance" in literary studies....This problem of asymmetric ignorance is not simply a matter of cultural cringe on our part or of cultural arrogance on the part of the European historians.... Our footnotes bear rich testimony to the insights we have derived from their knowledge and creativity. The dominance of Europe as the subject of all histories is a part of a much more profound theoretical condition under which historical knowledge is produced in the third world.[8]

Wrestling with *the inequality of ignorance* between the West and *the Rest,* one needs first to decenter the *cosmopolitanism moments* in the existing genealogy of cosmopolitanism, and then to constantly diversify the genealogy because no one race, ethnicity, or culture owns the virtue of the great spirit. Cosmopolitanism should treat every individual human being as equal and free—as the *citizen of the cosmos* regardless *who/what one is*.

Tracing back to the genealogy of the cosmopolitan mentality in the philosophical tradition in the West, one encounters the constitutive side of modernity, and realizes that coloniality is the hidden side of the very modernity that laid the groundwork of Western imperialistic global design to *control* the entire world. The Spanish missionaries, for instance, set up the parameters in order to judge human intelligence and civilization in the sixteenth century in terms of whether the people were able to do "alphabetic writing."[9] The Western global design is the beginning of imperial universalization and normativization of modern European knowledge and language in the world. In this process of colonial normativizing, non-European knowledge became devalued, dismissed, ignored, and eventually *subalternized*. Immanuel Kant's cosmopolitanism, for instance, is in fundamental contradiction with his racial and sexual prejudices and Eurocentrism, although his cosmopolitanism has made a significant contribution to laying the groundwork for contemporary cosmopolitan discourse.

Grounded in a Eurocentric imperialist construction of knowledge, people have regarded European philosophy and knowledge as *universal* and viewed the knowledge from outside the West as somehow irrational, backward, indigenous, local, exotic, or primitive, as lacking *universal* connotations and *authenticities* of knowledge. Finding an alternative to restituting the colonial subalternization of knowledge is, however, not simply reversing the position of the center and margin or the superior and inferior. *Deuniversalizing* and *provincializing* the Western knowledge and desubalternizing the non-Western knowledge, for instance, can happen neither by relocating the non-Western, subaltern knowledge in the center, nor by simply replacing the Western knowledge with the non-Western through such an exotic, romanticizing phrase as *the Wisdom of the East*. It is important to keep in mind that the solution to Western discursive imperialism is not naïve *nativism* that uncritically romanticizes or idealizes the so-called *indigenous* non-Western culture and philosophy.

Thus, my inclusion of Taoist philosophy in a genealogy of cosmopolitanism derives not from a nativist desire to demonstrate the *unique* virtue of the East. Instead, my inclusion derives from a postcolonial intention to *diversify* the channels of genealogies of the greatness of the human ideas to affirm and reaffirm the sheer truth that "no race possesses a monopoly of beauty, of intelligence, of force."[10] Deuniversalizing and provincializing the West are possible by desubalternizing the non-West, where different ways of knowing and practicing mingle together to liberate and enlarge human possibilities regardless of who/where/what one is. The postcolonial task of *provincializing the West* does not mean to simply deny the significant achievements of the intellectual, philosophical, political, or theological tradition of the West. I do not overlook the reality that all the significant concepts "such as citizenship, the state, civil society, public sphere, human rights, equality before the law, the individual, distinctions between public and private, the idea of the subject, democracy, popular sovereignty, social justice, scientific rationality, and so on all bear the burden of European thought and history."[11] Having borne the European trace in all the political, economic, or theological concepts that we are dealing with today, one cannot discuss contemporary socio-politico-theological issues without these concepts that were constructed in Europe, regardless of one's geopolitical location.

As one can see in Kant, the idea and vision of the Enlightenment of *universal* humanism or cosmopolitanism of Europe was great. It critically failed, however, in its practice in a concrete reality in the course of colonialism, denying its own principle of *universal humanism* for the colonized by becoming the colonizer. Imperialist Europe ended up being at war with its own humanism in the course of colonialism. My question follows: Is it necessary or possible to collectively deny the Enlightenment vision for the equality and freedom of every individual human being of ethical singularity, at least in principle if not in practice? Or do we need to create a "New Enlightenment," of which Jacques Derrida speaks, which is free of the illusions of the old Enlightenment? [12]

Along the line of Nietzsche, Derrida advocates an *active forgetfulness* [*Vergesslichkeit*], which is "an attribute boldly chosen by the philosopher in order to avoid falling into the trap of 'historical knowledge.'"[13] Through this *active forgetfulness,* one needs to deuniversalize and denormativize Europe, but, at the same time, one must reuniversalize, resituate, and renormativize the great spirit of human equality, justice, and freedom that the European Enlightenment happened to construct. Postcolonial perspective invites one to become committed to the indispensably *universal* notion of what it means to be human, of which significant value Frantz Fanon did not give up, even when he realized that "European imperialism had reduced that idea to the figure of the settler-colonial white man [*sic*]."[14] Fanon declares:

> [T]he European game has finally ended; we must find something different.... Europe has done what she set out to do and on the whole she has done it well; let us stop blaming her, but let us say to her firmly that she should not make such a song and dance about it....us stop envying her.... What we want to do is to go forward all the time....in the company of Man [*sic*], in the company of *all* men.... For Europe, for ourselves, and for humanity, comrades, we must turn over a new leaf, we must work out new concepts, and try to set afoot a new man.[15]

In his struggle for decolonization, Fanon seeks for a "new humanism,"[16] still adhering to the universal notion of human inherited from the European Enlightenment. Like Fanon, most of us, raised and educated in democratic public institutions, are standing and writing within this inheritance of the European Enlightenment and the nineteenth century, and could not deny that it "is now itself a part of the global heritage of all postcolonial thinkers."[17]

I entirely concur with what Gilles Deleuze rightly argues: "A theory is exactly like a box of tools. It has nothing to do with the signifier. It must be useful. It must function.... A theory does not totalize; it is an instrument for multiplication and it also multiplies itself."[18] Being born and raised in Asia, and teaching and living in the U.S., I am writing from a liminal space between the *imagined* categories of the West and the East. Wherever the *wisdom* comes from, I am willing to take it as long as it is *useful* and *functions* as an effective *tool* to complexify, multiply, and diversify the current configuration of *what-it-is* and eventually enlarge the circle of inclusion of people regardless who/what they are. The geographical origin of a discourse does not matter to me; nor does the gender, race, or ethnicity of the signifier of the knowledge, theory, or discourse. What matters to me the most is whether the discourse, theory, knowledge, or *wisdom* is effective and useful in liberating and enlarging human possibilities regardless *who* one is, *what* one is, or *where* one is. In this sense, Foucault's new way of locating the function of the author is thought provoking:

> No longer the tiresome repetitions:
> "Who is the real author?"
> "Have we proof of his [*sic*] authenticity and originality?"
> "What has he revealed of his most profound self in his language?"
> New questions will be heard:
> "What are the modes of existence of this discourse?"
> "Where does it come from; how is it circulated; who controls it?"
> "What placements are determined for possible subjects?"
> "Who can fulfill these diverse functions of the subject?"[19]

Cosmopolitan discourse would "unfold in a pervasive anonymity"[20] regardless of the authors, or the *author-function.* Although there are *authors* in the course of the public development of specific cosmopolitan discourse, it is important to note, "the author enters into his [*sic*] own death....it is languages which speak, not the authors."[21] Cosmopolitanism, not necessarily the *authors* of the cosmopolitan spirit, *speaks* about the urgent need for and the significance of relocating our discourse on, and current practice of, the scope and application of rights and justice for every singular human being regardless of the origin of the person's birth and belonging.

Cosmopolitan Condition: Cosmic Citizenship and Equality of Beings

The notion of cosmic citizenship and equality of beings that I present both from Greek and Taoist philosophies must not have had a geopolitical ramification for the contemporary world in its respective time and context. I would argue, however, that the very idea of *ontological equality* of all beings in Taoist philosophy and of *cosmic belonging* in Greek philosophy can offer significant epistemological grounding for further development and expansion of the cosmopolitan ideal today.

Cosmic Citizenship in Greek Philosophy

The ancient Greek term *kosmopolites,* a combination of *kosmos* and *polites,* is the origin of the word *cosmopolitan* in English, which simply signifies *citizen of the cosmos*. Diogenes of Sinope (ca. 390–323 B.C.E.), who coined the term, stated, "I am a citizen of the cosmos [*kosmopolites*],"[22] when asked where he came from. Some suggest that Socrates predates Diogenes as the first thinker to regard himself as a *world citizen*. When asked where he was from, Socrates also replied, not "Athens," but "the world/cosmos," thereby embracing the universe as his city.[23] Here, however, the meaning of *citizen of the world* must be different from how we now tend to perceive it because Athenian *citizenship* at that time explicitly excluded women, slaves, and foreigners.[24] People have translated the word *kosmopolites* into English in three ways: a citizen of the world, a citizen of the cosmos, and a citizen of the universe. Although the most generally used translation of *kosmopolites* in English is *a citizen of the world,* I adopt *a citizen of the cosmos* because the Greek usage of the fourth century B.C.E. connects the word *kosmos* to "its full force of 'universe,'"[25] which is larger than the *world*. Considering the fact that Diogenes tried to extend the sphere of operations of citizenship beyond the world of human beings in his use of the word *kosmos,* it seems appropriate to me to use *a citizen of the cosmos* rather than a *citizen of the world*. Diogenes lived as a street philosopher, a life of being marginalized as a *resident alien* in Athens without citizen rights or firm economic resources for daily survival. But it is interesting to see that Diogenes considered himself a *citizen* and that his *citizenship* functioned not just in a polis, but more *in the cosmos,* the largest community that a human could ever imagine.

The Cynic movement lasted for almost a millennium in Greek antiquity and engendered a significant range of ideas that influenced various areas of thoughts. Cynics adopted innovative forms of parody, satire, dialogue, diatribe, and aphorism and did not construct *theories*. Therefore, most resources on Cynicism are mostly of an anecdotal-biographical kind, such as by Diogenes Laërtius, which are the most important sources of the Cynic tradition.[26] Although there are various assumptions about the origin of and reasons for the name *Cynics,* meaning literally *dog-like,* the following four reasons seem plausible:

> First because of the *indifference* of their way of life, for they make a cult of indifference and, like dogs, eat and make love in public, go barefoot, and sleep in tubs and at crossroads.... The second reason is that the dog is a shameless animal, and they make a cult of shamelessness, not as being beneath modesty, but as superior to it.... The third reason is that the dog is a good guard, and they guard the tenets of their philosophy.... The fourth reason is that the dog is a discriminating animal which can distinguish between its friends and enemies.... So do they recognize as friends those who are suited to philosophy, and receive them kindly, while those unfitted they drive away, like dogs, by barking at them.[27]

Therefore, it seems obvious that the label Cynics is socially ascribed, not self-claimed. Diogenes of Sinope, one of the representative figures of Cynic tradition, dedicated his life to demonstrating the value of nature beyond human-constructed culture, and to *defacing* the false human values of the existing dominant custom. He identifies himself as follows: "A homeless exile, to his country dead. A wanderer who begs his daily bread."[28] Diogenes refused to respect people on the basis of social rank or position and disregarded conventional norms. When Alexander the Great offered, "Ask of me any boon you like," Diogenes replied, "Stand out of my light."[29] This anecdote about Diogenes and Alexander shows how free and unconventional the consciousness of Diogenes was.

It is, however, important to note that the *kosmopolites* by Diogenes and other Greek philosophers does not exemplify someone who has multicultural tastes, manners, or values and who would feel at home everywhere, as people today often perceive. The expression *kosmopolites* takes *citizen* in the phrase *citizen of the cosmos* in a metaphorical sense. It does not envision a *cosmic citizenship* in a literally geopolitical sense. What we can envision with this metaphoric expression, however, is a world where we treat *others* as fellow-citizens, co-habitants, neighbors, friends, or relatives. We can find the ground of this *ontological-family-tie* simply in the sheer fact that we humans belong to the *cosmos* as fellow-humans. Here ethnicity, race, gender, religious affiliation, citizenship, or nationality is not the primary identifier of human worth. Moreover, we can extend the scope of justice, fair treatment, or care to both humans and non-humans, as we all belong to the cosmos. It is problematic if we take Diogenes as *the* originator of cosmopolitanism because he did not ground his *cosmic citizenship* in the notion of the cosmopolitan mentality that endorses *planetary community*, which transcends one's national boundary especially in terms of the scope of justice, peace, and equality. However, his idea of *kosmopolites* has triggered people to construct a significant cosmopolitan ideal that one should not confine one's belonging just to a national/ geographical boundary but extend it to a larger community—the cosmos.

Stoicism furthermore strengthens a theoretical ground and support for the cosmopolitan spirit. Zeno, for instance, contends: "Our household arrangements should not be based on cities or local populations, each one marked out by its own legal system, but we should regard all people as our fellow-citizens and local residents, and there should be one way of life and one order, like that of a herd grazing together and nurtured by a common law."[30] Zeno offers a radical vision for the ideal community, a utopian vision of a human community, where people regard others as fellow-citizens. Interestingly, Zeno is skeptical about general culture and shows a radical view of conventional gender dress code by arguing that "men and women should wear the same dress and keep no part of the body entirely covered."[31] Through his cosmopolitan spirit and utopian vision, Zeno paved a way for two interrelated and significant ideas of moral universalism and natural law.[32] Seneca, one of the Roman Stoics, also offers a significant cosmopolitan spirit with the following statement:

> Let us grasp the idea that there are two commonwealths—the one, a vast and truly common state, which embraces alike gods and men [*sic*], in which we look neither to this corner of earth nor to that, but measure the bounds of our citizenship by the path of the sun; the other, the one to which we have been assigned by the accident of birth.[33]

Seneca differentiates between the citizenship by *the path of the sun* and by *the accident of birth* and makes clear that this dual citizenship and double belonging is not in contradiction. Moreover, emphasizing the *accidentality* of one's birth, he rejects the idea of innate privilege that one comes to possess by the birth origin. Marcus Aurelius also articulates this cosmopolitan sentiment by portraying the "Universe" as a "Commonwealth," a "Common City" for entire human race:

> If mind is common to us all, then also the reason, whereby we are rational beings, is common. If this be so, then also the reason which enjoins what is to be done or left undone is common. If this be so, law also is common; if this be so, we are citizens; and if this be so,

> we are partakers in one constitution; if this be so, the Universe is a kind of Commonwealth. For in what other common government can we say that the whole race of men [*sic*] partakes? And thence, from this common City, is derived our mind itself, our reason and our sense of law, or from what else?[34]

Aurelius goes on to claim, as fellow-citizens of the universe, "[W]e have come into the world to work together, like feet, like hands, like eyelids, like the rows of upper and lower teeth" and "[t]o work against one another therefore is to oppose Nature...."[35]

Aurelius' cosmopolitan paradigm is to envision the earth and the sky as one's home but does not exclude all attachments to and preferences for one's immediate family nor disregard one's particular ties to local communities. It is significant to note that what the Stoic cosmopolitanism offers is not a proposition for a grand world-state but the ideal of *cosmic citizen*, which is "strategically valuable in social life."[36] The ideal cosmopolitanism may appear to imply anti-nationalism because of its emphasis on the cosmic citizenship, rather than national citizenship. However, when one takes a binary approach of *either-or*—either nationalism or cosmopolitanism—to human reality, it is hard to capture the complexity of human reality and the spirit of cosmopolitanism. Cosmopolitanism moves beyond the binary approach and does not necessarily have to be in opposition against nationalism. Cosmopolitan justice is, however, incompatible with distorted forms of nationalism such as Nazism or Fascism.

Cosmic Equality of Beings in Taoist Philosophy

In 1920, before he published *I and Thou,* Martin Buber published a translation of and commentary on the work of Chuang Tzu, one of two primary Taoist philosophers along with Lao Tzu. Although he based his translation of Chuang Tzu's work heavily on English translations with minimal knowledge of the Chinese language, it is plausible that there is a "*thematic resonance*"[37] between Buber's view of Chuang Tzu and his later work, *I and Thou.* Regarding Tao and its profound meaning, Buber contends, "Tao is a singular and ineffable cosmic principle that is accessible in the form of an obliterating oneness that nevertheless provides an ontological basis for the transformation of things," which can offer "a glimpse of the eternal Thou."[38] The Taoist influence on Buber's thought is intriguing and Buber's *I and Thou* may represent "the crystallization of an ongoing reception of *Chuang Tzu.*"[39] Immanuel Kant mentions Taoist philosopher Lao Tzu in a negative tone. Kant posits Lao Tzu's philosophy of *nothingness* as a "monstrous system of the *supreme good,* which is supposed to consist of *nothingness* [*im Nichts*], i.e., in the consciousness derived from annihilating his [*sic*] personality, of *feeling* oneself flowing into and being swallowed up in the abyss of the divinity."[40] There is no clear information as to what resource Kant is referring to about Lao Tzu's philosophy, but he concludes his remarks on Lao Tzu's philosophy of nothingness with an overgeneralized and rather sarcastic statement: "Chinese philosophers exhaust themselves in dark rooms with their eyes closed trying to think and have sensations of their nothingness."[41] Whether misguided or appropriately understood, the assessments of Lao Tzu vary.

Taoist philosophy, represented primarily by Lao Tzu and Chuang Tzu, has utopian elements in the sense that it seeks an alternative world that transcends the existing sociopolitical reality. Lao Tzu consciously criticizes Confucian ethics, and Chuang Tzu's doctrine is fundamentally grounded in the philosophy of Lao Tzu. Therefore, in order to understand the Taoist philosophy of Lao Tzu and Chuang Tzu in a wider discursive context, one must realize that they harshly criticize the Confucians. Although the issue of the relation of Taoism to Confucianism can be still debatable, I entirely concur with Toshihiko Izutsu's argument that Taoist philosophy primarily by Lao Tzu and Chuang Tzu apparently "intended to be a conscious criticism of Confucian ethics" and that one cannot properly understand the Taoist philosophy "unless we place them against the background of a Confucian philosophy standing already on a very firm basis."[42] If one views Confucianism as a kyriarchal religion/philosophy, Taoism can be a counter-religion/philosophy that profoundly carries the egalitarian, deconstructive, poststructuralist ethos. In this context, it is not unthinkable that "Confucian knowledge was masculine and managing: the Taoists condemned it and sought after a feminine and receptive knowledge which could arise only as the fruit of a passive and yielding attitude in the observation of Nature."[43] Taoist exaltation of the feminine character in its portrayal of Tao is significant not simply because of its femininity per se but because of its iconoclastic function as counter-discourse to a kyriarchal philosophy.

Throughout the history of Chinese thought, a shamanistic mode of thinking has prevailed that sharply contrasts with the realistic and rationalistic mode of thinking of Confucianism. Lao Tzu and Chuang Tzu were shamans, on the one hand, and intellectual thinkers, on the other hand.[44] Unlike in Confucianism, there is historical evidence of the equal participation of women and men in Taoist religious leadership, and of women shamans' significant influence on the male Taoist leaders.[45] Moreover, some Chinese texts mention individual Taoist women as great laboratory alchemists, roles in which they created an elixir of immortality and served as a microcosm of the transformation of the universe.[46] Although Taoism as a religion coexisted along with Buddhism and Confucianism in China, Taoists were socio-religiously at the lowest level of the social hierarchy, as women were: "Since the men who wrote Chinese history were for the most part (at least publicly) Confucian, the Taoist was always relegated (with women) to the last place in the biographies of famous people in the dynastic histories."[47] Among the classical Taoist texts, the *Chuang Tzu* is most critical of Confucius and of what Confucius represents. Lao Tzu also criticizes the essential ideas of Confucianism such as *jen* [humaneness] and *i* [righteousness], which are the most basic human virtues in Confucianism.

Taoist philosophy seeks for an alternative utopian world where people live in perfect harmony and peace regardless of who they are, which one can express in the term *Great Equality* or *Great Peace* (*t'ai-p'ing*).[48] Here, it is significant to note that the notion of *harmony* in Taoism differs strikingly from Confucianism notions. Whereas the harmony in Taoism is fundamentally horizontal and egalitarian, the Confucian notion of harmony is vertical, and the hierarchy in interpersonal relationship is highly crucial. Despite its cosmological principle of the seeming complementarity of *yin* and *yang*, Confucianism resembles imperialist desire because "it is the first principle of imperialism that there is a clear-cut and absolute hierarchical distinction between ruler and ruled."[49] Feminists and ecologists have emphasized the ideal of interrelationality between humans, and human and nature, in a form of "ethics of inseparability,"[50] opposing the traditional definition of maturity as autonomy, separation, and independence. In this context, many scholars often take Asian philosophy such as Confucianism as an alternative discourse to that of individualistic Western philosophy and culture. Confucian emphasis on *interrelatedness* among humans, for example, might seem extremely ideal.

However, it is important to note that in the very relationship in Confucianism, one particular role carries the duty of exercising authority and power, and the other obedience. People under the Confucian influence have always formulated and practiced duties and roles on the basis of hierarchical and androcentric presupposition both in the private and public sphere. In Confucianism, maintaining the hierarchical relationship based on social class and status, age, gender, or educational background is crucial in fostering peace and harmony within a community. Claiming women's ontological, sociopolitical, or familial equality with men in its full sense is impossible in Confucian discourse and practice because of its fundamental assumptions of male supremacy.[51] In spite of the strong emphasis on the *harmony* and the *interrelationality* between humans, the Confucian notion of human interrelationality is problematic because of its extremely androcentric and hierarchal nature based on gender, social class, marital status, and age.

The International Adoption Statistics for 2010 reveal the five countries that sent the most children to families in the U.S. for adoption—the People's Republic of China, Ethiopia, Russia, South Korea, and Ukraine.[52] South Korea takes the fourth rank for exporting its children to the U.S. despite the fact that South Korea ranked fourteenth in its nominal GDP in 2010 among 193 countries in the world, and twelfth in purchasing power parity (PPP), belonging to one of the G-20 major economies.[53] It is certainly not because of economic factors that South Koreans export their parentless children. Instead, the reason for the high export rate of its parentless children is due to a sociocultural factor under the influence of the Confucian value system that places great significance on paternal bloodlines, paternal-family ties, and an absolute value on *purity* in blood.

The ideals of *filial piety* are the most important tenets of Confucianism, which require the existence of male posterity from a direct paternal bloodline. Adopting a child into one's family has been taboo in South Korean society due to the *impurity* of the adopted child in terms of paternal bloodline. Mencius, one of the key Confucianists, states, "[T]he root of the empire is in the state, and the root of the state is in the family,"[54] and he goes on to say, "[T]here are three things which are unfilial, and to have no posterity is the greatest of them."[55] The *posterity* in Mencius's statement refers only to the male child, and the patrilineal-family is the center of the Confucian discourse and practice of *filial piety*. There are seven traditional grounds for a husband to initiate the divorce of his wife in Confucian teaching—disobedience to a husband's parents, failure to bear a son, promiscuity, jealousy, having an incurable disease, talking too much, and stealing. However, a wife never had any grounds for initiating a divorce against her husband under any circumstances.[56] Only sons can perform an ancestral ritual that is significant in exercising Confucian filial piety for the paternal family and its ancestors, but not for the maternal ancestors. *The Book of Filiality* or *Hsiao Ching*, one of the Confucian Classics, is exclusively dedicated to the issue of filiality/filial piety. *The Book of Filiality* emphasizes the significance of filiality as follows:

> In reverencing one's father, nothing [is] greater than making him a companion of heaven.... How can there be anything in the virtue of the sage that passes beyond filiality? Because of the love shown by parents during childhood, the child's reverence for his parents—while supporting them—grew daily.... The relation between father and son is rooted in nature and develops into the proper relation between prince and ministers. Parents give one life; no bond could be stronger. They watch over their child with utmost care; no love could be greater. Therefore, to love others without first loving one's

> parents is to act against virtue. To reverence other men without first reverencing one's parents is to act against propriety. If we model right upon such perversity, the people have no true norm to follow. In this there is no goodness, it is all evil.[57]

Confucian teaching considers that all virtues are nothing other than manifestations of the one virtue: *filiality*. The father-son relationship is the center of the Confucian teaching of the filiality, excluding women in any form. Only in spring 2005 did the Constitutional Court of South Korea, one of the most Confucian countries in the contemporary world, reach a conclusion that the core articles of the so-called *Family-Head System* are incompatible with the Constitution. The National Assembly passed the alternative bill for the Civil Code that dismantled the Family-Head System, effective on January 1, 2008. Since the inception of the Family-Head System in South Korean family law in 1957, women lawyers, activists, and women's organizations have criticized the patriarchal family law that legalizes the priority of a male as the *head* of a household. The Confucians [*Yurim*], who otherwise have not been socially salient on other matters, have been the main opposition group against the change of the Family-Head System in the name of virtuous *tradition*.[58] The South Korean family law is a "legacy of Korea's own version of Confucianism, founded on the tradition of male ancestor worship."[59] Here, I am not problematizing the Confucian emphasis on filiality itself. What I am problematizing is the extreme androcentric and misogynic nature of the notion of filiality exclusively grounded in the paternal bloodline. The Confucian androcentric and hierarchical nature is exclusionary and repressive and is fundamentally against the cosmopolitan spirit that requires moving beyond the phallocentric desire for *purity-in-paternal-bloodline*. The problem with the desire for purity-in-paternal-bloodline is its rigidification of one's authentic belonging only to the *biological* father.

Walter Mignolo observes that Western tradition has highly stressed the values of literateness and taken it as equivalent with being cultured and civilized. However, in Confucian tradition one can see exactly the same phenomena in terms of connecting "literacy with power, respect, high culture, civilization, intelligence."[60] The following passage in the *Great Leaning*, one of the *Four Books* of Confucian canonical works, presents the spirit of Confucianism:

> The ancients who wished to illustrate illustrious virtue throughout the kingdom, first ordered well their own States. Wishing to order well their States, they first regulated their families. Wishing to regulate their families, they first cultivated their persons. Wishing

> to cultivate their persons, they first rectified their hearts. Wishing to rectify their hearts, they first sought to be sincere in their thoughts. Wishing to be sincere in their thoughts, they first extended to the upmost their knowledge. Such extension of knowledge lay in the investigation of things.[61]

The foundational words of this passage, such as "*order* the state" and "*regulate* the family," make clear the target audience of this text. In order to *order* the state, *man* has to be able to *regulate his* family in a proper way. At the same time, in order to regulate his family, he has to cultivate himself. Here it is obvious, considering the patriarchal ethos of the Confucian time, that those who are entitled to *order* the state or *regulate* the family are not women but men from the noble family. The primary goal of Confucian education is, therefore, the cultivation of the male self from the noble class family of society, which is the core of Confucian Enlightenment. It is not surprising to see that the Confucian family and education system are extremely kyriarchal and androcentric in their philosophy and institutional practice.

While Confucianism builds its principles upon law and order and upon moral distinctions and cultivation, Taoism moves beyond such rigid moral distinctions and strongly emphasizes the unity of all in the ground. It is interesting to see the contrast between the Taoist view of *morality* and that of Confucianism:

> When the great Tao is forgotten,
> Kindness [*jen*] and morality [*i*] arise.
> When wisdom and intelligence are born,
> The great pretense begins.
> When there is no peace within the family,
> Filial piety [*hyo*] and devotion arise.
> When the country is confused and in chaos,
> Loyal ministers appear.[62]

Lao Tzu views those most important Confucian virtues, *jen* (humaneness, benevolence, kindness), *i* (righteousness, morality), *hyo* (filiality) as secondary, as something that one needs to give up, by saying that "Give up kindness [*jen*], renounce morality [*i*], and men [*sic*] will rediscover filial piety and love."[63] In this sense, the "Taoists were opposed to the Confucianists' treatment of *jen* [benevolence] and *yi* [righteousness]."[64] Whereas Taoism advocates the equality of all beings, Confucianism promotes a hierarchy among humans and a distinction of ranks, in terms of one's family origin of birth, social class, gender, age, or marital status, and sees the hierarchy as a necessary measure to obtain order and harmony in family and state. According to the

Confucian teaching, "[T]o be a woman means to submit"[65] and a woman must obey her father and elder brother; when married, her husband; when her husband is dead, her son.[66] It is not surprising to see the contrast also in symbol system between Taoism and Confucianism. While Confucianism uses a male-dominant symbol system, Taoism emphasizes feminine symbols for Tao in a culture of extreme patriarchy that has adopted Confucianism as a state ideology. The Tao is the most all-embracing symbol both in Confucianism and Taoism, albeit also the source of the critical difference in their interpretation and application. To Confucians, Tao is a system of moral truth, the expression of Heaven, representing a general, ethical ideal. It is the way of concrete and appropriate conduct for an individual and a state. Tao in Confucianism is also an entity because an individual or a state possesses or lacks the Tao, which means Tao stands for the right way of ethical, social, and political action.[67] However, Tao in Taoism is a metaphysical notion, in the sense that it cannot be an *entity* nor fathomable, and therefore is elusive and intangible. The following chapters of *Tao te ching* show the Taoist core understanding of Tao:

> The Tao that can be told
> is not the eternal Tao;
> The name that can be named
> is not the eternal name.[68]
>
> The Tao is elusive and intangible…
> …. …. …. …. …. …. . . .
> The Tao is forever undefined.[69]

The first chapter of *Tao te ching* is a direct criticism of logocentric perception of the Tao and reveals the unfathomability and unexplainability of the ever-evolving Tao, which clearly entails the ethos of deconstruction. In fact, there are "striking affinities"[70] between Taoist philosophy and the discourse of Derridean deconstruction. The *deconstructionist* Lao Tzu also offers a philosophical ground for an *apophatic* theology, which "means (to say) very little, almost nothing, perhaps something other than something"[71] because *Tao te ching* emphasizes the indefinability, intangibility, and unknowability of the Tao, as *apophatic* theology highlights the unknowable, indefinable, unfathomable God:

> What God is one knows not: He [*sic*] is not light, not spirit,
> Not delight, not one [Not truth, unity, one], not what is
> called divinity;
> Not wisdom, not intellect, not love, will, goodness:

No thing, no no-thing either, no essence, no concern:
He is what I, or you, or any other creature,
Before we became what He is, have never come to know.[72]

This Derridean understanding of God is strikingly similar to Lao Tzu's description of Tao: "The Tao of the Absolute has no name."[73] Chuang Tzu also offers a view of the Tao similar to that of Lao Tzu by saying, "Tao had no name," and, "Great Tao is beyond description."[74] The Taoist tendency to constantly destabilize binary oppositionality and to dedoxify the Tao is what Derrida tries to achieve through deconstruction. According to Derrida, the binary oppositionality pervades the entirety of Western thought, which he identifies as "logocentrism and the metaphysics of presence as the exigent, powerful, systemic, and irrepressible desire for such a signified."[75] Such a *desire for presence* has created and maintained the binary oppositionality that tends to divide human reality into binary oppositions such as man-woman, spirit-body, reason-emotion, logos-pathos, culture-nature, speech-writing, etc., which, in fact, cannot be fixed opposites, but rather complement each other. Western *metaphysics of presence* has always privileged the first term of each over the other.

People might view the cosmological principle of *yin* and *yang* in Asian philosophical tradition as differing from the binary oppositionality of the West. One can find the cosmological foundation for this elaborate code of subordination in ancient Chinese beliefs dating from the first millennium B.C.E. These held that the universe consisted of two interacting elements, *yin* the female and *yang* the male. The *yin* elements displayed dark, weak, and passive attributes in contrast to the *yang* elements, characterized by all that was bright, strong, and active. While man, as *yang*, was endowed with the firm nature of heaven, woman, as *yin*, partook of the yielding nature of the earth. The originally conceived cosmological belief, incorporated as interacting and complementary, was soon arranged in a hierarchical relationship juxtaposing superiority to inferiority and goodness to evil. In time, *yin* elements came to stand for all that was negative and inferior in the universe. From this cosmic pattern, people often deduce that the position of women in the human order should be lowly and inferior like the earth, and that the proper behavior for a woman is to be yielding and weak, passible and still like the earth. People have incorporated this revised cosmological principle into the teachings of Confucius and his disciples, and have used the principle of *yin* and *yang* as a *kyriarchal* ideology, which has justified and perpetuated the submission of women to men, of lower class to the noble class, of the young to the old.

> On sophisticated levels of philosophical thinking, the yin and yang were regarded as equally necessary for the functioning of the cosmos and therefore as mutually complementary, even though the yin, like a wife to her husband, was recognized as subordinate to the dominant yang. Popular thinking, however, tended to look at the two principles in more absolute and Manichaean terms: the yang as desirable and good, the yin as undesirable and evil.[76]

The cosmological principle of *yin* and *yang* is not binary oppositional in principle. However, in reality the allegedly complementary principle has functioned as a binary oppositional system. In the structure of the family, upon which Confucianism based its conception of society, people ordered the relationship between members according to the *fixity* of the *yin* and *yang* cosmological principles: "Yin and Yang are different in nature; Men and women are different in behavior; Yang is powerful [virtuous] because he is hard [firm]; Yin is functional because she is soft."[77] Although the cosmology of *yin* and *yang* portrays human relationship in a complementary way in principle, when people materialize the principle into the reality, it functions as a principle of binary oppositionality based on gender, age, marital status, or class. Chuang Tzu philosophizes the need to move beyond this mode of binary thinking:

> Every thing can be a "that"; every thing can be a "this." One man [*sic*] cannot see things as another sees them. One can only know things through knowing oneself. Therefore it is said, "'That' comes from 'this,' and 'this' comes from 'that'"— which means "that" and "this" give birth to one another.... Thus, the sage does not bother with these distinctions but seeks enlightenment from heaven. So he [*sic*] sees "this," but "this" is also "that," and "that" is also "this." ....When there is no more separation between "this" and "that," it is called the still-point of Tao.[78]

Here, Chuang Tzu is fully aware of the fundamental problem of the binary oppositionality and suggests that we should transcend beyond the conventional epistemology by adopting a Taoist position that sees everything as equal with everything else. The cosmopolitan ideal is impossible without a constant deconstruction of existing boundaries, fixed perception of what-it-is for something undeconstructable, as Derrida contends: justice.[79] The Taoist position by Chuang Tzu rejects "the absolute categories of predication which we bring to our perceptions."[80] However, I do not concur with the claim that Chuang Tzu is relativist, whereas Derrida is not.[81] For what

Chuang Tzu offers is not the relativity of all values but the fundamental rejection of the rigidity and fixity of a truth-claim that distorts the very essence of the truth that one searches for. In this context, Chuang Tzu claims the "absolute reversal of values,"[82] or the "*transvaluation of all values*"[83] in a Nietzschean sense. Not surprisingly, Graham Parkes regards that some of Nietzsche's ideas about nature correspond to the Taoist position, although "there is no evidence that Nietzsche knew anything about Taoism."[84] My point of mentioning the striking affinity between Derrida and Chuang Tzu is neither to make a blindly simplistic comparison between the two, which is still debatable in many ways, nor to *Westernize* Taoist philosophy and to *Easternize* Western philosophy,[85] but to *diversify* the genealogy of the discourse of deconstruction, as people often regard its existence only in the Western philosophical thoughts. The ethos and idea of deconstruction have been evident in Taoist philosophy, although Taoist philosophers have not named their works as *deconstruction*. It is important to note that deconstruction is not a *method* but an *act/event* of reading that questions, reverses, displaces, and destabilizes the whole system of thought and the mode of binary thinking and world view, which is manifest not only in Derrida's philosophy but also in Taoist philosophy. Here, deconstruction is truly, "an endless act of reading" in *singularity*, which allows "the other to speak."[86]

Lao Tzu portrays the Tao as the water, the child, the Great Mother, the Mysterious Female, or the Uncarved Block.[87] Here, I am not celebrating a mere idealization of feminine values or a mere existence of *mother* or *female* in Taoist symbols because the existence of a goddess in a religion, for instance, does not automatically guarantee women's equality and liberation in a given society. In spite of the marginal status of Taoism in society, the Taoist symbols offer a significant meaning for constructing a cosmopolitan ideal. After all, these symbols for Tao signify the unfixity, non-doxification, namelessness, ever-becoming, non-dominating, non-controlling, ever-embracing, non-hierarchy, or non-polarity. The Taoist way of portraying things is deconstructive, allowing the voiceless to speak and seeking Tao in the invisible and in the marginalized. In this sense, the Tao in Taoism does denaturalize, dedoxify the *world-as-it-is* and invites one to envision the *world-to-come*.

Taoist philosophy not only rejects androcentric and anthropocentric values in its understanding of Tao and nature, but it also claims the ontological equality of beings—both human and non-human. According to Lao Tzu, the Tao is impartial,[88] in the sense that people should treat everything on equal footing, which resonates what Paul says: "God shows no partiality" (Rom. 2:11). In Taoist philosophy, everything is "ontologically equal."[89] In the Taoist ordering of beings, human beings do not receive any special status, and thereby anthropocentrism is simply absent. Humans are part of nature, and the world of nature and of human is not separable. Humans can actualize their wellbeing as human beings only in their abilities to follow the Tao, and the Tao is impartial to everything as it generates, comprehends, transforms, and preserves all things. The Taoist notion of *ontological equality of beings* offers a radical form of cosmopolitanism by extending its kinship not only to humans but also to nature. Whereas this notion of ontological equality of every being is implicit in Lao Tzu, it is very explicit in Chuang Tzu, who further elaborates this concept. According to Chuang Tzu, all beings are ontologically equal because they are formed as a result of a process of self- and mutual-Transformation:

> Once Chuang Chou dreamt he was a butterfly, a butterfly flitting and fluttering around, happy with himself and doing as he pleased. He didn't know he was Chuang Chou. Suddenly he woke up and there he was, solid and unmistakable Chuang Chou. But he didn't know if he was Chuang Chou who had dreamt he was a butterfly, or a butterfly dreaming he was Chuang Chou. Between Chuang Chou and a butterfly there must be *some* distinction! This is called the Transformation of things.[90]

The idea of *Transformation of things* (*wu hua*) is one of the most significant thoughts in Chuang Tzu's philosophy.[91] Here all living beings are ontologically equal in the sense of being both self-activating and mutually determining, in which there is no ontological hierarchy of beings. Transcending one's essentially fixed identity as human or butterfly means gaining another identity as butterfly or human. Izutsu argues that Chuang Tzu's view of Transformation deessentializes the distinction between *me* and *you* and presents its distinction only in terms of appearance. Chuang Tzu's concept of Transformation presents two important points. First, it refers to a metaphysical situation, in which "all things are found to be 'transmutable' to one another, so much so that ultimately they become merged into an absolute Unity."[92] In this sense, Taoist philosophy offers a radically cosmopolitan idea, in which all things are equally one in its singularity; all things *are* the Reality itself in its plurality.

The key premise of the Taoist philosophy of Lao Tzu and Chuang Tzu is *the unity of existence in multiplicity*, acknowledging that one's singular existence is a co-existence in its plurality, which brings a unity as co-existence but without collapsing the singularity of being into the uniformity of sameness. I see a conceptual resemblance between Jean-Luc Nancy's notion of "being singular plural"[93] and the Taoist notion of the *unity of existence in multiplicity*. In the light of the idea of the Transformation of things, all things are relational, what Izutsu calls an "existentialist position" against the "essentialist" position of Confucians.[94] Second, Chuang Tzu's notion of Transformation signifies metaphysically a *temporal process,* constituting an *ontological circle of equality of beings*. Chuang Tzu further elaborates the ontological equality of all beings as follows: "You were born in a human form, and you find joy in it; Yet there are ten thousand other forms endlessly transforming that are equally good, and the joy in these is untold."[95] The Taoist notion of the ontological equality of beings captures the ultimate claims of cosmopolitan spirit.

According to Chuang Tzu, "Great knowledge is all-encompassing; small knowledge is limited."[96] Lao Tzu or Chuang Tzu did not of course use the term cosmopolitanism. It is, in fact, so challenging for me to find an appropriate translation for the word *cosmopolitanism* into Chinese or Korean, due to its complex nature and scope of discourse, that people would likely misperceive it as *globalization* once it gets translated into these Asian languages. However, it is clear to me that Taoist philosophy carries the spirit of cosmopolitanism and provides a cosmopolitan condition in the sense that all beings are equal regardless of who one is, all belonging to the cosmos of Tao. Lao Tzu's statement, "Love the world as your own self; then you can truly care for all things,"[97] clearly carries a reconceptualized universal humanism of responsibility and compassion, a notion of trans-nation-state community—a community of cosmic citizens, where all beings love and are loved without any precondition. Taoist philosophy that calls for *the love of the world as oneself* radicalizes Jesus' message of *love your neighbor-enemy as yourself* by replacing *neighbor* with *the world*. Taoist philosophy further creates an iconoclastic power by adopting feminine symbols for the Tao, the Divine, reversing the privileged statue of the masculine over the feminine. The Taoist reversal of the existing Confucian *kyriarchal* values also has a power to offer an alternative view of the others and the world of non-hierarchy.

Along with the Cynics and Stoics, Taoist philosophy provides a firm ground for a *cosmopolitan condition* that we should grant every individual human being equal rights and freedom as a citizen of the cosmos. The notion of cosmic citizenship is significant in promoting a better world where justice, freedom, and equality among/between people prevail. There is an urgent need for a new configuration of the citizenship in our world because the current configuration of citizenship can neither "define a cultural, linguistic, or, in general, historical participation" nor "cover all these modes of belonging."[98] Although the question as to whether the cosmopolitan spirit in Taoist philosophy has political ramifications remains debatable, the

Taoist philosophy of ontological equality of beings clearly offers a significant discursive ground for the politics and ethics of cosmopolitanism. A Taoist objection to essentialist claims of reason, law, order, morality, intelligence, and androcentric and anthropocentric norms provides a profound ground in formulating a discourse and practice of equality, justice, rights, and dignity of all living beings, which are the key issues that cosmopolitanism attempts to address in the contemporary world.

Cosmopolitan Rights and the Vision for the *Kindom of Ends*

The term *Kindom of Ends* that I use here is a variation of Kant's *Kingdom of Ends*. I replace the word *Kingdom* with *Kindom* to depatriarchalize and dehierarchalize the significant vision that Kant portrays in his *Kingdom of Ends*. The word *kingdom* presupposes a hierarchy between the king and the subordinate, and a patriarchy that naturalizes male-King as the center of power. I am fully aware that even the word *kindom* also carries its own baggage from the past in the sense that the *kinship* in most traditional societies, except a few matrilineal and matrilocal societies, is androcentric and hierarchical according to the rank within the kin. However, the word *kindom* is more redeemable than *kingdom* in terms of its possibility of reconceptualization with a new meaning that would carry and promote a more egalitarian and democratic ethos.

Kant's vision for the world community of all human beings as free, equal, interdependent, and rational beings whom people should treat as *an end,* not as a means, is extremely significant. To treat other human beings with respect is a central theme in Kant's moral philosophy. In his proposal of *kingdom of ends,* Kant contends "all rational beings stand under the law that each of them should treat himself [*sic*] and all others never merely as means but always at the same time as an end in himself."[99] It is imperative, according to Kant, to "act in such a way that you treat humanity, whether in your own person or in the person of another, always at the same time as an end and never simply as a means."[100] Kant further contends: "The concept of every rational being as one who must regard himself [*sic*] as legislating universal law by all his will's maxims, so that he may judge himself and his actions from this point of view, leads to another very fruitful concept, which depends on the aforementioned one, viz., that of a kingdom of ends."[101] Through his *kingdom of ends,* Kant envisions an ethical ideal that may be unattainable in human political reality. However, the *unattainability* in reality does not diminish the meaning of the ethical imperative of the *kingdom of ends*. Instead, through such an ethical imperative, one comes to *remember* the future of the community of the ends that has to come. Furthermore, the very ethical ideal is significant because it also offers a vision of the interconnectedness of the *I* and the *you,* which promotes a strong sense of indispensable *we-ness.* In the *kingdom of ends,* the *I* relates to everyone else in the following way:

> I must make your ends and reasons mine, and I must choose mine in such a way that they can be yours. Generalised to the Kingdom of Ends, my own ends must be the possible objects of universal legislation, subject to the vote of all. And this is how I realise my autonomy. Paradoxically if you like, my ends and actions are most truly my own when they are chosen under the restrictions of a possible reciprocal relation—a kind of friendship—with everyone.[102]

The ideal of the *kindom of ends* is an ongoing reference to the concrete practice of the community of ends in reality, and as a "universal civic society"[103] in accordance with cosmopolitan rights, it can offer a liberative potential of the concrete geopolitical situation that we now face with such pressing issues as refugees, pleas for asylum, migrant workers, undocumented people, and so on. It is debatable what would be the fundamental reason for Kant's argument that one must respect others and treat them as an end.[104] Whether Kant grounds his argument for respecting others and treating the others as an end on the inner value or worth (*Wert*) of human beings, or on a practical, categorical imperative, I believe Kant's metaphysics of morals that urges us to always treat others with respect and dignity as fellow inhabitants of the earth, *fellow citizens of the cosmos,* offers a significant framework for promoting cosmopolitan rights for the contemporary world. The question as to whether a human being possesses an indispensable value and dignity is for me not a disputable matter, as each and every human being has her/his unique, singular *face* that no one can deny.

Cosmopolitanism in its contemporary use is based upon the inherent human dignity and equality of human beings. Therefore, people often use cosmopolitanism in association with universal human rights. Kant's idea of the *kingdom of ends* and the cosmopolitan condition for *perpetual peace* hold that every human being has both a natural right to freedom and a responsibility to enter into a civil condition covered by a social contract in order to realize and preserve that freedom. In his notion of *perpetual peace,* Kant argues for cosmopolitan values that defend the equal claim of every individual person to recognition and protection, and universal obligations of justice that cross borders of nationality and particular local community. Kant bases his advocacy of cosmopolitanism on his recognition of the fact that people have entered in varying degrees into a universal community and it has developed to the point that a violation of rights in one part of the world is felt everywhere. The cosmopolitanism that I employ starts its conceptual framework from Immanuel Kant, especially from his notion of cosmopolitan rights and universal hospitality. In his seminal essay "Perpetual Peace," Kant rightly argues:

> The people of the earth have thus entered in varying degrees into a universal community, and it has developed to the point where a violation of rights in *one* part of the world is felt *everywhere*. The idea of a cosmopolitan right is therefore not fantastic and overstrained; it is a necessary complement to the unwritten code of political and international right, transforming it into a universal right of humanity. Only under this condition can we flatter ourselves that we are continually advancing towards a perpetual peace.[105]

Kant's emphasis on the interconnected nature of the life of the *people of the earth,* and thereby on the significance of implementing the idea of a *cosmopolitan right,* is very important, especially in an era of globalization. What Kant concerns himself with is not *philanthropy* but *right,* in which context "*hospitality* means the right of a stranger not to be treated with hostility when he [*sic*] arrives on someone else's territory."[106] The ontological ground of this *planetary hospitality* lies in the sheer truth that "no-one originally has any greater right than anyone else to occupy any particular portion of the earth."[107] Kant clearly depicts the philosophical principles for achieving *perpetual peace* among nations, and, at the same time, portrays cosmopolitanism as the fullest measure of human achievement. In his thesis on "civil constitution," he argues that the civil constitution of every state shall be *republican*. Kant grounds his argument on three principles: "firstly, the principle of *freedom* for all members of a society (as men [*sic*]); secondly, the principle of the *dependence* of everyone upon a single common legislation (as subjects); and thirdly, the principle of legal *equality* for everyone (as citizens)."[108]

Scholars have widely adopted Kant's articulation of a *perpetual peace* based on cosmopolitanism, especially in relation to the issues of global justice and inequality in the era of globalization. Global, political, and economic inequality and injustice have become more serious issues because "these inequalities are mostly greater today than 50 or 100 years ago, and there is reason to believe that the gap will continue to grow."[109] Unlike other Enlightenment thinkers, such as John Locke or Voltaire, who believed that most essential to human advancement is the increase of knowledge, Kant regarded "the increase of knowledge in and of itself to have no such beneficial effects."[110] Knowledge can be "empowering and salvific" to individuals or society only when it "can be put in the service of appropriate ends."[111] Kant's ideas of a cosmopolitan condition for perpetual peace and its implication for human rights can be significant guides to practice. Although there is a huge discrepancy between Kant's understanding of the world and humans and the contemporary reality, Kant's idea of cosmopolitan rights can offer a point of departure for an international humanitarian framework for dealing with the violation of human rights by nation-states or individuals, although not a point of arrival due to his limited vision of *abstract universalism*. Kant's idea of cosmopolitan rights assures, at least in principle, that every singular individual has rights as a citizen of the world, which are *above* and *beyond* the positive law of nation-states. As Kant defines it, a "cosmopolitan right shall be limited to conditions of universal hospitality" and "no one had a greater right to any region of the earth than anyone else."[112] One of the most positive evaluations of Kant's cosmopolitanism follows:

> The greatness of spirit that Kant showed was to stand up to the rising nationalism of his time and to defend the best traditions of enlightenment universalism.... Kant did not simply abstract the cosmopolitan ideal from history and society, as is sometimes alleged, but rather he fought against a view of history and society that cannot see beyond what already exists and cannot reach for another form of life. Kant's so-called "abstract ideal" was his attempt to stem the growing tide of nationalism and harmonize the principle on which the world revolution was turning, namely the independence and sovereignty of the state, with the universalism of enlightenment.[113]

The issue of *rights* is extremely complex because the nature of rights would have a different meaning in each different historical context. In the sixteenth and seventeenth centuries, for instance, people discussed *rights* in relation to human and Christian believers, whereas in the eighteenth centuries they discussed rights in terms of human and national citizenship. It is only after World War II that people discussed *rights* in terms of humanity.[114] Cosmopolitan rights concern both issues—without forgetting the colonial practice in the West—with the idea of abstract universality: human rights and cosmic citizenship. It is also important to note that Cynic, Stoic, or Kantian cosmopolitanism did not yet develop a comprehensive sense of equality in terms of gender, sexuality, or race and ethnicity, although their cosmopolitan ideal would embrace all genders, races, and sexualities *in principle*. Expanding the areas of the application of cosmopolitan rights with a hypersensitivity to the marginalized will be an ongoing task. Kant connects his notion of *cosmopolitan right* to *hospitality* as he contends "the right of an alien not to be treated as an enemy upon his [*sic*] arrival in another's country" and "cosmopolitan right shall be limited to conditions of universal hospitality."[115]

Thinking *with* Kant *against* Kant: The Contradiction between Cosmopolitanism and Human Geography

If people retain, unwittingly and unconsciously, a desire for *coherent purity* in the intellectual world of a *great* thinker such as Immanuel Kant, it is probable that they end up with a great disappointment when they find out otherwise. One is hardly *homogeneous, coherent,* or *pure* in one's view of the world and is often self-contradictory. There is a fundamental self-contradiction between Kant's Eurocentric hierarchical theory of race and his cosmopolitan ideal that regards every individual human being as equal as citizens of the world. The contradiction that Kant has in his thought reveals a fundamental problem of the modern notion of *abstract universality*. People in the sixteenth century had already formulated the so-called idea of the *universal* rights of the people, but within an extremely limited planetary consciousness that located the Occident as the center of the universe and the primary frame of reference. Due to the epistemological blindness in this limited *planetary* consciousness, colonization of people of the non-West was possible without the conquerors being aware of the fundamental contradiction between the idea of the universal rights of the people and the colonial system that they exercised in non-Occidental parts of the world. In this sense, one needs to link the notion of cosmopolitanism and its universal rights of the people on the earth to the hidden agenda and colonial desire for modernity in Western Europe, in which people exercised and justified the "expulsion of the Moors and the Jews from the Iberian Peninsula" and "the beginnings of the massive contingent of African slaves in the Americas."[116] The coloniality of the West in multiple forms is what Walter Mignolo calls the *darker side* of modernity and the European Enlightenment.[117]

In his book *Race and the Enlightenment,* Emmanuel Chukwudi Eze compiles several writings from eighteenth-century philosophers such as Carl von Linne, Georges-Louis Leclerc, David Hume, Immanuel Kant, Johann Friedrich Blomenbach, Thomas Jefferson, Georges Leopold Cuvier, and Georg Wilhelm Friedrich Hegel and points out that people in Europe have constructed, wittingly or unwittingly, *race* on the ground of white Eurocentrism, and often used their works for the justification of European imperialism.[118] Assuming Negroes and whites are the basic races, Kant, for instance, divided the human race into four categories: "1) the race of the *white*, 2) the *Negro race*, 3) the *Hunnish* (Mongolian or Kalmuckian) race, 4) the Hindu or *Hindustani* race,"[119] and also came up with the following *natural causes of their origin* as follows:

> *First race* High blondes (Northern Europeans) from humid cold.
> *Second race* Copper-reds (Americans) from dry cold.
> *Third race* Blacks (Senegambia) from humid heat.
> *Fourth race* Olive-yellows (Indians) from dry heat.[120]

Kant assumes that the Negroes and White are the basic human races and shows his extremely biased perception about the *Negroes*: "[A]ll Negroes stink.... Incidentally, humid warmth is beneficial to the robust growth of animals in general and, in short, this results in the Negro, who is well suited to his climate, namely strong, fleshy, supple, but who, given the abundant provision of his mother land, is lazy, soft and trifling."[121]Kant goes on to argue: "All inhabitants of hot lands are exceptionally lazy; they are also timid and the same two traits characterize also folk living in the far north. Timidity engenders superstition and in lands ruled by king, leads to slavery."[122] He also contends in his work *On the Feeling of the Beautiful and the Sublime* that "the German ....has a happy mixture in the feeling of the sublime as well as the beautiful,"[123] and that the "Negroes of Africa have by nature no feeling that rises above the ridiculous."[124] Kant's idealizing the German as the best combination of the sublime and the beautiful sounds, unfortunately, like the Nazi's praise of the German. Kant concludes in his *Physical Geography* that the whites are the most perfect race:

> In the hot countries the human being matures in all aspects earlier, but does not, however, reach the perfection of those in the temperate zones. *Humanity is at its greatest perfection in the race of the whites.* The yellow Indians do have a meager talent. The Negroes are far below them and at the lowest point are a part of the American people.[125]

If one follows what Kant argues in terms of human race and geography, one must accept that *geography is destiny* not only for humans but also for non-human animals because Kant further claims "all dogs that are brought from Europe to Africa become dumb and bald and produce only similar offspring thereafter."[126] In his book, *Ideas on the Philosophy of the History of Mankind,* J. G. von Herder, a former student of Kant, criticized Kant, and Kant's response to Herder in his review of Herder's book created one of "the most lively public intellectual debates of eighteenth-century Germany."[127] Herder disagreed with Kant's race categorization based on skin color and also criticized Kant for his cultural prejudice because Herder believed that each culture carries its one beauty and value and cannot be regarded as inferior of superior to another. Kant harshly rebutted Herder's position.[128] Scholars regarded Kant's remarks on human geography as "nothing either fresh or particularly geographical" and "almost identical in form and content with those of Montesquieu."[129] However, the scholars of geography, not philosophers, positively received Kant's view of the role of geography in education as a "propaedeutic" and his later proposal for a "physical, moral, and political geography" as a new integrated discipline.[130] According to the lecture notes taken by one of his students during 1763–64, Kant introduced physical geography as "(a) a teacher of morality, which reveals the unaffected savage; (b) an instrument for political geography; (c) a summary of natural history and the key to theoretical physics; (d) also to theology, etc.; (e) it also brings ennobling satisfaction."[131]

Kant never traveled in his entire life beyond Königsberg, where he was born, raised, and taught. But he must have had a great interest in geography. Kant taught geography for forty years regularly until his retirement in 1797, and he first introduced geography into the curriculum at the University of Königsberg in 1756. Kant offered 72 courses in anthropology (24 times) and geography (48 times), whereas he taught logic 54 times, metaphysics 49 times, moral philosophy 28 times, and theoretical physics 20 times.[132] In this regard, Kant's interest in race and its biological, geographical, and cultural distribution must have been as significant as other philosophical issues. Even when the university reduced his teaching load, he did not give up teaching geography until his retirement from teaching. Kant viewed geography, a study of nature, and anthropology, a study of human being, as constituting the main aspects of the knowledge of the world (*Kenntnis der Welt*), and he believed "they become useful not merely for *school* but rather for *life* and through which the accomplished apprentice is introduced to the stage of his [*sic*] destiny, namely, the *world*."[133] He did not have an official textbook for the geography course, and therefore the course was an exceptional case for the customary regulations. The following official decrees from the Minister of Education revealed the background context of Kant's geography course:

> The worst compendium is certainly better than none, and the professors may, if they are wise enough, improve upon the author as much as they can, but lecturing on dictated passages must be absolutely stopped. From this, Professor Kant and his lectures on physical geography are to be excepted, as it is well known that there is yet no suitable text-book in this subject.[134]

It seems obvious that Kant must have had a very strong personal enthusiasm about geography, as he continued to teach the course even when there were no proper textbooks on geography. Reading on geography was Kant's favorite activity for mental amusement throughout his entire life, and he considered geography as the preparatory study for knowledge of the world. It is, however, surprising that few Kantian scholars have paid attention to Kant's attachment to geography and his work on physical geography, especially in relation to the *race question*. Although some geographers recognize that Kant's interest in geography assured an honorable statue of geography within the sciences and offered a justification for the existence of geography, most Kantian scholars seem to regard Kant's work on geography as irrelevant and show no interest.[135] That there is no English translation of Kant's *Physical Geography* in its entirety, even now, is telling. Only a part of *Physical Geography* is available in an English translation in *Race and the Enlightenment,* published in 1997, and in a book chapter, "The Color of Reason: The Idea of 'Race' in Kant's Anthropology" by Emmanuel Chukwudi Eze in *Postcolonial African Philosophy*. The first full English translation of Kant's *Physical Geography* will be published in the volume, *Kant: Natural Science* as one of the series of the Cambridge Edition of the Works of Immanuel Kant.[136] A 1999 article in *Le Monde* comments on Kant's *Physical Geography,* saying that reading Kant's geography "comes as a real shock" due to its "an unbelievable hodge-podge of heterogeneous remarks, of knowledge without system, of disconnected curiosities."[137] Those philosophers drawn to Kant's philosophical anthropology, including Martin Heidegger and Michel Foucault, made no mention of Kant's *race question,* and I find it strange that *A Kant Dictionary,* for instance, has no entry on *race*.[138]

When asked whether there is a place for geography in the archaeology of knowledge, Foucault replied with a firm *yes* because "[f]inding a place for geography would imply that the archaeology of knowledge embraces a project of global, exhaustive coverage of all domains of knowledge," and it is "possible to conduct an archaeology of geographical knowledge."[139] He goes on to affirm that "the formation of discourses and the genealogy of knowledge need to be analyzed, not in terms of types of consciousness, modes of perception and forms of ideology, but in terms of tactics and strategies of power,"[140] and geography takes the center of his concern. According to Foucault, in the nineteenth century people treated space "as the dead, the fixed, the undialectical, the immobile," while treating time as "richness, fecundity, life, dialectic."[141] Foucault rightly argues about the significant intersectionality of time and space in the present epoch:

> The great obsession of the nineteenth century was, as we know, history: with its themes of development and of suspension, of crisis and cycle, themes of the ever-accumulating past, with its great

> preponderance of dead men and the menacing glaciation of the world.... The present epoch will perhaps be above all the epoch of space. We are in the epoch of simultaneity: we are in the epoch of juxtaposition, the epoch of the near and far, of the side-by-side, of the dispersed. We are at a moment, I believe, when our experience of the world is less that of a long life developing through time than that of a network that connects points and intersects with its own skein. One could perhaps say that certain ideological conflicts animating present-day polemics oppose the pious descendants of time and the determined inhabitants of space .... [I]t is not possible to disregard the fatal intersection of time with space. [142]

However, it is surprising to see that Foucault did not mention Kant's geography and his race question, although he worked on Kant for his dissertation. I notice that this *ignorance* or *omission,* whether intentional or unintentional, of Kant's race question in relation to his human geography is also visible in the major works on Kant. *A Companion to Kant,* for instance, has thirty-three chapters with five hundred thirty pages, but there is no one chapter that deals with Kant's race question and his human geography. *The Cambridge Companion to Kant and Modern Philosophy* has eighteen chapters with seven hundred twenty-two pages, yet there is no single chapter that addresses Kant's race question.[143] This *ignorance/omission* seems to me a typical example of what Gayatri Chakravorty Spivak calls *sanctioned ignorance* in her critique of Michel Foucault as a self-contained Western intellectual, focusing on his *blind spot* in his appropriation of space. Spivak quotes from Foucault's own words to point out the *sanctioned ignorance* in his work: "One can perfectly well not talk about something because one doesn't know about it, not because one has a knowledge which is unconscious and therefore inaccessible."[144]

Kant may or may not be a racist in his personal attitude toward people of different races, but his view on human geography certainly carries the *racialist* view that there is an *essential* difference between races, which can be a pretext for scientific racism. Here it is helpful to acknowledge the difference between *racist* and *racialist.* Kwame Anthony Appiah makes a distinction between *racialism* and *racism*. According to Appiah, people practicing racialism believe that there *are* races, whereas those practicing racism argue that different races deserve different treatment.[145] Although *racialism* itself is not dangerous, people can use its so-called *equal but different* treatment as a justification of racism. In this sense, although Kant himself may not be a racist in his personal life, his biased race-thinking can result in extreme racism, implicitly or explicitly. Hannah Arendt's insights about this race matter are important when she warns that people turn to race-thinking when they need its explanatory power to achieve a goal and that "[t]he tremendous power of persuasion inherent in the main ideologies of our times is not accidental. . .[and] is not possible without appeal to either experiences or desires, in other words to immediate political needs."[146] It is not surprising to see that the racist inclination in David Hume, who is one of the important thinkers in the construction of Western philosophy, is also noticeable as he explicitly articulates his view on the *Negroes*:

> I am apt to suspect the Negroes to be naturally inferior to the Whites. There scarcely ever was a civilized nation of that complexion, nor even any individual, eminent either in action or speculation. No ingenious manufactures amongst them, no arts, no sciences.... Not to mention our colonies, there are Negro slaves dispersed all over Europe, of whom none ever discovered the symptoms of ingenuity; though low people, without education, will start up amongst us, and distinguish themselves in every profession. In Jamaica, indeed, they talk of one Negro as a man of parts and learning; but it is likely he is admired for slender accomplishments, like a parrot who speaks a few words plainly.[147]

Kant cited David Hume's racist remarks on *Negroes* in his "On the Feeling of the Beautiful and Sublime" and agreed with Hume that no Negro has shown any talent.[148] In this sense, Kant's hierarchical race-thinking is reflecting his time, during which Western thought regarded the white as the most supreme race and the *Negroes* as inferior to the white.

Kant's Eurocentric white supremacy presented in his human geography becomes a major ground for criticism of his cosmopolitanism as "a mask for the pursuit of hidden interest for the idealization of the Western power and the depiction of the other as an enemy of humankind itself."[149] In this context, Kant's *knowledge* about human race and its relation to geography can function as a form/ground of power that disseminates, perpetuates, naturalizes, and justifies the racist and racialist discrimination as *natural* on both the personal and institutional level. As Arendt rightly points out, racists "were the only ones who consistently denied....the principle of equality and solidarity of all peoples guaranteed by the idea of mankind [*sic*]."[150] Ironically, Kant clarifies in the announcements of the course from 1765 and 1775 that the purpose of the geography course is to cultivate students to become *citizens of the world*. In this sense, Kant connects his cosmopolitanism to his lecture on physical geography and anthropology, which he associates under the title, "*pragmatische Weltkenntnis* [practical world-knowledge]."[151] *Knowledge of the world* for Kant is "extensive knowledge of *things* in the world, for example, animals, plants and minerals from various lands and climates—but only when it contains knowledge of the human being as a *citizen of the world*."[152]

After I learned not only about Kant's cosmopolitanism but also Kant's hierarchical human geography, I had to face and wrestle with the following question: How one could deal with the fundamental contradiction between Kant's knowledge production of human geography, in which racist "knowledge" becomes *natural* on the one hand, and his remarkable cosmopolitan ideal for the perpetual peace for humanity on the other? In spite of Kant's biased human geography, I come to conclude, one cannot simply deny that Kant's significant ideal of cosmopolitanism has influenced scholars and writers who envision the ideal world of justice and peace beyond national boundaries. I found a helpful clue to the answer about my question regarding Kant's discursive contradiction in his "What Is Enlightenment?" in which Kant himself offers a universal principle with which one can think *with* Kant and at the same time move *beyond* and *against* Kant:

> Would a society of pastors, perhaps a church assembly or venerable presbytery, not be justified in binding itself by oath to a certain unalterable symbol in order to secure a constant guardianship over each of its members and through them over the people, and this for all time: I say that this is wholly impossible. Such a contract, whose intention is to preclude forever all *further enlightenment of the human race,* is absolutely null and void, even if it should be ratified by the supreme power, by parliaments, and by the most solemn peace treaties. One age cannot bind itself, and thus conspire, to place a succeeding one in a condition whereby it would be impossible for the later age to expand its knowledge, to rid itself of errors, and generally to increase its enlightenment. That would be *a crime against human nature,* whose essential destiny lies precisely in such progress; subsequent generations are thus completely justified in dismissing such agreements as unauthorized and criminal.[153]

It would be what Kant calls a *crime against human nature* if one did not to seek for a *further enlightenment* by simply remaining within Kant's sociopolitical *situated-knowledge* of race. Kant would be against the idea of us regarding his thought as a fixed doctrine on race because his thought is, as he argues, a "continuous process of new insights and new questions."[154] Kant's insights into a cosmopolitan condition, the only condition for the possibility for the harmony of justice and peace, and a peaceable *federation of nations* remain highly relevant and significant especially to contemporary hope for global justice in an era of globalization. Although numerous thinkers have offered theories of right and law or of the state, Kant is the one who "makes room for an international and even global perspective,"[155] which is one of the reasons I do not wish to abandon Kant simply because he is not *pure* in his ethnocentric racialist remarks. What one needs to do is to discover cosmopolitanism *through* and *with* Kant and radicalize its vision *against* and *beyond* Kant, as long as his cosmopolitan idea can function as a useful *box of tools* to enlarge the possibilities and freedom of every individual human being regardless of who one is.

Moving beyond Kant's inherent Eurocentrism requires a postcolonial endeavor and a constant rewriting of the historical moments of cosmopolitanism. Kant himself offers a principle of *crime against human nature* for the proper application of thinking-*with*-Kant-*against*-Kant, or thinking-*with*-Kant-*in-spite-of*-Kant in the course of examining cosmopolitanism discourse. In spite of his whitecentric view of the human race, Kant's vision for the *kingdom of ends* (*Reich der Zwecke*) of humanity in his idea of the perpetual peace is impossible to ignore. A group of scholars argues that he changed his racist view on race and even abandoned the concept of race itself.[156] Pauline Kleingeld also argues that although Kant consistently holds his hierarchical view on race during the 1780s and early 1790s, "Kant radically changes his mind" and during the 1790s "drops his hierarchical account of the races in favour of a more genuinely egalitarian and cosmopolitan view."[157]

There are other counter-arguments about the change of Kant's view of race. Robert Bernasconi, for instance, points out that "in Kant a certain cosmopolitanism and a certain racism do not seem to conflict with each other."[158] Both contradicting interpretations of Kant's view on race may have their own *truth* in a respective way. Kant is a product of his own time, in which a *universalist* ideal and a *racist* view often coexist. Kant may or may not have changed his hierarchical view of race over time during his life journey. However, it seems to me more plausible that Kant must have changed the hierarchical view on race that he once had. "Of the Different Races of Human Beings (1775)," "Determination of the Concept of a Human Race (1785)," and "On the Use of Teleological Principles in Philosophy (1788)" constitute the so-called Kant's trilogy on the natural history of the human species,[159] in which Kant defended racial hierarchy among different races. However, it is later, in "To Perpetual Peace (1795)" that Kant explicitly forbids the colonial conquest of foreign lands:

> [O]riginally no one had a greater right to any region of the earth than anyone else .... Compare this [cosmopolitan right] with the inhospitable conduct of civilized nations in our part of the world, especially commercial ones: the injustice that they display towards

foreign lands and people (which is the same as *conquering* them) is terrifying.[160]

Kant's hierarchical view of race and the views of other thinkers, such as David Hume, can be the *darker side of the Enlightenment* that Walter Mignolo points out.[161] There are, however, reasons for the contemporary relevance of Kant: Kant is the first thinker who has lifted up the notion of peace to the position of a foundational concept of philosophy;[162] who has connected the notion of peace to human rights; and who has extended this peace with a cosmopolitan perspective. Furthermore, Kant's notion of *kingly people* is significant in the sense that the *kingly people* are *the people,* not an elite group, "who rule themselves by the laws of equality."[163] One of the significant reasons for the contemporary relevance of Kant for me is that he offers, with his notion of cosmopolitan rights and perpetual peace, room for a transnational and planetary perspective in theories of human rights, law, or hospitality. In this sense, Kant gives the ideal of cosmopolitanism a philosophical and theopolitical meaning in *doing* theology. Therefore, I believe *thinking with Kant against Kant*[164] and *beyond Kant* is a significant way of using Kant's cosmopolitanism that is still relevant today.

Cosmopolitan Justice and Crimes against Humanity

In the dedication of *Otherwise than Being,* Emmanuel Levinas writes: "To the memory of those who were closest among the six million assassinated by the National Socialists, and of the millions on millions of all confessions and all nations, victims of the same hatred of the other man [*sic*], the same anti-semitism."[165] Here Levinas establishes a notion of *crime against humanity* by making the victims of the Holocaust and the victims of hatred equivalent because it is "the same hatred" that people exercise, which is, in fact, the hatred of humanity. The hatred of the other human is the hatred of humanity and is the foundation of any pattern of *antihumanism* because those victims of hatred, "be they Jews, gypsies, blacks, or Vietnamese, symbolize humanity as such: they are hostages, subjected to suffering and persecution, humiliation and death."[166] In this sense, Levinas offers a profound insight: the hatred of the other, on whatever ground, is the source of evil, crime, and injustice and it is a *crime against humanity*.

If people begin to change their perception of the others whose nationality and skin color are different from theirs and regard them as *fellow humans,* as fellow *cosmic citizens,* the way people respond to what happens to the others would be entirely different. If someone oppresses the other on whatever ground, personally or sociopolitically, people would feel that the oppression is not just oppression against woman, black, LGBT, Muslim,

Jew, disabled, or non-documented immigrant worker but *oppression against humanity*. For this oppression is a fundamental denial of who/what one is. When the Nazis persecuted and killed Jews, Gypsies, the homeless, or homosexuals, these murders were not just crimes against Gypsies, the homeless, homosexuals, or Jews, but also *crimes against humanity*, as they all are fellow humans who are sharing cosmic belongingness. Following the so-called "Final Solution," the Nazis and their collaborators killed nearly two-thirds (six million) of all European Jews (nine million)—one million were children; two million were women; and three million were men. The Nazis' killing also included 200,000 Gypsies; 200,000 mentally/physically disabled patients in institutions through the so-called "Euthanasia Program"; racial minorities such as Poles and Russians; and other groups such as Communists, Socialists, Jehovah's Witnesses, and homosexuals.[167] It is interesting to see that the Nazis categorized gays as a *racial danger* that diminished Germany's reproductive potential, whereas it did not regard lesbians as a threat to Nazis' racial polities and therefore did not persecute them along with non-German gays unless they had relationships with German gays. The Nazis sent German gays to the "racial community" to get "racially conscious" and change their lifestyle.[168] It seems the Nazis regarded gays as *anti-social*, but not *sub-social*, who could change who they were through *proper* education and training.

I often receive questions from my students as to whether men can be feminists, whether the white can *do* black liberation theology, or whether non-Jews can talk about the Holocaust. These kinds of questions usually come from the collectively categorized groups—both the *victimizer-group* and the *victimized-group*. There are some women, for instance, who believe that men cannot be feminists and should not claim to be feminists because of the biological difference. There are also groups of *people of color* who firmly believe that white people cannot *do* postcolonial theology. So those who carry the *collective markers of oppressors* such as male, white, heterosexual, and so on get questioned about their *authenticity* and ability to do feminist, liberation, postcolonial, or queer theology. Without any hesitation, my answer is always decisive, simple, and firm: "Yes, you can and you must." For sexism, racism, homophobism, classism, colonialism, or anti-Semitism are not just oppression against a certain group of people but also *oppression against humanity*.

Oppression or liberation from oppression is not about one's *essence* but about *position* and *rights* that derive from simply being human. So as humans, people must concern themselves about various forms of social oppression, discrimination, or exclusion of others on whatever ground. Besides, no one can claim an *ownership*, based on one's biology or cartographical location, of movements for human rights and justice. Showing concern for and joining in the works for human freedom, rights, and liberation are the endless duty of and responsibility for humanity to other fellow humans. In this context, the notion of *crimes against humanity* is extremely helpful for one to move beyond such sentiments of ownership of the social movement, biological/cultural essentialism, or historical determinism that hinders us from being in solidarity with the marginalized and working together for the betterment of the world. Here I adopt the notion of *crimes against humanity* in a more universalized way, although the public emergence of the notion of *crime against humanity* has its own particular historical context: World War II. I regard remaining awakened to not only the *historicality* but also the *transhistoricality* of the notion of crime against humanity equally significant in the work for justice in multiple contexts. The cosmopolitan view of human beings allows us to see others as fellow humans, regardless of one's nationality, citizenship, gender, religion, race, or sexuality, and gives birth to a significant notion, *crime against humanity*.

It is Rafael Lemkin, a Polish Jewish lawyer and a refugee from Nazism, who coined the term *genocide* and led the international movement to adopt the U.N. Convention on Genocide in 1948.[169] He identified and pushed genocide as an international crime, not only during wartime but also during peacetime. It is significant to see how Lemkin himself defines genocide in his book:

> Genocide is effected through a synchronized attack on different aspects of life of the captive peoples: in the political field (by destroying institutions of self-government and imposing a German pattern of administration, and through colonization by Germans); in the social field (by disrupting the social cohesion of the nation involved and killing or removing elements such as the intelligentsia, which provide spiritual leadership—according to Hitler's statement in Mein Kampf, "the greatest of spirits can be liquidated if its bearer is beaten to death with a rubber truncheon"); in the cultural field (by prohibiting or destroying cultural institutions and cultural activities; by substituting vocational education for education in the liberal arts, in order to prevent humanistic thinking, which the occupant considers dangerous because it promotes national thinking); in the economic field (by shifting the wealth to Germans and by prohibiting the exercise of trades and occupations by people who do not promote Germanism "without reservations"); in the biological field (by a policy of depopulation and by promoting

> procreation of Germans in the occupied countries); in the field of physical existence (by introducing a starvation rationing system for non-Germans and by mass killings, mainly of Jews, Poles, Slovenes, and Russians); in the religious field (by interfering with the activities of the Church, which in many countries provides not only spiritual but also national leadership); in the field of morality (by attempts to create an atmosphere of moral debasement through promoting pornographic publications and motion pictures, and the excessive consumption of alcohol).[170]

I find it extremely interesting to see that he lists seven fields of possible genocide alongside with the Jewish Holocaust: the political, social, cultural, economic, biological, religious, and moral fields. For those who want to absolutize the Holocaust as a unique genocide, Lemkin's definition and description of genocide may look utterly inappropriate, seemingly diluting the indescribable suffering and killing of the Jewish people under the Nazi regime. However, the *logic* Lemkin adopts in this long list of the fields of possible genocide has a significant implication. Genocide is not just the immediate destruction and mass killing of a nation or people. It is also the "destruction of essential foundations of the life of national groups, with the aim of annihilating the groups themselves."[171] Lemkin points out that genocide aims at this "destruction" with two phases: "the destruction of the national pattern of the oppressed group; the other, the imposition of the national pattern of the oppressor."[172]

According to Lemkin's concept of genocide, it is clear that genocide happens when people exercise the *politics of sameness,* which does not see the values and beauty of diversity and thereby does not allow people of difference to live with *us*. The politics of sameness is what Emmanuel Levinas calls *exercise of the same,* which is a desire "to receive nothing of the Other but what is in me, as though from all eternity I was in possession of what comes to me from the outside—to receive nothing or to be free."[173] The *politics of sameness* results in the exercise of the tyranny of binarism: *we* versus *they*. The *we-they* binarism is tyrannical because it justifies the discrimination, hatred, and killing of *they* by *we* when *we* possess the power over *they*. Therefore, Lemkin argues the importance of dismantling genocide based on his understanding of the beauty and value of human diversity as follows:

> Our whole cultural heritage is a product of the contributions of all nations. We can best understand when we realize how impoverished our culture would be if the people doomed by Germany, such as the Jews, had not been permitted to create the Bible or to give birth

> to an Einstein, a Spinoza; if the Poles had not had the opportunity to give to the world a Copernicus, a Chopin, a Curie; the Czechs a Huss, and a Dvorak; the Greeks a Plato and a Socrates; the Russians, a Tolstoy and a Shostakovich.[174]

The concept of *crimes against humanity* came to light in the Charter of the International Military Tribunal, which four principal Allied powers—the Americans, British, French, and Soviets—signed during the London conference on August 8, 1945.[175] This document turned out to be the crucial legal reference for the Nuremberg trial, especially with Article 6, which specifies the types of crimes—such as Crimes against Peace, War Crimes, and Crimes against Humanity. Article 6 of the Charter of the International Military Tribunal defines *crimes against humanity* as follows:

> Namely, murder, extermination, enslavement, deportation, and other inhumane acts committed against any civilian population, before or during the war, or persecutions on political, racial, or religious grounds in execution of or in connection with any crime within the jurisdiction of the Tribunal, whether or not in violation of domestic law of the country where perpetrated.[176]

Article 6 strongly emphasizes the responsibility of the *individual,* rather than nation-state, in its statement that "the following acts, or any of them, are crimes coming within the jurisdiction of the Tribunal for which there shall be individual responsibility."[177] So an individual cannot use the state law as an excuse for the crimes. As an individual human being, one has to take full responsibility for the crimes against humanity that one commits, even if it is an act of obeying one's state law or orders, because "laws of humanity"[178] override the positive law of a nation-state. The Nuremberg Trial of 1945–1946 is extremely significant because it innovated the notion of *crimes against humanity*.

Karl Jaspers depicts the Nuremberg Trial as "a feeble, ambiguous harbinger of world order, the need of which mankind [*sic*] is beginning to feel" and "the world order is not at hand by any means.…but it has come to seem possible to *thinking humanity*," [179] and goes on to say: "[T]he Eichmann trial is unsettling.… Its significance is not in its being a legal trial but in its establishing of historical fact and serving as a reminder of those facts for humanity.…"[180] Arendt replies to Jaspers, in which she highlights the significant notion, *crimes against humanity*:

> The concept of *hostis humani generis*—however one translates it, but not: crime against humanness; but, rather, against humanity—is

> more or less indispensable to the trial. The crucial point is that although the crime at issue was committed primarily against the Jews, it is in no way limited to the Jews or the Jewish question.[181]

Jaspers says to Arendt that the Eichmann trial is about humankind and one should not reduce the trial to an Israeli issue.[182] The *universalization* of the particularized notion of the *crime against humanity* is crucial because of the effectiveness of the notion that people can adopt in a different context from the particular historical background.

After World War II, concern grew about interdependence of the globe, especially with the notion of *crime against humanity*. Giorgio Agamben problematizes the use of the term *Holocaust* or *Shoah* because it gives a mystical stature to the brutal reality of the process of extermination.[183] When people use such terms, people tend to view Auschwitz as a place of mystery or theology that relates Auschwitz to the question of God or G-d. Auschwitz, according to Agamben, is a time and place, in which biopolitics exercises its power on *homo sacer* in God's absence. Auschwitz as the camp is "the place in which the most absolute *conditio inhumana* that has ever existed on earth was realized"[184] and "*the space that is opened when the state of exception begins to become the rule*."[185] In this sense, for Agamben, Auschwitz is a political and ethical space, where God was absent. Using such terms as Holocaust or Shoah *mystifies* a space of biopolitics, which can result in *sanctifying* the process of horrible extermination of masses of corpses of *homo sacer*. *Homo sacer*, by its definition, may be killed but cannot be sacrificed.[186] Taking Bartleby as an example, Agamben postulates the survivor as a space in which "to listen to what is unsaid," and the voice of "testimony says ....human beings are human insofar as they bear witness to the inhuman.'"[187] Agamben contends that Holocaust victims and survivors are models of the universal subject because they bear witness to *desubjectification*:

> Remembrance restores possibility to the past, making what happened incomplete and completing what never was. Remembrance is neither what happened nor what did not happen but, rather, their potentialization, their becoming possible once again. It is in this sense that Bartleby calls the past into question, re-calling it—not simply to redeem what was, to make it exist again but, more precisely, to consign it again to potentiality.[188]

Agamben raises the issue of the impossibility of speaking, the beyond-word-ness of the language of the witnesses: "Poets—witnesses—found language as what remains, as what actually survives the possibility, or impossibility, of speaking.... What cannot be stated, what cannot be archived is the language in which the author succeeds in bearing witness to his incapacity to speak. In this language, a language that survives the subjects who spoke it coincides with a speaker who remains beyond it."[189] Here Agamben is talking not about *aesteticization* of testimony but about the ethical responsibility of listening to *what cannot be stated, what cannot be archived*. Agamben invites us to think about "the new ethical territory."[190] Auschwitz/Holocaust is an important ethico-political issue and one has to regard the camp simply "not as a historical fact and an anomaly belonging to the past (even if still verifiable) but in some way as the hidden matrix and *nomos* of the political space in which we are still living."[191] For the "anonymous mass," whom "[o] ne hesitates to call them living: one hesitates to call their death death, in the face of which they have no fear, as they are too tired to understand,"[192] are still around the world today. The language and testimony of the horrible reality of Auschwitz offers invaluable ethico-political lessons about what Agamben calls *the camp as nomos,*[193] and we need to bear in mind that *nomos* and narratives in ethics, law, and religion are inextricably intertwined.

The notion of cosmopolitan human rights expands the horizon of the U.N. Universal Declaration of Human Rights proclaimed on December 10, 1948. Article 1 states: "All human beings are born free and equal in dignity and rights. They are endowed with reason and conscience and should act towards one another in a spirit of brotherhood."[194] At least theoretically, the U.N. Declaration of Human Rights seems to make a shift from an *international* to a *cosmopolitan* idea of justice and rights when it states *all human beings are born free and equal in dignity and rights*. However, it reveals its limits in its preamble because the "all human beings" are not literally "all" human beings but only those "among the peoples of Member States themselves and among the peoples of territories under their jurisdiction."[195] Therefore, the precondition for attaining human rights is being a "member state," excluding those who do not belong to any member states.

Hannah Arendt takes up Kantian ideas of universal rights and hospitality in her dealing with the *stateless* people, the displaced, the dislocated—the *Heimatlosen*.[196] She argues that the declaration of human rights from an international organization still has its limits because it "operates in terms of reciprocal agreements and treaties *between sovereign states*; and, for the time being, a sphere that is above the nations does not exist."[197] Arendt invites us to reevaluate the term *human rights* because *human rights,* by the very definition of the term, should be the rights of individual human beings, not of citizens of a particular nation-state. Here one encounters the tensions between *the particularity of positive law,* operated by the institutions of specific nation-states, and *the universality of natural law/ethical obligations* toward individual persons regardless of their national citizenship.[198] Arendt criticizes nationalism and its impact on the formulation of personal identity. Heinrich Blücher also expresses his skepticism about nationalism:

> The nation-state is the genuine political community transformed into a lie.... Nationalism is just as dangerous an ideology as capitalism, socialism, racism, imperialism, and it has been mixed with all of them to produce the most poisonous of cocktails.... With the aid of the national concept, genuine attachment to one's native people and land was distorted into the lies of racism and national superiority.... Nationalism has always led to imperialism by way of jingoism and chauvinism.... This is why reflection on the "national" is so necessary and is in itself a political event.[199]

In fact, at least theoretically, the U.N. Declaration of Human Rights in 1948 made a shift from an "international" to a "cosmopolitan" ideal of justice and rights when the General Assembly of the U.N. declared in December of that year that:

> All human beings are born free and equal in dignity and rights.... Everyone is entitled to all the rights and freedoms set forth in this Declaration, without distinction of any kind, such as race, colour, sex, language, religion, political or other opinion, national or social origin, property, birth or other status. [200]

How can then one treat those *Heimatlosen* as equal, as fellow human beings? Jacques Derrida elaborates on this idea by coining a new phrase, *free city,* where "one could retreat in order to escape from the threat of injustice."[201] The idea of a *free city* is significant because when one deals with the issues of hospitality or refuge, it could lift one up above nation-states or unshackle oneself from them. A significant task for our time, when the interconnectedness of the globe is becoming a daily reality, is then a construction of discourse that reconciles the universality of human rights with the particularity of positive law. Here it is important to note that the *particular* rights and the *universal* rights are not antagonistic—not once we enlarge the circle of inclusion of *particular* community until the circle can embrace the entire world, in which the *particular* community can be a component of the *cosmopolitan* community.

For Derrida, the notion of a *crime against humanity* is also important in that it constitutes a *performative event*. It is important to ask when and how people use the notion of a crime against humanity because people can misuse the notion. *Publicizing* or *universalizing* crime marks the play of repentance and forgiveness and authorizes its own authenticity. What Derrida calls *theatrical space* is a new public space for the acknowledgment of criminal acts against humanity. Derrida points out the problem in a *performative event* in the sense that "[t]his sort of transformation structured the theatrical space in which grand forgiveness, the grand scene of repentance which we are concerned with, is played, sincerely or not."[202] Although Derrida acknowledges the significance of the creation of a new public space for a "reaffirmation of human rights, or a new Declaration of Human Rights,"[203] Derrida warns against the possible danger of the popularization of the notion of *crime against humanity* after WWII:

> However, the simulacra, the automatic ritual, hypocrisy, calculation, or mimicry are often a part, and invite parasites to this ceremony of culpability. Here is a humanity shaken by a movement which would like itself to be unanimous; here is a human race which would claim to accuse itself all at once, publicly and spectacularly, of all the crimes committed, in effect, by itself against itself, 'against humanity.'[204]

Derrida criticizes the "fake, banal ritual of semi-forgiveness for guilt over crimes in the past by nation-states, and the avowal of them on occasion for state-based economic advantages, since the guilt and the forgiveness are not genuine and will not lead to real respect."[205] Arendt is also critical of the uncritical use of the notion of a *crime against humanity* in terms of including "genocide if practiced against non-Jewish peoples (such as the Gypsies or the Poles) and all other crimes, including murder, committed against either Jews or non-Jews, provided that these crimes were not committed with intent to destroy the people as a whole."[206] If one lumps together all kind of ordinary crimes into the category of crimes against humanity, people will misunderstand the fundamental reason for this new category, *crimes against humanity,* which refers to "the act of genocide which was perpetrated against a people simply because it existed on the face of this earth as *this specific kind of people*."[207] Adolf Eichmann, one of the well-known Nazi criminals, said at his trial in Jerusalem in 1961, "I am not the monster I am made out to be ....I am the victim of a fallacy."[208] Arendt concludes her observation of Eichmann's trial and his act in the face of his own death at the gallows: "It was as though in those last minutes he was summing up the lesson that this long course in human wickedness had taught us—the lesson of the fearsome, word-and-thought-defying *banality of evil*."[209] The notion of genocide and crimes against humanity in international law dealing with the Holocaust and other war crimes is the evolution of cosmopolitan justice that Kant, Arendt, and Jaspers awaited.

Karl Jaspers, an opponent and victim of the Nazis during the twelve-year Third Reich, laid the groundwork of the notion of *crimes against humanity* and linked the Nuremberg Trial to the Kantian cosmopolitan vision. Unlike other philosophers in his time, such as Martin Heidegger, Jaspers did not compromise with the Nazi regime. Jaspers took an active leadership role as one of thirteen members on the "Committee for the Reconstruction of the University," mediating between the American occupation officials and German academics. The committee was composed of "unincriminated professors," with its task to be the "planning of the form of the future university."[210] In his book *The Question of German Guilt (Die Schuldfrage),* parts of a lecture on the intellectual situation in Germany at Heidelberg University in the winter of 1946 that he published later, Jaspers distinguishes four levels of guilt: criminal, political, moral, and metaphysical. Whereas criminal and political guilt are public, moral and metaphysical guilt are private. Criminal guilt is the result of acts capable of objective proof and unequivocal laws. Jaspers also argues that all Germans are politically guilty "for the acts committed by their state,"[211] and therefore responsible for what the Germans allowed the *Reich* to do. Jaspers himself attests: "Every German is made to share the blame for the crimes committed in the name of the Reich. We are collectively liable. The question is in what sense each of us must feel co-responsible."[212] However, having a political guilt in public is not sufficient. Each and every German should go through an individual self-scrutiny with a question: "How am I guilty?"[213]

One cannot establish a sense of moral guilt collectively. It is up to an individual person's self-judgment, because "the moral guilt exists for all those who give room to conscience and repentance."[214] Jaspers suffers from his own *moral guilt* in his lament: "Camouflage had become a basic trait of our existence...." and "weighs on our moral conscience."[215] Defining metaphysical guilt as "the lack of absolute solidarity with the human being as such," Jaspers states, "I am guilty of being still alive," and, "We are guilty of being alive."[216] However, the moral/metaphysical guilt is not something that an external party can impose upon others, as Jaspers experienced in the process of *denazification* of Heidelberg University.[217] The real collective transformation becomes possible when the individuals begin to recognize the moral level of guilt, and then the metaphysical one. This sense of moral and metaphysical guilt should come out of neither self-pity nor pride, but rather "humility and moderation" before God, the "only fixed point."[218] Jaspers closes his essay on German guilt with the story of Jeremiah, asking people for seriousness before God with a remarkable final sentence: "Our share is humility and moderation."[219] According to Anson Rabinbach, "[N]o single intellectual in immediately postwar Germany contributed more to the reorientation of German philosophy toward a reconceptualized Western humanism than Karl Jaspers."[220]

The evolution of cosmopolitan justice and the notion of crimes against humanity trigger people like Arendt and Jaspers to ask the question about the responsibility not only for fellow citizens (nationals) but also for *fellow human beings,* transcending nationality and citizenship. Taking the *individual* human being, regardless of one's nationality or citizenship, to be the primary unit of ethico-political and theological concern requires a cosmopolitan consciousness that regards every individual human with a *proper name* of ethical singularity—or a *face* in the Levinasian sense—as a fellow citizen of the cosmos. In this cosmopolitan consciousness, issues of justice and human rights transcend national borders, and therefore what cosmopolitanism offers is justice and human rights *beyond* borders, not only *inter*-national but also *trans*-national because it should include those stateless, *Heimatlosen,* in the circle of inclusion. In his speech on August 22, 1939, Adolf Hitler said:

> I have put my death-head formations in place with the command relentlessly and without compassion to send into death many women and children of Polish origin and language. Only thus *we* can gain the living space that *we* need. Who after all is today speaking about the destruction of the Armenians?[221]

Here it is obvious that the *we* for Hitler is extremely exclusionary and repressive in opposition to others—to racial/ethnic others, sexual others, religious others, sociocultural others, political others. His knowledge of who *we* are depends on his total exclusion of others. Cosmopolitanism seeks a *we* that does not rely on the exclusion of *others* but, instead, recognizes and confirms each other as part of the planetary *we*. The cosmopolitan *we* is not grounded in a monolithic sameness but in a constant alterity and *ethical singularity* of each individual human person regardless of one's national origin and belonging, religious affiliation, gender, race and ethnicity, class, ability, or sexuality. Seeking for a cosmopolitan planetary *we* in the notion of *crimes against humanity* is one way to respond to Karl Jaspers' question of a metaphysical guilt—"the lack of absolute solidarity with the human being as such."[222] Jaspers' notion of metaphysical guilt is significant not only in the process of denazification after the *Third Reich* but also in the construction of public theological discourse and practice today. The crime against humanity is, by definition, unforgivable, as "men [*sic*] are unable to forgive what they cannot punish" and "they are unable to punish what has turned out to be unforgivable."[223] However, the notion of *crimes against humanity* helps us establish a sense of *planetary-we-ness* and *solidarity-in-alterity* because it stresses our infinite responsibility for the other as a fellow citizens of the cosmos.

4

Cosmopolitan *Trans-Religious* Solidarity

Beyond Religious Tourism

One is a self among other selves.

—Charles Taylor[1]

No tradition can claim to possess the religious truth of humanity.

—Luce Irigaray[2]

The Rhetoric of Religious Plurality: Other Religions—Tokens or Significant Others?

Interest in religion, both in academia and in public debate, has been growing, especially after September 11, 2001. The Bush government of the United States declared the so-called War on Terror after the September 11 event and linked Al-Qaeda and the phenomenon of international terrorism to Islamic radicalism. Religion began playing a more distinctive role in U.S. foreign policy, since George W. Bush combined his evangelical Christian faith with his administration's foreign policy. In his official biography, Bush made clear that his role as the president of the U.S. was to achieve a victory of *good* over *evil*, and that his being president was working for God's will. In September 2002, he invited five leaders from the Abrahamic religions—three Christian, one Jewish, and one Muslim—to the Oval Office to get support from the religious leaders for his War on Terror. He asked them to pray for him with the following remarks: "I had a drinking problem. Right now I should be in a bar in Texas, not the Oval Office. There is only one reason I am in the Oval Office and not in a bar. I found faith. I found God. I am here because of the power of prayer."[3] I wonder how the Jewish and Muslim leaders, who were there alongside the three Christian leaders, felt about Bush's *God*. I wonder about their feeling because it is not hard to presume that Bush, from his evangelical Protestant point of view, would base his notion of God on an exclusive view of other religions, and that the only absolute savior would be the *Jesus* of Christianity. Thus, the very *God* in Bush's theology would be incompatible with the G-d in Judaism or Allah in Islam, especially as those two religions deny the divinity of Jesus as the incarnated God and do not acknowledge Jesus as the only true savior for all of humanity. When asked who his favorite philosopher was during his 2000 campaign, Bush, an evangelical Protestant guided by Billy Graham, replied, "Jesus."[4]

People can interpret this statement in various ways, but it would not be exaggerating to say that Bush sees everything in the light of his *evangelical* Christianity, and that *Jesus* for him represents the eternal victor of good over evil. Needless to say, such terms as *good* and *evil* that Bush frequently uses are primarily religious, not political. Adopting such religious terms in his political statement on the *axis of evil,* indicating Iraq, Iran, and North Korea, for instance, the U.S. foreign policy under the Bush administration became more *religious* than political. Bush based his American exceptionalism on his belief that "God has singled out America to be his [*sic*] chosen instrument,"[5] which has justified the U.S. hegemony in the world as a product of the divine will. His public statement to a reporter, "I'm in the Lord's hand,"[6] indicates his *Christianized* understanding of the War on Terror. In this context, he would perceive destroying the *axis of evil* as a divine mission to carry out God's will, which is an exemplar statement of what I would call the *crusade mentality*. One should ask such questions as *who* is making such a statement and *in what circumstances* in order to see its theopolitical implications, because one's religious statement is far from being neutral, especially when one is in a position of extreme political power. Bush's statement, "I am in the Lord's hand," sacralizes and justifies his War on Terrorism as if it has a divine sanction, as if God is leading him to a militant policy that destroys countless lives. The growing public interest in religion in the U.S., especially in Islam, is implicitly grounded in the Christian superiorism that regards other religions as inauthentic, less-true, if not *evil*.

The resurgence of religious fundamentalism in various regions of the world and the rise of popular interest in spirituality could also be some of the reasons for the recent sociopolitical turn to religion. Furthermore, due to immigration and its impact on demographic trends, the U.S. has become a more religiously pluralistic nation than ever, which has generated a drastic change in the religious demography in the U.S.[7] For these various reasons, *religion* has become more popular than ever as a topic of public discourse and interest. In the context of religious plurality in the U.S., in spite of Christian dominance of politics especially under the Bush government, the public urge to acknowledge the very existence of various religions has focused primarily on easing or preventing conflict and tension among and between various religions. Most religions have placed, at least in principle, the highest value on peace, love, equality, and compassion. However, one can easily find the link between religion and violence in many parts of the world as religion has justified violence for a *sacred* or *higher* cause. Thus, it is likely that violence "finds its prime model—its source, force, and counterforce—in key elements of the tradition called the religious," and that violence "can be seen as the very element of religion."[8] In this sense, there seems "no violence without (some) religion; no religion without (some) violence."[9] In the context of violence and war in the name of religion and the *sacred* cause, teaching and learning about religious plurality should eventually mean inspiring students to commit themselves to promoting peace, justice, equality, and freedom by attending to the issues of ethico-theological approaches to religions, the underlying *power* asymmetry among religions, or the geopolitics of religions, rather than taking students on a *religious tour* that does not require any commitment to effect change for the betterment of the world.

Teaching and learning *religious plurality* should not mean treating *other* religions as just *tokens*. Without seriously examining one's own theology of religion, the rhetoric of religious plurality can easily fall into the trap of *religious tokenism*, as one can see in the case of Bush's invitation of five religious leaders from three religions to visit his Oval Office. Bush did invite *other* religious leaders along with the Christian leaders, which may have given the impression that he *recognizes* religious plurality. However, when his theology exclusively sees Christianity as the *only* true religion among other religions, and fails to question his own theological presupposition about other religions, the seeming *recognition* of other religions by the dominant power can easily be an act of *religious tokenism*. In this context, one must note that *practicing* a rhetoric of religious plurality and a politics of recognition requires Christians to wrestle with the fundamental presuppositions of Christian theology, soteriology, and Christology that dismiss other religions, and with the justice issues involving power disparities between Christianity and other religions. Only through the fundamental reexamination of one's own theological perceptions can the rhetoric of religious plurality help one recognize the authentic dignity of *religious others* as *significant others*,[10] whose presence is significant in one's own existence, and implement this idea into social, political, educational, and theological discourse and practice.

Politics of Recognition and Its Theological Implication

In his seminal essay "Politics of Recognition," Charles Taylor contends that Jean-Jacques Rousseau and Immanuel Kant are the originators of the discourse on politics of recognition and politics of equal dignity.[11] One can examine the politics of recognition in the context of religions in the light of multiculturalism and multireligionism, because a politics of recognition of religious plurality shares similar issues with multiculturalism. There are, however, a few unique issues in multireligionism that multiculturalism does not have to deal with: the issue of absolute *truth-claim* in religions, for one. When a marginalized people, on the basis of their gender, race, ethnicity, or sexuality, begin claiming their own identity as legitimate, they also demand *recognition*. Therefore one can interlink the demand for recognition with the issue of identity-claim. Charles Taylor rightly points out:

> [O]ur identity is partly shaped by recognition or its absence, often by *mis*recognition of other, and so a person or group of people can suffer real damage, real distortion, if the people or society around them mirror back to them a confining or demeaning or contemptible picture of themselves. Nonrecognition or misrecognition can inflict harm, can be a form of oppression, imprisoning someone in a false, distorted, and reduced mode of being.[12]

Therefore, people usually interlink *politics of recognition* to the *politics of identity* of various marginalized groups, such as women, LGBT, physically challenged, racial-ethnic minorities, or religious minorities, who demand a social, political, or legal *recognition* of who/what they are. The politics of recognition in the light of multiculturalism deals with one's culture—whether it is language, custom, daily practice, tradition, religion, or some other characteristics. Although one can approach multiculturalism in many different ways, the primary focus of the current discussion on multiculturalism is on the political and legal aspects of *recognition* of different ethnic and cultural aspects in a given society.[13] Multiculturalism contrasts with monoculturalism and is a product of critical resistance to the rhetoric of the *melting-pot* of monocultural assimilation. However, multiculturalism has taken different forms with various political commitments and practices, and is never a unitary discourse in its discursive implication and political implementation. In this context, Peter McLaren examines four different types of multiculturalism and differentiates "critical and resistance multiculturalism" from conservative or corporate multiculturalism, liberal multiculturalism, and left-liberal multiculturalism.[14]

According to McLaren, multiculturalism poses a danger when it takes a form of conservative, liberal, or left-liberal multiculturalism, in which people in the dominant culture want to officially "distance themselves from racist ideologies" but "pay only lip service to the cognitive equality of all races," and give "the white cultural elite the excuse they need for unreflectively and disproportionately occupying positions of power."[15] In *conservative multiculturalism,* for instance, people try to create a *common* culture through such policy and practice as "delegitimization of foreign languages and regional and ethnic dialects, a persistent attack on nonstandard English, and undermining of bilingual education."[16] In this case, the conservative multiculturalists use their celebration of *diversity* only to "cover up the ideology of assimilation."[17] Here left-liberal multiculturalists homogenize, exoticize, and essentialize ethnic groups, and then members of the ethnic groups become just entertaining *add-ons* to or *tokens* for the dominant culture. In conservative, liberal, and left-liberal multiculturalism, people *naturalize* the colonialist legacy of white supremacy without any transformation of existing sociocultural-political systems that privilege the Western over the non-Western culture. One should note that just celebrating *diversity*—whether the diversity is cultural or religious—without any willingness to transform the existing relations of power-differential among diversities could be just another form of assimilation to the larger social order. Thus, what we need to exercise is *critical and resistance multiculturalism,* in which "diversity itself is not a goal" but "must be affirmed within a politics of cultural criticism and a commitment to social justice."[18]

There are a lot of similarities between the rhetoric of religious plurality and the rhetoric of cultural diversity and multiculturalism, and there could be, thus, conservative, liberal, left-liberal, and critical and resistance multireligionisms in teaching religious plurality. If Christian supremacy remains intact, implicitly or explicitly, in the class on religious plurality, teaching and learning religious plurality ends up reducing other religions as *add-ons* to Christianity. In this case, having a course on religious plurality in a Christian theological school may appear to indicate the school is open, progressive, ecumenical, or politically correct. However, if educators of religious plurality homogenize, exoticize, or *a*historicize other religions in their teaching, the course on religious plurality is nothing but *religious tourism, religious tokenism,* or *religious add-on*. It is not an act of a *politics of recognition* but of a *politics of misrecognition,* despite the school's good intention. Such theological *misrecognition* of other religions is not just *a lack of due respect,* but a suppression of a "vital human need" for who/what they are.[19]

Therefore, in a form of conservative, liberal, or left-liberal multireligionism, distorted recognition or "withholding of recognition can be a form of oppression."[20] Here, the *politics of theological recognition* should not mean differentiating all other religious groups by a unitary category of religion as if a religion is a fixed, unitary, homogeneous entity. On the part of Christianity, a politics of *authentic recognition* starts with *deabsolutizing* and *provincializing* Christianity in relation to other religions, as Christianity has been placing itself at the center of the world, not only religiously but also culturally, economically, and politically. An *authentic* recognition also requires *destereotyping* other religions, as a dominant group tends to construct its hegemony by indoctrinating the image of inferiority and inauthenticity in the subjugated group.

Theological educators usually design courses on religious plurality or world religions in colleges and universities to offer students some basic knowledge *about* various religions, and they appear plainly *value-neutral*.[21] The dilemma of this seeming *value-neutrality* of the courses results from the fact that in this process of providing knowledge *about* other religions from a perspective of *value-neutrality*, stereotypization, homogenization, idealization, romanticization, or degradation of other religions than Christianity tends to occur. Idealization or romanticization of a religion has the same dangerous function as degradation because both attitudes distort the complex nature and development of a religion and the materialized reality of the people within the religion. The educators of the courses on religious plurality usually recognize and celebrate differences between different religions while taking out any sort of *politico-ethical* approach to the very religions that they teach. Under the banner of multireligionism, the *politics of recognition* based on the rhetoric of religious plurality shares similar strengths and, at the same time, limitations with multiculturalism when it lacks a *critical* analysis of the power-asymmetry and power-disparity within, among, and between religions (*cultures* in the case of multiculturalism) and believers (*people* in the case of multiculturalism).

The most significant strength of multireligionism, in conjunction with multiculturalism, is its *recognition* of the differences and existence of religions other than one's own, without applying a sense of superiority or inferiority of one religion/culture over the other. Needless to mention, acknowledging and celebrating *difference* and *plurality* among cultures and religions are the primary steps toward finding significant antidotes to religious conflicts and wars. Teaching and learning *religious plurality* therefore involves, in principle, this *politics of recognition* and *politics of difference*, whether or not educators explicitly indicate these aspects through the courses they offer. As soon as one notices that any religion or culture cannot be a unitary, homogeneous, ahistorical entity but is always a heterogeneous, multiple, interest-bound, and historical product in the midst of a historical-political power struggle and identity construction, one realizes the power-laden reality of religions and cultures.

Moreover, one recognizes that the so-called *value-neutrality* of the course can become in fact a basis of overlooking the lived life-experience of the people who bear the social markers of race, gender, sexuality, etc., within the boundary of a given religion and culture. One can hardly deny that the politics of recognition of religious plurality are still very much grounded in Western and Christian initiative and motivation. When people engage in the practice of multiculturalism in the West, the *cultures* they imagine are usually other than the Western culture, and this assumption holds true in the case of multireligionism. The absence of the West and the Christian from the surface of the rhetoric of multireligionism has the danger of *normativizing* the West and the Christian in the discourse and practice of *religious plurality*. Therefore, the questions one needs to ask regarding the politics of recognition of religious plurality are: *By whom* does a religion or a culture need to be *recognized*? Why? *Whose interest* does such recognition serve? Does the *recognition of religious plurality* necessarily require an acceptance of theological *religious pluralism*?

The term *religious pluralism* is a contested concept and used differently depending on the disciplinary contexts. In the context of a theology of religion, scholars use *religious pluralism* in opposition to *religious exclusivism*, a concept based on the traditional paradigm of the axiom *Outside-the-Church-no-salvation* (*Extra ecclesiam nulla salus*). Scholars of religion can ground their notion of religious pluralism on multiple angles such as Theocentric, Christocentric, or ecclesiocentric, for instance. The primary claim of religious pluralism is that there are *plural*, not *singular*, paths unto salvation, which fundamentally challenges and contrasts with religious exclusivism or religious inclusivism. Religious inclusivism is obviously different from exclusivism, but it still maintains the Christian-centric view of religion, with "the claim to Christianity's unique finality as the locus of the only full divine revelation and the only adequate saving event."[22]

Although theologians of religious pluralism argue, "Non-Christians can be saved because, unknown to them, Christ is secretly 'in a way united' with them,"[23] they still base their *recognition* of other religions on an absolute Christian-superiorism. Religious pluralism, as one of the three typical positions in Christian theology of religion, along with exclusivism and inclusivism, searches "for the meaning in God's design for humankind of the plurality of living faiths and religious traditions."[24] There are two interpretations of theological religious pluralism: one affirming "independent validity and equality of the various religious traditions" while denying "the possibility of any one of them being universally normative" and the other one asserting a religious "pluralism that is universally valid."[25] In the context of sociology, *religious pluralism* refers to the diversity of religions within the same sociocultural space and the "interaction of religious actors with one another and with the society and the state around concrete cultural, social, economic, and political agendas."[26] Therefore, religious pluralism from a sociological perspective stands for a politics that incorporates with other religious communities while respecting and maintaining distinctive religious ethics and ethos that each religion may have. In this sense, one can relate *religious pluralism* in a sociological sense to a politics of recognition in the sense it *recognizes* the religious plurality as a sociocultural phenomenon in a democratic society that guarantees individual religious freedom and the interaction of diverse religious communities, and that protects individuals and groups with different religions from violence and unnecessary tension based on religious difference.

However, it is important to note that the sociological approach to religious pluralism does not have to deal with a fundamental theological question, while teaching religious plurality in theological schools and institutions means encountering root questions about the nature of religious truth-claims: How far can a Christian, for instance, *recognize* the theologically legitimate existence of other religions? How far should one *tolerate* other religions? How would the politics of recognition *function* in one's ministerial and theological formation? Can proselytization be compatible with the politics of recognition in religion? These are the pressing issues with which those teaching and learning about *religious plurality* must wrestle. In this sense, the politics of recognition in multireligionism requires an entirely different pedagogical and epistemological approach from the politics of recognition in multiculturalism. *Culture* does not have to get involved with a *truth-claim* issue, but can grant a simple *tolerance* and *recognition*, whereas *religion* gets engaged with the issue of *truth-claim*. In this context, one cannot adopt and teach the politics of recognition of religious plurality from a position of so-called *academic value-neutrality*. If one does, teaching students on religious plurality becomes nothing but *religious tourism* that provides only *information* about other religions while avoiding critical theological and epistemological questions about the nature of the religious *truth-claim* that always arises from discussions about different religions.

One needs to critically engage with at least three fundamental questions when teaching and learning about religious plurality, especially in the context of Christian theological schools, seminaries, and institutions. The first question involves the *truth-claim* religions make. When one recognizes that there are many religions other than Christianity, and that every religion has its own *truth-claim,* the initial question that arises is whether these *truth-claims* from different religions are compatible with one another in general, and with the Christian truth-claim in particular. Recognizing religious plurality in the world means facing this question: What can a minister/theologian say about the Christian truth-claims in Jesus' statement, for instance, "I myself am the Way—I am Truth, and I am Life. No one comes to Abba God but through me" (Jn. 14:6, Inclusive)? This question always arises in courses that deal with the issue of *religious plurality* at my school—a university-based divinity school, a majority of whose students pursue a parish ministry after their study. Christians have "Christianized" Jesus' statement as if Christianity had existed even in Jesus' time. One must interpret this kind of statement outside the institutionalized Christian box and in relation to the other teachings by Jesus about neighbor-love and hospitality.

The second question one needs to wrestle with in teaching and learning *religious plurality* involves one's *theological confidence*. How can one maintain a theological confidence in what one claims to be *true* while acknowledging the existence of multiple religions that also claim to be *true*? Although there is a different level of theological confidence in one's epistemological journey, this question of *confidence* requires in-depth theological configuration and critical reflection. Usually people interlink the issue of *confidence* with the question of *religious belonging*. How can one be sure that one is making the *best* choice of religion, when so many other religions make *truth-claims*? If one is learning religious plurality seriously, one should struggle with this theological challenge with the frustration of losing the *absolute* confidence that one once had.

The third question one may have to ask is about *religious others* who are outside of one's religious boundary and belong to a religion other than one's own. One can perceive and relate to *religious others* in many diferent ways. One can take a position of toleration, separation, conversion, or full recognition of the religious other as a *religious neighbor* or even as a *significant other*. When one tries to *tolerate* others, for instance, the very act of *toleration* implies a fundamental disapproval of the other because, unless one disapproves of or dislikes the other, one does not need to *tolerate* the other—whether the other is a person, a group, or a religion. Therefore, tolerance "implies a moral judgment on error and the consequent adoption of a moral attitude, based on charity, toward the good faith of those who err."[27] This question about *religious others* is also interlinked with the question of Christian mission and proselytization. Retheologizing the traditional *mission texts* in the Bible, such as, "Go therefore and make disciples of all the nations. Baptize them in the name of Abba God, and of the Only Begotten, and of the Holy Spirit" (Mt. 28:19, Inclusive), is an ongoing task in the process of teaching and learning religious plurality in Christian theological schools, because these mission texts have served as the grounds for condemning other religions and militantly proselytizing the *heathens* in Christian history.

Beyond Religious Tourism: Teaching and Learning Religious Plurality as Creating a *Religious Culture of Dissent*

Teaching and learning *religious plurality* often ends up privileging religious *texts* over *practice* and largely ignoring the social and historical contexts and the lived experience of people who shape, situate, and structure these religious texts. Furthermore, adopting the politics of recognition as a pedagogical principle in teaching can lead to an *uncritical silence* about the various forms of oppression and domination of certain religious groups. Here people often use *religious difference* as a *religious alibi* for the oppression or violation of human rights of certain groups of people, such as women or LGBT people. When one challenges an exclusion of women's leadership role in a certain religion, for instance, one often gets a response that one should not intervene in another religion because the exclusionary practice is a religious difference. People often turn a question of justice into a question of mere difference. I believe a religion can be meaningful not for its own claim to truth and divine authority but for the ways in which it serves to liberate and enlarge human freedom, possibility, and peace—not just *spiritually* but *holistically* in a materialized human reality. In this context, teaching and learning *religious plurality* should be: (1) a process of awakening to the universal values of hospitality, human rights, justice, and equality, and the dignity of and respect for the individual person through an exposure to other religions; (2) a process of theological and spiritual formation of a commitment to the betterment of the world, beyond one's own religious boundary; (3) a process of self-critical examination of one's own and other religious teaching and practices in the light of justice perspectives of various forms, such as racial justice, gender justice, ecological justice, geopolitical justice, sexual justice, etc; and (4) a process of strengthening a *deep ecumenism* that pursues the *unity* of humanity in its holistic sense.

Here one should not perceive *unity* as a homogenized, idealized, romanticized notion that simply chants, *We-are-one*, but as referring to a state of the world in which we achieve human equality, dignity, justice, and peace within, among, and between religions and individual persons. In this sense, teaching and learning religious plurality in a Christian context require a fundamental reexamination and reconstruction of one's perception of God, Jesus Christ, salvation, and the mission of the church. Acknowledging *religious plurality* would mean turning *religious others* into *religious neighbors* or *significant others,* and, as a result of this epistemological shift, the theological exclusivism that condemns religions other than Christianity loses its legitimacy.

Teaching and learning *religious plurality* involves two critical considerations: First, it is important to note that the liberal notion of multireligionism often places *religious differences* or *cultural differences* within the context of *false equality* among religions, disregarding the geopolitical power-asymmetry between religions, and within the context of a depoliticized and dehistoricized notion of homogeneity (consensus). Teaching and learning *religious plurality* means to replace this *liberal* multireligionism with a *critical* multireligionism of religious difference, power, and religious citizenship, which recognizes the power disparities between, among, and within religions in the construction of individual and collective religious identities and practices. Second, teaching and learning *religious plurality* should mean offering students a *space for translating* the core values of religions—such as human freedom, equality, peace, compassion, and justice—into human concrete everyday reality, not interpreting religious values as *apolitical* and *ahistorical* attributes. This act of radical *translation* of religious values would mean reevaluating the religious values within various religious practices and their application so that a believer or a community of believers can apply the significant values of a religion to every individual human being, regardless of his or her gender, sexuality, race, marital status, ability, age, or citizenship, and to every dimension of human life. Here one should not separate human *spirituality* from human *physicality/materiality,* which often occurs within religious communities and traditions, because such separation of spirituality from human materiality has perpetuated a binary approach to human beings and their reality. Educating students about *religious plurality* is, therefore, neither about taking students to a *religious supermarket* where one can do some *eye-shopping* nor acting as a *religious informant* or *religious tour-guide* who offers students a *religious tour*. In the age of the Internet, all the *information* about a certain religion is always *out there* to be found. What students need to learn in the era of multireligionism is not mere *information* but a deep and critical *perspective* through which they can find not only the *visible* information-out-there but also the hidden, distorted, suppressed, *invisible* knowledge about a specific religion and its relation to other religions so that they commit themselves to a radical engagement with the everyday reality in which people should materialize the religious core values in their day-to-day reality.

What we need to do in teaching and learning *religious plurality* concerns not simply differences or similarities between religions but the creation of a *religious culture of dissent* within theological schools and institutions, and among the communities of believers. *Religious cultures of dissent* would mean "creating spaces for epistemological standpoints that are grounded in the interests of people and which recognize the materiality of conflict, of privilege, and of domination" and would further entail "taking the politics of everyday life seriously as teachers, students, administrators, and members of hegemonic academic cultures."[28] Marnia Lazreg talks about the *ethnocentrism* in academic feminist scholarship and argues for an understanding of *intersubjectivity* as the basis for comparative studies across cultures and histories:

> To take intersubjectivity into consideration when studying Algerian women or other Third World women means seeing their lives as meaningful, coherent, and understandable instead of being infused "by us" with doom and sorrow. It means that their lives like "ours" are structured by economic, political, and cultural factors. It means that these women, like "us," are engaged in the process of adjusting, often shaping, at times resisting and even transforming their environment. It means they have their own individuality; they are "for themselves" instead of being "for us." An appropriation of their singular individuality to fit the generalizing categories of "our" analyses is an assault on their integrity and on their identity."[29]

To teach and learn religions other than Christianity requires a *philosophy of intersubjectivity* that helps one not to homogenize, orientalize, or essentialize other religions but to acknowledge the simple truth that a religion is always in the making and ever-evolving in the same way Christianity has been. When one views and teaches other religions as exotic, monolithic, homogeneous, or unchanging, a dangerous discursive distortion begins by suppressing the heterogeneity, hybridity, and multiplicity of religion. Educators and learners of religious plurality need to always remember that every religion, including Christianity, is a shifting sphere of heterogeneous borders in which different histories, languages, experiences, and voices intermingle amid diverse relations of power and privilege. Teaching and learning religious plurality should be, eventually, an act of creating a space of hope in the midst of hopelessness, where one can learn how to listen to the voiceless, the marginalized, and the excluded in the world of power and domination in multiple forms in an era of globalization and neo-imperialism. For religion should be about hope, solidarity, and peace for every living being, not about domination, control, or power.

Cosmopolitan *Trans-Religious* Solidarity

Traditional Christian theology and its practices have contributed to the construction of its *religious other* in the world of religions. Christian theology of religion and ecumenism has evolved around the issue of interreligious dialogue, primarily grounded in a *politics of tolerance*. The genealogy of the politics of tolerance has Christian origin marked by a religious war between Christians and non-Christians, and therefore the term *tolerance* has its own limit as it presupposes the conditions and circumstances of being tolerated. The *religious other* can enjoy the politics of tolerance only if they comply with the conditions that the *tolerators* set. In this sense, tolerance is *a form of charity*. In a current configuration of religious diversity, in which Christianity plays a major role in terms of interreligious relations, the politics of *tolerance* is a form of Christian charity, although other religions might appropriate the term *tolerance* in other contexts. Engaging in a politics of religious tolerance is like saying "to the other from [an] elevated position, I am letting you be, you are not insufferable, I am leaving you a place in my home but do not forget that this is my home ...." [30] Although tolerance has its merit and is much better than intolerance, it still "remains a scrutinized hospitality, always under surveillance, parsimonious and protective of its sovereignty.... In the best of cases, it's ....conditional hospitality."[31] In this politics of tolerance, people may idealize or compliment the religious other as long as the religious other remains a safe and "toothless other."[32]

Whenever one comes to the table for interreligious dialogue, there is what I would call an *ecumenical taboo* that one has to comply with. The *ecumenical taboo* does not exist in a written document, but people tend to practice it around the dialogue table. One should not raise, for instance, such questions as gender justice, sexual orientation issues, religious constructions of the other, multiple forms of violence in a religious community, or religious cooption with neo/imperialism. Each religion has its own *history of sin* that has justified and perpetuated oppression and exclusion of certain groups of people through its own religious teaching, doctrine, and practice. In order to be *nice* and *tolerant* to one another, interreligious dialogue has not challenged the fundamental issues of injustice that a particular religion has practiced, justified, and perpetuated in various ways. I do not disregard that most ecumenists have based interreligious dialogue on a politics of tolerance, and this has played a significant role in easing the antagonism between religions, at least among the leaders of established religions. However, we should ground an authentic ecumenism and theology of religion in a *politics of affirmation and transformation*, rather than a *politics of tolerance*. Furthermore, encounters with one another should involve a process of revisiting, reexamining, rechallenging, recontesting, and reconstructing the very foundations of each religious discourse and practice from the perspective of cosmopolitan justice, for religious discourse and practice impinge on the lives of ordinary people. In so doing, interreligious encounters and teaching/learning religious diversity will serve to dismantle the way a religion constructs its discourse and identity, which has contributed to the construction of *the other* in multiple ways—not just a religious *other* but also a racialized, ethnicized, gendered, sexualized, or culturally essentialized *other*.

An ultimate goal of teaching and learning religious diversity and building interreligious relations is to work for the justice and betterment of the *cosmos*. Unless we pursue a fundamental transformation of our own theological discourses and practices, multireligious education and interreligious dialogue will be nothing but *religious voyeurism* and/or *ecumenical tourism*. Working for *trans-religious solidarity* does not mean that everyone thinks the same way. Instead, it begins when people of different religions have the confidence to disagree over issues because they believe in transformation for the betterment of the world, not merely in coming up with doctrinal common ground among different faiths and religious traditions. This cosmopolitan *trans-religious solidarity* would maximize mutual interaction, challenge, and transformation, rather than pursuing a *neutral* balance between and among different religions. Human community, as a large community of co-habitants who belong to the cosmos, is not about homogeneity that results in imposing one's way of religious/spiritual life onto others. Seeing others from different religions than one's own as co-habitants in this cosmos is significant in *doing* theology. The cosmopolitan consciousness helps one realize that the *cosmic* community is much larger than a particular religious community, and that we all belong to the cosmos that the Divine created and will constantly create, and that one's particular belonging to a religion does not have to be in contradiction with one's universal belonging to the cosmos. In the end, no one religion can claim absolute ownership of the truth, virtue, beauty, and goodness that the Divine has revealed and continues to reveal.

5

Cosmopolitan Theology of *Natality*

Toward Neighbor-Love as Passion for an Impossible Community of Justice

My sense of the holy is bound up with the hope that some day my remote descendants will live in a global civilization in which love is pretty much the only law.

—Richard Rorty[1]

If one is not a human being, what is one?

—Achille Mbembe[2]

Natality—the Miraculous Event of Ever-New Beginning

The overall theme of theology can be twofold: the search for meaning and the responsibility one has to the others. This chapter is, in a way, an attempt to seek how one can be responsible to oneself and the other-self in the sense that one cannot and should not separate oneself from one's neighbor/enemy-self. Jesus' radical commandment to love one's *neighbor-and-enemy-as-oneself* is a radical call for dissolving the seemingly rigid boundaries between the triad of *I-neighbor-enemy*—the boundaries that appear to be impossible to transgress, to dissolve. How can it be possible for one to love one's neighbor and enemy as oneself? What constitutes *loving* one's neighbor-enemy as oneself in one's everyday life? How is it possible for one to embrace and love the whole being of an enemy as oneself? Religion is, in this sense, about this impossible love, impossible hospitality, and impossible responsibility to oneself and to others: *the passion for the impossible.* Here I follow Angelus Silesius' prophetic theological insight:

> Go there where you cannot go, to the impossible, it is indeed the only way of going or coming. To go there where it is possible is not to surrender, rather, it is to be already there and to paralyze oneself in the in-decision of the non-event.[3]

The endless responsibility to the others makes one ponder about the precondition for this responsibility of love, the unconditional hospitality to others. I contend that unless one can acknowledge the ever-newness in oneself and in others, it is impossible to exercise Jesus' radical commandment of love and responsibility to the others, and that the belief in ever-newness in oneself and in others is one of preconditions for this *impossible* commandment. According to Hannah Arendt, "[L]ove of neighbor does not mean to love the other in his [*sic*] mortality, but to love what is eternal in him, his very own 'whence.'"[4] What is eternal in each and every individual human being is not mortality but *natality*.

Human birth, *natality*, marks the entrance of a human being into the world and establishes the very possibility of human experience in her/his existence as a human. Yet the significant implications of this event of birth have been largely absent from theological discourse, although human life itself is a transition between birth and death, between natality and mortality. The notion of *virgin-birth* or *new-birth* is significant in Jesus' life and teaching. The *virginal birth* of Jesus, for instance, reveals the secret truth of the "nonhistory of absolute beginnings."[5] His birth has no previous memory, history, tie, cause, or origin, but itself alone constitutes the very credential for who he is. Jesus' Virgin Birth in Matthew, who starts his gospel, paradoxically, with a genealogy of Jesus, is in a "radical discontinuity with Hebrew genealogy."[6] In order to understand Jesus' Virgin Birth in Matthew, one must deconstruct the very genealogy of Matthew. In the process of deconstruction, of radical discontinuity with the very tradition, one can reencounter, reinterpret, reconceptualize, recontextualize, and reconstruct the meaning of the tradition as if one is inventing a new tradition out of nothingness—a *nonhistory of absolute beginnings*.

When visited by Nicodemus, Jesus declares to him that no one can see the *kindom* of God unless one is born again. Here Jesus' metaphor *born-again, new-birth,* is certainly not a biological rebirth, as Nicodemus asks Jesus how one can enter one's mother's womb a second time and be born.[7] The metaphor *born-again* that Jesus uses would mean the *impossible possibility of the nonhistory of an absolute new beginning*.

One can also find the crucial significance of the *nonhistory of an absolute new beginning* in Abraham's life story. When God commands Abraham to leave his own country, his kin, and his father's house at the age of seventy-five years old (Gen. 12:1), Abraham accepts and obeys the divine call for a radical plan to be *born-again*, the *nonhistory of an absolute new beginning*. Accepting God's call for a radical discontinuity from his past, tradition, familiarity, origins, customs, and authority, Abraham encounters the absolute unknown *nothingness* of his own future. Derrida articulates the importance of the absolute new beginning regarding the issue of being just or unjust in applying a law:

> To be just, the decision of a judge, for example, must not only follow a rule of law or a general law [*loi*] but must also assume it, approve it, confirm its values, by a reinstituting act of interpretation, as if, at the limit, the law [*loi*] did not exist previously—as if the judge himself invented it in each case.... In short, for a decision to be just and responsible, it must [*il faut*], in its proper moment, if there is one, be both regulated and without regulation, it must preserve the law [*loi*] and also destroy or suspend it enough to have [*pour devoir*] to reinvent it in each case, rejustify it, reinvent it at least in the reaffirmation and the new and free confirmation of its principle. Each case is other, each decision is different and requires an absolutely unique interpretation, which no existing, coded rule can or ought to guarantee absolutely.[8]

Hannah Arendt draws attention to the notion of natality, to the uniqueness of each and every birth, as a substantial human condition for action in the world. According to Arendt, human beings are "*initium*, newcomers and beginners by virtue of birth," which "is not the same as the beginning of the world."[9] Arendt thinks of human beings primarily as *natals*, rather than *mortals*. With the creation and birth of human beings, the principle of beginning and the principle of freedom were created and came into the world. *Natality* is, in this sense, the *ontologically rooted* human capacity to act *freely*.[10] In this sense, human natality, being born into the world, is the basis of the political and, therefore, "natality as opposed to mortality is without doubt the central category of political thought as opposed to metaphysical thought."[11]

There is no agreement among the scholars who dedicate their works to the concept of Arendt's natality about the origin of the concept. Some argue that Arendt's notion of natality is a philosophical theme and that she employs the concept of natality from Heidegger's *Sein und Zeit*.[12] However, there is no clear *evidence* that Arendt took her idea of natality from Heidegger's analysis of human life. Scholars often translate *natality* in German as *Gebürtigkeit* or *Gebürtlichkeit*. However, the word that Heidegger uses is the adjective, "gebürtig, "[13] not "Natalität" that Arendt uses.[14] I employ Arendt's notion of natality, not within a Heideggerian philosophical framework, but within the discourse of *biopolitics* in Giorgio Agamben's sense. It is worthy to note that there is a lexical bifurcation between *biopolitics* and *biopower*. Whereas *biopolitics* means "a politics in the name of life," *biopower* denotes "a life subjected to the command of politics."[15]

The creation story from Genesis indicates the significance of human birth into the world. God creates human(s), unlike other species, *singularly*, not collectively, and gives humans freedom. In this sense, human natality becomes the condition of human freedom.[16] The *singularity* of the nature of human birth, in which every individual human being is unique and singular, becomes the ground of the human *plurality* in terms of one's thinking, judging, and acting. Therefore, the ontological nature of human *singularity* and the sociopolitical nature of human *plurality* are not in contradiction. Instead, the human condition of *singularity in natality* is interlinked to the human condition of plurality in relation to other humans because being in the world (*Dasein*) means being in the world *with* others (*Mitsein*). Arendt's notion of *natality* symbolizes an ever-present possibility of a new being. Although a number of *political philosophers* have discussed Arendt's concept of natality, few *theologians* have dealt with her notion of natality. I contend that Arendt's concept of *natality* is one of her most significant contributions to the construction of the theological discourse of faith, hope, and love—the three fundamental virtues of Christianity. Arendt posits:

> The miracle that saves the world, the realm of human affairs, from its normal, "natural" ruin is ultimately the fact of natality, in which the faculty of action is ontologically rooted. It is, in other words, the birth of new men and the new beginning, the action they are capable of by virtue of being born. Only the full experience of this capacity can bestow upon human affairs faith and hope, those two essential characteristics of human existence.... It is this faith in and hope for the world that found perhaps its most glorious and most succinct expression in the few words with which the Gospels announced their "glad tidings": "A child has been born unto us."[17]

Here, Arendt seems to bring this announcement of *glad tidings* from the gospel of Luke, not from Isaiah, and she explicitly connects her citation to Christian gospels.[18] It is debatable why Arendt, a Jew, often brings her citation from the Christian Bible and whether she uses the Christian Bible because she wants to escape/deemphasize her Jewishness, or to emphasize the universal nature of the event of *birth,* connecting it not necessarily to a divine incarnation but to a universal human natality.[19] However, what is clear in Arendt's citation is that one can connect the event of Jesus' birth as a result of God's love and hope for and faith in the world, and that humans need to celebrate every birth as a unique *glad tiding*. Jesus' *factual natality,* being born into the world with his physical body, is a manifestation of God's *amor mundi,* because "God so loved the world as to give the Only Begotten One... God sent the Only Begotten into the world" (Jn. 3:16–17, Inclusive), in which humans and other beings reside.

In Arendt's view, natality occurs during three human experiences: first, *factual natality*—physical birth into the world; second, *political natality*—mental birth into the space of action; and third, *theoretical natality*—birth into the timelessness of thought. For Arendt, *factual natality* denotes the supreme capacity of human beings, *political natality* manifests itself in political freedom, action, and the mutual creation of public spaces, and *theoretical natality* is the promising, hopeful capacity of the life of the human mind, which is manifested in thinking, willing, and judging.[20] With these three notions of natality, Arendt introduces the context of human natality into the realm of *amor mundi,* the human potentiality of new beginnings directed toward *the love for the world*—the space we humans hold in common. Starting from the *factual natality,* Arendt further articulates the notion of *natality* in the course of her attempt to draw the significance of the ever-present possibility that someone, somewhere, sometime might say or do something that makes possible a fresh start in the realm of human affairs. She characterizes this possibility as the *miracle that saves the world* from ruin. The great symbol of the ever-present possibility is the announcement of "glad tidings: a child has been born unto us."[21] It is this Christian figuration of the miraculous through the image of the new-birth that gives Arendt the term *natality*. In her own words, "the new beginning inherent in birth can make itself felt in the world only because the newcomer possesses the capacity of beginning something anew."[22] By grounding natality in a biological inevitability, in which humans are uniquely and constantly born into the world, Arendt tries to signify a space of potential provocation and hope against hope in the midst of the hopelessness of human affairs.

However, it is thus not just a biological birth that Arendt means by natality. Arendt does complexify the human experience of natality and deepen it as profound philosophical and theological concepts. For Arendt, natality is like a *second birth* or a *constant-born-again* state. The possibility and experience of *ever-newness* in natality does not refer only to unprecedented events or ideas. Instead, it refers to the moments in which individuals take the initiative in attempting to forge new realities. Therefore, natality denotes the everyday *miracles* that occur whenever human beings take the initiative and rekindle their passion for seemingly impossible change in the world. Here the concept of *miracle* that Arendt posits might seem odd when the word *miracle* seems to have disappeared from theological discourse in the post-Enlightenment era. However, Franz Rosenzweig, for instance, makes *miracle* one of his central theological themes in his book *The Star of Redemption*, having a separate section "On the Possibility of Experiencing Miracles."[23] If the identification of the Enlightenment with the victory of reason/rationality over superstition, emotion, miracle, or myth is admissible, it is not surprising that Rosenzweig focuses on the concept of miracles while he deals with not just one but "a number of enlightenments."[24] He criticizes the disappearance of *miracles* from post-Enlightenment theological discourse and argues that the "miracle was based on an entirely different circumstance, namely, on its having been predicted, not on its deviation from the course of nature as this had previously been fixed by law.... Miracle and prophecy belong together."[25]

For Arendt, *beginning* is the supreme capacity of humans, and each new birth guarantees the beginning. Furthermore, the primary experience of natality is fundamentally a potentiality for action. Human natality makes it possible for humans to dedicate themselves to and for the world—the *love of the world*. In this sense, the human capacity for *natality* makes neighbor-love as self-love possible, and one can extend the capacity for natality to the love of the world. Arendt's natality offers us a hope and possibility that one can transform individual persons, institutions, communities, and the world into *newness*—the *miracle*. As Rosenzweig poetically puts it, "[L]ove of the neighbor always newly arises; it is always a new beginning"[26] Arendt draws her concept of natality from human biological birth, *factual natality*, and makes a shift from the biological experience to philosophical natality.[27] However, I would like to argue that if one understands the shift she makes is only from biological to philosophical, one limits the implication of Arendt's concept of natality to a realm of abstraction, because such interpretation tends to overlook the profound implication of the concept of natality for biopolitics and politico-theology. Therefore, I would like to highlight the biopolitical and theopolitical implications of Arendt's natality to examine how natality can be a mobilizing concept for deepening and promoting political and theological discourse and the practice of *neighbor-love-as-self-love*, which one can also interlink to the love for God.

Cosmopolitan consciousness, which regards oneself and others primarily as citizens of the cosmos, requires a constant reformulation of one's identity, deterritorialization of master narratives of certainty, and defamiliarization of custom. In this cosmopolitan consciousness, "[t]he purpose of history....is not to discover the roots of our identity but to commit itself to its dissipation."[28] Only through the deterritorialization of certainty and fixity of what/who one is and the defamiliarization of one's sociocultural custom does the creation of new subjecthood becomes possible. Theologically speaking, the creation of new subjecthood is Jesus' calling for an *ever-becoming-born-again.*

Jesus gave Nicodemus this answer:

> "The truth of the matter is,
> Unless one is born from above,
> One cannot see the kindom of God."
> Nicodemus said, "How can an adult be born a second time? I can't go back into my mother's womb to be born again!"
> (Jn. 3:3–4, Inclusive)

Remembrance of history and familiarization of custom hinder the possibility of one's *being-born-again* because history and custom form one's subjecthood within a frame of continuity of the past tradition through a mere inheritance and transmission. When asked *why,* the person of custom and history would respond simply, "This is the way it has always been done." In this sense, as long as one attaches oneself firmly to custom and past fixed history, one cannot see a possibility of ever-being-born-again because "custom operates as if it were a second nature."[29] Unless one *deterritorializes, defamiliarizes,* and *deremembers* one's history, custom, and memory, ever-being-born-again is not possible.

Christian churches have misinterpreted Jesus' calling for *being-born-again* exclusively in the context of a missionary zeal to convert the *heathens* to Christianity or in the context of a *romanticized* experience of the Holy Spirit. However, considering the simple fact that Christianity, as an institutionalized religion, did not come into being in Jesus' time, it is unthinkable that Jesus would have had the *Christian* churches in mind, as many Christians would interpret, when he made such a statement about *being-born-again.* Furthermore, there is no indication in the gospels that it matters to Jesus whether or not one is a member of an institutionalized religion. The stories of the good Samaritan in Luke 10 or the last judgment in Matthew 25, for instance, clearly indicate that what matters the most to Jesus is the way one relates to others, and the way one cares and takes responsibility for the neighbors in need and the Least. Jesus' story about the last judgment should be a significant biblical ground that constitutes the nature of the mission of the church and

Christians and the theological framework for the cosmic neighbor-love that transcends national ties, cultural custom, religious doctrines and affiliation, or spatial territories. *Religious territorialization* and *doxification* of what Jesus reveals to us to follow is, in fact, a serious distortion of Jesus' spirit and his vision for the world. I regard Jesus' calling for a mandate of *being-born-again* as an invitation to practice a discourse of prophetic critique and transformation of self, world, and others.

Thanatopolitics—Impotence of *De*politicized Neighbor-Love in the Face of the *Unperson*

According to Michel Foucault, sovereign power is the power of life and death, the power to take one's life or to let one live.[30] In the seventeenth and eighteenth centuries, the transition from sovereign power or the juridico-institutional power to *biopower* took place in politics via the control of individuals through *disciplinary power*. *Disciplinary power*, as "nonsovereign" power, "cannot be described or justified in terms of the theory of sovereignty" because it is "radically heterogeneous and should logically have led to the complete disappearance of the great juridical edifice of sovereignty."[31] Whereas people or the state exercise the *sovereign power* by means of law and violence, they exercise *biopower* through *normalizing* biological mechanisms, through the "methods of power capable of optimizing forces, aptitudes, and life in general."[32] Here politics becomes a power over life. This power over life is the other side of the power to "disallow life to the point of death."[33] Primo Levi describes the horrible experience of the biopower that totalitarian regimes exercise in "the Larger," which is "pre-eminently a gigantic biological and social experiment."[34] Levi illustrates the way in which the totalitarian regimes dehumanize human life through his portrayal of *Muselmänner* in the Larger:

> All the musselmans who finished in the gas chambers have the same story, or more exactly, have no story .... Their life is short, but their number is endless; they, the Muselmänner, the drowned, form the backbone of the camp, an anonymous mass, continually renewed and always identical, of non-men who march and labour in silence, the divine spark dead within them, already too empty to really suffer. One hesitates to call them living: one hesitates to call their death death, in the face of which they have no fear, as they are too tired to understand.[35]

Giorgio Agamben refers to these dehumanized, "faceless presences"[36] of human life as *bare life*, and the bearer of such *faceless* life as *homo sacer*, whose life people no longer recognize as a human life. Here Agamben criticizes

Foucault's distinction between biopower and sovereign power because for Agamben it is not possible to differentiate sovereign power from biopower. According to Agamben, the production of *bare life* is the original activity of sovereign power over life. By introducing the Roman practice of *homo sacer,* "who may be killed and yet not sacrificed,"[37] Agamben argues that Foucault's thesis overlooks the fact that the production of *homo sacer*—"the realm of bare life that is originally situated at the margins of the political order—gradually begins to coincide with the political realm, and exclusion and inclusion, outside and inside, *bios* and *zoe,* and right and fact, enter into a zone of irreducible indistinction."[38] In this sense, the production of *homo sacer* is "the hidden foundation on which the entire political system rested."[39] When biological life becomes a primary object of the modern state, the hidden connection between sovereign power and biopower gets revealed. The sovereign power, according to Agamben, excludes *bare life* from the political realm, in which lies the invisible bond between biopower and sovereign power.

Agamben recounts the notion of *bare life*. Under archaic Roman law, a criminal declared a *homo sacer* was an *unperson* whose life the gods neither receive as sacrifice nor humans protect against any kind of homicide. The *homo sacer,* in this ancient sense, is "the one whom the people have judged on account of a crime,"[40] and the people ban the *homo sacer* from the juridical-political community. Since the gods of the underworld already hold the *homo sacer,* the *homo sacer* cannot be the object of sacrifice. Yet the state will not punish anyone who kills the *homo sacer*. The *homo sacer* is completely different from the criminal in the sense that a criminal could claim certain legal protection and formal procedures. Yet, the state completely "unprotects" the *homo sacer* and reduces the *homo sacer* to a mere physical existence—a *bare life*. From the beginning of all politics, "[t]he original political relation is the ban"[41] that establishes a borderline and inaugurates a space that deprives the protection of the law from people, which is "zone of indistinction between outside and inside, exclusion and inclusion."[42] The sovereign power permits the killing and does not regard the homicide done to *homo sacer* as a sacrilege. *Homo sacer* presents a paradoxical existence both imposed and shunned by human society— a *bare life*. When the sovereign political power strips all recognition and rights as human, banishes into an *alien* status, and denies any kind of protection, the *homo sacer* becomes simply a *bare life*—the *living dead*. Here Agamben asks: "What, then, is the life of *homo sacer,* if it is situated at the intersection of a capacity to be killed and yet not sacrificed, outside both human and divine law?"[43]

Agamben's analysis of the *homo sacer* as a mere *bare life* presents the figure of *homo sacer* as a theoretical concept that informs the political situation not only in the ancient past but also in contemporary biopolitics. The *bare life* does not refer to a natural nakedness, but to an *artificial product* created by sovereign biopolitical power. It reveals the political mechanism of rule and exception through the institutionalization of the "bare life (*zoe*)," "rightless existence," and the "political existence (*bios*)."[44] Agamben uses *the camp* (see below) not just "as a historical fact and an anomaly belonging to the past.... but in some way as the hidden matrix and *nomos* of the political space in which we all still living."[45] As Agamben says:

> [I]f the essence of the camp consists in the materialization of the state of exception and in the subsequent creation of a space in which bare life and the juridical rule enter into a threshold of indistinction, then we must admit that we find ourselves virtually in the presence of a camp every time such a structure is created, ... The stadium in Bari into which the Italian police in 1991 provisionally herded all illegal Albanian immigrants before sending them back to their country, the winter cycle-racing track in which the Vichy authorities gathered the Jews before consigning them to the Germans, ... In all these cases, an apparently innocuous space....actually delimits a space in which the normal order is de facto suspended and in which whether or not atrocities are committed depends not on law but on the civility and ethical sense of the police who temporarily act as sovereign.... [46]

Agamben argues that when a state's decision on one's life turns out to be a decision on one's death, biopolitics is essentially "thanatopolitics."[47] The situation of the *homo sacer* reflects the experience of what Arendt calls *stateless people,* the *Heimatlosen,* in the sense that the state completely deprives them of its protection, rights, and official recognition.[48] Agamben's analysis of biopolitics and thanatopolitics reveals how the nation-state can mark undesired people, the unwelcome, those from unwanted categories of class/race/ethnic background/sexual identity as so mere undifferentiated, biological units, as *bare life,* by decertifying, delegitimating, denationalizing them, which results in the inevitable degradation of biopolitics into thanatopolitics. The Nazi extermination of Jews, Gypsies, homosexuals, physically challenged children, and mentally ill people was an example of how the sovereign biopolitics turned the undesired people into *bare lives,* and of how people who conducted the killing of *bare lives* did not perceive the lives they terminated as human lives with value. Arendt refers to those living a *bare life* as *living corpses* whose *individuality* and *uniqueness* the totalitarian regime destroys.[49] The total domination of totalitarian regimes starts with killing the "juridical person in man [*sic*]" by placing "certain categories of people outside the protection of the law and forcing at the same time, through the instrument of denationalization, the nontotalitarian world into recognition of lawlessness."[50] In this way, *biopolitics* can turn into *thanatopolitics—necropolitics,* the use of *death* for sustaining and mobilizing politics.

Politicizing the Neighbor with the Face of the Contemporary *Homo Sacer*

Agamben's notion of *homo sacer* offers a significant insight when one thinks of *neighbor-love* and neighbors relevance today. Willem Schinkel, for instance, regards *irregular immigrants,* a term he intentionally uses as an alternative to *illegal* immigrants, as *homo sacer,* and views the detention center for those *illegal immigrants* as a space of exception in Agamben's sense.[51] The *illegal immigrants, refugees*—the *stateless* people in Arendt's term, or *non-documented* people, would be a significant determining face of the twenty-first century when it comes to issues of justice, categories of neighbor, hospitality, human rights, or citizenship in this era of globalization. Agamben argues that *the camp* is not just a "historical fact and an anomaly belonging to the past," but "the hidden matrix and nomos of the political space in which we are still living."[52] The invention of the detention center by states in Western Europe, Schinkel points out, "turns local spaces into sites that have a complex matrix."[53] It is *the camp* or *non-place*. Those *illegal* immigrants or refugees in the detention center are from the *dark side of the earth,* the so-called Third World, and the sovereign states of their current physical existence place the mark of the *illegal* on their bodies. According to U.N. estimates, the number of international migrants worldwide was about 214 million in 2010, whereas the number of internally displaced persons in the world in 2009 was 27.1 million, and refugees number 15.2 million in the world today.[54] The *irregular immigrants* are in fact a byproduct of globalization or its *free market* policies and asymmetrical distribution of the wealth between the First World and *the Rest*. Although the *irregular immigrants* provide cheap labor, societies/states treat them as *human waste* simply because "they do not 'exist' as civilians before the law."[55]

As Agamben observes, " The original political relation is the ban" and "[t]oday it is not the city but rather the camp that is the fundamental biopolitical paradigm of the West."[56] The *ban* of illegal immigrants is often exercised in a manner of *saving* the states. California, for instance, passed Proposition 187, known as the "Save Our State" initiative, with 59 percent of the vote on November 8, 1994, which banned all undocumented immigrants and their children from enrollment in public schools and colleges, denied non-emergency public health care, and cut off social welfare services. The "Save Our State" initiative, Proposition 187, made the following claims:

> The People of California find and declare as follows:
>
> That they have suffered and are suffering economic hardship caused by the presence of illegal aliens in this state.
>
> That they have suffered and are suffering personal injury and damage caused by the criminal conduct of illegal aliens in this state.
>
> That they have a right to the protection of their government from any person or persons entering this country unlawfully.
>
> Therefore, the people of California declare their intention to provide for cooperation between their agencies of state and local government with the federal government, and to establish a system of required notification by and between such agencies to prevent illegal aliens in the United States from receiving benefits or public services in the State of California.[57]

The xenophobic sentiments of the *citizens*, the *People* of California, criminalize the non-persons, the *illegal* aliens as those whose *criminal conduct* caused them "injury and damage." This xenophobic, racist anti-immigrant law is in fact the "culmination of 150 years of politics."[58]

In "From Homo Sacer to the Neighbor," Slavoj Zizek shares his experience in Berlin when he witnessed an actual racial harassment by a German of a Vietnamese. It was what he calls a "soft harassment" because the German did not use any physical violence. Instead, the German just blocked whichever way the Vietnamese tried to turn without physically touching him. Zizek was astonished by the fact that "the people who were passing by…simply ignored—or, rather, pretended to ignore—the event, averting their eyes while hurrying along as if nothing special was going on."[59] He goes on to argue that this *soft harassment* is worse than the physical attack by a neo-Nazi skinhead because it "precisely allowed the passers-by to ignore it and accept it as an *ordinary event*."[60] Christians, who may well have memorized the Bible verse about *loving your neighbor-enemy as your self*, need to fundamentally rethink the categories of neighbor-enemy that they usually draw. *Who is my neighbor?* the question to Jesus from a lawyer who seeks to *inherit eternal life* (Lk. 10:25), is becoming a more serious politico-theological question today. When the neighbor-love becomes apoliticized or depoliticized, the rhetoric of neighbor-love is nothing but an empty, impotent chant, which cannot have its public relevance in the world. Can the contemporary *homo sacer* be one's neighbor? What will happen if all the *Christians* in the U.S., for instance, begin to regard the contemporary *homo sacer* as their *neighbors* whom Jesus commands them to love as themselves? If such a thing occurs, what will happen to the U.S. international policies or immigration laws in every state?

In the face of *bare life,* the question that one must ask is: How can one practice neighbor-love without acknowledging the contemporary existence of *homo sacer,* the turning of humans into *bare life,* into *non-persons*? When Christians separate the notion of neighbor-love from politics and then lay claim to universal Christian love, the neighbor-love becomes impotent in the world. When the rhetoric of neighbor-love becomes an *apoliticized* affirmation of love and life, the neighbor-love can be meaningless and even dangerous because it romanticizes *love* while ignoring the thanatopolitics that turns the undesired, the undocumented, the unwelcome into *bare life*—a being without any kind of protection. Frantz Fanon analyzes historical associations of Western humanism between knowledge, love, benevolence, and romanticism. Claiming that "the black man is not a man: There is a zone of nonbeing, an extraordinarily sterile and arid region, an utterly naked declivity where an authentic upheaval can be born,"[61] Fanon contends that apoliticized *love* is one of the destructive effects of the coalition between Western humanism and colonialism. Here the Black people become *bare life,* non-persons, located in a zone of *homo sacer* and at the lowest point of *ontological declivity*. The colonial space of *lovelessness* is a space of *camp* in Agamben's sense. In this regard, the Christian ideal of neighbor-love-as-self-love has institutionally and systemically failed in the Western history of colonialism.

> Christian Ideology of Love formed a supportive partnership with knowledge procedures imposed upon the colonized. Administrative practices, cartography, road-building, extraction of natural resources, agriculture, anthropology, botany, and geology—along with systems of education, language, cultural assimilation, and religious conversion—represent epistemological projects demanded by colonialism. Within these projects, love is the basis for a benevolent rhetoric of the West dutifully marching alongside the imperialist project and justifying its systems of information gathering and domination—the ideological foundation for moral and economic salvation.[62]

It is impossible to separate religion from politics in human reality. What one needs is not to simply disconnect any religious discourse from politics in the face of the failure. Instead, one must critically reconnect religion to politics so that religion and politics can serve to enlarge the circle of inclusion in the daily reality of the people, and unconditionally expand the zone of equality and rights of every singular person as a fellow cosmic citizen—epistemologically, spiritually, ontologically, systemically, institutionally, and politically. The unconditional possibility of *cosmic neighbor-love* will be effective only when the rhetoric of neighbor-love becomes materialized in the daily lives of the people through politics and its institutional practices.

Cosmopolitan Theology of *Natality*: Toward a *Community of Justice*

In thanatopolitics, one's *existence* as human does not automatically bring one's *life* as human. What it means to be human becomes not only philosophical speculation but also a biopolitical and theological question, because human "[e]xistence must be alive through and through" and "[l]ife and existence do not overlap—yet."[63] How then can theologies become mobilizing discourses to foster an *affirmative* biopolitics that resists and counters thanatopolitics, a *destructive* biopolitics? Constructing mobilizing discourses that promote an affirmative biopolitics can be one of the urgent theological tasks in the contemporary world, in which human existence and life still do not overlap and the production of human *bare life, bare existence,* in the politics of our everyday reality threatens the fullness of human life in various ways. I would argue that when people spiritualize, apoliticize, or depoliticize theological discourse on neighbor-love, it is not just problematic but dangerous because people can use the rhetoric of neighbor-love as a weapon for promoting a thanatopolitics that makes a thanatopolitical distinction between *we-neighbor* and *they-non-neighbor* (*they-bare-life*) in concrete reality, where human domination and subjugation are still a daily reality based on one's citizenship, nationality, gender, race, sexuality, and so on.

Arendt's concept of *natality* can serve as a counter-concept to the thanatopolitical concept of *bare life,* which is implicit in modern biopolitics, as Agamben points out. Arendt's natality implies an *affirmative* biopolitics that avows human life with one's uniqueness, singularity, and individuality, whereas the *destructive* biopolitics that destroys human uniqueness and individuality turns out to be *thanatopolitics*—the necropolitics, or the politics of death. In this regard one can divide biopolitics into two: *life-affirming* and *life-denying* biopolitics,[64] or *affirmative* and *destructive* biopolitics. Arendt's *factual natality* signifies life back to an origin that receives the name of creation, of a birth into the world. Theologically speaking, the human *natality,* as a biological and ontological condition of the uniqueness and singularity of the individual human being, could be a theological ground for an ever-affirmation of the freedom of human life, and the dignity of every individual human person as being created in *imago dei* regardless who/what the person is. Arendt refers to Genesis in order to affirm that God creates the human species so that life can have a beginning—*the moment of natality*.

> It is in the nature of beginning that something new is started which cannot be expected from whatever may have happened before. This character of startling unexpectedness is inherent in all beginnings and in all origins.... The fact that man [*sic*] is capable of action means that the unexpected can be expected from him, that he is able to perform what is infinitely improbable. And this again is possible only because each man is unique, so that with each birth something uniquely new comes into the world.[65]

In this regard, Arendt's notion of natality becomes a significant theological ground of *love*. One can follow the biblical commandment *love your neighbor as yourself* only through one's passion for *natality* in oneself and others. It would be impossible for one to truly love oneself and others, if one does not have a belief in the possibility of an ever-present new-start of the person one loves. Extending one's self-love toward the other involves allowing the other a space of ever-present renewal and transformation—a *space of natality*. Interestingly, Arendt makes a distinction between Jesus and Paul in their use of creation stories.[66] Jesus adopts the first creation story to emphasize the equal partnership of male and female by saying: "Have you not read that the one who made them at the beginning 'made them male and female'?" (Mt. 19:4). Yet Paul takes the second creation story to argue the female's submissive position to males, as one can see in his remarks: "For a man ought not to have his head veiled, since he is the image and reflection of God; but woman is the reflection of man. Indeed, man was not made from woman, but woman from man. Neither was man created for the sake of women, but woman for the sake of man" (1 Cor. 11:7–9).

Natality contrasts to *mortality* and marks the human capacity for *beginning something anew,* not ending. We humans emerge through natality into the world, which is only possible through the care, love, and solidarity of those around us. In his *Works of Love,* Søren Kierkegaard claims that the only good, ideal neighbor that one should love is a "dead one." His reasoning is surprisingly simple. According to Kierkegaard, since loving one's neighbor means equality, one should "forsake all distinctions so that you can love your neighbor."[67] However, it is only in death that all distinctions disappear because "death erases all distinctions, but preference is always related to distinctions."[68] Kierkegaard's notion of an *ideal neighbor* as a *dead one* reminds us of the impossibility of neighbor-love in the human condition. Theodore Adorno points out that Kierkegaard's concept of the ideal neighbor as dead would mean that the "neighbor no longer exists"[69] in modern society, and that "the neighbor cannot behave spontaneously to the neighbor for longer than an instant."[70]

Arendt takes Augustine's leitmotif, "I have become a question to myself,"[71] and develops from it a concept of love as a way of working through the dichotomy of *withdrawal* from and *action* within the world. Arendt's notion of *natality* marks the *beyondness* of objectivizing consciousness, invites one to a relationship with the other as "*non-knowable,*" and supports an unconditional welcoming of the other's being-in-the-world and her/his *alterity.* Through natality, every individual human person gains one's own mastery as a subject, whereas one loses it through *mortality*. In the possibility of natality, one can effect one's own transformation into *being-in-the-world,* being-there (*Dasein*) because one must carry out one's own natality. At the same time, with one's belief in one's own natality, one can see the possibility of natality in others: As I am born and I give birth, you are born and you give birth. Here *natality* signifies a fundamental leap from one mode of being to another whose essential trait is *non-knowing* and becomes the precondition for the possibility of love of self and others. In this sense, natality *is* a precondition and condition of neighbor-love-as-self-love and of love for the world.

Natality as a precondition of the possibility of *neighbor-love-as-self-love* becomes more clear when one reads Jesus' commandment to love not only neighbor but also enemy (Lk. 6: 27). I would argue that the only way that one can turn an *enemy* into *neighbor* is through one's belief in the *natality* of each and every individual human person—the ever-present possibility of newness. It can be the ground and source of hope—individual and societal hope. The Christian rhetoric of love has mostly become that of *worldlessness,* and the rhetoric of neighbor love has been often apolitical/ depolitical, separating the Christian message of love from the public realm, separating theology from politics. As *amor mundi* is the natality's deepest interest, Arendt juxtaposes human natality with a love for the world,[72] which resonates God's *amor mundi* manifested in God's creation of all being and incarnation. Shifting from the *worldlessness of love* to the *worldliness of love* forces one eventually to acknowledge the invisible, voiceless neighbors whose lives get turned to *bare life*. The neighbor-love-as-self-love should be radically ecumenical and should not have even a religious boundary, as Augustine contends: "You should consider every person your neighbor, even before he [*sic*] is a Christian. For you do not know how he stands with God, furthermore, you do not know how God may have foreknown him."[73]

When asked, "Who is my neighbor?" (Lk. 10:29), Jesus does not offer a direct answer, as usual. Instead, he tells the so-called parable of the good Samaritan (Lk. 10:30–35). In this parable, Jesus moves beyond the traditional boundary of friend-neighbor-enemy by using two people—a Jew and a Samaritan, whom people used to consider *strangers/enemies* to one another. It is the *stranger/enemy,* the Samaritan, rather than the traditional *neighbors,* the priest and the Levite, who shows compassionate love to the traveler wounded by robbers. It is also interesting how Jesus makes a shift of the question itself from "Who is my neighbor?" to "Which of these three, do you think, was a neighbour to the man who fell into the hands of the robbers?" (Lk. 10:36). This shift of the question invites us to realize that *I* can be a neighbor to the other, but, at the same time, *I* can be in a desperate situation in which I need the hospitality of a *neighbor*. Being a benefactor or recipient of hospitality as a *neighbor* would depend on the *event* in one's life journey.

In Jesus' story of the last judgment (Mt. 25:31–46), the standard by which the Last Judge separates sheep from goats is not based on one's religious citizenship or doctrinal confession. Instead, the standard is based on the radical category and practice of *neighbor-enemy-love*. Those in the category of *goats* ask the questions: "Lord, when was it that we saw you hungry or thirsty or a stranger or naked or sick or in prison, and did not take care of you?" (Mt. 25:44). The Judge answers: "Truly I tell you, just as you did not do it to one of the least of these, you did not do it to me" (Mt. 25:45). One of the significant theological tasks today is to foster the *knowing* of the existence of various neighbors, because of the following reasons: First, the neighbors are often unrecognizable, undesired, unwelcome, unlikable, undocumented; second, the *knowing* requires a deep socio-politico-theological sensitivity and awareness, which does not come automatically simply with one's confession *I love my neighbor/Jesus/God*; third, the *not-knowing* or *ignorance* cannot be an excuse for taking no responsibility for the neighbor; and, finally, loving neighbors is inseparable from loving God/Jesus since, as Jesus declares, "just as you did it to one of the least of these who are members of my family, you did it to me" (Mt. 25:40).

In this regard, religion is about hospitality, neighbor-love, and redemption. The redemption here is not a doctrinal set of propositions but the meaningfulness of/in one's life. Franz Rosenzweig places redemption at the center of his theological writing and connects redemption to the act of love for neighbor and love for God:

> The effect of the love of "neighbor" is that "Anyone" and "all the world" thus belong together and, for the world of redemption, thereby generate a factuality which wholly corresponds to the reality effected, in creation, through the collaboration of that which is general in a limited sense with that which is distinctive in a limited sense. For the world of redemption, absolute factuality derives from

> the fact that be momentarily my neighbor represents all the world for me in full validity.[74]

The love for neighbor is interlinked with the love for God because "[l]ove for God must be externalized in love for the neighbor."[75] The love for neighbors is not based on their merit but is grounded in the fact that the neighbors are "only a representative" of the world that God creates, in which God reveals Godself. Therefore, the neighbors are not loved for themselves, are not loved for their "beautiful eyes," but only because they are "just there," because they are "just my neighbor."[76] As Meister Eckhart says, love is "without why" and is "letting the other be."[77] Redemption is possible only when one can enter the space of "Kingdom" and the "Kingdom, the *vitalization of existence,* comes from the beginning."[78] Through reading Augustine, Arendt affirms that humans are like family, because they all are the descendants of Adam. Coming from the same beginning, Adam, humans are kin to one another, and the kinship among one another is the ground of human equality.[79] The question that we must ask is not whether we love God but, as Augustine asks, "What is it then that I love when I love my God?"[80] One actualizes love for God in one's love for neighbor-enemy as oneself and in the belief in the natality, the possibility of ever-newness, of and in every person. Furthermore, the *true* neighbor-love would mean one reaches the point at which "Ich bin du, wenn ich ich bin" [I am you, when I am I].[81] The neighbor-love is inextricably in relation to the self-love—the core of Jesus' teaching: Love your neighbor as yourself. Loving one's neighbor does not and should not mean avoiding oneself. Rather one should fundamentally associate true *neighbor-love* with true *self-love.* How is the neighbor-love possible when people do not love or do not know how to love themselves? Nietzsche warns against the dissociation of neighbor-love from self-love:

> [Y]our love of the neighbor is your bad love of yourselves. You flee to your neighbor from yourselves and would like to make a virtue out of that: but I see through your "selflessness.... You cannot endure yourselves and do not love yourselves enough: now you want to seduce your neighbor to love.... You invite a witness when you want to speak well of yourselves; and when you have seduced him [*sic*] to think well of you, then you think well of yourselves.[82]

What, then, is love? Spivak rightly illustrates that love means the very concrete act of *mindchanging,* of changing the laws and legislation, the health care system:

> We are talking about using the strongest mobilizing discourse in the world in a certain way, for the globe, not merely for Fourth

> World uplift. I say this again because it is so easy to dismiss this as quixotic moralism. This learning can only be attempted through the supplementation of collective effort by love. What deserves the name of love is an effort—over which one has no control yet at whichone must not strain—which is slow, attentive on both sides—how does one win the attention of the subaltern without coercion or crisis?—mindchanging on both sides, at the possibility of an unascertainable ethical singularity that is not ever a sustainable condition. The necessary collective efforts are to change laws, relations of production, systems of education, and health care. But without the mind-changing one-on-one responsible contact, nothing will stick.[83]

The *mindchanging* love that Spivak talks about is neither *religious* nor *secular* because the act of loving moves beyond any artificial boundary of the religious or secular and should not need to draw any boundary—as in Jesus' radical call for the *neighbor/enemy-love-as-self-love*. Unfortunately, we are living in a world in which the religious right misuses the notion of love in an extremely distorted way. Peter Sprigg, senior fellow of the Family Research Council in the U.S., for instance, makes a public statement that he wants to deport gays and lesbians out of the Unites States and also wants to pass laws designed to put gays and lesbians in jail.[84] He goes on to firmly argue: "People are afraid of the homosexual activists .... Nobody wants to be accused of participating in 'hate'.... On the contrary, everything we do is motivated by love for the people who are hurt by this lifestyle."[85] A statement like this, coming from the Family Research Council, the Christian right organization with a motto of "advancing faith, family and freedom,"[86] reveals the reversal of the very religious message of neighbor-love-as-self-love that they want to "advance" in its dismissing *who-one-is* of LGBT people.

The awareness of mortality leads one to think about the absolute loneliness: One dies alone. On the contrary, the awareness of natality awakens us to the absolute interrelationality and interdependence of our being with others simply because one cannot be born alone. The sheer awareness of natality brings us an epistemological shift from the idea that one is the ground of one's being to the idea that the ground of one's being is interdependent on others. One is born into the world with the good will, care, love, hospitality, and solidarity of others; lives in midst of the world (*Dasein*) with others (*Mitsein*); and retreats from the world through mortality. Being awakened to human natality as well as mortality, one eventually comes to acknowledge the fundamental human condition: We humans should *become* equal in sociopolitical community, even if we are not born equal in our biological/physical environment. A cosmopolitan theology of natality invites us to envision a community of *equality-in-alterity*, where people acknowledge the *ethical singularity* of each individual human being as a fellow-citizen of the cosmos and celebrate the *plurality* of who-one-is. Whereas human *singularity* refers to the dimension of our being with one's own unique *face* and distinctiveness in relation to others, human *plurality* points the way to who/what one is to oneself with one's own constitution and creation of the world. Acknowledging human plurality moves one beyond a fixed, singular identity that confines one to just one thing. Treating human beings as members and citizens of the cosmos is the epistemological ground of cosmopolitanism, whose life in the world is under the same human conditions: natality, mortality, singularity, and plurality. Connecting Arendt's political anthropology of *natality* to theological anthropology offers the profound meaning of neighbor-love as a passion for a community of justice, where one can be and must be born and reborn in order to "work out your own salvation"(Phil. 2:12, Inclusive), and to think, judge, and act, in the world in the existential condition of the possibility of freedom.

6

Cosmopolitan Theology of *Planetary Hospitality*

Love the world as your own self;
then you can truly care for all things.

—LAO TZU[1]

The word I means here I am, answering for everything and for everyone.

—EMMANUEL LEVINAS [2]

Religion is responsibility or it is nothing at all.

—JACQUES DERRIDA[3]

Being Religious: An *Event of Facing* the Face of the Other

Cosmopolitan discourse emphasizes the *cosmic belonging* of all individual human beings as the ground of our hospitality, solidarity, justice, and neighbor-love. Cosmopolitan discourse is about turning a *compassionate gaze* onto others regardless of one's nationality and citizenship, origin of birth, religion, gender, race and ethnicity, sexuality, or ability. Here the compassion in the *compassionate gaze* is neither pity nor altruism. Instead, compassion is "the disturbance of violent relatedness"[4] with the others, who inhabit this cosmos as *us*. I find the lucidity of a particular TV commercial theologically profound. The advertisement starts with various statements by people from different genders, races, ages, and social classes, and ends with a simple but powerful statement:

I am not a statistic;
I am not a target, market, or a demographic;
I am not data, and I am not a patient.

I am a person, a mom, a daughter, a butcher, a teacher;
who just happens to have type 2 diabetes;
who happens to have high cholesterol;
who has high blood pressure.
....
I am a human being.[5]

"*I am a human being*" is a powerful statement from those who demand their rights as human beings, regardless who/what they are. In his "Perpetual Peace," Kant elaborates his notion of *kingly people,* who "rule themselves by laws of equality."[6] One can distinguish the *kingly people* not by their prestigious education or royal background but by the way they practice justice. As long as people follow and govern themselves by the laws of equality and justice, people are the *kingly people.* When one makes a decisive statement, *I am a human being,* it is an appeal to the cosmopolitan right, which claims that every individual singular human being who shares the surface of the earth has all of his or her rights simply by being human. The statement, *I am a human being,* is not only a *self-affirmation* but also *an appeal* to responsibility to and solidarity with one another.

Jesus, a primary point of reference for those who identify themselves as *Christians,* both affirmatively and critically, presents the core of his teaching in the following statement: "The truth is, every time you did this for the least of my sisters or brothers, you did it for me" (Mt. 25:40, Inclusive). His encounter with Zacchaeus (Lk. 19:1–10) indicates the essential meaning of *being religious* as having the *gaze* of planetary love and hospitality that sees people as simply human beings. Therefore, the cosmopolitan gaze of planetary love and hospitality *is* what constitutes *being religious.* One should regard one's religious or denominational affiliation as a point of departure, a point of entry, not the point of arrival because one cannot confine God to a particular religion or faith tradition, and therefore should not claim one's exclusive ownership of God. Regarding one's religious or denominational affiliation as *accidentality,* not as *inevitability,* is important in religious discourse and practice because such a sense of *accidentality* of one's affiliation allows a space of *alterity,* of reciprocal contestation and challenge, and a space of planetary gaze that sees others as fellow human beings, *regardless.*

No matter who and what one is, we, the entire humanity, inhabit and belong together in the *cosmos.* The realization of this *cosmic we-ness* is not to operate the *exercise of the same,* which is "to receive nothing of the Other but what is in me."[7] The *exercise of the same* arises from a *desire for totalization* that is manifest in a tradition—whether it is a philosophical, national, or religious tradition—that attempts "to reduce the universe to an originary and ultimate unity by way of panoramic overviews and dialectical syntheses."[8] Cosmopolitan theological discourse originates not from a *desire for totalization* but from an exercise of an *ethical singularity* that sees every individual human being in its infinite alterity and that creates a space for a new kind of *we-ness*. Jean-Luc Nancy poetically contends: "We are Meaning."[9] Looking out for meaning, as if *meaning* is out there to be found, is pointless because meaning *is* in the midst of our *being-with-one-another* and, therefore, "*meaning is itself the sharing of Being*."[10] The realization of *being-with-one-another*, this *we-ness*, could be the beginning of *becoming-religious*. However, *we-ness* is neither an abstract universalism that suppresses the singularity, heterogeneity, and plurality of an individual being nor a romantic longing for the *wholeness* of sameness. *We-ness in alterity* is the "paradoxical 'first-person plural.'"[11]

The cosmopolitan theology that I propose responds to the question of what it means to *be religious, be Christian* today. Cosmopolitan theology is a discourse and practice that I ground in the idea that we are to treat every individual human person as human, and that simply being human is a sufficient ground for human dignity and rights regardless of one's origin of birth, nationality and citizenship, religion, gender, sexuality, or ability. We live in an era when we are overwhelmed by the presence of the others, whose rights to life, to freedom, or to survival are *categorically* denied through laws, biases, conventions, value systems, or religious teachings and practices. Today, countless places, people, or groups experience bloody conflicts, extreme poverty and hunger, oppression, hate crime, and killing. *Planetary* hospitality, solidarity, and responsibility toward the other foster an ethics and politics of *singularity*, which is, I believe, what religion is all about. The purpose of cosmopolitan theology is to respond to the *face* of the other and, therefore, is an *event of facing*. Here *facing* is not based on a *philosophy of reflection* in which the "'I' sees itself reflected in the other but does not see the other looking back" and as a result the "other is reduced to a mirror for oneself."[12] Furthermore, the *event of facing* is not the imposition of *unity and sameness* that situates *alterity* of the other within a horizon where totality prevails and denies *alterity*—its very otherness in the other.

The *philosophy of reflection* and *politics of non-alterity* are inherent in the discourse and practice of imperialism and colonialism, whether it is geopolitical, sociocultural, theopolitical, or philosophical imperialism and colonialism. The Levinasian notion of the *face* of the other "brings us to a notion of meaning prior to my *Sinngebung* and thus independent of my initiative and my power."[13] The *faces* of the others that we see everywhere *disturb* our being *at home* with ourselves, when we can see there are ongoing conflicts, discriminations, dominations and subordinations, exclusions, wars, or social, political, religious, and physical killings. Becoming religious in this sense would mean *being-deeply-disturbed* and *not-being-at-home* any longer: an event of *facing* the face of the other. *Feeling at home,* not being disturbed by the face of the other, becomes unethical and unreligious and therefore "no one is at home."[14] In a world that one characterizes by its hostility and the absence of solidarity, the "way of the I against the 'other' of the world consists in *sojourning,* in *identifying oneself* by existing here *at home with oneself.*"[15] Here *at home* would not mean simply being in a shelter but being in a space where one can be who one is and completely free. My being-free inextricably relies on *your* being-free and on my being-*with*-you. Therefore, my feeling-*at-home* should be possible only if the other also feels *at home,* but not as a result of the *imperialism of ontology,* the suppression of alterity of the other, where domination and exploitation over the other in difference become a general practice. In this sense, the Heideggerian ontology is, according to Levinas, a form of imperialism because it "subordinates the relationship with the Other to the relation with Being in general, remains under obedience to the anonymous, and leads inevitably to another power, to imperialist domination, to tyranny."[16]

In this context, constructing a cosmopolitan theological discourse is first to prioritize the *face* of the other, who *brings us to a notion of meaning* while rejecting the idea that one can categorically reduce the other human being into mere data, statistic, or nomenclature, of which connotation and denotation mark the absence of the *singular face.* Such a nomenclature as "Indian," for instance, is "a simulation and loan word of dominance"[17] and a suspension of alterity of singular persons. I believe recognizing the presence of the *face* of the other as existent, no matter who/what one is, is one of the core messages of Jesus' teaching. Cosmopolitan theology is, therefore, an *event of facing* the face of the other, who is in the world *before* me, *with* me, and *after* me. Second, constructing cosmopolitan theological discourse is to theopoliticize *being disturbed* by the face of the other as a way of *being religious.*

Theopoliticizing begins with an act of *deromanticizing* and *materializing* Jesus' command for *neighbor-love-as-self-love* that is inextricably interrelated to God-love, and of mediating it by the command for justice, solidarity, and radical hospitality in our geopolitical reality. Furthermore, *being religious* is being compelled to acknowledge, ethically and geopolitically, the presence of the face of the other as being in its infinity beyond totalizing, categorizing, or classifying. Unless one is being deeply *disturbed,* one cannot *be religious* in a world where dehumanization, marginalization, domination and subjugation, oppression and exploitation, ostracization, or stereotypization still prevail and kill so many anonymous *faces*—physically, socially, politically, culturally, or spiritually. Cosmopolitan theology claims that *being religious* means answering the call by the face of the other to be accountable, to be responsible, to be hospitable, and to be in solidarity. Here, *being religious* means to bear the burden of being *disturbed,* the burden of responsibility that we would rather want to ignore, dismiss, deny, or resist, but eventually have to take: an *event of facing* the face of the other in singularity.

Thinking *with* Paul *against* Paul: Pauline Cosmopolitanism as a Foundation for *Universal Singularity*

One must not value religious faith merely for its claims to absolute truth, but for the ways and practices in which it serves to liberate, expand, and enlarge human liberation, inclusion, hopes, and possibilities. The idea of cosmopolitanism is to ever-enlarge the circle of inclusion and extend the scope of justice, which is implicit in various biblical texts. The biblical texts with cosmopolitan ideas can provide a foundational teaching for a religious practice that transforms the view of the other and ever-enlarges the circle of inclusion. One can find one of the powerful theological grounds of *cosmopolitan citizenship* in Paul's statement about *fellow citizenship*: "So then you are no longer strangers and aliens, but you are citizens with the saints and also members of the household of God" (Eph. 2:19). By designating *foreigners* as *co-citizens* with the saints and members of the household of God, Pauline cosmopolitanism radicalizes and politicizes the dimension of religious practice fundamentally related to the question of hospitality and neighbor-love. Here it is misreading if one perceives "members of the household of God" simply as the *Christians-only-circle,* because Christians cannot and should not claim an exclusive ownership of God as if they were the only *God's people.* Besides, Christians, as a religious entity, had not yet come into being when Paul made this cosmopolitan statement. Theologically speaking, the God who creates the cosmos refuses a *proper name.* When asked about the name, God declares: "I AM WHO I AM" (Ex. 3:13–14). "I AM WHO I AM" is a divine refusal to be named, to be categorized, or to be owned. Therefore, no one particular religion can claim an absolute ownership of God.

Paul's statement, "There is no longer Jew or Greek, there is no longer slave or free, there is no longer male and female; for all of you are one in Christ Jesus" (Gal. 3:28), also offers a cosmopolitan ethos that urges one to dismantle the discriminatory boundaries of race, class, and gender, and that emphasizes *equal citizenship* in Jesus Christ. There can be an exclusively doctrinal interpretation of the phrase "in Christ Jesus"as implying that the equal citizenship applies only to *Christians* who have their official membership in the institutionalized Christian churches. How one interprets "in Christ Jesus" would depend on how one understands the profound meaning of *following* Jesus Christ—becoming a Christian, a Christ-follower. Here it is theopolitically important to note that one should locate Jesus, God's incarnated being, in the context of the divine refusal to be owned by a particular religious group or community of faith, because the Jesus as the divine incarnation refuses to be owned by a particular institutionalized religious group with a proper name: *JESUS-IS-WHO-JESUS-IS* as *GOD-IS-WHO-GOD-IS*.

The name "Jesus" symbolizes a *substitution,* which entails a *being-with-and-for-the-other*. *I-in-Jesus-Christ* in Pauline cosmopolitan text, the *ipseity,* comes to mean "I" as "*here I am*, answering for everything and for everyone,"[18] an endless responsibility, solidarity, and hospitality *for, with*, and *to* the other—a passion for the impossible. *I-in-Jesus-Christ* should mean not *I* as an institutionally *Christianized ipseity*, but *I* as *here-I-am,* who is "under the weight of the universe, responsible for everything."[19] *Here-I-am* (Isa. 6:8) does not at all state, "I believe in God," a doctrinal statement that may confirm one's religious belonging in reality. Therefore, as Levinas rightly points out, to "bear witness to God is precisely not to state this extraordinary word" but to signify "me in the name of God at the service of men [*sic*] that look at me."[20] As soon as one dedoxifies such bible verses, they can reveal the depth of the messages that are relevant today.

Understanding Pauline cosmopolitanism requires one to see Paul not as a founder of a religious institution, nor as an apologist of Christendom, but as a *philosopher theologian* who addresses the issues that concern philosophy—such as justice, law, violence, hospitality, ethics, and politics. If one defines the *philosopher* as "one who specialized in generalities," Alain Badiou contends, Paul is then an *antiphilosopher* because what the philosopher must do is not "the production of universal truths, but rather the organization of their synthetic reception by forging and reformulating the category of Truth."[21] Paul is an *antiphilosopher-philosopher* in the sense that Paul grounds his truth claim, not on the fixed, static, philosophical foundation, but on the *event,* which is never fixed nor static. That Paul's truth/faith claim has "no origin or foundation in philosophy is what makes Paul of "foundational importance for philosophy."[22] Paul's so-called conversion on the way to Damascus was beyond one's calculation or anticipation, and began with Paul's enunciation as a subject rather than with any external force. Through this Damascus *event,* according to Badiou, Paul institutes a new subjecthood by declaring:

"By the grace of God I am what I am" (1 Cor. 15:10a). The enunciation of *I-am* as a *speaking subject* lays the ground for one's truth-claim, or what Badiou calls the "(re)surgence [(re)surrection] of the subject."[23]

If one takes Paul as an *antiphilosopher-philosopher* in Badiou's sense, not as an apologist or philosopher in a traditional sense, one can realize that the issues Paul raises are sociopolitical, theopolitical, and philosophical, rather than Christian-centered doctrinal. Badiou views Paul as a "poet-thinker of the event."[24] Badiou adopts Paul, not to connect him with an institutionalized religion but to articulate the notion of the *subject* as a *universal singularity*. According to Badiou, one must give exclusive credit to Paul for establishing that "the fidelity to such an event [Christ-event] exists only through the termination of communitarian particularisms and the determination of a subject-of-truth who indistinguishes the One and the 'for all.'"[25] In this sense, Badiou argues, Paul is "a founder, in that he is one of the very first theoreticians of the universal."[26] Here *theoretical* is opposite to *real*, not to *practical*. Religious discourses have usually made their truth-claim according to a totalized system of *unchanging* doctrines, whereas Paul's discourse on truth "begins from the Christ-event itself, refusing to subject that event to any preconceived framework in order to proclaim its truth."[27]

Theodore Jennings also attempts to read Paul outside the institutionalized and privatized religious ghetto, and sees him as someone who opens up to the philosophical and political realm with concerns for justice.[28] Slavoj Zizek complexifies the perception of Paul by contending that Paul did not belong to "Christ's inner circle" and "betrayed Christ by not caring about his idiosyncrasies, by ruthlessly reducing him to the fundamentals, with no patience for his wisdom, miracles, and similar paraphernalia."[29] Zizek also points out that through the reading of Paul's epistles, one can easily recognize that Paul is notably indifferent toward Jesus as a living human person in the gospels, who is not yet Christ, and that Paul pays no attention to Jesus' actual teachings, acts, or stories. Since Paul was not a part of Jesus' inner circle, he was able to "elevate Christianity from a Jewish sect into a universal religion (religion of universality)."[30] Reading Paul as an outsider of Christ's circle makes it possible for one to comprehend "*Christianity-in-becoming*."[31] In order to see Paul from a new angle, one needs to defamiliarize, dedoxify, and de-Christianize Paul and read him *within* and *beyond* Jewish tradition. Regarding Paul's letter to the Romans as a text of foundational significance for Western thought about law and politics, Giorgio Agamben proposes to revive Paul's letters as the messianic text and argues: "[T]wo thousand years of translation and commentary coinciding with the history of the Christian church have literally cancelled out the messianic, and the word *Messiah* itself, from Paul's text."[32]

Another interesting angle through which one can see Paul in a nontypical way is from Friedrich Nietzsche. Nietzsche de-idealizes Paul by describing him as "one of the most ambitious and importunate souls" and "a very tormented, very pitiable, very unpleasant man who also found himself unpleasant."[33] Nietzsche goes on to say that Paul "suffered from a fixed idea, or more clearly from a *fixed question* which was always present to him and would never rest: What is the Jewish law really concerned with? and in particular, what is the *fulfillment of this law*?"[34] Paul, according to Nietzsche, as "fiery, sensual, melancholy, malevolent in hatred as he was—*could* not fulfill the law."[35] One's encounter with Paul can be so multiple and various. Elsa Tamez, for example, examines Paul as "a Jew, an artisan, and a prisoner,"[36] who restlessly suffered from ongoing persecution, various conflicts, imprisonment, being on the margin. His restless struggles both with his external and internal world must have led him to passionately envision a world of justice, peace, and equality and to long for a "community in which there will be no discriminatory differences,"[37] which is explicit in his radical egalitarian statement, "there is no longer Jew or Greek, there is no longer slave or free, there is no longer male and female" (Gal. 3:28). Considering the multiple layers of Paul, I believe Paul's statement, "God shows no partiality" (Rom. 2:11), can also provide a firm ground for philosophical and theological cosmopolitanism along with other statements that Paul made. The various angles used for approaching Paul help one recognize the necessity to *dedoxify* Paul in order to locate Paul in his own specific context and to retrieve the relevant meaning from his works.

However, one cannot deny that no sooner did Paul establish the principle of radically cosmopolitan equality for every individual human being, than he betrayed the very principle of revolutionary egalitarianism by his extremely patriarchal statements in other texts. Pauline injunctions, such as, "For the husband is the head of the wife just as Christ is the head of the church, the body of which he is the Savior" (Eph. 5:23), or, "But I want you to understand that Christ is the head of every man, and the husband is the head of his wife, and God is the head of Christ" (1 Cor. 11:3), remind me of the Kantian cosmopolitanism and, at the same time, his extreme prejudices that lead me to confirm the formula of *thinking with Kant against Kant* that I use in chapter 3. Retrieving Pauline cosmopolitanism from the variety of biblical texts also requires an attitude of *thinking with Paul against Paul* with his apparent patriarchal/kyriarchal injunction. If one moves beyond the *desire for purity* in a figure, Paul's cosmopolitanism, in spite of his extremely patriarchal injunctions, can offer significant ground for a construction of cosmopolitan theology and for the *universal singularity* of individual human being. *Purity* does not exist in *any* thinker, simply because one is always historically and socioculturally situated, bound, and limited, and, therefore, no one is epistemologically *innocent*. My primary interest in Pauline cosmopolitanism is to use it as a *theopolitical tool* for constructing and promoting a cosmopolitan ethos both *within* and *beyond* faith communities. One can extend his unconditional notion of hospitality, for instance, through his injunction "extend hospitality to strangers" (Rom. 12:13) and "welcome one another" (Rom. 15:7) to the issue of immigration, asylum, or undocumented workers today. If one is able to dedoxify Paul's various texts, Pauline texts can become profound resources for radical notions of hospitality and cosmopolitanism, which go beyond the boundary of Christian confinement of Paul's thought.

Cosmopolitan Theology of *Solidarity of Singular-Plurality*

Sameness and Singular-Plurality

The issue of solidarity has been emerging as one of the pressing challenges of the twenty-first century. In constructing a theology of solidarity, I would like to pay attention to both the notion of the *absolute alterity* that Emmanuel Levinas and Jacques Derrida have elaborated upon and the notion of *singular-plurality* that Jean-Luc Nancy has articulated. I would argue that the notion of *absolute alterity* does not discount the notion of *singular-plurality* and vice versa. I contend that both concepts, *absolute alterity* and *singular-plurality*, complement one another. It is not, however, my intention to cross-examine two line of thoughts—the Levinas/Derrida and the Nancy. Instead, juxtaposing two types of solidarity, *solidarity of sameness* and *solidarity of singular-plurality*, I base my theological construction of cosmopolitan solidarity on the notion of *singular-plurality* that deeply embeds within it the notion of the *absolute alterity* of human beings. Singularity and plurality of the nature of being are not as in opposition as they may sound. The concept of singular-plurality reveals the significant layers of who one is and the mystery, I believe, of the be-ing.

In his *Totality and Infinity*, Emmanuel Levinas highlights the notion of *absolute alterity*. Levinas points out that the concept of totality dictates Western philosophy. He characterizes the ethics as calling into question the "exercise of the same" and "calling into question ....my spontaneity by the presence of the Other."[38] Levinas focuses his ethico-philosophical discourse on the notion of *absolute alterity*, in which an essentializing, homogenizing, totalizing, reductive way that makes the other of *the same* is the fundamental sin. Derrida engages in Levinas' notion of alterity and reaffirms Levinas: "Beneath solidarity, beneath companionship, before *Mitsein*, which would be only a derivative and modified form of the originary relation with the other, Levinas already aims for the face-to-face, the encounter with the face."[39] Levinas and Derrida's evolution of Levinasian thought has made the theme of *the same and the other* significant for an ethico-philosophical discourse. Taking the theme of *the same and the other* as a significant theological term brings light to the cosmopolitan theological view of the human being that highlights the *singularity* of being in its cosmic uniqueness and, at the same time, the inextricably interconnected nature of being with one another in cosmic fellow citizenship, not *because of* the sameness of the other with me but *in spite of* the difference of the other from me. Acknowledging the complementarity and interrelatedness of self and other makes one realize the fundamental problem of the binary approach to the theme of the self and the other in a manner of *totality of the same*. Here Jean-Luc Nancy's concept of *singular-plurality* helps one to understand the seemingly paradoxical nature of being. Nancy addresses the issue of alterity with his elaboration of the notion of irreducible plurality of a coexistence that never becomes the same in the first place: the truth of the paradox, "first-person plural."[40] With his notion of *singular-plurality*, Nancy eloquently and lucidly articulates the profound depth of the meaning of solidarity by declaring, "Existence *is with*: otherwise nothing exists."[41]

Nancy lists the recurring tragedies of "Bosnia-Herzogovina, Chechnya, Rwanda, Bosnian Serbs, Tutsis, Hutus, Tamil Tigers, Krajina Serbs, Casamance, Chiapas, Islamic Jihad, Bangladesh, the Secret Army for the Liberation of Armenia, Hamas, Kazakhstan, Khmers Rouges, ETA militia, Kurds (UPK/PDK), Montataire, the Movement for Self-determination, Somalia, Chicanos, Shiites, FNLC-Canal Historique, Liberia, Givat Hagadan, Nigeria, the League of the North, Afghanistan, Indonesia, Sikhs, Haiti, Roma gypsies of Slovenia, Taiwan, Burma, PLO, Iraq, Islamic Front Salvation, Shining Path, Vaulx-en-Velins, Neuhof."[42] Moving beyond the binary of *the same* and *the other*, the *sameness* and the *alterity*, Nancy contends that the recurring tragedies in the world reveal that we, humanity, have been unable to expunge our recourse to an essentializing, totalizing *we* that operates with the self-identity of an *I*. The question that preoccupies Nancy is not the question of *alterity* but the question of *plurality*. I believe the importance of *we-ness* as being-together in a non-totalizing way and being open to alterity runs through both Levinasian and Nancean thought.

The Nancean *plurality* is primordial and irreducible, which denotes *relation*, not identity, alterity, or dissemination. Here, *I* does not precede *we*. Instead, one needs to regard being as relation, as "the primordial, ontological condition of being-with or being-together.... 'being-with-one-another.'"[43] Therefore, the *singular* does not precede the *plural* and vice versa. It is important to note that the singular is not the individual, which is separate and indivisible. The individual is nothing but "the residue of the experience of the dissolution of community.... [A]s its name indicates, it is the atom, the indivisible—the individual reveals that it is the abstract result of a decomposition."[44] As Nancy tries to indicate with his term *singular plural,* one should not dissociate the singularity from the plurality because *singular-plural* being is in relation and therefore inseparable, whereas the individual is separate. Nancy contends:

> It is a singularity taking refuge in its affirmation of Being, a touch of meaning. It is not an other Being; it is the singular of Being by which the being *is,* or it is of Being, which *is being* in a transitive sense of the verb (an unheard of, inaudible sense—the very meaning of Being). The touch of meaning brings into play its own singularity, its distinction, and brings into play the plurality of the "each time" of every touch of meaning, "mine" as well as all the others, each one of which is "mine" *in turn,* according to the singular turn of its affirmation.[45]

According to Nancy, self is not "in itself, or by itself, or for itself, but rather 'one of us.'"[46] Therefore, being is *being-together,* not an anonymous *one,* of which characteristics are mutuality and sharing. There is no originary unity that grounds the *singular-plurality* because "being-in-common excludes interior unity, subsistence, and presence in and for itself" and "[b]eing with, being together and even being 'united' are precisely not a matter of being 'one.'"[47] Nancy makes an important distinction between *plurality* in his term *singular-plurality* and *multiplicity*. Being constitutes the existence of all existences—the co-existences. However, co-existence does not mean that the self disappears into the site of oppositional beings of the other. The unique singularity of being/self and its plurality in co-existence with the other are the defining aspect of who we humans are. Here plurality is not multiplicity that one can *count*. Plurality means *more,* the *more-ness,* being different from *numerous,* and an "increase or excess of origin in the origin,"[48] which is to say: "the One is more than one; it is not that 'it divides itself,' rather it is that one equals more than one, because 'one' cannot be counted without counting more than one."[49] The profound meaning of singularity is significant to an understanding of the conception of the *singular-plurality*:

> The singular being is neither the common being nor the individual. There is a concept of the common being and of the individual; there is a generality of what is common and of the individual. There is neither of these for the singular being. There is no singular *being*: there is, and this is different, an essential singularity *of being* itself (its finitude, in Heidegger's language). That is to say, the "singular

> being" is not a kind of being among beings. In a sense, every being is absolutely singular; a stone never occupies the space of another stone.[50]

Nancy's notion of singular-plurality and the meaning of the *with* offers a profound depth of cosmopolitan solidarity. For the being-together, being-*with*-ness as singular-plurality is the inevitable precondition of cosmopolitan solidarity. Here, the self and the other are not in an oppositional position and they are inextricably entangled and interconnected. Nancy eloquently asserts: "Being is at the same time in the same place only on the condition of the spacing of an indefinite plurality of singularities. Being is with Beings.... We are each time an other, each time with others."[51] Here, Nancy's notion of the *with* echoes the spirit of cosmopolitan solidarity. Being as *being-together* or *being-with* in its unique singularity without fusion or collapsing into a fixed identity or a unitary group is the core of cosmopolitan spirit. The *proximity-in-distance,* the *Mitdasein,*[52] is the ground of our solidarity that makes us *us*.

Mechanical Solidarity and Organic Solidarity

In his *The Division of Labor in Society,* published in 1893, Emile Durkheim makes a distinction between two types of solidarity: *mechanical* and *organic*. *Mechanical* solidarity or solidarity by similarities, which prevails in primitive society, derives from resemblances and it binds the individual directly to the group or society. I find Durkheim's concepts of *organic solidarity* are insightful for the construction of cosmopolitan solidarity. The division of labor in a society yields dissimilarity and thereby it becomes a cause of power-differential between people. *Mechanical solidarity* can be conceivable under conditions of minimal power-differentiation. In a society in which people regard differences between people lightly, the concern for justice cannot be primary. Only when there is sensitive recognition of an extreme power-differential between people does justice come to be crucial to the ethical and theological imperative. In order to avoid and prevent the misuse of power-differential, the contractual relationship is significant in a society. Justice, in this sense, is the ethical norm that shepherds fairness and equality in a contractual relationship. In this sense, Durkheim points out: "Agreement between the parties concerned cannot make a clause fair which of itself is unfair. There are rules of justice that social justice must prevent being violated, even if a clause has been agreed to by the parties concerned."[53] Mechanical solidarity gets the individual persons together within the community. However, modern society functions in the differentiated spheres of life, and division of labor necessitates interdependency. The division of labor creates what he calls *organic solidarity,* which prevails in modern society. Whereas *mechanical solidarity* consists of similarities and binds the individual persons directly to society, *organic solidarity* consists of dissimilarities or difference and binds the individual persons indirectly to society.

There is an inseparable connection between the division of labor, solidarity, and morality, as Durkheim argues: "In short, since the division of labor becomes the predominant source of social solidarity, at the same time it becomes the foundation of the moral order."[54] In a way, Durkheim's two types of solidarity, *mechanical* and *organic*, carry their own paradoxical meaning in terms of similarity/sameness and dissimilarity/alterity between the individual members of society. While mechanical solidarity contributes to the immediate integration of the individual persons into society, *organic solidarity* leads to indirect integration through the web of interdependencies it creates. Durkheim juxtaposes these two solidarities in a contradicting way: *mechanical solidarity* is small, backward in a way, homogeneous, and without a sense of individuality, whereas *organic solidarity* is large, advanced, heterogeneous, differentiated, and with a strong sense of individuality. In *mechanical solidarity* people like each other because they are alike, whereas in *organic solidarity* people like each other because they are dissimilar. Although Durkheim makes a distinction between these two types of solidarity primarily in a sociohistorical context—primitive and modern—I think that these two types of solidarity still co-exist in society, depending on the nature of groups.

It is important to note that the act of sociopolitical and religio-theological solidarity requires one's passion for *justice,* taking the misuse of the power-differential between/among individuals seriously, which is different from *charity*. Durkheim postulates a fundamental difference between the duties of justice and the duties of charity: "Between the two [duties], it is agreed there is a kind of hiatus or break in continuity. They seem to derive from ideas and sentiments that have nothing in common. In justice, there is a further division as between distributive justice and commutative justice. "[55] Although Durkheim's notion of justice is not new, it is interesting to see that the concern for justice is central to Durkheim's construction of moral order and to his works. However, one should not approach the issue of charity and justice in a binary sense, because the act of charity is inextricably interlinked to sustaining a sense of justice. The total absence of a sense of charity would kill the sense of compassion that feeds the passion and longing for justice, for the *world-as-it-ought-to-be*.

Therefore, distinguishing charity from justice, even when one makes a distinction, is only a *strategic* distinction, but not an oppositional, bipolar, binary differentiation. The act of charity in Christianity is not one's choice but a *duty* as humans, not just as Christians, which Jesus' parable of the last judgment in Matthew 25 eloquently illustrates. In Jesus' parable about the last judgment, the acts of charity, such as feeding the hungry with food and water, welcoming the stranger, offering clothing to the naked, taking care of the sick, or visiting the imprisoned, are inseparable from the issues of justice if one takes the parable both literally and theopolitically. There is no precondition of one's religious affiliation for one's *redemption* in the final judgment in Jesus' parable. The only measurement for the final judgment is how one has exercised and practiced the acts of charity *and* justice, not the nature of one's religious belonging or one's sexuality, for instance. When the way people exercise charity becomes too personal, too individual, or too private, and when the rise of diversification, or individualism among/between people becomes serious, justice comes to be more urgent and crucial than charity, although the ultimate question is not about whether one chooses *either* justice *or* charity but about how we can make *both* justice *and* charity operational.

Derrida asserts that justice is not deconstructable and is incalculable, whereas law is "the element of calculation."[56] Although the notion of justice is too complex and incalculable to simply define, it is clear that justice seeks a just relation in the asymmetrical power relationships between and among people. As Deuteronomy 1:16—17a indicates: "Give the members of your community a fair hearing, and judge rightly between one person and another, whether citizen or resident alien. You must not be partial in judging: hear out the small and the great alike." In this sense, the justice that a sociopolitical and religious-theological solidarity seeks is to accomplish the moderation of just relations between people in the use and misuse of asymmetrical power and privilege. Those who have all the power and privilege, for instance, would think that they do not need solidarity with others because they are self-sufficient. In this sense, solidarity begins with questioning the power-differential and asymmetrical power relationships, and gives attention to individuals who are victims of the misuse of asymmetrical power differentials among people. In this sense, justice calls for a universalistic value and orientation, whereas charity endorses a particularistic relationship among people and does not question the power-differential among members of society. When the act of charity becomes one aspect of this profound dimension of justice, embracing both the particular and universal ties among people, the passion and solidarity for justice-to-come would not lose its humane face.

Solidarity and We-Question: We-in-Sameness and We-in-Alterity

Cosmopolitan discourse is in a way a response to the issue of solidarity. Although the precondition for solidarity can be a *community*, solidarity requires more intentional commitment and performance than does community.

Solidarity implies an intentional, conscious, and singular claim that individuals have on each other's passion, compassion, and commitment. Needless to say, one of the preconditions for solidarity is a sense of *we-ness*. In this sense, the question of solidarity is a *we-question*. Nowadays, the *we-discourse* has become popular since the emergence of identity politics in the late 1960s. Jodi Dean argues that the 1980s were the *me*-decade, whereas the 1990s were the *we*- decade.[57] I would argue, however, that, since the emergence of various identity politics, the *me-ness* and *we-ness* have hardly been separable from and reducible to one another because both—the *me-ness* and *we-ness*—get inextricably intertwined. Yet, it becomes clear that the multiple types of newly constructed *we* emerge. The claims for *we-ness,* such as *we-women, we-Asians, we-Afro-Americans, we-Latinas/nos,* or *we-queers,* for instance, evoke a sense of solidarity among those who belong to the circle of *we,* which I would characterize as a *solidarity-in-sameness*. There are double edges in the claim for *we-ness* of this kind and its *solidarity-in-sameness*. On the one hand, the claim for *we-ness-in-sameness* can strengthen the bond among the marginalized and raise people's political consciousness for change of the existing systems of racism, sexism, classism, ableism, and heterosexism. Various sociopolitical movements that call for change have heavily relied on the rhetoric of *we-ness-in-sameness*. Therefore, I fully recognize there is an urgent need for constructing the *strategic we-ness-in-sameness* and promoting the *solidarity of sameness*. The sheer realization of the inextricable interconnectedness of I-ness/me-ness and we-ness/us-ness is the ground for an authentic solidarity with one another in spite of and regardless of the difference.

On the other hand, however, one needs to remember that this type of *solidarity-in-sameness* should be only *strategic* and *context-specific,* not *permanent* and *context-unlimited*. It is important to remain constantly aware that there is a *double-edged* sword in the discourse and practice of *we-ness-in-sameness,* and that it can operate in an extremely destructive way. Here, one needs to apply hypersensitivity to the issues of standardization, centralization, and authentication of *we-ness-in-sameness* by those who have the power to construct the very discourse and practice of *we-ness*. "We-British" during the colonization era, "We-Germans" during the Third Reich, "We-Japanese" during the colonization of Asian countries, or "We-Bosnian-Serbs" during the ethnic cleansing, for instance, evoke the horrors of cruel imperialist practice, ethnic cleansing, genocide, or crimes against humanity. In this terrible, exclusive *we-ness,* a claim based on *sameness,* there is a deep-seated *desire for purity* or *desire for totalization,* which ends up suppressing, oppressing, or distorting any possibility of *alterity* in the other. In this sense, one of the dilemmas of the politics of *we-ness-in-sameness* is its tendency to overlook, ignore, or refuse to acknowledge the internal differences and heterogeneity among and within the alleged *sameness*. Identifying himself as "a gay academic living in New York City," Ed Cohen, for instance, expresses the dilemma and uneasiness that he has experienced at a lot of gay and lesbian studies meetings. Although he enjoyed "the potential for conviviality and comradery that these occasions provide,"[58] he found himself wondering, "'I' have no idea who 'we' are."[59] He then came to realize:

> So, although the assumption that "we" constitute a "natural" community because we share a sexual identity might appear to offer a stable basis for group formations, my experience suggests that it can just as often interrupt the process of creating intellectual and political projects which can gather "us" together across time and space. By predicating "our" affinity upon the assertion of a common "sexuality," we tacitly agree to leave unexplored any "internal" contradictions which undermine the coherence we desire from the imagined certainty of an unassailable commonality or of incontestable sexuality. Hence we almost inevitably render ourselves vulnerable to personal and political crisis whenever such putative certainty is destabilized from within the body, the psyche, the collectivity, or the polity.[60]

Here, Cohen rightly reveals the deep-seated dilemma of the politics of *we-ness-in-sameness:* when people ground the sameness in *essence,* not in *position*. The politics of *we-ness-in-sameness* operates in most movements from the socially marginalized group. However, the functionality of *essentialized sameness* as unchanging and homogenized entity easily becomes more constraining than liberating in the long run. The discursive and practical dilemma of the argument that *we*-are-different-from-*them,* in terms of gender, race/ethnicity, class, sexuality, religion, nationality, citizenship, or ability, is the fact that it finds its self-expression only through a *category*. So the *categorical-we* (as Asian, women, gay, Afro-American, Latina/o, Christian, Muslim, etc.) is claiming heterogeneity of *us* from *them*. However, when the claim for heterogeneity comes to *us,* it turns into the category of the homogeneity, which functions as what R. Radhakrishnan calls: "[T]otal violation of the decentered and nonauthoritarian spirit of heterogeneity."[61]

Here, I find Radhakrishnan's distinction between a *categorical* heterogeneity and an *acategorical* heterogeneity extremely helpful for understanding the complex and paradoxical nature of the politics of identity that is based on the logic of the *sameness* among *we* on the one hand, and the essential *difference* between *we* and *they* on the other. According to Radhakrishnan, an *acategorical* heterogeneity "finds its 'self-expression' through the breakdown of the 'categorical,'" whereas a *categorical* heterogeneity is "construed by the homogeneous logic of the 'category.'"[62] He also further makes a distinction between "heterogeneity as bohemianism, anarchism, and political indifference and heterogeneity as political destiny."[63] In the politics of *categorical heterogeneity*, what I call *we-ness-in-sameness*, there is often a *policing and authenticating gaze* to determine the nature of the *authentic we-ness*. Here, people often expect one's *me-ness* to get collapsed into the *we-ness* in *we-Asians*, for instance, and *Asians* then becomes a *categorical heterogeneity*, which claims its heterogeneity in relation to *non-Asians*, but, at the same time, often homogenizes the *we* as Asians and overlooks the diversity and heterogeneity within and among that very *we*. Therefore, there are two kinds of *we-ness*: *we-ness-in-sameness* and *we-ness-in-singular-plurality*. The *we-ness-in-sameness* essentializes, homogenizes, and rigidifies the *we*, whereas *we-ness-in-singular-plurality* celebrates singularity and heterogeneity and pluralizes the effective identities within the *we*. It is important to note that the *we* here is not an *essential* but a *positional* strategic *we* for survival and solidarity for the sake of justice, which is an empowering vision for solidarity-in-alterity.

Cosmopolitanism promotes a sense of new *we-ness* as regarding every individual human being as a citizen of the cosmos. However, the *we-cosmic-citizens* are not to promote the *we-ness-in-sameness*, but rather the *we-ness-in-alterity*. Unlike the solidarity-in-sameness, cosmopolitan *solidarity-in-alterity* celebrates the singularity and difference of each individual human being, while not denying the historical necessity of the strategic construction of *we* to challenge the very sociopolitically imposed category.

> [T]he greater irony is that, to the extent that the activists did succeed in advancing the situation of gays and lesbians, they undermined the logical supports for their own arguments.... How do you protest a socially imposed categorization, except by organizing around the category? Just as blacks cannot fight the arbitrariness of racial classifications without organizing *as blacks*, so gays could not advocate the overthrow of the sexual order without making their gayness the very basis of their claims.[64]

In this context, there is a historical and political *necessity* and urgency of forming *we* around a socially ascribed category and then shifting the very socioculturally *ascribed-category* to sociopolitically *claimed-category*, while recognizing the very paradoxicality that it is impossible to rigidify the *we* as the unchanging sameness. *We-ness-in-alterity* embraces the paradoxical reality of *necessity* and *impossibility* of *we-ness-in-sameness*. There is an "*inessential* commonality"[65] in *we,* and what matters the most in the solidarity of the *we-ness-in-alterity* is one's existence as co-existence, but not one's existence as co-essence. The affirmation of the *cosmic-sameness* invites us to embrace and celebrate the micro-difference because the cosmic-sameness and the micro-difference are not, in the end, in a binary opposition.

Cosmopolitan Solidarity in Singular-Plurality: Politics of Border-Traversing

I firmly base my construction of cosmopolitan theology on a politics *of solidarity* for justice and compassion. The cosmopolitan theology that I propose is a theological discourse and practice that cultivates planetary solidarity for justice, peace, and equality for all living beings. It embraces and transcends the diverse *subject-positions* in a world of extreme inequalities. According to the data for 187 countries in the world, the inequality of a child's life expectancy reveals the extreme *unevenness* of the world in which we humans live. A child born in Japan has a life expectancy at birth of 83.4 years, in Switzerland of 82.3 years, in Italy and Australia of 81.9 years, in Canada of 81.0 years, in the Republic of Korea of 80.6 years, and in the United States of 78.5 years. Unfortunately, however, a child born in Chad has a life expectancy at birth of 49.6 years, in Central African Republic and Democratic Republic of the Congo of 48.4 years, in Guinea-Bissau of 48.1 years, and in Sierra Leone of 47.8 years.[66] Furthermore, in Luxemburg, GDP per capita is 83,820 dollars; in the Unites States, it is $45, 989 dollars; and in Democratic Republic of the Congo, it is only $319.[67] It is clear that we humans on the planet are living in an *uneven* world of unprecedented inequality between and among nations, regions, and peoples. Cosmopolitan theology attempts to offer the opportunity for us to engage the multiple realities that constitute different cultural, political, economic codes, and invites us to cross the borders in order to practice an impartial neighbor-love and to be theopolitically in solidarity with those on the margins across various borders. The factual description about the unevenness of the world is an invitation for Christians to revisit, rethink, recontextualize, and retheologize Jesus' story of the last judgment in Matthew 25, especially about the mandate of *feeding the hungry* and its connection to the love for God.

> About 1.75 billion people in the 104 countries covered by the MPI [Multidimensional Poverty Index]—a third of their population—live in multidimensional poverty—that is, with at least 30 percent of the indicators reflecting acute deprivation in health, education and standard of living. This exceeds the estimated 1.44 billion people in

> those countries who live on $1.25 a day or less (though it is below the share who live on $2 or less).[68]

Global political and economic inequality and injustice become serious issues because "these inequalities are mostly greater today than 50 or 100 years ago, and there is reason to believe that the gap will continue to grow."[69] It is obvious that we are living in an age that requires human solidarity with other beings in multiple forms. Every theological discourse that concerns justice and human liberation needs to wrestle with the issue of solidarity. However, the discourse and practice of solidarity is not as simple as it may sound, especially when solidarity operates with a notion of *membership, sameness,* or *similarity* that is both exclusionary and repressive. It is not my intention to propose a politics of solidarity grounded in membership, sameness, or commonality, which often ends up denying differences, dissimilarities, and alterity among people who one wants to be in solidarity with. The politics of *solidarity-in-sameness,* as I call it, tends to create an exclusionary norm and to expose the problems of essentialization, homogenization, and exclusion, requiring people to sacrifice their alterity. I ground cosmopolitan *solidarity-in-singular-plurality* not just in sameness, commonality, agreement, or consensus but more in difference, dissimilarities, disagreement, or dissent. Cosmopolitan *solidarity-in-singular-plurality* means to practice one's humanity, with its planetary scope and depth, and to promote justice while respecting an *ethical singularity* of the individual persons with whom one is in solidarity. It is attuned to the universality within particular identities of heterogeneity, and it no longer blocks one from one's *alterity*.

Experimentally, while not excluding one from the other, I would like to differentiate two politics: politics of identity and politics of *border-traversing.* The politics of border-traversing takes cosmopolitan *solidarity-in-singular-plurality* as a point of arrival, while taking the politics of identity as a *strategic point of entry* for a necessary movement for social transformation. Identifying Jesus as a radical *border-traverser,* a politics *of border-traversing* views the human subject as contradictory, multilayered, and plural, and challenges the liberal notion of the unified, unchanging, fixed, and essentialized view of human identity. I problematize the liberal notion of *celebrating diversity* that links difference between different identity groups within the horizon of a false equality and a *depoliticized* notion of solidarity. *Doing* theology is an act of *border-traversing,* constantly moving in and out of borders epistemologically, ontologically, and theopolitically. These borders include cultural borders, physical borders, geopolitical borders, religious borders, borders of meaning, and borders between different *identities* and alterity. However, I do not intend to simply replace politics of identity with politics of solidarity. My intention is to articulate a theological/philosophical discourse that moves beyond the binary approach to identity and solidarity and to stress that claiming one's identity is more a question of political strategy and *positionality* rather than a question of one's *essentiality*. I ground cosmopolitan solidarity in the ethics of *singular-plurality*, not the politics of identity-of-sameness. A powerful act of solidarity is the *solidarity-in-singular-plurality* that sees every individual human being in its *singularity*. Agamben rightly observes:

> What the State cannot tolerate in any way ....is that the *singularities form a community without affirming an identity*, that humans *co-belong without any representable condition of belonging* (even in the form of a simple presupposition).... Whatever singularity, which wants to appropriate belonging itself, its own being-in-language, and thus rejects all identity and every condition of belonging, is the principal enemy of the State. Wherever these singularities peacefully demonstrate their being in common there will be a Tiananmen, and, sooner or later, the tanks will appear.[70]

Grounded in humans' co-belongingness "without any representable condition of belonging"[71] and in a "common and absolutely exposed singularity,"[72] cosmopolitan theology seeks to build solidarity based on the *we-hermeneutics* in the sense that "I am because we are; and we are because I am."[73] Here one should not base the *we* on the hierarchical relationships, as is the case in *cosmopolitanism from above*, but on a radical egalitarian democratic relationship among, across, and beyond gender, age, race, ethnicity, class, orientation, culture, and religion. Furthermore, the *we* in *we-hermeneutics* is not a concept/group for the *swarming of individualities*, as is often the case in the politics of ethnic/racial/gender/sexual identity, which is mostly *unitary*. I attempt to derive cosmopolitan *we-hermeneutics* from a hermeneutics of *acategorical heterogeneity* and to epistemologically ground this hermeneutics in a politics of heterogeneity as a *political destiny*. In a politics of heterogeneity, one does not collapse one's *I-ness* into the *we-ness-in-sameness* of the *swarming individualities*, and the I-We is no longer a binary category but an interlinked web of human life. In this sense, Agamben's observation on Spinoza's reflection on human *inessential commonality* is truly insightful:

> All bodies, he [Spinoza] says, have it in common to express the divine attributes of extension (*Ethics*, Part II, Proposition 13, Lemma 2). And yet what is common cannot in any case constitute the essence of the single case (*Ethics*, Part II, Proposition 37). Decisive here is the idea of an *inessential* commonality, a solidarity that in no way concerns an essence. *Taking-place, the communication of singularities in*

> *the attribute of extension, does not unite them in essence, but scatters them in existence.*[74]

Agamben's idea of an *inessential commonality* is significant in cultivating a new type of solidarity that does not look for an essentialized, homogenized commonality as its point of departure, but takes the passion for justice as its decisive point of entry, with its full acknowledgment of one's *being-such, being-singular-plural*—an *inessential commonality* we humans share.

The relevance and meaning of *neighbor-love* can manifest itself only in one's exercise of hospitality and solidarity toward the others—both the *concrete* and *distant* others. When asked what one must do to inherit eternal life, Jesus mentions nothing about religious affiliation/belonging, but shares the story of a Samaritan who exercises neighbor-love through solidarity and hospitality to the other in need (Lk. 10:25–37). If one dedoxifies and de-Christianizes Jesus' response to the question of inheriting eternal life, one can surprisingly notice that Jesus' reply is neither *religion-specific* nor *doctrine-based*. Instead, he firmly and lucidly confirms that the way one can inherit eternal life, attaining *salvation* in a Christian term, is to practice neighbor-love, hospitality, and to be in solidarity with those in need. Jesus' parable on the last judgment (Mt. 25:31–46) strongly reaffirms and explicitly indicates that *salvation* is possible only through one's practice of neighbor-love, hospitality, and solidarity, not through one's religious affiliation or membership. Being in solidarity with the hungry, the thirsty, the stranger, the naked, the sick, and the imprisoned, as Jesus listed, is the core of Jesus' teaching and should be the core of Christian discourse and practice if one admits that the word *Christian* simply denotes the *Christ-follower*. Instead of being occupied with claiming the *ownership* of Jesus and confining Jesus to exclusively Christian doctrines, Christians need to liberate Jesus from these rigid, exclusive doctrines and a religiously institutionalized interpretation of salvation.

In this sense, the theological discourse and ministerial practice around the issue of *extra Ecclesiam nulla salus* (outside the church, there is no salvation) does not resonate and is indeed in contradiction with what Jesus confirms about how one can *inherit eternal life*—salvation. The church, as an institutionalized form of a community of believers, can be meaningful when it constantly views itself only as what John Caputo calls "plan B."[75] If the church absolutizes the meaning of its existence in the world as if it is *plan A*, "were Jesus to return in the flesh, he would be executed again, not by the world but by the church."[76] The church should constantly seek for the *church-to-come* and understand the current configuration of the *church-as-it-is* always as plan B. Only then can the church work out its own salvation with *fear and trembling*, as Paul instructs (Phil. 2:12), but never with absolute certainty, self-sufficiency, and self-righteousness. In this sense, the church should never feel *at-home,* but rather on the *constant-move*. When the church and Christians feel *at-home,* self-sufficient, and self-righteous, they can easily become against-Christ, against-church, and against-humanity in the extremely uneven world in which we live today.

Christian promise of a *new heaven and a new earth,* where "death will be no more; mourning and crying and pain will be no more"(Rev. 21:4), offers a vision of the *world-to-come* that is inextricably connected to the *world-of-already*. The intimate connection between the *world-of-not-yet* and the *world-of-already* seems to foreshadow the possibility of and responsibility for changing the world. All that is necessary to establish *a new heaven and a new earth* might be the *slight displacement* of a stone, a cup, or a brush. However, "this small displacement is so difficult to achieve and its measure is so difficult to find that, with regard to the world, humans are incapable of it and it is necessary that the Messiah come."[77] Here the question that I would like to pose is, What it would mean for us today to imagine a *world-to-come* in which "everything will be as it is now, just a little different"?[78] What would constitute this *little difference*? I would suggest that we must find our vision for the *world-to-come, the world-of-not-ye*t in the midst of the *world-of-already,* in which biopolitics, normalization of the *state of exception,* and unceasing commodification of humans prevail.

The cosmopolitan *solidarity-in-singularity* that I propose is not a romantic longing and an idealized yearning for *wholeness* but a fierce love for the world (*amor mundi*) where we humans, in our singular-plurality, work for *a little difference* in the midst of the dissonance, catastrophe, darkness, and disparity in which we live. Furthermore, the cosmopolitan *solidarity-in-singularity* that I attempt to articulate is by no means to construct a metanarrative on solidarity that would not take us anywhere, because one cannot base a *blind* metanarrative on a human specific-materialized context. The cosmopolitan *solidarity-in-singularity* is to call upon others to maintain connection with and to act upon *us-ness* in a concrete context, in which the concept of *us* is much more complex and deeper than *us-in-sameness* in terms of *same* race, gender, sexuality, nationality, religion, affiliation, denomination, and so forth. What the cosmopolitan solidarity-in-singularity seeks and affirms is the *planetary us-ness-in-singular-plurality*. Cosmopolitan solidarity-in-singularity means to regard every individual human being as a fellow citizen of the cosmos because, as Paul declares, "So then you are no longer strangers and aliens, but you are citizens with the saints and also members of the household of God" (Eph. 2:19).

What Agamben calls the *coming community* resonates what the community of cosmopolitan *solidarity-in-singularity* envisions. Agamben's concern for the new form of singularity without identity that he calls "whatever being" or "being-*such*"[79] is to imagine a life of endless potentialities that could escape the hold of sovereign power that dehumanizes and controls humans by fixing of human identities into categories and presupposing exclusionary forms of belonging and border-control to police the borders of identity and entitlement. One way to escape such a *thanatopolitics,* a politics of death, Agamben argues, is to contest the *fixity* of identity and to envision a new form of community without fixed, essentialized, homogeneous identity-as-such. In this new *coming community,* humans can use the self that entails the denaturalization, defixation, and desacralization of the self, which exists as a complete *singularity,* rather than confining the self to a particular identity-group. The new identity-in-singularity does not fall into the binary trap of *either* the universal, claiming mere abstract rights of humanity, *or* the particular, claiming *only* exclusively factional rights.

The notion of human singularity, what Agamben terms *whatever-being* or being-*such,* offers the possibility of a human community free of any essential, homogeneous precondition of belonging, shared destiny, or categories of inclusion or exclusion. Cosmopolitan *solidarity-in-singularity* is to envision and work for a community of being-together of human existences-in-singularity, rather than a community of unchanging essence, or a community of sameness, in which people confine the appeal to solidarity only to those-in-sameness. The *beings-in-singularity,* the *whatever-beings,* have no unitary, essentialized, homogeneous, unchanging identity that would make it possible to shape a community presupposed on a *logic of inclusion-exclusion*. The act of *authentic* solidarity is possible not merely out of obligation and duty but out of love and compassion for the other. Here, we should connect the meaning of *singularity* to the notion of love, as Agamben contends:

> Love is never directed toward this or that property of the loved one (being blond, being small, being tender, being lame), but neither does it neglect the properties in favor of an insipid generality (universal love): The lover wants the loved one *with all of its predicates,* its being such as it is. The lover desires the *as* only insofar as it is *such*—this is the lover's particular fetishism. Thus, whatever singularity (the Lovable) is never the intelligence of some thing, of this or that quality or essence, but only the intelligence of an intelligibility.[80]

The emphasis on human existence in being-in-singularity is not to reject a particular tie to a group but to denote "the non-predicative property par excellence that belongs to each member of a class and at the same time makes its belonging an aporia."[81] Human existence as *being-thus,* or *being-such,* is *the*

Irreparable: "The Irreparable is that things are just as they are, in this or that mode, consigned without remedy to their way of being. States of things are irreparable, whatever they may be: sad or happy, atrocious or blessed. How you are, how the world is—this is the Irreparable."[82] Solidarity-of-singularity can happen when one can accept the human innermost exteriority, a *face*, as the determination of everything. Singularity, what Agamben terms being-*such*, being-*thus*, or *the Irreparable*, is "neither an essence nor an existence, neither a substance nor a quality, neither a possibility nor a necessity.... It is not *thus*, but rather it is *its* thus....[I]t is only its mode of being."[83] Loving *human-in-singularity* is "letting others be"[84]—*Gellassenheit* in Meister Eckhart's sense.

Needless to say, solidarity is what makes human beings hold together, and is a promising ethico-theopolitical metaphor and norm. God's incarnation, for instance, signifies the very meaning and act of solidarity—the *divine solidarity with humanity*. Cosmopolitan solidarity-of-singularity is for the world-to-come, in which "nation shall not lift up sword against nation, / neither shall they learn war any more" (Isa. 2:4), and for the common well-being of all individual human beings in their *singular faces*. One cannot separate *knowing* God from loving others, being in solidarity with others, because "whoever does not love does not know God, for God is love" (1 Jn. 4:8). The act of love is not just a romantic desire. It requires a passion for justice in multiple forms, a fierce passion for the impossible, a commitment to solidarity with the concrete and distant others, which regards every individual being as *being-thus*, as in its mode of being without any identity markers. In this context, solidarity is impossible without a *radical affirmation of the other*, and, at the same time, a *radical neighbor-love*.

Cosmopolitan theology invites us to fundamentally ask and redefine who *the other* is and who *the neighbor* is in our time and specific context. Once, the neighbor was very ethnocentric in Israelite/Jewish tradition, and then became *religio-centric* in Christian tradition through its invention of the *religious other* through its construction of doctrine, theology, and institutionalized practice. Theologians need to transform the nature of Christian discourse concerning the others from a r*eluctant tolerance* to a *radical affirmation* of the formerly constructed *other* and to a radical inclusion of the other into the community of neighbors—epistemologically, theologically, institutionally, and systemically. I base cosmopolitan solidarity-of-singular-plurality on a Christology that envisions Jesus as the one who is ever-affirming the *other*—the racialized other, gendered other, sexualized other, religiocized other, ethnicized other, and so forth. Jesus' radical affirmation of the other is, I believe, not based on doctrinal grounds nor personal merit, but on a radical neighbor-love and compassion for the whole of being in the cosmos—including both human and non-human. Cosmopolitan solidarity-of-singularity is an ideal, a *passion for the impossible*. However, as Derrida posits: "But why not recognize there [Gelassenheit] love itself, that is, this infinite renunciation which somehow *surrenders to the impossible*?"[85]

Cosmopolitan Theology of *Planetary Hospitality*

"I am a stranger and an alien residing among you."—GENESIS 23:4A

"I am a stranger on the earth."—Psalm 119:19, NIV

After the slaughters of WWII…the notion of neighbor lost its innocence.[86]

We do not know what hospitality is.
Hospitality can only take place beyond hospitality.—JACQUE DERRIDA[87]

Double Bind: The Impossibility and Necessity of Hospitality

Jacques Derrida made an address at the International Parliament of Writers in Strasbourg, France, in 1996, on the issues of cosmopolitanism and cosmopolitan rights, and their implication for such areas as international law, immigration, refugees, immigrants, and asylum-seekers in a time of new justification of xenophobia. His address on cosmopolitan rights at the International Parliament of Writers, an organization that advocates for writers whose home countries regard them as dissidents, proves and reconfirms that deconstruction is not an *a*political or purely abstract discourse but "a concrete intervention in contexts that is governed by an undeconstructable concern for justice."[88] The type of cosmopolitanism that I adopt is about the scope of justice, and justice is about responsibility, about hospitality—the welcoming the other. As Derrida contends, "Religion is responsibility or it is nothing at all," and, "the demonic is ….nonresponsibility."[89] I find what Derrida points out about the core of religion to be truly intriguing and significant in understanding the nature and accountability of religion. Attending to the issue of hospitality in an uneven world means responding to the religious mandate to take responsibility for what is happening in the world, because taking responsibility would mean offering and exercising hospitality, the neighbor-love, in a complex sense.

Discourse on hospitality has moved to the center of sociopolitical, economic, philosophical, and religious controversy, especially over such pressing issues as illegal immigrants, undocumented workers, refugees, asylum, and multiculturalism. One can relate the issue of hospitality to the context of globalization, internationalization, citizenship, or immigration, especially in public policy about inclusion and exclusion as political or religious instruments of *othering* the other. Although hospitality is primarily about a relationship between the host and the guest, the questions of *who-is-the-host* and *who-is-the-guest/stranger/foreigner* in a specific context, and how one should practice hospitality as either an individual, a group, or a state, are far from being as simple as they may appear. Examining how an individual person, society, or a state perceives a *guest/foreigner,* for instance, is a significant way to measure the nature and scope of hospitality in a concrete context.

What constitutes hospitality is a complex issue that requires one to examine discourse, perception, and practices both on personal and institutional levels. The hospitality discourse also revolves around the issues of forgiveness, friendship, gift, *face,* mourning, and the *ethical singularity* of an individual human being. When people apoliticize, depoliticize, or simply romanticize the notion of hospitality, however, the hospitality discourse ends up being another discourse on blind-charity. There are numerous works on hospitality within the Christian tradition. However, few works connect the notion of hospitality to the complex sociopolitical dimension and to sophisticated theological discourse, which require one to revisit and reshape the conceptual framework of the very ground of Christianity.[90] A discourse of romanticized hospitality tends to mislead the understanding of hospitality in our concrete reality, where the exercise of hospitality is always interlinked with state regulation and control.

It is important to note how differently an individual or a state perceives and exercises hospitality. For instance, in 1793 France expelled the foreigners whose homelands were at war with France, making some exceptions for those who were able to prove their loyalty to France. However, France forced them to bear a special marker—a tricolor ribbon—all the time, as it declared: "Those who will have been deemed worthy of staying will have to wear a tricolor ribbon bearing this word: *Hospitality*. They will also carry their *certificate of hospitality*."[91] It is extremely disturbing to learn that people used the word *hospitality* in such a dehumanizing and distorted way *and* that such a tragic practice of state "hospitality" in 1793 France has not disappeared, but has existed in various parts of the world in many different forms to this very day.[92] The *certificate of hospitality* can be a metaphor for the failure of the *laws of hospitality*—the conditional hospitality, the *politics* of hospitality—that is in a permanent tension with the *Law of hospitality*—the unconditional hospitality, the *ethics* of hospitality. As Levinas rightly points out, "[P]olitics bears a tyranny within itself; it deforms the I and the other who have given rise to it, for it judges them according to universal rules, thus as in absentia."[93] The state through its sovereign power regulates and controls the boundaries between private and public, between *friends* and *enemies,* between the legality and illegality of the other. The issues of immigration, refuge, or asylum, for instance, could be the key areas in which one can see how differently people can define hospitality in severely contradicting ways. Furthermore, the immigration issue reveals the huge disparity between state hospitality and individual hospitality, as the state can always *police* the private, individual practice of hospitality for those illegal/undocumented immigrant workers. These two terms, *illegal* and *undocumented,* may look interchangeable, but they have strikingly different sociopolitical connotations.

In the summer of 1996 in France, there was a high-profile "*sans-papiers* (undocumented) movement," in which French intellectuals actively got involved by organizing a committee of mediators when the French government ordered a cruel evacuation of the Church of Saint Bernard in Montmartre on August 23, 1996. In the Church of Saint Bernard, 300 African women and men had protested against the government for months, and ten of the "illegal" immigrants were on a long hunger strike, which got intense national media attention. The movement, called "*affaire des sans-papiers de Saint-Bernard* (the affair of the undocumented immigrants of the Church of Saint Bernard),"[94] became a moment during which people began to replace the word *illegal* with *undocumented.* Although simply altering one word, from *illegal* to *undocumented,* may not bring an actual legal change of status to the undocumented immigrant, a public use of the term *undocumented,* instead of *illegal,* may open up a public horizon to approach the immigrant question in a more hospitable way, for the term *illegal* already implies a negative public attitude that justifies repressive measures, making the immigrants look like an *enemy* or *threat* to the state.

Connecting the discourse and practice of hospitality to the immigration issue can be one of the most urgent theological issues that Christians need to wrestle with, especially in the age of globalization. Whether or not people use the word explicitly, the complex notion of *hospitality* is in fact at the center of various political, socioeconomic, multicultural, and multireligious controversies today, and these controversies revolve around the issue of immigration—concerning, for instance, documentation, religious affiliation and establishment, cultural practices, use of public language at school, medical and educational benefit for the children of undocumented immigrants, etc. The state hospitality affects the lives of all immigrants, both the documented and undocumented, in their daily reality, and shapes the public view of the guests, the strangers, the *foreign* bodies, languages, cultures, religions, and knowledge systems.

It is significant to note the differentiation between an *ethics* of hospitality (an unconditional hospitality) and a *politics* of hospitality (a conditional hospitality) that Jacque Derrida lucidly makes through the work of Emmanuel Levinas.[95] Although Levinas himself rarely highlights the word *hospitality,* his notion of *welcome-of-the-face* in his *Totality and Infinity* is "an immense treatise *of hospitality,*"[96] in which he underlines the significance of one's face: "To begin with the face as a source from which all meaning appears, the face in its absolute nudity ....is to affirm that being enacted in the relation between men [*sic*] ....[97] The question that one encounters in dealing with the issues around hospitality is: In what degree can one *welcome* the other—the guest, stranger, foreigner, or the absolute other even without a proper name, nationality, or any other identity marker? What would constitute *welcoming* the other, when Paul says "welcome one another" (Rom. 15:7)? On an individual/private level, it is the very *face,* not the proper name, that invites one to genuinely welcome even the absolute other. There is no need to know the proper name in order genuinely to welcome someone, especially when people often use one's proper name as a primary identity marker on legal documents. The ethics of *unconditional* hospitality does not require one's identity document or sociopolitical marker. The very face of *who-one-is,* rather than *what-one-is,* itself becomes the *Law* (with an upper case "L" in singular) of hospitality—the *unconditionality* of hospitality. On an official state level, however, the *welcoming* is based on the proper name in the sense of a legal identity marker, the *what-one-is* (rather than *who-one-is*). And the *laws* (with a lower case "l" in plural) of hospitality regulate the state hospitality toward the guest/foreigner, which would require one's proper name, legal identity document, and national belonging. In this sense, there is always huge disparity between the *unconditional* hospitality and *conditional* hospitality, which are in constant tension.

It seems almost impossible for one to fully comprehend the profundity of the scope of *hospitality* as a word of a "troubled and troubling origin, a word which carries its own contradiction incorporated into it, a Latin word which allows itself to be parasitized by its opposite, 'hostility.'"[98] Derrida further argues: "Hospitality is a self-contradictory concept and experience which can only self-destruct ....or protect itself from itself, auto-immunize itself in some way, which is to say, deconstruct itself—precisely—in being put into practice."[99] It is interesting to examine the Latin root of the word *hospitality* as Derrida introduces it. *Guest* in Latin is both *hostis* and *hospes,* the combination of which is *hosti-pet.* So one may interpret *hosti-pet* as arising from an abstract noun *hosti* and consequently means one who predominantly personifies hospitality, and therefore *hosti-pet* can mean hospitality itself. The original notion of *hostis* initially denotes "equality by compensation" and "*a* hostis is one who repays my gift by a counter-gift."[100] *Hospes* goes back to *hosti-pet-s*, and the *pet* signifies *master*. So the literal meaning of *hospes* is the *guest-master*, and the *master* represents *husband* in marriage and *chief* in a clan or tribe.[101] However, the *hostis* in Latin, which corresponds to *gasts* of Gothic, interestingly also means *enemy*. This ironic dual meaning of *hostis* as both guest and enemy is derived from *stranger*, in which "favorable stranger" became "guest," whereas "hostile stranger" developed to "*enemy*."[102] In this context, Derrida repeatedly points out the ambivalence of the term *hospitality* and coins the term "hostipitality (*hostipitalité*)" [103] to show the entanglement of hostility and hospitality, raising a fundamental question of the nature and the subject of hospitality. Derrida's *hostipitality* invites one to realize the undecidability, entanglement, and fine line between *friend* (favorable stranger) and *enemy* (hostile stranger), between *hospitality* and *hostility*, and to approach the issue of hospitality from a fundamentally new way.

One can find a provisional answer to the question of the subject of hospitality in a French word, *hôte*. *Hôte* in French means both the giver (*donne*) and the receiver (*reçoit*) of hospitality.[104] There is always an interchangeability of host and guest, as "the visitor radically overwhelms the self of the 'visited' and the *chez-soi* of the *hôte*."[105] Derrida brings our attention to an extremely ambivalent relationship between the moment of *hospitality* and that of *hostility*, when one has an initial encounter with the other. The moment of initial encounter with the other is a liminal space between *acceptance/hospitality* and *rejection/hostility*, which is also the moment of *undecidability* on the part of the host, and *uncertainty* on the part of the guest. When there is a differential of rights and power between two subjects—the host and the guest, the other—hospitality means fundamental welcoming, unconditional receptivity by the host toward the other, because "radical hospitality consists, would have to consist, in *receiving without invitation*, beyond or before the invitation."[106]

In a society, the position between these two subjects—the host and the guest—often hinges on one's citizenship, race, gender, nationality, class, ability, or ethnicity. However, this reversibility of the stance of *hospitality* and *hostility* in our everyday encounters with countless *others* is extremely complex and significantly entangled. Derrida provokes us to rethink the profound and complex meaning of hospitality by repeatedly placing the phrase before us: "We do not know what hospitality is [*Nous ne savons pas ce que c'est que l'hospitalité*]."[107] Reminding the readers/audience that he is speaking this sentence in French, his own language, Derrida highlights the interlinkedness of language and the issue of hospitality. Being able to speak in one's own language indicates that one is *at home*, the host, in a position of welcoming the others. As a person who has been studying and teaching in three different language zones—Korean, German, and English, I can understand, not only by theoretical analysis but also by my lived experience, how deeply the issue of language and hospitality gets often intertwined.

As a Korean native and Korean speaker, for instance, I may act, as long as I am in Korea, as a host toward those *foreigners* whose primary languages are not Korean. Those whose locations socioculturally allow them to communicate and speak in their heart-language, the mother-tongue, play the role of the *host,* while those whose heart-language becomes *foreign*-language and are expected to speak in an acquired language become the permanent transient, the guest, the foreigner, the stranger. Being uprooted from their own language makes them ontologically and sociopolitically the permanent *guests in exile.* One's mother tongue indicates one's belonging, a clear identity marker. In this sense, the *ipseity,* the I-ness, is closely associated with power, "the mastery and sovereignty"[108] of the host who *can* welcome in his/her *mother-tongue* the stranger speaking in a *foreign-tongue.*

My speaking in German in Germany or English in the U.K. or the U.S., which are not my mother-tongues, often leads the *native* people to ask the question: "Where are you from?" Here, this *where-are-you-from* question becomes a political undertaking that comes to imply, with or without the questioner's intention and awareness, the claim of ownership of the space, and a drawing of a line between the host and the guest, wittingly or unwittingly. However, it is important to note that not all languages have an equal power when it comes to *native* or *foreign,* as there is certainly a political hierarchy of power among different languages in the contemporary world, where English becomes more and more a universal language, and other European languages such as French, German, or Spanish are still the *international* languages that people would easily and willingly translate.[109]

Through the seemingly simple phrase, "We do not know what hospitality is," Derrida illustrates a profound depth and complex scope of the nature and practice of hospitality, which is one of the urgent and pressing issues today. First, Derrida's claim, *we do not know what hospitality is,* denotes the paradoxical aspect of the *double bind* of hospitality: the necessity and the impossibility. As soon as the host offers hospitality to the guest with the opening remarks, *make-yourself-at-home,* the limit of the hospitality gets established with or without the intentionality of the host. For the act of offering hospitality becomes an act of confirming the boundary between the host and the guest. The guest needs the hospitality because the door exists between the host and the guest. In the liminal space between the host and the guest, there lies the door. The existence of the door symbolizes the rigid boundary between the host, as one who has the key to the door as the owner of the house, and the guest, as one who needs to be admitted. In this sense, "hospitality always in some way does the opposite of what it pretends to do and immobilizes itself on the threshold of itself."[110] The existence of the door implies that authentic, genuine, unconditional hospitality is impossible and at the same time necessary. In this sense, "from the outset hospitality limits itself as its very beginning, it remains forever on the threshold of itself, it governs the threshold ....[I]t becomes the threshold."[111] Here hospitality is possible only when it overcomes the sort of hospitality that "paralyzes itself on the threshold which it is" and thereby "hospitality can only take place beyond hospitality."[112]

Second, the *not-knowing* in Derrida's address, the *we do not know what hospitality is,* indicates a significant aspect of hospitality. Since there is always a huge disparity between unconditional hospitality and conditional hospitality, *knowing* hospitality in its entirety is impossible. In this sense, hospitality is never a concept or a calculable knowledge that one can simply grasp. Instead, hospitality is an *event* that one can hardly comprehend in its full entirety. The acknowledgment of the dimension of *not-knowability* of hospitality is rebelling "against any self-identity or any consistent, stable, and objectifiable conceptual determination"[113] because hospitality is "not only an experience in the most enigmatic sense of the word, ...but is also an intentional experience which proceeds beyond knowledge toward the other as absolute stranger, as unknown."[114] Hospitality is, therefore, not "in the mode of being-present, unless it is that of the law of the should-be or obligation, the law of hospitality, the imperative of which seems moreover contradictory or paradoxical."[115]

Third, there is also another dimension of the significance of *not-knowing.* The *not-knowing* is not only about the meaning of hospitality but also about the host's attitude toward the guests. At the very moment one assumes one *knows* who/what the other, the guest, the stranger, the foreigner is, one begins establishing the "circles of conditionality"[116] of hospitality. In this sense, the acknowledgment of *not-knowing* is essential for an unconditional hospitality because it allows one to completely open oneself to the guest without building any precondition for receiving hospitality. Fourth, the phrase, *we do not know what hospitality is,* implies there is a dimension of *not-yet-ness* in hospitality: Hospitality is always *to-come,* beyond our comprehension. The history of universal hospitality by Kant in terms of the *rights* of the stranger has not fully disclosed what hospitality truly is. Therefore, *not-knowing-hospitality* encompasses "we do not yet know who or what will come, nor what is called hospitality and what is called in hospitality, knowing that hospitality, in the first place, is called, even if this call does not take shape in human language."[117]

Derrida further elaborates the relationship between "*the* law of unlimited hospitality" and the "law*s* (in the plural) of hospitality."[118] In other words, *the laws-of-hospitality* is a political site of *the law-of-hospitality* that is an unconditional ethical responsibility and duty. The *laws-of-hospitality* deal with the question of *how* to practice the law of hospitality, which requires rethinking democratic politics. Derrida contends:

> In other words, there would be an antinomy, an insoluble antinomy, a non-dialectizable antinomy between, on the one hand, *The* law of unlimited hospitality (to give the new arrival all of one's home and oneself, to give him or her one's own, our own, without asking a name, or compensation, or the fulfillment of even the smallest condition), and on the other hand, the law*s* (in the plural), those rights and duties that are always conditioned and conditional, as they are defined by the Greco-Roman tradition and even the Judeo-Christian one, by all of law and all philosophy of law up to Kant and Hegel in particular, across the family, civil society, and the State.[119]

In our reality, one can hardly deny that there is always a tension between the law-of-hospitality and the laws-of-hospitality. The spirit of *the* law of unlimited hospitality transcends a particular time and space. In this sense, this unconditional law of hospitality is a "law without imperative, without order and without duty. A law without law."[120] If one offers hospitality *out of duty* or *out of imperative*, as in the Kantian sense, it is no longer an unconditional, absolute hospitality because the hospitality out of duty becomes an act of paying a debt of hospitality. Here the law*s* of hospitality, the conditional hospitality, are historical, which means the laws are always culturally and sociopolitically situated in a particular time and space. So whenever one improves, creates, transforms, or overturns the law*s*, s/he is practicing a form of deconstruction. For Derrida, hospitality is therefore "a name or an example of deconstruction."[121] He further contends that "justice in itself, if such a thing exist, outside or beyond law, is not deconstructible.... Deconstruction is justice."[122] Here Derrida makes a distinction between law and justice. Whereas one can or should deconstruct the law, one cannot deconstruct justice because justice is not an idea, form, or regulative principle, and is never reducible to the law*s*. Derrida's notion of the law of unlimited hospitality echoes the Taoist notion of the great Tao:

> The great Tao flows everywhere, both to the left and to the right.
> The ten thousand things depend upon it; it holds nothing back.
> It fulfills its purpose silently and makes no claim.

It nourishes the ten thousand things,
And yet is not their lord.
It has no aim
. . . .
It does not show greatness,
And is therefore truly great.[123]

The unconditional hospitality is like the great Tao that flows without boundaries, frames, and borders, without making any claim for return on the debt of hospitality. The unconditional hospitality includes both the invitation and the visitation of the guest. Offering hospitality is, therefore, to open up the borders and frames of *protection* of the host. The idea of the unconditional hospitality offers the possibility of an authentic communication beyond the borders, boundaries, and frames of *protection,* a communication that is form-less, border-less, and boundary-less, like flowing water: Tao. God's incarnation claims the visitation to humanity and the act of unconditional hospitality of visitation.

Tension between Private Hospitality and Public Hospitality

Exercising hospitality is not just a purely religious or humanitarian act, but an *ethico-political* one. What will happen when one's individual/private hospitality is in conflict with state/public hospitality? How do we deal with the dilemma of hospitality, especially when one tries to love one's neighbor/enemy as oneself by offering unconditional hospitality to the stranger? In 1997 in France, for instance, a French citizen named Jacqueline Deltombe got arrested due to her *criminal* act: She allowed an undocumented immigrant to stay at her flat.

> According to the ordinance of November 2, 1945, modified by the August 24, 1993, Pasqua law on immigration, this act is punishable by a five-year prison sentence and a Fr 200.000 fine. Yes, five years in prison for having neglected to ask a stranger for his [*sic*] identification papers. The discrepancy between the crime and the severity of the punishment was such that the prosecutor himself pleaded for clemency. He did not ask for any penalty to be imposed on Deltombe at the public hearing on January 28, arguing that "it could not established [*sic*] that she had deliberately broken the law." One week later, she was nonetheless found guilty as charged.[124]

Deltombe's case clearly indicates the conflict between the individual hospitality and the state hospitality, in which the ethics of hospitality and the politics of hospitality fundamentally clash. Furthermore, Deltombe's case shows that one cannot separate the public/state hospitality from the *legal* identity of the guest. In order to abide state hospitality, one must practice one's individual hospitality only in so far as one is able to confirm the *legality* of the identity of the guest.

The ongoing conflict between private hospitality and official, public hospitality was evident when Arizona Governor Jan Brewer, for instance, signed an immigration bill on April 23, 2010, that legally sanctioned police to stop anyone and request proper documentation to prove one is not *illegal* immigrant. This Arizona immigration law "would require anyone whom police suspect of being in the country illegally to produce 'an alien registration document,' such as a green card or other proof of citizenship, such as a passport or Arizona driver's license."[125] The Arizona governor made these opening remarks right before she signed the bill in her office in front of the press: "We in Arizona have been more than patient waiting for Washington to act .... But decades of federal inaction and misguided policy have created an unacceptable situation."[126] Who would be the *we* in her remarks and what would be an *unacceptable situation*? The governor used *we* as if there were a community of action within which "to establish a *we* on the basis of the work that had been done, a *we* that would also be likely to form a community of action."[127] Foucault makes an observation about the problem of the abstract *we*:

> [T]he problem is ....to decide if it is actually suitable to place oneself within a "we" in order to assert the principles one recognizes and the values one accepts; or if it is not, rather, necessary to make the future formation of a "we" possible, by elaborating the question. Because it seems to me that the "we" must not be previous to the question; it can only be the result—the necessarily temporary result—of the question as it is posed in the new terms in which one formulates it.[128]

In the officially defined notion of *legality* in the Arizona case, it becomes clear that the hospitality question is truly the *foreigner question*. Here, not just one's nationality or citizenship, but the skin color of one's body, becomes a crucial determinant of whether one can be a potential-criminal, which can legally result in police interrogation, scrutinization, and being locked behind bars until one can provide a legal document. When one is a Hispanic, for instance, s/he "just became a suspect and open to police harassment."[129] Now people in Arizona may come to cultivate distrust of the darker body, and to perceive a *foreigner* with a darker skin color as a potential suspect for illegality. When Arizona legalizes this kind of xenophobic reaction, the state of Arizona is, in fact, promoting people's negative perceptions of *foreigners* with darker skin as *somehow* illegitimate, or suspicious, even when they may visit Arizona as good customers, intending to spend their money through commercial tourism. This kind of action on the part of the state results not only in *racial profiling* but also in *bioprofiling* based on the color of one's body. Now the state of Arizona can legally exercise its explicit *biopower* over a *foreign body* by means of the new immigration law, which can be what Foucault calls one of the "diverse techniques for achieving the subjugations of bodies and the control of populations."[130]

Therefore, the conflict between personal hospitality and state hospitality is a serious dilemma in practicing hospitality, because "the implied consequence of the state's right to interfere in the definition of what constitutes an authorized guest is that the host's house is a subset of the national territory and that private gestures of hospitality are always a subcategory of national hospitality."[131] Here, in order not to get criminalized by the state, the host must become an *identity checker*, policing the guest to determine whether the guest can be an *authorized guest* or not. However, the Bible message clearly connects neighbor-love-as-self-love with an unconditional hospitality toward an alien: "Do not mistreat the foreigners who reside in your land. The foreigner who lives among you must be treated like one of your own. Love them as you love yourself, for you too were a foreigner" (Lev. 19:33–34, Inclusive). In this context, the Christian notion of neighbor-love encounters a fundamental dilemma: How can one practice neighbor-love when the state defines the nature and scope of that very neighbor-love, and when hospitality, a substantial form of neighbor-love, is only a subcategory of state/public hospitality? How far can Christians "extend hospitality to strangers" (Rom. 12:13)? In a contemporary world where a nation-state regulates and dictates all forms of hospitality and *neighbor-love* by individuals, there are so many cases in which the issue of hospitality, as a form of neighbor-love, is not just a matter of the relation of an individual host and the guest, but a matter for the host-guest-state—the "triangular structure."[132] The triangular structure of hospitality in our reality indicates that a theology of hospitality as neighbor-love needs to be always *context-specific*, and that there is no way we can practice *hospitality as neighbor-love* in an idealized, romanticized, universalized manner.

Derrida makes a distinction between *relative hospitality* and *absolute hospitality*. Relative hospitality is *hospitality of invitation*, in which *I* am the one who chooses who gets to be invited and remain as the *master* of the house. When *I* offer this hospitality of invitation, *I*, as the initiator of the invitation, set the boundaries—such as: "'Come, come to me, feel at home,' 'But you should respect my house, my language, my rules, the rules of my nation,

....'You are welcome, but under some conditions.'"[133] However, in the case of absolute hospitality, I am neither choosing the guests nor initiating the invitation because it is *hospitality of visitation*. It is an unexpected *visitation*, and the unexpected visitor just comes and is welcomed without any preconditions or rules. It "falls upon" me, "comes over me," and just "happens" as an "event" without predictability.[134] Here, with the unconditionality of welcoming, the absolute hospitality moves beyond the borderline between the host and the guest.

Derrida rightly contends that the question of hospitality is a *foreigner-question*.[135] At the age of twelve in Algeria, he got expelled from school because of his being Jew. Although he got to return to school after a year, he "never forgot how it felt to be a victim of discrimination, deprived of civil rights, and treated as an unwanted foreigner in his own land."[136] Derrida became a *foreigner* in his homeland, deprived of his citizenship with "the brutality of a unilateral decision."[137]

> I was very young at that time, and I certainly did not understand very well—already, I did not understand very well—what citizenship and loss of citizenship *meant to say*. But I do not doubt that exclusion—from the school reserved for young French citizens—could have a relationship to the disorder of identity. . .[138]

There are over 14 million refugees in the world, according to the *World Refugee Survey 2008*.[139] This figure does not include boat people, migrant workers imported by the industrial nations, *foreign* domestic and child care workers, seasonal agricultural workers whose legal status nations have categorized under *undocumented*, and also those who are characterized as homeless, who are dislocated from their home. In the twenty-first century, an increasing numbers of people have become dislocated or displaced from ethnic, national, regional locations. In the midst of all forms of displacements and dislocations, how people receive the *new arrivant*—individually and collectively, personally and institutionally, culturally and sociopolitically—becomes a more and more significant theological issue.

Gender-Troubling Hospitality: A Massive Failure of Hospitality

It is impossible to discuss hospitality without acknowledging the gender-troubling issue in the discourse and exercise of hospitality. There is a clear elimination of the women figure as part of the host-guest pair in the *exemplary* hospitality story. There are two examples of distorted gender-troubling practice of hospitality in the Bible: hospitality by Lot in Genesis 19 and by a Levite in Judges 19. The problem with these two stories about hospitality lies in its extreme violation of the *rights* of women to protect the rights of men, the guests. Lot offers his daughters to "the men of Sodom, both young and old, all the people to the last man, [who] surrounded the house" (Gen. 19:4), in order to offer hospitality to two male guests: "Look, I have two daughters who have not known a man; let me bring them out to you, and do to them as you please; only do nothing to these men, for they have come under the shelter of my roof" (Gen. 19: 8). While the guests were enjoying the protection of hospitality by the host, two voiceless women were facing extreme hostility from their own father, who is completely disregarding the human dignity of his own daughters. In another story of hospitality in Judges, there is a case of gender-troubling hospitality similar to the story in Genesis 19. A master of the house offers his hospitality to his male guest, a Levite, and protects his guest from the mob through the act of offering the lives of two women:

> "No, my brothers, do not act so wickedly. Since this man is my guest, do not do this vile thing. Here are my virgin daughter and his concubine; let me bring them out now. Ravish them and do whatever you want to them; but against this man do not do such a vile thing." (Judg. 19: 23–24)

When the crowd did not listen to the word of the master of the house, the Levite, the guest, seized his own concubine and took her out to the male crowd, who "wantonly raped her, and abused her all through the night until the morning" (Judg. 19:25). Here the story of hospitality does not reveal whether the woman who is repeatedly gang-raped until morning is still alive when her master stumbles over her on the threshold the next day, because there is no voice from her. But what is certain is that the guest-Levite, upon his return to his home, "took a knife, and grasping his concubine he cut her into twelve pieces, limb by limb, and sent her throughout all the territory of Israel" (Judg. 19:29). The host-man of the house uses women as a *gift* to exercise hospitality to his guests. The author of this story of hospitality deliberately opts for the *absence*, the *invisibility* of the women that the host uses as the *gift* to the "men of the city" as a way of exercising hospitality to his guest.

These biblical stories about hospitality in Genesis and Judges have one thing in common: The hospitality to male guests at the expense of women. The male hosts perform the exercise of hospitality to one party (male *beings,* the guests) in the same space they perform acts of extreme hostility toward the other party (female *non-beings*). The male hosts treat those women as nonbeings, *living-dead,* the *homo sacer*. The scenes of hospitality *for* the male guests and *by* the male hosts turn into scenes of the brutal hostility of (potential or actual) betrayal, abuse, violence, rape, and murder for the woman-other, who does not belong to the primordial guests-hosts figures. The female-being appears neither as a host nor as the guest, but only as a victim of hostility in the name of hospitality toward the male-guests.

Christians have often used the story of Sodom as the biblical ground for the demonization of homosexuality. In his *The Invention of Sodomy in Christian Theology,* Mark Jordan rightly contends: "[T]he Old Testament story about the destruction of Sodom cannot be read as a lesson about divine punishment of same sex copulation. If any lesson is wanted from the story, the lesson would be about hospitality."[140] In spite of his sensitivity to the homophobic interpretation, however, he does not seem to recognize the unbelievably violent patriarchal nature of the *lesson* about hospitality in the story of Sodom. *Sodom* is symbolic not for the sin of homosexuality but for the sin of hostility to the angels, guests, strangers, or foreigners. Debunking the homophobic interpretation of the Bible passage is of course important. At the same time, however, scrutinizing the extreme patriarchal practice of hospitality is significant in freeing the text from the distorted interpretation and uncritically and monolithically constructed *lesson* that often overlooks the voices of the voiceless victims. These two biblical stories about hospitality indicate that "rules of hospitality in Israel protect only males.... and no hospitality safeguards" women.[141] As one can see in these stories of hospitality in the Bible, a *non-inclusive* hospitality can be against the very principle of hospitality and can easily turn out to be the exercise of hostility toward the other.

In these biblical stories of hospitality, the hosts, the mobs, and crowds are men, who are at the center of power. In these scenes of the practice of hospitality, women do not have even voice, as if they are *nonbeings*—the *subalterns,* the *absolute victims*. One must note that the subaltern is not simply the oppressed, the exploited, the excluded, or the marginalized. The subaltern is "structurally and systemically written out or excluded from any hegemonic ideology, official history, developed economic structure, or political system of representation."[142] The *subaltern,* as the spoken subject/object, is the name given by the namers, but not by the subaltern her/himself. The subaltern can be present only in complete absence. *Its-possible-presence-only-in-complete-absence* is what/who the subaltern is. The *subaltern* is, therefore, the *absolute victim* "who cannot even protest ....cannot even identify the victim as victim ....cannot even present himself or herself as such ....is totally excluded or covered over by language, annihilated by history, a victim one cannot identify."[143] In this sense, Spivak concludes, "the subaltern cannot speak"[144]and "if the subaltern can speak then, thank God, the subaltern is not a subaltern any more."[145] Even if the subaltern speaks, who will listen? What constitutes *speaking* here would always relate to *listening* or *being listened.*

Those women in the two bible stories about hospitality can be *spoken objects* but never *speaking subjects*, not because they lack a physical voice, but because no one would listen even if they . To my question about the issue of the *subalternspeaking,* Spivak replies: "When the subaltern attempts to speak, she is not heard .... [I]f the person is somehow heard collectively, then the subalternity is not."[146] In this sense, the question of what constitutes *speaking* is the question of what constitutes *listening,* and these two acts, *speaking* and *listening,* are inextricably intertwined. Those women who become the victims of the hosts' offering of hospitality in the Bible are the *subalterns,* the absolute victims whose very *singular* existences get denied by the hosts who attempt to offer an *unconditional* hospitality to the strangers. The male hosts exercise such unconditional hospitality to the male strangers through the act of an unbelievable hostility toward the women's singular existence. These female victims may have *spoken,* but no one *listened,* as there is no trace of their *voice* in the Bible story of hospitality: a *gender-troubling* hospitality. These voiceless and nameless women are the witnesses to the *massive failure of hospitality,* to both the limit and extent of Abrahamic hospitality. The biblical configuration of Abrahamic hospitality reveals the double-edges of hospitality: the impossibility and necessity of cosmopolitan planetary hospitality. Abraham, who practiced unconditional hospitality to the three *strangers*—the distant others—denies the protection of the *rights* of his own *family*—the concrete others: Hagar and Ishmael. Furthermore, Abraham, who decisively exercises unconditional hospitality to God, practices hostility toward his son Isaac.

In contrast to the discourse of hospitality in the Bible, in which women are completely absent and muted, Derrida takes woman's maternity as an important site of hospitality. Derrida symbolizes hospitality as a pregnancy, and the pregnant mother as both host and hostage to her child inside of her. Welcoming her child (the unknown guest) requires the mother (the host) to go through a long period of waiting, to engage in intense labor, to take risks, and to locate herself in an extremely vulnerable position. So the woman in pregnancy becomes both host and hostage to the guest, the awaiting child. In this sense, Derrida posits:

> [T]he question of hospitality is also the question of waiting, of the time of waiting and of waiting beyond time .... [W]hat belabors hospitality at its core [*ce qui travaille l'hospitalité en son sein*], what works it like a labor, like a pregnancy, life a promise as much as a threat,

> what settles in it, within it [*en son dedans*], like a Trojan horse, the enemy (*hostis*) as much as the *avenir,* intestine hostility, is indeed a contradictory conception, a thwarted [*contrariée*] conception, or a contraception of awaiting, a contradiction of welcoming itself. And something that binds, perhaps, as in Isaac's pregnancy [*la grossesse d'Isaac*], the laughter at pregnancy, at the announcement of childbirth. Abraham ….laughs, like Sarah, at the announcement of Isaac's birth.[147]

Derrida connects the woman's maternity to the issue of *non-substitutable substitution,* which is completely different from substitutable substitution. The non-substitutable substitution, or what Derrida calls *true substitution,* is an "absolutely singular and irreplaceable existence that, in a free act, substitutes itself for another, makes itself responsible for another, expiates for another, sacrifices itself for another outside of any homogeneous series" and is "not the indifferent replacement of an equal thing by an equal or identical thing."[148] In this *true substitution,* it is impossible to regard one as "you, for example,"[149] which implies the replaceability of one's being with another. It is stimulating to see how Derrida attends to the issue of women's absence in the discourse of hospitality by presenting women's maternity as an example of sacred hospitality, which has been missing and distorted in the traditional discourse and practice of Abrahamic hospitality. The Abrahamic prayer of Sodom, according to Louis Massignon, is the "reassertion of sacred hospitality in exactly the place where it had been violated, and offering that prayer Abraham signaled for his entire tradition the necessity for ultimate acceptance of otherness at the heart of what is regarded as proper to one's self."[150]

Hospitality as Welcoming of the Epiphany of the Face

I have been traveling for most of my adult life, and travel seems to be an *act of certainty* rather than a process of question. The itinerary of my travel always seems to offer the certainty of clear points of departure and arrival. However, the more I travel, the more I become puzzled about this very certainty of the act of travel. The seeming certainty that the itinerary seems to provide is, in fact, a fundamentally vulnerable uncertainty, because the certainty of my departure or arrival entirely depends on the attitude of the permitter of my departure or the receiver of my arrival. If the receiver, the gatekeeper at my arrival, does not allow me to arrive in the very territory of my arrival, there is no way that I can actually arrive. The certainty of my arrival is entirely dependent on the receiver of me as a new arrivant. When one arrives, one's existence is in an extremely vulnerable position. So *being a new arrivant* is a matter of vulnerability and resistance, confinement and freedom, acceptance and rejection, hospitality and hostility. Whenever I arrive, the most common question that I have to deal with is, "Who are you?" The receiver of a new arrivant gets to ask the question "*Who are you?*" which in fact means, "What *are you?*" in a legal sense. Here, the question "*Who/What are you?*" is in between *located* and *dislocated, placed* and *displaced.* In this context, it is true that one can link the question of hospitality *to* and *of* the question of the foreigner/stranger.[151]

This everyday, ordinary question, "*Who are you?*" which involves asking one's singular *proper name,* is a *liminal* question, which can be either an opening gesture of welcoming invitation or an opening for interrogation of one's membership, belonging, citizenship, or identity. The question is on the threshold that can lead to the door of either hospitality or hostility. In this regard, the "*Who are you?*" question falls between hospitality and hostility. Derrida calls this ordinary, everyday question a "question of hospitality," a question that can reject or accept, exclude or include, the *arrivant,* the stranger, the *foreigner*:

> [T]his foreigner who has the right to hospitality in the cosmopolitan tradition ....is someone with whom, to receive him [*sic*] you begin by asking his name; you enjoin him to state and to guarantee his identity; as you would a witness before a court. This is someone to whom you put a question and address a demand, the first demand, the minimal demand being: "What is your name?" or then "In telling me what your name is, in responding to this request, you are responding on your own behalf, you are responsible before the law and before your hosts, you are a subject in law.[152]

Whether the "*Who are you?*" question is a hospitable *welcoming* question or a hostile *interrogating* one would depend on the *face* of the receiver of the new arrivant. One cannot *welcome* the newcomer without smile, laughter, or tears of joy. One's face, even without a spoken word, conveys the message to the arrivant. When one is *welcoming* the arrivant, one looks into the eyes of the arrivant with an expression of welcoming. The arrivant also presents him- or herself in his/her face. Thus, according to Levinas, the ethical relation is the "face-to-face relation."[153]

Whenever I travel overseas, I have to go through passport control. Although I have been to so many countries, there is no *face* that I encounter from the passport control booth that I have had to go through. The relationship between the officer in the booth and myself is entirely a judicial one, not an ethical one. S/he and I do not make genuine eye contact, nor exchange any genuine friendly smile. When I enter into the U.S. site, the fact that I do not possess a *strong passport,* having citizenship from a country other than the U.S. or Western Europe, makes the officer turn to the mode of judicial suspicion about my arrival. The "*Who are you?*" question, without face-to-face relation, without exchange of welcoming smile, laughter, or tears of joy, becomes an opening question of investigation for a site of power-exercise. This is the moment when the *singularity* of *who-I-am* with a singular face collapses into the anonymous, collective *they,* whose primary identity markers are national belonging. I become an anonymous *arrivant* without a singular *face*. The officers may have seen countless faces of *foreigners,* but they do not look at the *face* of *the arrivant* with a proper name and existence of singularity. Here, one's *face* becomes a profound metaphor for cosmopolitan hospitality, resistance, and responsibility.

Emmanuel Levinas eloquently claims that "the face resists possession, resists my powers"[154]and "the face speaks to me and thereby invites me to a relation incommensurate with a power exercised, be it enjoyment or knowledge."[155] He further contends:

> The face opens the primordial discourse whose first word is obligation, which no "interiority" permits avoiding .... The face in its nakedness as a face presents to me the destitution of the poor one and the stranger; but this poverty and exile which appeal to my powers, address me, do not deliver themselves over to these powers as givens, remain the expression of the face. The poor one, the stranger, presents himself [*sic*] as an equal. He comes to *join* me ....By essence the prophetic word responds to the epiphany of the face . . .[156]

In this sense, the human *face* precedes speaking and writing in human encounter and communication. When one encounters the other person—the singular person—the two look at the faces of one another, and the initial response to this encounter comes from both sides through/with/in their *faces*. Therefore, the face is "of itself visitation and transcendence"[157] and, at the same time, is "*visit* and *visitation*."[158] As Levinas rightly contends, the neighbor as the other is *face,* and the other's *face* is "not a metaphor, not a figure ....does not signify, does not present itself as a sign, but expresses itself, offering itself in person, in itself . . ."[159] Cosmopolitan *gaze* is to look at the individual person in the *face* and to acknowledge the fundamental value and rights simply because of being human with *face*. One's *face* precedes, I argue, one's proper name and any kind of identity marker. In this sense, one should ground cosmopolitan justice and rights not in one's citizenship, national belonging, or any identity marker, but rather in the very *face,* the bearer of human singularity. One of the examples of this *cosmopolitan gaze* is Jesus' gaze in the story of his encounter with Zacchaeus. The initial act of Jesus was looking at the *face* of Zacchaeus. Jesus did not preach nor criticize him for being wrong. Instead, Jesus just looked into his *face.* When Jesus looked at his face, a *miracle,* an unexpected transformation, happened. No one was able to predict what would happen between Jesus and Zacchaeus, or explain why it happened:

> A man was there named Zacchaeus; he was a chief tax collector and was rich. He was trying to see who Jesus was, but on account of the crowd he could not, because he was short in stature. So he ran ahead and climbed a sycamore tree to see him, because he was going to pass that way. When Jesus came to the place, he looked up and said to him, "Zacchaeus, hurry and come down; for I must stay at your house today." So he hurried down and was happy to welcome him. All who saw it began to grumble and said, "He has gone to be the guest of one who is a sinner." Zacchaeus stood there and said to the Lord, "Look, half of my possessions, Lord, I will give to the poor; and if I have defrauded anyone of anything, I will pay back four times as much." Then Jesus said to him, "Today salvation has come to this house, because he too is a son of Abraham. For the Son of Man came to seek out and to save the lost." (Lk. 19:2–10)

In this story, Jesus looks at Zacchaeus' *face.* For Zacchaeus, as a short person and tax collector, it must have been the first time in his life time that someone truly looked at his *face* with a nonjudgmental, embracing, affirming, genuinely humane gaze—he whom most people around him must have hated, dismissed, and, at best, failed to unrecognized. What Jesus did was to look at the *face* of Zacchaeus, and Zacchaeus also was able to see the face of Jesus. Jesus did not set any precondition for his affirming of Zacchaeus as who he was, such as repentance or religious conversion. There was also no hierarchy of beings between these two faces. The *event* of the face-to-face encounter was in liminal time. No one could make a prediction of this *event,* of this face-to-face encounter. Jesus' first act was looking at Zacchaeus in his face, and his first utterance was, "I must stay at your house." There is no question of *whether, shall I,* or *may I.* The very liminal space between *hospitality* and *hostility* turns into the absolute willing of hospitality from both Jesus and Zacchaeus. Here the seemingly self-evident border between the host and the guest becomes blurry and pointless through Jesus' act of border-traversing. Zacchaeus completely welcomes the uninvited visitation, and Jesus offers an invitation of himself to Zacchaeus. Jesus initiates moving beyond the rigid boundaries between the home, the host, and the guest, and the borders between visitation and invitation. What happens at the moment two persons look at each other's *face* is beyond our ordinary perception of who is the inviter or invited. Here happens the absolute welcome of the epiphany of the face of the other as *uninvited* or *mutually-invited* guest: Jesus to Zacchaeus and Zacchaeus to Jesus. Numerous places in the Bible talk about being a *stranger/ foreigner:* "No matter where I am on earth, I am a foreigner" (Ps. 119:19, Inclusive). If we are *strangers/foreigners* on earth, who need to receive hospitality from others for our survival, then claiming the ownership of certain territory or patronizing others, as if there is a hierarchy of beings, become pointless. Abrahamic hospitality, for example, is a paradigmatic illustration of biblical hospitality: the unconditional welcoming of the epiphany of the *face* of strangers. Abraham "bowed down to the ground" (Gen. 18:2) to welcome the faces of the three strangers and then served the strangers with water, bread, and meat. Here the host, Abraham, offers his hospitality to the guests—who appear not by *invitation* but by *visitation*—without calculation or asking their *identity*. Therefore, "radical hospitality consists, *would have* to consist, of *receiving without invitation,* beyond or before the invitation."[160] In this sense, hospitality is about the rights of the guests, the strangers, the foreigners—not to be treated with hostility but with hospitality when they appear in the territory of the host *without invitation,* as Kant stresses. Quoting Louis Massignon, a Catholic scholar of Islam, Derrida highlights the significant meaning of hospitality—of welcoming the stranger, the other, the guest, in one's quest for *truth,* for the Sacred:

> The hôte is the messenger of God. Abraham's hospitality is a sign of announcing the final completion of the gathering of all nations, blessed in Abraham, in this Holy Land which must be monopolized by none. (…) This notion of sacred hospitality seems to me essential for a search after truth between men [*sic*], in our itineraries and our work, here below, and toward the threshold of the hereafter. (…) With hospitality, we find the Sacred at the center of our destinies' mystery, like secret and divine alms. (…) This mystery touches the very bottom of the mystery of the Trinity, where God is at once Guest [*Hôte*], Host [*Hospitalier*], and Home [*Foyer*].[161]

Theologically and ontologically speaking, we humans are indeed *foreigners* and *strangers* on the earth. As *guests* of this cosmos, we appear at the last moment of God's creation. No one should be *at-home,* because we are nothing *but strangers* in this cosmos. Derrida thus rightly contends: "Hospitality is the deconstruction of the at-home; deconstruction is hospitality to the other, to the other than oneself, the other than 'its other,' to an other who is beyond any 'its other.'"[162]How one can *love* one's neighbors would start with the proclamation, as Levinas says, "'Thanks to God' I am another for the others,"[163] and the recognition that the "passing of God, of whom I can speak only by reference to this aid or this grace, is precisely the reverting of the incomparable subject into a member of society."[164] In one's act of neighbor-love in a form of unconditional hospitality, it is impossible for one to operate a hierarchy between I and others. Frantz Fanon laments the current configuration of the hierarchy of being, and invites us to think about *neighborly love*:

> Superiority? Inferiority?
> Why not the quite simple attempt to touch the other,
> To feel the other,
> To explain the other to myself?
> Was my freedom not given to me then in order to build the world of the *You*?[165]

When there is no hierarchy of beings, there would be a genuine exchange of smiles and laughter between me and the others. Therefore, "it is difficult to dissociate a culture of hospitality from a culture of laughter or a culture of a smile,"[166] because "it is hard to imagine a scene of hospitality during which one welcomes without smiling at the other, without giving a sign of joy or pleasure, without smiling at the other as at the welcoming of a promise."[167] Simply attempting to *touch* the other, as Fanon invites us, can mean entering into a political risk of taking a side between the ethics of hospitality and the politics of hospitality. Therefore, the question one would wrestle with before touching the other would be, as Derrida asks:

> Does hospitality consist in interrogating the new arrival? Does it begin with the question addressed to the newcomer ....[W]hat is your name? tell me your name, what should I call you, I who am calling on you, I who want to call you by your name? What am I going to call you? It is also what we sometimes tenderly ask children and those we love. Or else does hospitality begin with the unquestioning welcome, in a double effacement, the effacement of the question *and* the name? Is it more just and more loving to question or not to question? to call by the name or without the name? to give or to learn a name already given? Does one give hospitality to a subject? to an identifiable subject? to a subject identifiable by name? to a legal subject? Or is hospitality *rendered,* is it *given* to the

> other before they are identified, even before they are (posited as or supposed to be) a subject, legal subject and subject nameable by their family name, etc.?[168]

Those questions that Derrida invokes convince one to concur with his statement that "the question of hospitality is thus also the question of the question."[169] Hospitality is, according to Derrida, constituted by a negotiation between two imperatives: *unconditional* hospitality and *conditional* hospitality. The unconditional imperative is to unconditionally welcome and receive the arrivant before asking questions, or knowing name or identity, whereas the conditional imperative is to welcome someone in particular, with a name and identity. Derrida goes on to say about this unconditional welcoming of the arrivant who does not have any identity marker or document except his/her face—the unconditional hospitality toward the *absolute arrivant* without host's invitation: "The absolute *arrivant* does not yet have a name or an identity."[170]

Radical hospitality, the unconditional hospitality, means to unconditionally receive the arrivant *without, beyond, before* the invitation, and is therefore *hospitality by visitation.*[171] Whereas the *unconditional* hospitality is ethical, the *conditional* hospitality is political. Here, the ethical and the political are the two poles that are irreducible to one another and, at the same time, they remain indissociable because the ethics of hospitality, the *unconditional* hospitality, is a permanent reference for the politics of hospitality, the *conditional* hospitality.

> Pure hospitality consists in welcoming the *arrivant,* the one who arrives, before laying down any conditions, before knowing or asking anything of him [*sic*], whether this is a name or a piece of identification. But this pure hospitality also presupposes that one addresses him, and singularly so, that one thus calls him and acknowledges a proper name for him. "What is your name?" Hospitality consists in doing everything to address the other; it consists in granting him, indeed in asking him, his name, all the while trying to prevent this question from becoming a "condition," a police interrogation, an inquest or an investigation, or a border check. The difference is subtle and yet fundamental, a question asked on the threshold of one's home and on the threshold between two inflections.[172]

The guest or arrivant is like an *event* that visits us but whom we cannot ultimately identify, anticipate, or foresee. The absolute arrivant, the uninvited guest, just falls upon us. In this regard, the unconditional hospitality is always "hospitality toward the event."[173] Here the *singularity* of the arrivant is significant because, whoever the arrivant is, the arrivant has her or his own uniqueness in simply being who s/he is as human. When there is a disparity of rights and power between two subjects—the host and the guest, the other, the foreigner—hospitality means fundamental welcoming, unconditional receptivity by the host toward the other. Jesus' parable of the last judgment in Matthew reveals how *hospitality* constitutes the core of Jesus' teaching:

> "The ruler will say to those on the right, 'Come, you blessed of my Abba God! Inherit the kindom prepared for you from the creation of the world! For I was hungry and you fed me;I was thirsty and you gave me drink. I was a stranger and you welcomed me; naked and you clothed me. I was ill and you comforted me; in prison and you came to visit me.... The truth is, every time you did this for the least of my sisters and brothers, you did it for me.'" (Mt. 25:35–46, Inclusive).

Here the boundary between neighbor, enemy, God, and I becomes blurry, as they are inextricably interconnected. When *I*, as the host, practice unconditional hospitality to others, what I do to the guest, both by invitation and visitation, becomes what I do to God, the final Judge. Jesus introduces a new commandment to his disciples in his farewell discourse: "I give you a new commandment, that you love one another. Just as I have loved you, you also should love one another. By this everyone will know that you are my disciples, if you have love for one another" (Jn. 13:34–35). Jesus' farewell address contains an extremely significant theological insight for the question what it means to be Jesus' disciples. Christians have regarded being Jesus' disciples as identical with having membership in a Christian church, or being a zealous proselytizer. However, Jesus' farewell address reaffirms the essential nature of being Jesus' disciples: practicing love, exercising an unconditional hospitality—showing compassion to the other, to the stranger, to the foreigner, to the guest.

There are numerous indications in Jesus' teaching that practicing hospitality is a way to *inherit eternal life*, and that loving oneself, neighbor, and enemy is in fact loving Jesus and God, in which neighbor/enemy-love-as-self-love becomes identical with Jesus-love/God-love. When a lawyer asked Jesus how one can inherit eternal life, Jesus' answer was direct and simple: Love God and neighbor as yourself. When asked who one's neighbor is, Jesus introduced the story of the Samaritan's hospitality as an exemplar of neighbor-love. A Samaritan offers unconditional hospitality to the unknown stranger who is half-dead by robbers: taking care of his wounds with oil and wine, taking him to an inn, and looking after him overnight. The next day, the Samarian offers money to the innkeeper and says, "Take care of him; and when I come back, I will repay you whatever more you spend" (Lk. 10:35). The Samaritan offers the gift of hospitality to the unknown stranger without checking the identity of the stranger, without expecting any return, without leaving him any debt of gift, of reciprocity. The story of the Samaritan is a profound example of an unconditional hospitality and compassion. One needs to free Jesus from the religiously doctrinated box in order to hear the profound message that Jesus conveys. There is no message about any kind of religious doctrine or religious belonging in Jesus' teachings about loving God, inheriting eternal life, or being Jesus' disciples, which are the key issues in Christian life and teaching.

The biblical example of unconditional hospitality reaches its peak at Jesus' Last Supper: "While they were eating, he took a loaf of bread, and after blessing it he broke it, gave it to them, and said: 'Take; this is my body.' Then he took a cup, and after giving thanks he gave it to them, and all of them drank from it. He said to them, 'This is my blood of the covenant, which is poured out for many'" (Mk. 14:22–24). Offering one's body and blood symbolizes offering one's entire being itself for the other. Here Jesus, as the host of the supper, offers all that constitutes who he is—body and blood—to his guests without condition, without debt of return, without questioning their identity or scrutinizing their loyalty or authenticity. There is no economy of hospitality in Jesus' unconditional offering of his whole being—body and blood—to the guests. Jesus' Last Supper is an exemplar of the cosmopolitan theology of hospitality, in which one can experience the unconditionality of hospitality—the absolute hospitality. Christian churches have instrumentalized Jesus' Last Supper through the institution of Eucharist. Unfortunately, however, Christian churches have doctrinated Jesus' act of unconditional hospitality into the logic of inclusion and exclusion, into a site of religious or denominational *identity-checking*. Contrary to what Jesus exercised, the unconditional love and hospitality, the institutionalization of the Last Supper turns into the institution of Eucharist, which has become an impetus for division within Christianity, and the focus of hostility toward the religious other among various churches in the history of Christianity.

Jesus' washing of his disciples' feet is another example of unconditional hospitality. The only thing that he asks of his disciples is to wash one another's feet as he has done to them (Jn. 13:3–15). Washing one's feet signifies an utmost act of hospitality and a humble offering of caring to the other. Practicing hospitality involves spiritual, physical, cultural, and sociopolitical dimensions of human reality. When Martin Luther says, "God Himself [*sic*] is in our home, is being fed at our house, is lying down and resting,"[174] this simple sentence symbolizes the nature and depth of unconditional hospitality in a concrete human reality. Religion in general and Christianity in particular are about neighbor-love, and neighbor-love is about hospitality. Being hospitable to those like-minded is not necessarily an act of hospitality. Practicing hospitality is a radically political act of risk-taking and boundary-crossing. When one romanticizes hospitality, hospitality becomes depoliticized, apoliticized, as one can see from the following remarks on hospitality:

> [T]o describe hospitality is to describe the delightfulness of being human. To be human is to know hospitality. In her bounty and beauty, Mother Nature, our planet Earth, provides hospitality so that we might live. Each human comes into the world after having enjoyed the hospitality of mother's body, of mother's sacred womb.[175]

Here the author connects hospitality to *Mother Nature* and a mother's womb without offering an explanation for who *mother* would be in our reality, if not just a biological mother. *Poeticization* of hospitality can offer an imaginative power to expand the horizon of hospitality. However, there is a danger in this romanticized attitude to hospitality, because, in the course of romanticization, that very hospitality becomes depoliticized, apoliticized, and anti-politicized—when, meanwhile, the hospitality in human day-to-day reality requires a politically impossible and ethically unconditional boundary-crossing such as one can experience, for example, among undocumented immigrants. When one romanticizes the concept of hospitality, she or he does not want to deal with the troubling side in practicing hospitality. If hospitality is about being hospitable to those like-minded, to those in the same *circles* based on religion, race, ethnicity, class, sexuality, and so on, it is not in fact an act of hospitality, an act of love, as Jesus says: "If you love those who love you, what credit is that to you? Even sinners love those who love them" (Lk. 6:32). In this regard, one locates hospitality discourse in a mode of *naturalized romanticization,* using the metaphor of *Mother Nature* as if there is no power-differential between/among people, religions, or nations, but only an endless giving and sharing of one's resources (here, *Mother Nature*) and space (here, *mother's sacred womb*) in our reality. Jesus' command to love not only one's neighbor but also one's *enemy* as oneself requires one to commit oneself to a passion for the endless border-crossing, unconditional hospitality that deterritorializes the very boundaries between self, neighbor, and enemy in human spheres of epistemology, ethics, and politics.

One can only *imagine* the nature of *planetary hospitality,* as we humans have never shown it in its entirety, which is to regard every individual being on the planet as deserving an ethical universal singularity as the ground of hospitality. In this sense, the cosmopolitan theology of hospitality that I propose is *planetary* in its scope and is *of singularity* in its nature: *planetary hospitality of singularity*. *Singularity* here does not mean an indifference to a communal belonging, such as being Christian, being Buddhist, being Asian, being women, being gay, etc. Instead, one should relate *singularity* to "only in its being *such as it is*," which is "neither universal nor an individual included in a series."[176] Agamben contends that singularity is "singularity insofar as it is whatever singularity,"[177] and he goes on to argue:

> In this conception, such-and-such being is reclaimed from its having this or that property, which identifies it as belonging to this or that set, to this or that class (the reds, the French, the Muslims)—and it is reclaimed not for another class nor for the simple generic absence of any belonging, but for its being-*such*, for belonging itself. Thus being-*such*, which remains constantly hidden in the condition of belonging ("there is an *x* such that it belongs to *y*") and which is in no way a real predicate, comes to light itself: The singularity exposed as such is whatever you *want*, that is, lovable.[178]

Therefore, the *hospitality of singularity* is the hospitality offered based on neither one's unchanging *essence-as-such* nor one's position of belonging, but on one's very existence-as-being-*such*, which is indefinable, non-fixed, irreplaceable, ever-becoming, and ever-evolving. When one dismisses another's *singularity*, the hospitality that one would offer to others is distorting and misleading.

Cosmopolitan Planetary Hospitality: Toward a Community-to-Come

Spivak makes a distinction between *globe* and *planet*. As she lucidly puts it: "The globe is in our computer. No one lives there ....The planet is in the species of alterity, belonging to another system and yet we inhabit it, on loan." Therefore, she declares, "I propose the planet to overwrite the globe. Globalization is the imposition of the same system of exchange everywhere."[179] However, she clearly differentiates her planet-talk from *unexamined environmentalism* because "[t]o talk planet-talk by way of an unexamined environmentalism, referring to an undivided 'natural' space rather than a differentiated political space, can work in the interest of this globalization in the mode of the abstract as such."[180] Planetary hospitality is to offer oneself, whether one is an individual person, community, or state, to the other because "to be human is to be intended toward the other."[181] Cosmopolitan discourse of planetary hospitality invites us to fundamentally rethink how we understand our responsibility to others, including the most vulnerable members of our community, and what constitutes membership in the community, when even so-called democratic communities tend to drift toward exclusion of people based on race, nationality, sexuality, gender, ability, citizenship, and so on. The issue of *hospitality* today is not only ethical and sociogeopolitical, but also a theological issue, and it should be for "the community of those who do not have a community."[182]

In this context, the hospitality discourse should be primarily a discourse of *rights* rather than a discourse of *generosity* or *charity*, as is often the case. The act of hospitality is a form of generosity by the host, whether an individual person or the state, but it often ends up being ruthless forms of the *non-rights* of the guests, once the guests seem to cross the borderline. Here the seemingly self-evident borderline between the host and the guest is, in fact, fundamentally problematic, especially when it comes to the issue of migrant workers, for instance, who help the host country build its cities and factories and do most "dirty" work. In a discourse of hospitality as a discourse of *rights*, the relationship between the host and the guest always presupposes equality. Since the context of the practice of hospitality varies, people often get caught in contradictions that are extremely hard to resolve in concrete daily reality. Derrida is clear in designating hospitality an issue of *rights*, when he argues, "The combat against xenophobia and racism *also goes* via this right to vote. So long as it is not gained, injustice will reign, democracy will be limited to that extent, and the riposte to racism will remain abstract and impotent."[183]

The *planetary hospitality of singularity* is a discourse of hospitality about the *rights* of every *singular* being as *guests* who are equal with *hosts*. It is also a discourse of hypersensitivity to the marginalized, the subjugated, the excluded, the colonized, and the subaltern, including the concrete other, the distant others, and animals. Planetary hospitality should be *of singularity*, in which everyone involved in the exercise of hospitality must be treated as a singular, unique being. No one should offer one's hospitality to the other at the expense of hostility to *another* other, as one can see in the examples of hospitality in Genesis and Judges in the Bible. Derrida, an "artist and poet of hospitality,"[184] calls for *the* law of unlimited hospitality:

> Let us say yes *to who or what turns up*, before any determination, before any anticipation, before any *identification*, whether or not it has to do with a foreigner, an immigrant, an invited guest, or an unexpected visitor, whether or not the new arrival is the citizen of another country, a human, an animal, or divine creature, a living or dead thing, male or female.[185]

A planetary hospitality of *singularity* is hospitality that opens to "[t]he other and the third party, my neighbors, contemporaries of one another."

Citing Isaiah 57:19, "Peace, peace to the neighbor and the one far-off," Levinas ever-extends the scope of hospitality to "the third party" who is "other than the neighbor, but also another neighbor, and also a neighbor of the other, and not simply his [*sic*] fellow."[186] Derrida extends "the third party" even to the animal, taking examples from the animals in Noah's ark and Jonah's whale.[187] Derrida's call for an unconditional, unlimited hospitality is not to romanticize it but to invite us to take cosmic responsibility and to see the disparity between unconditional and conditional hospitality as a call—a prophetic call. I base *planetary hospitality* on the notion of God as *always-yes*—an unconditional affirmation of *yes* to all beings, not only human but also non-human beings in this cosmos, because the name of God (Jah-weh) is *Yes,* "the affirmation at the limit, a limitless affirmation of the impossible":[188]

God said to Moses, "I am *yes*." He said further: "Thus shall you say to the Israelites, 'I am *yes* has sent me to you. The Impossible, the Incoming.'" (Ex.3:14, NRquasi-SV)[189]

For Derrida, the concept of cosmopolitanism signifies an "undeconstructable concern for justice."[190] I believe cosmopolitanism maintains principles of justice and compassion that transcend nationality, citizenship, and various boundaries, and defend the application of justice to all individuals of the cosmos as a whole. Paul's cosmopolitan statement, "There is no longer Jew or Greek, there is no longer slave or free, there is no longer male and female; for all of you are one in Christ Jesus" (Gal. 3:28), reflects the planetary oneness of humanity. Cosmopolitanism and its theological adoption is a theological response to the issues of global inequality, planetary crisis, and destruction that we have been facing. I would argue that cosmopolitan *impartiality* of the scope of justice and hospitality is in fact the very nature of Christian teaching of *neighbor-love-as-self-love.* It is important to note that cosmopolitan *impartiality* does not necessarily rule out *partiality* to one's local attachments and commitments. The spirit of cosmopolitanism requires us to radically extend the category of our *neighbor,* to cross and transcend various borders, and to embrace every singular person and the living beings on this planet as our *neighbors.* Practicing *neighbor-love* is practicing *planetary hospitality* as *gift-without-return,* beyond the economic calculation of giving and taking. Practicing *planetary hospitality* is engaging "profoundly with *one* person," and affirming and reaffirming one's ethical singularity, as "a secret encounter."[191] Acknowledging and embodying the notion of *ethical singularity* of the one person is significant in practicing planetary hospitality, because consciousness reminds us ofthe simple truth: One has to live "one's own existence as possibility or potentiality"[192] as being-*such.*

When one ever-extends the category of *neighbor* from a perspective of the cosmopolitan hospitality of singularity, one needs to fundamentally rethink and reconceptualize the discourse of *community*. People tend to romanticize the notion of *community* and construct the community in a form of *exercise of sameness*. The questions of how people constitute the category, scope, nature, and notion of community, and what is the sociopolitical implication of such *community-of-sameness,* are significant issues that we need to take into serious theological consideration and reflection. What does it mean to say, for instance, *Muslim* community, *Christian* community, *Asian* community, *women's* community, or *LGBTQ* community? What kinds of borders of inclusion/exclusion does this construction of community draw, and what sociopolitical and epistemological implications do such borders carry? Contesting and challenging the conception of *community* that people ground in the sense of sameness, unity-in-uniformity, or pseudo-universalism is an urgent theological task in the process of seeking a *planetary* community of and for those who do not and cannot have a community in an uneven world today.

In his *Imagined Communities,* Benedict Anderson, for instance, presents an uncritical conception of *community* by arguing that a nation is "imagined as a community, because, regardless of the actual inequality and exploitation that may prevail in each, the nation is always conceived as a deep, horizontal comradeship."[193] This kind of concept of community is extremely problematic, and even dangerous, because it contributes to justifying and perpetuating a distorted notion of community that people build upon collectivization and homogenization of members and dismissal of power-differential, inequality, and exploitation between people within the community. It also misguides the notion of the significance of the *horizontality* of members in the construction of community. The *horizontal comradeship* that Anderson talks about completely distorts the concept of community, because it is impossible to attain a true *horizontality* when there is an extreme power-differential that causes exploitation and inequality among people within the community. Anderson's concept of community, which resonates a typical concept of community, seeks to appeal to *sameness* and takes *sameness* as the foundation for societal values, in which people regard contestation, difference, disagreement, or dissimilarity as a *threat* or *danger* to community.

The *community-in-sameness* on whatever grounds precludes a possibility of a multiple sense of belonging to or affiliation with a community. The most serious problem of the *community-in-sameness* is its being premised upon tyrannical violence by dismissing, overlooking, and erasing difference, alterity, contradiction, and contestation. The collective and unified form of *community-in-sameness* does not allow a space of *alterity,* a space of *singularity,* because it does not align with the constitution of the community. When asked about *community,* Derrida responds: "If by community one implies, as is often the case, a harmonious group, consensus, and fundamental agreement beneath the phenomena of discord or war, then I don't believe in it very much and I sense in it as much threat as promise."[194] Here, constructing a radically new concept of community is necessary, such as a *community-without-community* by Jean-Luc Nancy, or a *coming-community* by Giorgio Agamben. According to Nancy, "Community without community is *to come*, in the sense that it is always *coming*, endlessly, at the heart of every collectivity (because it never stops coming, it ceaselessly resists collectivity itself as much as it resists the individual)."[195] The new concept of community does not guarantee the sameness, the essentialized homogeneity, or a unified collectivity. The *community-to-come* is a community of *singularity*, a community without "affirming an identity, that humans co-belong without any representable condition of belonging (even in the form of a simple presupposition)."[196] Here human singularity truly is the "passion of being."[197]

Cosmopolitan hospitality seeks a community with no ties to *essence*, and that refuses to link to *the foundational violence* in order to create a new community with new constitutions and presuppositions—which involves not what religion, gender, race and ethnicity, citizenship and nationality, or sexuality one belongs to but rather the very singularity in which each and every individual human exists. Cosmopolitan hospitality makes it possible to form and work for the *community-without-identity*, the *community-without-community*, the *community-to-come*, the *coming-community*, or the *community for those without community* by interrupting normative accounts of community, resisting the collectivity of community, and reconceptualizing community not as a passively fixed entity but as an *event* that is constantly active and becoming. The *community-to-come* that cosmopolitan hospitality intends to build is a community of singularity "without either representation or possible description—an absolutely unrepresentable community,"[198] which shakes the very foundations of a unified community based on collective identity and belonging, unified traditions, totalizing myths, homogeneous histories, and so forth. The *community-to-come* opens up the possibility of a new way of being *community-as-an-event*, as a process, a constant struggle to establish connections and relations among persons of singular-plurality in the very impossibility of their categorization, classification, and identification.

7

The Impossible Necessity of Dreaming the *Kindom*

Toward a Public Theology-to-Come

Each of us is the destiny of the other.
—Jean Baudrillard [1]

The kingdom is a kingdom of singularities.
—John D. Caputo [2]

My sense of the holy is bound up with the hope that someday my remote descendants will live in a global civilization in which love is pretty much the only law.
—Richard Rorty[3]

***Double Bind*: The Impossibility and Necessity of Dreaming the *Kindom* of God**

Today most people may consider themselves *worldwide* citizens who always connect themselves with the world on-line. What can then the spirit of cosmic citizenship and its theological discourse represent today? Reenacting the cosmic citizenship is not meant to reaffirm the liberal notion of individualism that does not question a structural injustice between different individuals and nation-states or the European ethnocentric notion of nation-state, liberalism, and abstract universalism. The spirits of the

Enlightenment, capitalism, or communism make claims for the worldwide recognition of the human as the bearer of universal rights, in one way or the other. However, the *worldly visions* that each of these traditions project is structured within the ideal frame of the sovereignty of national borders. Such *worldly visions* grounded in nationhood fail to address the urgent issues of those nationless, stateless people such as refugees, diaspora, and exiles who represent the spirit of the community of cosmic citizens. Cosmopolitanism is *situated-universalism,* completely different from abstract, faceless universalisms, and invites the latter to recognize their own situatedness in specific historical, cultural, sociopolitical, religious contexts.

What does it mean to be human, to continue to live as human, to remain *faithful* to the Divine while living in a cultural, sociogeopolitical, and religious world where power disparity between/among humans based on their nationality, citizenship, gender, race, class, sexuality, ability, religion, and so forth still prevails? The act of *theologizing* for me involves responding to these questions and stimulating the practice of liberating and enlarging human possibility in our daily reality. If the core message of Christianity, loving one's neighbor as oneself, is merely a *spiritualized* or *romanticized* rhetoric that people just chant in the church without rigorously wrestling with the hard questions such as *who* one's neighbors are, *to whom* I/we are neighbors, and *what* constitutes *loving* oneself and neighbors, then the significant value of *loving one's neighbor as oneself* entirely loses its profound meaning and sociogeopolitical implication for daily reality. In order to examine the present reality of *what-it-is,* one always needs a perspective of *what-it-ought-to-be*. The perspective of *what-it-ought-to-be* is a utopic perspective, a viewpoint of the ideal. There is an inextricable correlation between the perspective/reality of *what-it-is*—the current configuration of the world—and that of *what-it-ought-to-be*—the *world-to-come*.

People usually use the term *utopia,* coined by Thomas More in his book *Utopia,* [4] to designate a world that does not exist—*U-topia*. More suggests a world that would deserve full approval, a place of felicity, *Eu-topia*.[5] Constance Penley makes a distinction between *dystopian* and *utopian*. People ground the appeal to the future in dystopian thought in a form of nostalgic romanticism with its call for a return to a past. Therefore, dystopian thought, as an atrophy of utopian imagination, often "limits itself to solutions that are either individualist or bound to a romanticized notion of guerrilla-like small-group resistance," but "cannot conceive the kind of collective political strategies necessary to change to ensure that future."[6] Here, it is important to note that Karl Mannheim makes a distinction between the *absolute unrealizability* and the *relative unrealizability* of utopia. Utopia is "unrealizable only within the framework" of the existing order, where people "whose thoughts and feelings are bound up with an order of existence,"[7] but utopia is *realizable* when people move beyond the existing social order and the "limits of the status quo."[8]

Therefore, it is not surprising to see that those who are content with the existing reality tend to disregard the distinction between the *absolutely unrealizable utopia* and the *relatively unrealizable utopia*. Blurring the distinction between the various types of utopia would not only give a full endorsement for the *status quo, reality-as-it-is,* but also would suppress the significant prophetic function of utopian thoughts that long for an alternative *reality-as-it-ought-to-be,* the *world-to-come,* the *kindom of God*. If we trace the history of the women's movement, civil rights movement, anti-apartheid movement, or any form of liberation movement, for instance, it is not difficult to realize that the *utopian* dream, a strong vision for the *world-to-come,* has been essential to stimulate and motivate people into revolutionary acts and solidarity. No one in the late nineteenth century, when the U.S. government did not even give black people and women the right to *vote,* for instance, could have ever imagined such a *utopian* idea that Barack Obama, a non-white person whom people consider "black,"[9] could take the position of the President of the U.S. in the year 2009. Human history is, in a way, a history of multiple forms of *utopian* dreams and is always in the process of being realized in human reality. Utopian thought dreams *the impossible* and envisions the *world-to-come*. Mannheim articulates the importance of utopian thought, the dream of the impossible, as follows:

> [T]he complete elimination of reality-transcending elements from our world would lead us to a "matter-of-factness" [*Sachlichkeit*] which ultimately would mean the decay of the human will .... [T]he complete disappearance of the utopian element from human thought and action would mean that human nature and human development would take on a totally new character. The disappearance of utopia brings about a static state of affairs in which man himself [*sic*] becomes no more than a thing ....becomes a mere creature of impulses .... [W]ith the relinquishment of utopias, man would lose his will to shape history and therewith his ability to understand it.[10]

Mannheim further warns about the possible distortion of utopian thoughts when people try to implement them in reality. People can often distort the meaning of Christian neighbor-love and make it *unrealizable* when the society is not "organized on the same principle."[11] Utopian thoughts play the role of shattering the logocentric design/institutionalization of the reality that suppresses the powerless, the voiceless—the subaltern. Utopian thoughts expand one's perception of who-one-is/who-the-others-are and motivate one to seek for an alternative world that seems *impossible* in the present reality. The notion of utopia that I adopt is the one Mannheim defines. According to Mannheim, just leaving or simply moving beyond reality does not make one's state of mind *utopian* unless it offers "revolutionary possibilities"[12] that can transform the existing reality for a better world. In this regard, an effective utopia should be the work of both an individual and the society/community. Paul Tillich highlights the significant condition for the actualization of the utopic vision:

> A socially defined utopia loses its truth if it does not at the same time fulfill the person, just as the individually defined utopia loses its truth if it does not at the same time bring fulfillment to society.... [H]ealing of ills in society and social fulfillment cannot be achieved apart from wholeness in the person. This is the tragedy of the revolutionary movements of the past hundred years, all of which foundered inwardly, and many outwardly, because they expected to heal society without at the same time healing individuals who are the bearers of society.[13]

Imagining a world where people treat all living beings as fellow *citizens of the cosmos,* sharing the same *citizenship* in our sociogeopolitical reality, is truly a utopian vision—a vision for *the impossible*. However, such an impossible vision is for the *justice-to-come*. The cosmopolitan view of the others and citizenship has a strong metaphoric power of redescribing, reaffirming, resituating life. Therefore,

> Go there where you cannot go, to the impossible,
> it is indeed the only way of going or coming.
> To go there where it is possible is not to surrender,
> rather, it is to be already there and to paralyze oneself
> in the in-decision of the non-event.[14]

I regard constructing cosmopolitan theology as a *project*. A *project* is, by its nature, in process, never-ending. Therefore, in constructing a cosmopolitan theology as a *project,* one will need to continue to carry it on with different conceptual issues, angles, positionalities, and locationalties, especially in its discursive and practical implications and implementations. I am undertaking my cosmopolitan theological *project* out of a sense of *subversive* hope, the *impossible* hope that envisions the *world-to-come*. As a theologian-philosopher or philosopher-theologian who locates her primary religious affiliation in the Christian tradition, I regard Jesus, a primary reference for Christians, as a *prophetic utopian,* whose eschatological hope and vision for the *Kindom* of God is *the passion for the impossible,* the witness to the *subversive hope against hope*: "Nothing will be impossible with God" (Lk. 1:37).

> The reference to the eschatological Kingdom, the fully human community of love promised by God, discloses injustice and inhumanity in the best of social structures. The Christian hope is of its nature a searchlight which, turned on its social *milieu,* seeks out the opportunities for protest. The Gospel can never be at home in the world, and cannot fail to bring a true believer into conflict with any existing order of things. It is in essential and permanent tension with the world. This tension should be a fruitful one, from which awkward questions are continually being put to the world. Hope is a permanently unsettling force, seeking to prevent social institutions from becoming rigid and fixed, always inclined to treat the status quo with suspicion.... In this sense the Gospel is 'revolutionary'....[15]

A cosmopolitan theology that longs for the Kindom of God seeks to recover its revolutionary universalizing ethos in terms of hospitality, neighbor-love, and multiple solidarities that one can see in Jesus' teaching and ministry, without any imperialist, kyriarchal, hierarchical implications.

Cosmopolitan Theology as *Public Theology-to-Come*

One of the most distinctive movements within theology over the past few decades has been the emergence of the various theologies of liberation, such as Latin American and Black liberation theologies, feminist/womanist theologies, and LGBT (lesbian, gay, bisexual and transgendered) theologies. All theologies of liberation and transformation focus on the marginalized, the excluded, the silenced, or the oppressed as their priority. One of liberation theology's contributions is its repositioning the role and the task of theology in the world. As one can define public theology as a theology that gets involved in the public affairs of society, liberation theologies have paved a way for the emergence of public theology in our times. Cosmopolitan theology is a new form of public theology that concerns the oppressed and the marginalized in our society. Its goal is to resist all forms of *oppression against humanity* and to be in solidarity with the marginalized. It further wrestles with the intersecting issues of social oppression and discrimination in society today and the conflicts among various advocacy groups and particular bounded communities. I regard the prospect of cosmopolitan theology as public theology, which has to do with the public relevance of a theology that has a concern for the coming of the Kindom of God in the world of human history through the cosmopolitan justice of planetary neighborly love.

Cosmopolitanism is a discourse of hope and compassion that has not yet had the opportunity to actualize its utopian potential. In this regard, cosmopolitan theology is a *theology from the future* and transforms the goal of doing theology and the task of theologians. Traditionally, people have viewed theologians not as active participants in public affairs and the role of theologians was often that of transmitter or interpreter of *divine truth*. Yet I believe theologians must become *cosmopolitans*, who cross the borders of difference and are capable not just of interpreting but also of *reinventing* traditions that serve to liberate and enlarge human possibilities regardless of one's nationality, gender, race, ethnicity, ability, religion, or sexual orientation. Cosmopolitan theology represents the voice of an all-embracing affirmation of life. However, it challenges the liberal, humanist notion of the unified, essentialized subject, and views the subject as contradictory and multilayered. It rejects the politics of single group identity if it essentializes the subject, and invites us to rethink fundamentally how we constitute ourselves as subjects within a rapidly changing set of political, social, economic, cultural, and religious conditions. Cosmopolitan theology further calls for solidarity across borders, a community of radical inclusion, and deep compassion for the other regardless of who one is. It points to solidarity, community, justice, and compassion as essential aspects of how we experience the world and ourselves in a meaningful way.

Cosmopolitanism calls for *planetary neighborly love* and *deep and radical compassion* for living beings, which I believe should be the central message of Christianity. In *The Coming of the Cosmic Christ*,[16] Matthew Fox examines how compassion is dying in the face of all the contemporary crises throughout the world: Mother Earth is dying; hope is dying; the youth are dying; and native peoples, cultures, religions, and wisdom are dying. He calls us to enact the resurrection of the living Cosmic Christ in our beings and then in our actions to transform society and bring healing to all its suffering, broken parts through love, imagination, peacemaking, and environmental, moral, and social justice. Fox argues, with conviction and enthusiasm, that restoring the mystical mind of compassion, the Christian work of love, can bring a global renaissance to the entire world, including every aspect of society, from religion to sexuality, from peacemaking and disarmament to mentoring the young. Remaking the world will require *planetary love*—mindchanging love for the planet, as Spivak calls for.

Cosmopolitan theology envisions a new *Cosmic Christ* who urges us to begin a great work to live and build the Kindom of God on earth. We need to expand the sites of theology so that it resides not merely in theological schools and institutions but in the wider public sphere; in doing so we would be extending the possible terrains of struggle for justice as well. I would hope that theology addresses major social issues, fully engages matters of power and inequality in all aspects of daily life, and fosters in every way possible the imperatives of justice across all boundaries. Doing theology today may be one of the few spheres left for us to provide the conditions for people to become critically engaged social agents, and also to create the conditions for people to struggle anew to sustain the promise of the Kindom of God on earth and continuously expand into a world of new possibilities and opportunities for keeping justice and hope alive.

In this context, the theologian is an active participant in public affairs, not an objective and neutral observer, not just an academic scholar who resides only within an *ivory tower*. If *reading the signs of our times* is one of the roles of theologians, what constitutes *reading* becomes an important question, and redefining the role of theologians becomes an urgent task. Theologians are not to be passive transmitters of *divine truth* but active participants within multiple communities and public sectors, engaging with and providing theological discourses that foster and promote solidarities with the marginalized within, against, and between dominant powers and institutions on local and global levels. They are, in this sense, the boundary-crossers, who cross the boundaries of gender, nationality, race, ethnicity, physical/mental ability, sexuality, and religion, in order to bring the divine will to earth, where justice, peace, equality, and compassion will flow like a river. Here theologians are *artists* in the sense that they create and recreate religious traditions and their practices of transformation and liberation. The languages that theologians use, create, and construct should be the languages of boundary-crossing—radical inclusion and hope, transboundary-solidarity and justice. Theologians' public responsibility is to contest sociogeopolitical relations and institutions that keep privilege, exclusion, discrimination, and oppression of one group over against the other alive in daily life. Cosmopolitan theological discourse is, then, a public theology from the future—of a present, of *passion for the impossible, longing for the impossible, dreaming of the impossible, hope for the impossible.* What can theology offer in the public sphere and to political action? Asked in an interview, "How do you think philosophy could and should react to the problems mentioned with a kind of institutional fantasy?" Derrida replied: "All political innovation touches on philosophy. The *true* political action always engages with a philosophy. All action, all political decision making, must invent its norm or rule. Such a gesture traverses or implies philosophy."[17] Can theology function as philosophy does in political action? My answer is yes. Theology can be an ardent *interlocutor* in public discourse, disseminate its ideals in the public sector, and promote political action to enhance *planetary hospitality* for humanity.

Theology should be a discourse that helps the sociopolitical approach to justice to maintain its human face and not to become *impersonal.*

Cosmopolitan Theologians as *Public Theologians-without-Passports*

Who are theologians? What kind of self-identity could or should a theologian claim? Should a theologian be a defender or transmitter of Christian *tradition*? What if the *tradition* itself carries a dark side, implicitly or explicitly, bounded by religious or cultural superiorism, ethnocentrism, homophobism, exclusive nationalism, sexism, racism, and so forth? What kind of *identity* would then justify my role as a *theologian*? This question has been lingering in my mind throughout the time I have been working on cosmopolitan theology. It may sound simple, but for me the identity issue has been fundamental. The following remarks by Derrida resonate with what I think of as a proper language for the *identity* of a cosmopolitan theologian: cosmopolitan theologians, like philosophers in Derrida's sense, are those *without a passport*:

> In principle, a philosopher should not have a passport, or any kind of identity documents, he [*sic*] should never be required to have a visa! He should not represent any nationality, not even a national language. The will to be a philosopher, in principle and in relation to the most firm of traditions, is the will to make a contribution to the universal community. Not just cosmopolitan, but universal; beyond citizenship, beyond state, even beyond the cosmopolitan.[18]

Once one comes to possess an *identity document,* one is bound to the ground of that identity document, whether it is about national or religious affiliation, or a particular advocacy cause, etc. One begins, then, to get attached to the very ground of such *identity*. Here a *passport* symbolizes classification, categorization, homogenization, totalization, genderization, sexualization, racialization, ethnicization, and so forth. The *passport* fundamentally limits the endless dimension of one's *neighbors, friends,* to a certain *category,* especially when there is, in our reality, a *strong* passport and a *weak* one. *Theologians-without-passports* intentionally dissociate themselves from the dominant power, practice, or discourse that totalizes, categorizes, and classifies an individual person into a stereotypical box of numbers and data. *Theologians-without-passports* commit themselves to "make a contribution to the universal community," to the Kindom of God, where every individual human being is equal to everyone else, treated justly, accepted fully as who one is. The word *beyondness* captures the spirit of cosmopolitan theologians as public *theologians-without-passports*. Theologians are to look to the *beyond*-community—*beyond* nationality, skin-color, gender, sexual orientation, citizenship, religious affiliation—because God, the Divine, who is the primary frame of reference for theologians, is for, with, in, among those individual human beings. It is to reaffirm the sheer truth: No one is better or worse, superior or inferior than any other; and, "Ich bin du, wenn Ich Ich bin [I am you, when I am I]."[19] So, what does it mean to *do* theology in academia without having a *passport*? John Caputo puts eloquently what it means to do philosophy, which also echoes what it means to do theology without a *passport*:

> Philosophy is the right to ask any question about all that we hold sacred, even and especially about reason and philosophy itself .... The "right to philosophy," both to study and to teach it, to read and write, discuss and publish it, is everyone's ....Philosophy is not just one discipline among many, the one housed in the "philosophy department." Philosophy must be ex-posed, dis-located, ...made to understand that it cannot be wholly confined within the limits of a disciplinary specialization. Philosophy must be audacious and made to "cross the borders" of the disciplines.[20]

Doing cosmopolitan theology *without having a passport* is not romanticizing or spiritualizing a theological discourse and practice. Instead, it is an attempt to promote a concrete transformation of one's ethical, religious, and geopolitical perspective and a fundamental change of the structural, systemic, institutional, and judicial dimension, especially in the way people setup and exercise the standard of *membership* or *citizenship*. Cosmopolitan theology is a theology for *the impossible*. It dreams of the world that has been impossible. The world that cosmopolitan theology dreams is a world where all singular persons in all places, countries, cultures, regions, religions, and of all genders, sexualities, abilities with protean identities enjoy the cosmic conviviality as fellow-citizens-of-the-cosmos, which God creates and loves. Cosmopolitan theology is neither a *faceless universalism* nor an illusory dream. Ludwig Wittgenstein offers an insightful point for the direction of contemporary theological de/construction:

> The *words* that you utter, or what you mean when you utter them, is not what matters so much as the difference they make at various points in your life. How do I know that two people mean the same when each says he [*sic*] believes in God?.... A theology which insists on the use of *certain particular* words and phrases, and outlaws others, does not make anything clearer ....*Practice* gives the words their sense.[21]

Theological construction is not merely for repetition of the tradition, or justification of the doctrine, but for motivating people in church and society toward the better *practices* of what they confess. People value doctrinal confession or long-standing traditions not for their words/claims to truth and authority but for the ways in which they serve to liberate human freedom and possibility, and ever-enlarge the circle of inclusion and happiness for all singular persons in all places. Cosmopolitan theological discourse could motivate the *practices*, new *practices* of radical neighbor-love, radical inclusion, that cross the exclusive borders of citizenship, nationality, gender, race, class, sexuality, and ability, and regard all persons in all places as uniquely singular persons, each of whom has a proper name and unique face.

Cosmopolitan theology is not a theology that one operates according to particular *metanarratives*—overarching narratives of *cosmopolitanism*. Yet cosmopolitan theology only becomes meaningful when one enacts and embodies it in the concrete singular stories of persons with proper names and unique singular faces, and the concrete practices of particular groups and communities. Now the question we must ask is *not* whether a theology is based on metanarratives or petit-narratives, *but* what kind of *practices* it motivates, what kind of *gaze* onto others, the guest, the new arrivant, it offers us to carry with us; *not* who my neighbors are *but* to whom I am being a neighbor. Cosmopolitan theology that dreams of ever-enlarging the circle of neighbors—of singular persons, animals, plants, eco-systems, and God—is truly a theology of the *impossible*. Being a person of faith would mean being a *dreamer of the impossible*, as Jesus always dreams for the Kindom of God, "a world in which some fundamental principles of justice govern relations between all persons in all places."[22] The central question that cosmopolitan theology asks is how we create a theological and ministerial environment that is as hospitable as possible to the others, neighbors, distant others. Theology is offering the law of planetary hospitality that entails an unconditional embracing of and offering to the *stranger, neighbors* regardless of what/who they are. Planetary neighbor-love or hospitality is an unconditional *yes* to the new arrivant, regardless of who the new arrivant is. For Yahweh is *yes*:

> Let us say yes to who or what turns up,
> before any determination,
> before any anticipation,
> before any identification,
> whether or not the new arrival is
> the citizen of another country, a human, animal, or divine creature, a living or dead thing, male or female.[23]

A breadth and depth of scholarship, knowledge, and understanding means a certain catholicism, a cosmopolitanism that roams a world and its historical culture for the pleasure of identifying the resources needed to make interventions so the present society might transform to meet a higher set of almost impossible ethical ideals. Intellectuals who can do these things are themselves a resource.[24] Constructing a cosmopolitan theology is to critically and compassionately interrupt, contest, and invite each other, to bring each other to crisis, in order to make ourselves commit to an enlargement of the circle of inclusion, not only epistemologically and spiritually, but also institutionally, systematically, and politico-economically. I hope this *project* of cosmopolitan theology will open a new path of critical inquiry and provide broad possibilities for exploring, evaluating, and applying theological/philosophical vision and passion to the ends of Christian theo-political analysis of and engagement with the world. *Doing* cosmopolitan theology is a strengthening and nurturing endeavor that can advance more firm compassions and solidarities, alliances, and coalitions among every singular individual of the cosmos, regardless of one's citizenship; national belonging; religious affiliation; or sexual, racial, gender, or ethnic identity. As *citizens of the cosmos,* we will struggle and stay together "with the hope that some day my remote descendants will live in a global civilization in which love is pretty much the only law."[25]

If cosmopolitanism is theologically compelling, it is because it claims that we humans have obligations and responsibilities to others and because it profoundly resonates with Christian teachings of neighbor-love, compassion, and hospitality. If theologians, people of faith, and ministers are to carry out a more reflexive practice in cosmopolitan terms, then we will struggle with the questions: What are the relevant implications of our work for the communities with which we do that work? How does our intellectual construction of theological discourses help to reshape life-affirming identities of people? How can theological discourse promote compassion, equality, peace, and justice in the public world? My attempt to construct a cosmopolitan theology hopes to stimulate and promote religious/theological sensitivities to the problems of a troubling present in an *uneven* world. Cosmopolitanism is a mode of understanding the self, the others, the world; it is an ethic and a theology of responsibility, compassion, hospitality; and it is an ongoing exercise of interdependence in the face of violence, war, and exclusion. Let us humans then continue to dream an impossible dream for the Kindom of God—which is the ethico-political and theological space of *planetary conviviality.*

Notes

Preface

[1]For a publication of the presentation papers from the Transdisciplinary Conference, see *Planetary Loves: Spivak, Postcoloniality, and Theology*, ed. Stephen D. Moore and Mayra Rivera (New York: Fordham University Press, 2010).

[2]For this description of Derrida as a *person of tears and prayers,* I am indebted to John D. Caputo, *The Prayers and Tears of Jacques Derrida: Religion without Religion* (Bloomington, Ind.: Indiana University Press, 1997). I put *tears* first because for me *tears* precede *prayers,* although in Derrida both seem eventually inseparable/indissociable.

[3]Jacques Derrida, *Points…Interviews, 1974-1994*, ed. Elisabeth Weber, trans. Peggy Kamuf & Others. (Stanford, Calif.: Stanford University Press, 1995), 321.

[4]Roland Barthes, "The Death of the Author," in *Image, Music, Text,* trans. Stephen Heath (New York: Hill and Wang, 1977), 142 and 143.

Chapter 1

[1]Jacques Derrida, *Circumfession: Fifty-nine Periods and Periphrases*, in *Jacques Derrida*, Geoffrey Bennington and Jacques Derrida (Chicago: University of Chicago Press, 1993), 194.

[2]Jean-Francois Lyotard, *The Postmodern Condition: A Report on Knowledge*, trans. G. Benington and B. Massumi (Minneapolis: University of Minnesota Press, 1984), xxiv.

[3]Cf. Jean-Francois Lyotard, "The Differend," trans. Georges Van Den Abbeele, *Diacritics* (Fall 1984): 4–14.

[4]Edward Said, as quoted in Steven Howe, "Edward Said: The Traveller and the Exile," *Open Democracy* (October 2, 2003). http://www.opendemocracy.net/node/1516.

[5]Gilles Deleuze, as quoted in Michel Foucault, "Intellectuals and Power: A Conversation between Michel Foucault and Gilles Deleuze," in *Language, Counter-Memory, Practice,* ed. Donald F. Bouchard, trans. Donald F. Bouchard and Sherry Simon (Ithaca, N.Y.: Cornell University Press, 1977), 208.

[6]Paul Ricoeur, *Lectures on Ideology and Utopia*, ed. George H. Taylor (New York: Columbia University Press, 1986), 273.

[7]Ibid., xxi.

[8]Bharati Mukherjee-Blaise, "Mimicry and Reinvention," in *The Commonwealth in Canada,* ed. Uma Parameswaran (Calcutta: Writer's Workshop Greybird, 1983), 151.

[9]Theodor W. Adorno and Ernst Bloch, "Something is Missing: A Discussion Between Ernst Bloch and Theodor W. Adorno on the Contradictions of Utopian Longing," in *The Utopian Function of Art and Literature: Selected Essays*, ed. Jack Zipes and Frank Mecklenburg (Cambridge, Mass.: The MIT Press, 1988), 16.

[10]Jacques Derrida, *Learning to Live Finally*, trans. Pascale-Anne Brault and Michael Naas (Hoboken, N.J.: Melville House Publishing, 2007), 22.

[11]Gayatri Chakravorty Spivak, *The Postcolonial Critic: Interviews, Strategies, Dialogues,* ed. Sarah Harasym (New York & London: Routledge, 1990), 7. Italics added.

[12]Gayatri Chakravorty Spivak, as quoted in Foucault, "Intellectuals and Power," 206.

[13]Gayatri Chakravorty Spivak, *A Critique of Postcolonial Reason: Toward a History of the Vanishing Present* (Cambridge, Mass.: Harvard University Press, 1999) 382.

[14]Spivak, *The Postcolonial Critic*, 12.

[15]Cf. Michel Foucault, "What Is an Author?" in *Language, Counter-Memory, Practice*, ed. Donald F. Bouchard, trans. Donald F. Bouchard and Sherry Simon (Ithaca, N.Y.: Cornell University Press, 1977), 125–31.

[16]Michel Foucault, The *Archaeology of Knowledge* (1969; New York: Routledge Classics, 2002), 19.

[17]Spivak, *A Critique of Postcolonial Reason,* 383.

[18]Gilles Deleuze, as quoted in Foucault, "Intellectuals and Power," 205–206.

[19]Foucault, "Intellectuals and Power," 208.

[20]Martha C. Nussbaum, *Poetic Justice: The Literary Imagination and Public Life* (Boston: Beacon Press, 1995), xvi.

[21]Jacques Derrida, "Intellectual Courage: An Interview by Thomas Assheuer," *Culture Machine: Generating Research in Culture and Theory*, vol. 2 (2000). http://www.culturemachine.net/index.php/cm/article/view/303/288.

[22]Hannah Arendt, *The Origins of Totalitarianism* (1951; New York: Schocken Books, 2004), 355.

[23]Ibid., 365.

[24]Jean-Francois Lyotard, "The Differend, the Referent, and the Proper Name," *Diacritics*, vol. 14, no. 3: 10 and 13.

[25]Maurice Blanchot, *The Infinite Conversation*, trans. Susan Hanson (Minneapolis: University of Minnesota Press, 1993), 51–52.

[26]Jacques Derrida, *Circumfession: Fifty-nine Periods and Periphrases,* in *Jacques Derrida,* Geoffrey Bennington and Jacques Derrida (Chicago: University of Chicago Press, 1993), 194.

[27]Jacques Derrida, *On the Name,* ed. Thomas Dutoit, trans. David Wood, John P. Leavey Jr., and Ian McLeod (Stanford, Calif.: Stanford University Press, 1993), 75. Derrida goes on to cite Angelus Silesius, a German mystic in the seventeenth century:

"Geh hin, wo du nicht kanst;
Sih, wo du sihest nicht:
Hör wo nichts schallt und klingt, so bestu wo Gott spricht."

Chapter 2

[1]Gayatri Chakravorty Spivak, *Death of Discipline* (New York: Columbia University Press, 2005), 72.

[2]Seneca, *De Otio,* 4.1, in *Seneca: Moral Essays,* vol. 2, trans. John W. Basore (1932; Cambridge, Mass.: Harvard University Press, 1970), 187 and 189.

[3]Marcus Aurelius, *The Meditations* (Indianapolis: Hackett, 1983), 10:15.

[4]Cornel West, "The New Cultural Politics of Difference," in *Out There: Marginalization and Contemporary Culture*, ed. Russell Ferguson, Martha Gever, Trinh T. Minh-ha, and Cornel West (New York and Cambridge: The New Museum of Contemporary Art and MIT Press, 1990), 36.

[5]David Harvey, "Cosmopolitanism and the Banality of Geographical Evils," *Public Culture* 12 (2000): 529.

[6]Walter D. Mignolo, "Editor's Introduction," *Poetics Today,* vol. 15, no. 4, Loci of Enunciation and Imaginary Construction: The Case of (Latin) America, 1 (Winter 1994): 508.

[7]Gayatri Chakravorty Spivak, *A Critique of Postcolonial Reason: Toward a History of the Vanishing Present* (Cambridge, Mass.: Harvard University Press, 1999), 383.

[8]Ibid.

[9]Ibid.

[10]Ibid. 384.

[11]Friedrich Nietzsche, *Human, All Too Human: A Book for Free Spirits* (Cambridge, U.K.: Cambridge University Press, 1996), 196.

[12]Cf. Samuel Scheffler, "Conceptions of Cosmopolitanism," *Utilitas*, vol. 11, no.3 (November 1999): 255–76.

[13]For various uses of the label *cosmopolitan,* see Ulrich Beck, *Cosmopolitan Vision,* trans. Ciaran Cronin (Cambridge, U.K.: Polity Press, 2006), 3.

[14]Diogenes Laërtius, *Lives of Eminent Philosophers,* vol. II, trans. H.D. Hicks (Cambridge, Mass.: Harvard University Press, 1925), 65 [Book VI:63].

[15]Here, however, the meaning of " citizen of the world" must be different from how we now tend to perceive it because Athenian "citizenship" at that time explicitly excluded women, slaves, and foreigners. Cf. Jeremy Waldon, "Minority Cultures and the Cosmopolitan Alternative," *University of Michigan Journal of Law Reform* 25 (1992): 751–93.

[16]Patrick Hayden, *Cosmopolitan Global Politics* (Burlington, Vt.: Ashgate, 2005), 12.

[17]Aurelius, *The Meditations,* 10:15.

[18]Charles Jones, *Global Justice: Defending Cosmopolitanism* (Oxford, U.K.: Oxford University Press, 1999),16.

[19]Martha Nussbaum, "Kant and Cosmopolitanism," in *Perpetual Peace: Essays on Kant's Cosmopolitan Ideal,* ed. James Bohman and Matthias Lutz-Backmann (Cambridge, Mass.: The MIT Press, 1997), 31.

[20]For this argument, see Sharon Anderson-Gold, *Cosmopolitanism and Human Rights* (Cardiff, U.K.: University of Wales Press, 2001); Darrel Moellendorf, *Cosmopolitan Justice* (Cambridge, Mass.: Westview Press, 2002); Jones, *Global Justice*; Hayden, *Cosmopolitan Global Politics*; Luis Cabrera, *Political Theory of Global Justice: A Cosmopolitan Case for the World State* (London & New York: Routledge, 2004); Steven Vertovec and Robin Cohen, *Conceiving Cosmopolitanism: Theory, Context, and Practice* (Oxford, U.K.: Oxford University Press, 2002); Beck, *Cosmopolitan Vision.*

[21]Beck, *Cosmopolitan Vision*, 7.

[22]Martha C. Nussbaum, "Patriotism and Cosmopolitanism," in *For Love of Country: Debating the Limits of Patriotism,* ed. Joshua Cohen (Boston: Beacon, 1996), 4.

[23]Paul Rabinow, "Representations Are Social Facts: Modernity and Post-Modernity in Anthropology," in *Writing Culture: The Poetics of Ethnography*, ed. James Clifford and George E. Marcus (Berkeley: University of California Press, 1986), 258.

[24]Nussbaum, "Kant and Cosmopolitanism," 31.

[25]Anderson-Gold, *Cosmopolitanism and Human Rights*, 11.

[26]Cf. Bohman and Lutz-Bachmann, eds., *Perpetual Peace*.

[27]Emmanuel Levinas, *Difficult Freedom: Essays on Judaism* (Baltimore: The Johns Hopkins University Press, 1990), 22.

[28]Jacques Derrida, *The Gift of Death,* trans. David Willis (1992; Chicago: University of Chicago Press, 1995), 2.

[29]Kok-Chor Tan, *Justice without Borders: Cosmopolitanism, Nationalism and Patriotism* (Cambridge, U.K.: Cambridge University Press, 2004), 1.

[30]For this position, see Charles Beitz, *Political Theory and International Relations* (Princeton: Princeton University Press, 1979); id., "Cosmopolitan Ideals and National Sentiment," *Journal of Philosophy* 80 (1983): 591–600; Nussbaum, "Kant and Cosmopolitanism"; Tan, *Justice without Borders*.

[31]For the distinction of two types of cosmopolitanism, see Charles Beitz, "International Liberalism and Distributive Justice: A Survey of Recent Thought," *World Politics* 51 (1999): 269–96.

[32]Samuel Scheffler, *Boundaries and Allegiances* (Oxford, U.K.: Oxford University Press, 2001), 112.

[33]Jones, *Global Justice*, 15–17.

[34]Derrida, *On Cosmopolitanism and Forgiveness,* viii.

[35]Stuart Alan Clarke, "Fear of a Black Planet," *Socialist Review* 21 (1991): 46.

[36]R. Radhakrishnan, *Diasporic Mediations: Between Home and Location* (Minneapolis: University of Minnesota Press, 1996), 75.

[37]Michel Foucault, "Theatrum Philosophicum," in *Language, Counter-Memory, Practice: Selected Essays and Interviews* (Ithaca, N.Y.: Cornell University Press, 1980), 182.

[38]For a detailed discussion on this issue, see Namsoon Kang, "Who/What Is Asian: A Postcolonial Theological Reading of Orientalism and Neo-Orientalism," in *Postcolonial Theologies: Divinity, Hybridity, and Empire,* ed. Catherine Keller, Michael Nausner, Mayra Rivera (St. Louis: Chalice Press, 2004), 100–117.

[39]Ellen Willis, "Multiple Identities," *Tikkun* 6(6) (1991): 58.

[40]Clarke, "Fear of a Black Planet," 46.

[41]Marcus Aurelius, *Meditations,* trans. Robin Hard (London: Wordsworth Classics of World Literature, 1997), Book VI, 44.

[42]Seneca, *De Otio,* 187 and 189.

[43]For a more detailed discussion, see Sheila Greeve Davaney, "Continuing the Story, but Departing the Text: A Historicist Interpretation of Feminist Norms in Theology," *Horizons in Feminist Theology: Identity, Tradition, and Norms,* ed. Rebecca S. Chopp and Sheila Greeve Davaney (Minneapolis: Fortress Press, 1997).

[44]Edward W. Said, *Culture and Imperialism* (New York: Vintage Books, 1994), 336.

[45]Michele Wallace, "Multiculturalism and Oppositionality," *Afterimage* (October 1991): 6.

[46]Benedict Anderson, "Ice Empire and Ice Hockey: Two *Fin de siècle* Dreams," *New Left Review* 214 (November/December 1995): 150.

[47]Ulrich Beck, *Cosmopolitan Vision*, trans. Ciaran Cronin (Cambridge, U.K.: Polity Press, 2006), 3.

[48]Paul Rabinow, "Representations Are Social Facts: Modernity and Post-Modernity in Anthropology," in *Writing Culture: The Poetics of Ethnography*, ed. James Clifford and George E. Marcus (Berkeley, Calif.: University of California Press, 1986), 258.

[49]Bruce Robbins, "Introduction Part I: Actually Existing Cosmopolitanism," in *Cosmopolitics: Thinking and Feeling beyond the Nation*, ed. Pheng Cheah and Bruce Robbins (Minneapolis: University of Minnesota Press, 1998), 1.

[50]Amanda Anderson, "Cosmopolitanism, Universalism, and the Divided Legacies of Modernity," in *Cosmopolitics: Thinking and Feeling Beyond Nation*, ed. Pheng Cheah and Bruce Robbins (Minneapolis: University of Minnesota Press, 1998), 270.

[51]Tim Brennan, "Cosmopolitans and Celebrities," *Race & Class* 31, no. 1 (1989): 7.

[52]Anderson, "Cosmopolitanism, Universalism, and Divided Legacies of Modernity," 271.

[53]Tim Brennan, "Rushdie, Islam, and Postcolonial Criticism," *Social Text*, no. 31/32, Third World and Post-Colonial Issues (1992): 274.

[54]Frantz Fanon, *The Wretched of the Earth*, trans. Constance Farrington (1961; New York: Grove Weidenfeld, 1963) 149, 200.

[55]Tommie Shelby and Paul Gilroy, "Cosmopolitanism, Blackness, and Utopia," *Transition*, no. 98 (2008): 117.

[56]Ibid., 118.

[57]Tan, *Justice without Borders*, 13.

[58]Benjamin Aldes Wurgaft, "Starbucks and Rootless Cosmopolitanism," *The Journal of Good and Culture*, vol. 3. no. 4 (Fall 2003): 75.

[59]Salman Rushdie, *Imaginary Homelands: Essays and Criticism, 1981–1991* (London: Granta Books, 1991), 394.

[60]Kwame Anthony Appiah, "Cosmopolitan Contamination," *Cosmopolitanism: Ethics in a World of Strangers* (New York: W.W. Norton & Company, 2006), 113.

[61]Kwame Anthony Appiah, "Rooted Cosmopolitanism," *Ethics of Identity* (Princeton: Princeton University Press, 2005), 217.

[62]Ulrich Beck, "The Cosmopolitan Perspective: Sociology of the Second Age of Modernity," *British Journal of Sociology*, vol. 51, no. 1 (January/March 2000): 79.

[63]Ibid., 84. Italics in original.

[64]Ibid., 102.

[65]Bruce Robbins, "Introduction Part I: Actually Existing Cosmopolitanism," in *Cosmopolitics: Thinking and Feeling Beyond Nation*, ed. Pheng Cheah and Bruce Robbins (Minneapolis: University of Minnesota Press, 1998), 12–13.

[66]David Hollinger, *Postethnic America: Beyond Multiculturalism* (New York: Basic Books, 1995), 2.

[67]Ibid., 5.

[68]Ibid., 3.

[69]Ibid., 85–86. Italics added.

[70]Ibid., 84.

[71]Ibid., 172. Italics added.

[72]Ulf Hannerz, "Cosmopolitans and Locals in World Culture," in *Theory, Culture & Society* 7 (1990): 239, 242.

[73]Ibid., 243, 239.

[74]Ibid., 243.

[75]Pauline Kleingeld, "Six Varieties of Cosmopolitanism in Late Eighteenth-Century Germany," *Journal of the History of Ideas*, vol. 60. no. 3 (July 1999): 519.

[76]For the cover images of Cosmopolitan women, see the following link. http://www.google.com/search?q=cosmopolitan+megan+fox&hl=en&client=safari&rls=en&prmd=imvnso&tbm=isch&tbo=u&source=univ&sa=X&ei=9AJ-T9GwBOSY2wWsh52YDg&ved=0CEsQsAQ&biw=895&bih=557

[77]Walter Mignolo, "The Many Faces of Cosmo-polis: Border Thinking and Critical Cosmopolitanism," *Public Culture*, vol. 11, no 3 (Fall 2000): 721.

[78]Ibid., 721.

[79]Walter Mignolo, *Local Histories/Global Designs: Coloniality, Subaltern Knowledge and Border Thinking* (Princeton: Princeton University Press, 2000), 19.

[80]Mignolo, "The Many Faces of Cosmo-polis," 722.

[81]Ibid.

[82]Ibid., 722–23.

[83]Ibid., 723.

[84]Ibid.

[85]Ibid., 733.

[86]Ibid., 744,

[87]Ibid.

[88]Ibid., 745.

[89]Appiah, "Rooted Cosmopolitanism," 256.

[90]Martha Nussbaum, "Patriotism and Cosmopolitanism," in Martha C. Nussbaum with Respondents. *For Love of Country: Debating the Limits of Patriotism*, ed. Joshua Cohen (Cambridge, Mass.: Beacon Press, 1996), 9.

[91]Appiah, "Rooted Cosmopolitanism," 257.

[92]Pnina Werbner, "Vernacular Cosmopolitanism," *Theory, Culture & Society*, 23 (May 2006): 497.

[93]Alfredo Gonzalez-Ruibal, "Vernacular Cosmopolitanism: An Archaeological Critique of Universalistic Readon," in *Cosmopolitan Archaeologies,* ed. Lynn Meskell (Durham, N.C.: Duke University Press, 2009), 117.

[94]Ibid., 118.

[95]Jamil Khader, "Subaltern Cosmopolitanism: Community and Transnational Mobility in Caribbean Postcolonial Feminist Writings," *Feminist Studies,* vol. 29, no. 1 (Spring 2003): 76.

[96]James Clifford, "Traveling Cultures," in *Cultural Studies,* ed. Lawrence Grossberg, Cary Nelson, and Paula Treichler (New York: Routledge, 1992), 109.

[97]Ibid., 109.

[98]Aurora Levins Morales and Rosario Morales, *Getting Home Alive* (Ithaca, N.Y.: Firebrand Books, 1986), 76. Cited in Jamil Khader, "Subaltern Cosmopolitanism: Community and Transnational Mobility in Caribbean Postcolonial Feminist Writings," *Feminist Studies,* vol. 29, no. 1 (Spring 2003): 68

[99]Khader, "Subaltern Cosmopolitanism," 64.

[100]Ibid., 77.

[101]Ibid., 76.

[102]Gayatri Chakravorty Spivak, "Can Subaltern Speak?" in *Marxism and the Interpretation of Culture,* ed. Cary Nelson and Lawrence Grossberg (Urbana and Chicago: University of Illinois Press, 1988), 104.

[103]Gayatri Chakravorty Spivak, *The Postcolonial Critic: Interviews, Strategies, Dialogues,* ed. Sarah Harasym (New York & London: Routledge, 1990), 158.

[104]Stephen D. Moore, "Situating Spivak," in *Planetary Loves: Spivak, Postcoloniality, and Theology,* ed. Stephen D. Moore and Mayra Rivera (New York: Fordham University Press, 2011), 20.

[105]Ulf Hannerz, "The Global Ecumene," *Cultural Complexity: Studies in the Social Organisation of Meaning* (New York: Columbia University Press, 1992), 252.

[106]Ibid., 249.

[107]For the critical assessment of Hannerz's position, see Pnina Werbner, "Global Pathways: Working Class Cosmopolitans and the Creation of Transnational Ethnic Worlds," *Social Anthropology,* vol. 7, no. 1 (1999): 17–35.

[108]Gonzalez-Ruibal, "Vernacular Cosmopolitanism," 117.

[109]Homi K. Bhabha, "The Vernacular Cosmopolitanism," in *Voices of the Crossing: The Impact of Britain on Writers from Asia, the Caribbean and Africa,*" ed. Naseem Khan (London: Serpent's Tail, 2000), 134.

[110]Ibid., 135.

[111]Ibid.

[112]Ibid., 141.

[113]Ibid., 138.

[114]Ibid., 141.

[115]Ibid., 142.

[116]Homi Bhabha, "Unsatisfied: Notes on Vernacular Cosmopolitanism," in *Postcolonial Discourses: An Anthology,* ed. Gregory Castle (Oxford, U.K., and Malden, Mass.: Blackwell, 2001), 48.

[117]Gonzalez-Ruibal, "Vernacular Cosmopolitanism," 120.

[118]Slavoj Zizek, "Neighbors and Other Monsters: A Plea for Ethical Violence," in *The Neighbor: Three Inquiries in Political Theology*, ed. Slavoj Zizek, Eric L. Santner, and Kenneth Reinhard (Chicago and London: The University of Chicago Press, 2005), 163.

Chapter 3

[1]Lao Tsu, *Tao Te Ching*, trans. Gia-fu Feng and Jane English (New York: Vintage Books, 1972), chap. 13.

[2]Frantz Fanon, *Black Skin, White Masks*, trans. Charles Lam Markmann (1952; New York: Grove Press, 1967), 8.

[3]Emmanuel Levinas, *Otherwise than Being or Beyond Essence*, trans. Alphonso Lingis (1974; Pittsburgh: Duquesne University Press, 1998), 197.

[4]Michel Foucault,in *Language, Counter-Memory, Practice: Selected Essays and Interviews*, ed. Donald F. Bouchard, trans. Donald F. Bouchard and Sherry Simon (Ithaca, N.Y.: Cornell University Press, 1977), 5.

[5]Robert Fine and Robin Cohen, "Four Cosmopolitan Moments," in *Conceiving Cosmopolitanism: Theory, Context, and Practice*, ed. Steven Vertovec and Robin Cohen (Oxford, U.K.: Oxford University Press, 2002), 137.

[6]Ulrich Beck, *Cosmopolitan Vision*, trans. Ciaran Cronin (2004; Cambridge, U.K., and Malden, Mass.: Polity Press, 2006), 45.

[7]Albert Memmi, *The Colonizer and the Colonized* (1965; Boston: Beacon Press, 1967), 83.

[8]Dipesh Chakrabarty, *Provincializing Europe: Postcolonial Thought and Historical Difference* (Princeton: Princeton University Press, 2000), 28–29.

[9]Walter Mignolo, *Local Histories/Global Designs: Coloniality, Subaltern Knowledges and Border Thinking* (Princeton: Princeton University Press, 2000), 3. Derrida starts his book, *Of Grammatology*, whose main concern is to deconstruct the "complicity between alphabetic writing and Western foundations of knowledge," with quotes from Rousseau and Hegel, who glorify the alphabet: Rousseau concludes that "the alphabet corresponds 'to civilized people,'" and Hegel absolutizes the value of alphabet by saying, "Alphabet script is in itself and for itself the most intelligent." Jacques Derrida, "Writing before the Letter," in *Of Grammatology*, corrected edition, trans. Gayatri Chakravorty Spivak (1967; Baltimore: Johns Hopkins University Press, 1997), 3. Also see Walter Mignolo, *The Darker Side of the Renaissance: Literacy, Territoriality, and Colonization*, 2nd ed. (1995; Ann Arbor, Mich.: The University of Michigan Press, 2003), 318.

[10]Aime Cesaire, cited in Edward Said, *Culture and Imperialism* (1993; New York: Vintage Books, 1994), 280.

[11]Chakrabarty, *Provincializing Europe*, 4.

[12]Derrida speaks for "New Enlightenment," instead of poststructuralism or postmodernism. Cf. John Caputo, *What Would Jesus Deconstruct?: The Good News of Postmodernism for the Church* (Grand Rapids, Mich.: Baker Academic, 2007), 145.

[13]Gayatri Chakravorty Spivak, "Translator's Preface," in Jacques Derrida, *Of Grammatology*, corrected edition, trans. Gayatri Chakravorty Spivak (1967; Baltimore: Johns Hopkins University Press, 1997), xxxi. In Nietzsche, this "forgetfulness" is double-edged: one edge "as a limitation that protects the human being from the blinding light of an absolute historical memory, and the other edge as a self-chosen willing, an active forgetfulness, that makes possible to ward off the trap of "historical knowledge." Ibid.

[14]Chakrabarty, *Provincializing Europe*, 5.

[15]Frantz Fanon, *The Wretched of the Earth*, trans. Constance Farrington (1961; New York: Grove Weidenfeld, 1963), 312–16.

[16]Frantz Fanon, *Black Skin, White Masks*, trans. Charles Lam Markmann (1952; New York: Grove Press, 1967), 7.

[17]Chakrabarty, *Provincializing Europe*, 5.

[18]Michel Foucault, "Intellectuals and Power: A Conversation between Michel Foucault and Gilles Deleuze," in *Language, Counter-Memory, Practice: Selected Essays and Interviews*, ed. Donald F. Bouchard, trans. Donald F. Bouchard and Sherry Simon (Ithaca, N.Y.: Cornell University Press, 1977), 208.

[19]Michel Foucault, "What Is an Author?" in *Language, Counter-Memory, Practice*, 138. Note that the translators use gender exclusive language throughout the book, including this quote.

[20]Ibid.

[21]Roland Barthes, "The Death of the Author," in *Image, Music, Text,* trans. Stephen Heath (New York: Hill and Wang, 1977), 143.

[22]Cf. Diogenes Laërtius, *Lives of Eminent Philosophers,* vol. II, trans. H.D. Hicks (Cambridge, Mass.: Harvard University Press, 1925), 65 [Book VI:63]. Hereafter cited in the text as Diogenes Laërtius.

[23]Patrick Hayden, *Cosmopolitan Global Politics* (Burlington, Vt.: Ashgate, 2005), 12.

[24]Cf. Jeremy Waldon, "Minority Cultures and the Cosmopolitan Alternative," *University of Michigan Journal of Law Reform* 25 (1992): 751–93.

[25]John L. Moles, "Cynic Cosmopolitanism," in *The Cynics: The Cynic Movement in Antiquity and Its Legacy,* ed. R. Bracht Branham and Marie-Odile Goulet-Caze (Berkeley, Calif.: University of California Press, 1996), 113. Here Moles uses "a citizen of the cosmos" for *kosmopolites* (ibid., p. 107), where he also offers an explanation about the original meaning of the word, *kosmos,* as entailing the full force of the universe. For the use of "a citizen of the universe" for *kosmopolites,* see Martha Nussbaum, "Foreword" in Malcolm Schofield, *The Stoic Idea of the City* (Chicago: The University Press of Chicago Press, 1999), 133, and Branham and Goulet-Caze, "Introduction," in *The Cynics,* 24.

[26]Heinrich Niehues-Proebsting, "The Modern Reception of Cynicism: Diogenes in the Enlightenment," in Branham and Goulet-Caze, *The Cynics.*

[27]According to a scholium on Aristotle, cited in Donald R. Dudley, *A History of Cynicism: From Diogenes to the 6th Century A.D.* (London: Methuen & Co. LTD, 1937), 5.

[28]Diogenes Laërtius, *Lives of Eminent Philosophers,* vol. II, 39 [Book VI:38]

[29]Ibid., 41 [Book VI:38]

[30]Zeno, as quoted in A. A. Long, "The Concept of the Cosmopolitan in Greek and Roman Thought," The American Academy of Arts and Sciences, *Daedalus* (Summer 2008): 55.

[31]Diogenes Laërtius, *Lives of Eminent Philosophers,* vol. II , 145 [Book 7:33].

[32]A. A. Long, "The Concept of the Cosmopolitan in Greek and Roman Thought," 55.

[33]Seneca, *De Otio,* 4.1, in *Seneca: Moral Essays,* vol. 2, trans. John W. Basore (1932; Cambridge, Mass.: Harvard University Press, 1970), 187 and189.

[34]Marcus Aurelius, *The Meditations of the Emperor Marcus Antoninus,* ed. and trans. A. S. L. Farquharson, vol. I (Oxford, U.K.: Oxford University Press, 1968), 53 [Book IV:4].

[35]Ibid., 21 [Book II:1].

[36]Martha Nussbaum, "Kant and Cosmopolitanism," in *Perpetual Peace: Essays on Kant's Cosmopolitan Ideal,* ed. James Bohman and Mattias Lutz Bachmann (Cambridge, Mass.: MIT Press, 1997), 31.

[37]Jonathan R. Herman, *I and Tao: Martin Buber's Encounter with Chuang Tzu* (New York: State University of New York Press, 1996), ix. Cf. Martin Buber, *Reden und Gleichnisse des Tschuang-tse* (Leipzig: Insel-Verlag, 1910).

[38]Herman, *I and Tao: Martin Buber's Encounter with Chuang Tzu,* 154, 185.

[39]Ibid., 169.

[40]Immanuel Kant, "End of All Things," in *Perpetual Peace and Other Essays on Politics, History, and Morals,* trans. Ted Humphrey (Indianapolis, Ind., and Cambridge, Mass.: Hackett Publishing Company, 1983), 99. Italics in original.

[41]Ibid., 99.

[42]Toshihiko Izutsu, *Sufism and Taoism: A Comparative Study of Key Philosophical Concepts* (Los Angeles: University of California Press, 1983), 289.

[43]Joseph Needham, *Science and Civilization in China,* vol. 2 (Cambridge, U.K.: Cambridge University Press, 1956), 33.

[44]Izutsu, *Sufism and Taoism,* 300.

[45]Barbara E. Reed, "Taoism," in *Women in World Religions,* ed. Arvind Sharma (New York: State University of New York Press, 1987), 167.

[46]Joseph Needham, *Science and Civilization in China,* vol. 5 (Cambridge, U.K.: Cambridge University Press, 1983), 76.

[47]Michael Saso, *The Teachings of Taoist Master Chuang* (New Haven: Yale University Press, 1978), 4.

[48]Max Kaltenmark, "The Ideology of the T'ai-p'ing ching," in *Facets of Taoism: Essays in Chinese Religion,* ed. Holmes Welch and Anna Seidel (New Heaven: Yale University Press, 1979), 21.

[49]Edward Said, "Yeats and Decolonization," *Nationalism, Colonialism and Literature,* A Field Day Pamphlet, 15 (1988): 14.

[50]Cf. Catherine Keller, "Feminism and the Ethic of Inseparability," in *Weaving the Visions: New Patterns in Feminist Spirituality,* ed. Judith Plaskow and Carol Christ (San Francisco: Harper & Row, 1989).

[51]The Confucian canonical works are "The Four Books" and "The Five Classics." While "The Four Books" is the name given to *The Analects*, *The Great Learning*, *The Doctrine of the Mean,* and *Mencius*, "The Five Classics" is the name applied to *The Book of Change*, *The Book of History*, *The Book of Odes*, *The Book of Rites,* and *The Spring and Autumn Annals*. Since people believed Confucius to be their author or editor, they became canonical when Confucianism became the state ideology of China in the second century B.C.E. Cf. Miles Menander Dawson, *The Basic Thoughts of Confucius: The Conduct of Life* (New York: Garden City Publishing Co., 1939), xiii–xiv.

[52]http://www.legallanguage.com/legal-articles/adoption-statistics-2010/.

[53]http://www.thomaswhite.com/explore-the-world/south-korea.aspx.

[54]*Mencius,* in James Legge, trans., *The Four Books: Confucian Analects, the Great Learning, the Doctrine of the Mean, and the Works of Mencius* (1923; New York: Paragon, 1966), 698 [Bk. IV, Pt. I, Chap. V]

[55]Ibid., 725 [Bk. IV, Pt. I. Chap. XXVI, 1].

[56]Theresa Kelleher, "Confucianism," in *Women in World Religions,* ed. Arvind Sharma (New York: State University of New York Press, 1987), 137.

[57]*The Hsiao Ching,* trans. Mary Lelia Makra, ed. Paul K. T. Sih (New York: St. John's University Press, 1961), 20–21 (Chap. IX).

[58]Cf. Hyunah Yang, "Vision of Postcolonial Feminist Jurisprudence in Korea: Seen from the 'Family-Head System' in Family Law," *Journal of Korean Law,* vol. 5, no. 2 (2006): 12–28.

[59]Kay C. Lee, "Confucian Ethics, Judges, and Women: Divorce Under the Revised Korean Family Law," *Pacific Rim Law & Policy Journal,* vol. 4, no. 2 (1995): 482.

[60]Walter Mignolo, *The Darker Side of the Renaissance: Literacy, Territoriality, and Colonization,* 2nd ed. (1995; Ann Arbor, Mich.: The University of Michigan Press, 2003), 322.

[61]William Theodore De Bary, *Neo-Confucian Orthodoxy and the Learning of the Mind-and-Heart* (New York: Columbia University Press, 1981), 367–68.

[62]Lao Tsu, *Tao Te Ching,* trans. Gia-fu Feng and Jane English (New York: Vintage Books, 1972), chap. 18.

[63]Ibid., chap. 19.

[64]Fung Yu-lan, *The Spirit of Chinese Philosophy*, trans. E. R. Hughes (London: Kegan Paul, Trench, Triibner, 1947) 79. For a further discussion about the philosophical difference between Taoism and Confucianism, see Toshihiko Izutsu, "Lao-Tzu and Chuang-Tzu," in *Sufism and Taoism,* esp. 287–90.

[65]C. C. Chai and W. Chai, eds., *Li Chi, Book of Rites,* trans. James Legge, 2 vols. (1885; New York: University Books, 1967), IX:24.

[66]Ibid., X:24.

[67]Herrlee G. Creel, *Confucius: the Man and the Myth* (New York: Routeledge & Kegan Paul LTD, 1949), 122–23.

[68]Lao Tsu, *Tao Te Ching,* chap. 1.

[69]Ibid., chap. 21 and 32.

[70]Chi-hui Chien, "Theft's Way: A Comparative Study of Chuang Tzu's Tao and Derridean Trace," *Journal of Chinese Philosophy,* 17. 1 (1990): 32.

[71]Jacques Derrida, *On the Name,* ed. Thomas Dutoit, trans. David Wood, John P. Leavey Jr., and Ian McLeod (Stanford, Calif.: Stanford University Press, 1993), 50.

[72]Ibid., 52.

[73]Lao Tsu, *Tao Te Ching,* chap. 32.

[74]Chuang Tzu, *Chuang Tzu: Inner Chapters,* trans. Gia-Fu Feng and Jane English (New York: Random House, 1974), 37, 38.

[75]Jacques Derrida, *Of Grammatology,* trans. Gayatri Chakravorty Spivak (1974; Baltimore: The Johns Hopkins University Press, 1997), 49.

[76]Derk Bodde, *Festivals in Classical China* (Princeton, N.J.: Princeton University Press, 1975), 37.

[77]Pan Chao of Later Han, *Ts'ao Ta-Chia Nu Chieh*, chap. 3, 2b9-3al, cited by Diana Paul, "Portraits of the Feminine: Buddhist and Confucian Historical Perspectives," in *Studies in History of Buddhism,* ed. A. K. Narain (Delhi: B. R. Publishing Corporation, 1980), 212.

[78]Chuang Tzu, *Chuang Tzu: Inner Chapters,* 29.

[79]Jacques Derrida, "Force of Law," in *Acts of Religion*, ed. Gil Anidjar (New York and London: Routledge, 2002), 243.

[80]Benjamin Schwartz, *The World of Thought in Ancient China* (Cambridge, Mass.: Harvard UP, 1985), 219.

[81]Cf. Hongchu Fu, "Deconstruction and Taoism: Comparisons Reconsidered," *Comparative Literature Studies,* vol. 29, no. 3 (1992): 305.

[82]Cf. Toshihiko Izutsu, "Absolute Reversal of Values," in *Sufism and Taoism,* 430–41.

[83]Friedrich Nietzsche, *The Anti-Christ,* trans. H. L. Mencken (Tucson, Ariz.: See Sharp Press, 1999), 91.

[84]Graham Parkes, "Human/Nature in Nietzsche and Taoism," in *Nature in Asian Traditions of Thought: Essays in Environmental Philosophy*, ed. Baird Callicott and Roger T. Ames (Albany: State University of New York Press, 1989), 80.

[85]Hans-Georg Moeller, "The "Exotic" Nietzsche—East and West, *Journal of Nietzsche Studies*, no. 28 (Autumn 2004): 57. For contradicting views of the similarities and differences between Western and Taoist philosophy in ecological issues, see Paper Jordan, "'Daoism' and 'Deep Ecology': Fantasy and Potentiality," in *Daoism and Ecology: Ways within a Cosmic Landscape*, ed. N. J. Giradot, James Miller, and Liu Xiaogan (Cambridge, Mass.: Harvard CSWR, 2001), 9–18. For a debate over the issue of affinity between Derrida (deconstruction) and Chuang Tzu (Taoism), see Michelle Yeh, "Deconstructive Way: A Comparative Study of Derrida and Chuang Tzu," *Journal of Chinese Philosophy,* 10 (1983): 95–126 and Hongchu Fu, "Deconstruction and Taoism: Comparisons Reconsidered," *Comparative Literature Studies,* vol. 29, no. 3 (1992): 296–321.

[86]Martin McQuillan, "Introduction: Five Strategies for Deconstruction," in *Deconstruction: A Reader,* ed. Martin McQuillan (Edinburgh: Edinburgh University Press, 2000), 7.

[87]For the various symbols for Tao, see Tao Te Ching, chap. 8, 32, 34, 66, and 78 for water; chap. 10 and 55 for child; chap. 25 and 52 for Mother; chap. 6, 28, and 61 for female; and chap. 19 and 32 for the uncarved block.

[88]Lao Tsu, *Tao Te Ching,* chap. 16

[89]Chang Chung-ying, "Chinese Philosophy: A Characterization," in *Introduction to Chinese Philosophy,* ed. Ame Naess and Alastair Hannay (Oslo: Universitesforlaget, 1972), 149.

[90]Chuang Tzu, *The Complete Works of Chuang Tzu,* ed. Burton Watson (New York: Columbia University Press, 1968), 49 (chap. II).

[91]Toshihiko Izutsu, *Sufism and Taoism,* 311. Izutsu points out that Chuang Tzu's concept of Transformation does not mean that "the soul goes on transmigrating from one body to another," but means that "everything is a phenomenal from one body to another," but means that "everything is a phenomenal form of one unique Reality which goes on assuming successively different forms of self-manifestation." Ibid., 316.

[92]Ibid., 313.

[93]Cf. Jean-Luc Nancy, *Being Singular Plural,* trans. Robert D. Richardson and Anne E. O'Byrne (1996; Stanford: Stanford University Press, 2000).

[94]Toshihiko Izutsu, *Sufism and Taoism,* 326.

[95]Chuang Tzu, *Chuang Tzu: Inner Chapters,* chap. 6, trans. Gia-Fu Feng and Jane English (New York: Random House, 1974), 123.

[96]*Ibid.*, 22.

[97]Lao Tsu, *Tao Te Ching,* chap. 13.

[98]Jacques Derrida, *Monolingualism of the Other; or, The Prosthesis of Origin,* trans. Patrick Mensah (1996; Stanford, Calif.: Stanford University Press, 1998), 14–15.

[99]Immanuel Kant, *Grounding for the Metaphysics of Morals: On a Supposed Right to Lie because of Philanthropic Concerns,* trans. James W. Ellngton (Indianapolis: Hackett Publishing Company, 1993), 39.

[100]Ibid., 36.

[101]Ibid., 39.

[102]Christine Korsgaard, *Creating the Kingdom of Ends* (Cambridge, U.K.: Cambridge University Press, 1996), 193.

[103]Kant, "Idea for a Universal History with a Cosmopolitan Intent (1784)," *Perpetual Peace and Other Essays on Politics, History, and Morals,* trans. Ted Humphrey (Indianapolis, Ind., and Cambridge, Mass.: Hackett Publishing Company, 1983), 33.

[104]For the debate over this issue, see Oliver Sensen, "Dignity and the Formula of Humanity," in *Kant's Groundwork of the Metaphysics of Morals: A Critical Guide,* ed. Jens Timmermann (Cambridge, U.K.: Cambridge University Press, 2009), 102–118. Here, Sensen concludes that Kant bases his argument for respecting others on the categorical imperative, not on the inherent value in human beings.

[105]Immanuel Kant, "Perpetual Peace: A Philosophical Sketch," in *Kant's Political Writings,* ed. Hans Reiss, trans. H.B. Nisbet (Cambridge, U.K.: Cambridge University Press, 1971), 107–108. In my book, I use two books for Kant's "Perpetual Peace" to find the better translation: one from *Kant's Political Writings,* ed. Hans Reiss, trans. H.B. Nisbet and the other from *Perpetual Peace and Other Essays on Politics, History, and Morals*, trans. Ted Humphrey (Indianapolis, Ind., and Cambridge, Mass.: Hackett Publishing Company, 1983).

[106]Kant, "Perpetual Peace," in *Kant's Political Writings*, 105.

[107]Ibid., 106.

[108]Ibid., 99.

[109]Charles Beitz, "Does Global Inequality Matter?" in *Global Justice,* ed., Thomas W. Pogge (Oxford, U.K.: Blackwell, 2001) 106.

[110]Ted Humphrey, "Translator's Introduction," in Immanuel Kant, *Perpetual Peace and Other Essays on Politics, History, and Morals,* trans. Ted Humphrey (Indianapolis, Ind., and Cambridge, Mass.: Hackett Publishing Company, 1983), 1–2.

[111]Ibid.

[112]Kant, *Perpetual Peace,* trans. Ted Humphrey, 118.

[113]Robert Fine and Robin Cohen, "Four Cosmopolitanism Moments," in *Conceiving Cosmopolitanism: Theory, Context, and Practice,* 144.

[114]Cf. Walter Mignolo, "The Many Faces of Cosmo-polis: Border Thinking and Critical Cosmopolitanism," *Public Culture,* vol. 11, no 3 (Fall 2000): 721–48.

[115]Kant, *Perpetual Peace,* trans. Ten Humphrey, 118.

[116]Mignolo, "The Many Faces of Cosmo-polis," 731.

[117]Ibid., 722.

[118]Emmanuel Chukwudi Eze, *Race and the Enlightenment: A Reader* (Malden, Mass.: Blackwell, 1997).

[119]Immanuel Kant, "Of the Different Races of Human Beings," in *Anthropology, History, and Education,* ed. Günter Zöller and Robert B. Louden, trans. Mary Gregor, et al. (Cambridge, U.K.: Cambridge University Press, 2007), 87. Italics in original.

[120]Ibid., 95. Italics in original.

[121]Ibid., 93. For Kant's assumption about Negroes and Whites as the basic human races, see ibid., 88.

[122]Immanuel Kant, "Physical Geography," quoted in J. A. May, *Kant's Concept of Geography and Its Relation to Recent Geographical Thought* (Toronto: University of Toronto Press, 1970), 66.

[123]Immanuel Kant, "On the Feeling of the Beautiful and Sublime," in *Anthropology, History, and Education,* 55–56.

[124]Ibid., 59.

[125]Kant, "Physical Geography," in Emmanuel Chukwudi Eze, *Race and the Enlightenment: A Reader* (Malden, Mass.: Blackwell, 1997), 63. Italics added.

[126]Ibid., 62.

[127]Emmanuel Chukwudi Eze, "The Kant-Herder Controversy," in *Race and the Enlightenment,* 65.

[128]Kant, "Kant's Review of Herder's Ideas on the Philosophy of the History of Mankind, Part Two (1785)," in Eze, *Race and the Enlightenment,* 66–70.

[129]Tatham, "Environmentalism and Possibilism," in *Geography in the Twentieth Century,* ed. Griffith Taylor, 3rd edition (London: Methuen, 1957), 130–31. Quoted in May, *Kant's Concept of Geography,* 68.

[130]See for further discussion about the reception and influence of Kant's idea of geography, see J. A. May, "Kant's Influence," *Kant's Concept of Geography,* 73–83.

[131]Erich Adickes, *Kant als Naturforscher,* vol. II (Berlin: W. de Gruyter, 1925), 380. Quoted in May, *Kant's Concept of Geography,* 68. The handwritten copies of Kant's lectures were broadly passed around and even the Prussian Minister of Culture, who was a Kant admirer, read them. May, ibid., 73.

[132]May, *Kant's Concept of Geography,* 3–4. For Kant's life, see "Life and Philosophical Development," in Otfried Höffe, *Immanuel Kant,* trans. Marshall Farrier (1992; Albany, N.Y.: State University of New York, 1994), 9–30.

[133]Kant, "Of the different races of human beings," *Anthropology, History, and Education*, 97. Italics in original.

[134]Friedrich Paulsen, *Immanuel Kant: His Life and Doctrine,* trans. J. E. Creighton and Albert

Lefebvre, 2nd ed. (1902; New York: Frederick Ungar, 1963), 60. Quoted in May, *Kant's Concept of Geography,* 5.

[135]May, *Kant's Concept of Geography,* 9. For a wide range of perspectives on Kant's interest in geography and its complex implication, see Stuart Elden and Eduardo Mendieta, eds., *Reading Kant's Geography* (Albany, N.Y.: State University of New York Press, 2011).

[136]Cf. Emmanuel Chukwudi Eze, *Race and the Enlightenment;* and id., "The Color of Reason: The Idea of 'Race' in Kant's Anthropology," in *Postcolonial African Philosophy: A Critical Reader,* ed. Emmanuel Chukwudi Eze (Cambridge, Mass.: Blackwell, 1997); Immanuel Kant, "Physical Geography (1802)," in *Kant: Natural Science,* ed. Eric Watkins, the Cambridge Edition of the Works of Immanuel Kant (Cambridge, U.K.: Cambridge University Press, 2012). Regarding the full information about the publication of Kant's *Physical Geography,* see Elden and Mendieta, eds., *Reading Kant's Geography,* 2.

[137]*Le Monde,* 5 February 1999, quoted in David Harvey, "Cosmopolitanism and the Banality of Geographical Evils," *Public Culture,* vol. 12, no. 2 (2000): 532.

[138]Cf. Eze, *Race and the Enlightenment,* 3; and Howard Caygill, *A Kant Dictionary* (Oxford, U.K.: Blackwell Publishers, 1994).

[139]Michel Foucault, "Questions on Geography," in *Power/Knowledge: Selected Interviews and Other Writings 1972-1977,* ed. Colin Gordon, trans. Colin Gordon, Leo Marshall, John Mepham, Kate Soper (New York: Pantheon Books, 1980), 66, 67.

[140]Ibid., 77.

[141]Ibid., 70.

[142]Michel Foucault, "Of Other Spaces," *Diacritics* 16, no.1 (Spring 1986): 22.

[143]Cf. Granham Bird, ed., *A Companion to Kant* (Oxford, U.K.: Blackwell, 2006); and Paul Guyer, ed., *The Cambridge Companion to Kant and Modern Philosophy* (Cambridge, U.K.: Cambridge University Press, 2006).

[144]Foucault, "Questions on Geography," 66. Quoted by Spivak, "Can Subaltern Speak?" in *Marxism and the Interpretation of Culture,* ed. Cary Nelson and Lawrence Grossberg (Urbana and Chicago: University of Illinois Press, 1988), 291.

[145]Kwame Anthony Appiah, *In My Father's House: Africa in the Philosophy of Culture* (Oxford, U.K.: Oxford University Press, 1992), 13.

[146]Hannah Arendt, "Race-Thinking Before Racism," in *The Origins of Totalitarianism* (1951; New York: Schocken Books, 2004), 211.

[147]David Hume, "Of National Character (1748)," in *The Philosophical Works of David Hume,* vol. III (Bristol: Thoemmes Press, 1996), 228.

[148]Kant, "On the Feeling of the Beautiful and Sublime," in *Anthropology, History, and Education,* 59, 61.

[149]Steven Vertovec and Robin Cohen, eds., *Conceiving Cosmopolitanism: Theory, Context, and Practice* (Oxford, U.K.: Oxford University Press, 2002), 140.

[150]Arendt, "Race-Thinking Before Racism," 214.

[151]Holly L. Wilson, *Kant's Pragmatic Anthropology: Its Origin, Meaning, and Critical Significance* (Albany, N.Y.: SUNY Press, 2006), 8.

[152]Immanuel Kant, *Anthropology from a Pragmatic Point of View,* ed. and trans. Robert B. Louden (Cambridge, U.K.: Cambridge University Press, 2006), 4. Quoted in Elden and Mendieta, eds., *Reading Kant's Geography,* 9

[153]Immanuel Kant, "An Answer to the Question: What Is Enlightenment?"(1784) in *Perpetual Peace and Other Essays on Politics,* trans. Ted Humphrey, 43–44. Emphasis added.

[154]Otfried Höffe, *Immanuel Kant,* trans. Marshall Farrier (1992; Albany, N.Y.: State University of New York Press, 1994), 26.

[155]Otfried Höffe, *Kant's Cosmopolitan Theory of Law and Peace,* trans. Alexandra Newton (2001; Cambridge, U.K.: Cambridge University Press, 2006), 13.

[156]Cf. Susan Meld Shell, *The Embodiment of Reason* (Chicago: University of Chicago Press, 1996); Peter Fenves, *Late Kant* (London: Routledge, 2003); and Sankar Muthu, *Enlightenment against Empire* (Princeton: Princeton University Press, 2003).

[157]Pauline Kleingeld, "Kant's Second Thoughts on Race," *The Philosophical Quarterly,* vol. 57, no. 229 (October 2007): 573.

[158]Robert Bernasconi, "Kant's Third Thoughts on Race," in *Reading Kant's Geography,* ed. Stuart Elden and Eduardo Mendieta, 295

[159]Kant, *Anthropology, History, and Education,* 83.

[160]Immanuel Kant, "To Perpetual Peace: A Philosophical Sketch (1785)," in *Perpetual Peace*, trans. Ted Humphrey, 118, 119.

[161]Walter D. Mignolo, "The Darker Side of the Enlightenment: A De-Colonial Reading of Kant's Geography," in *Reading Kant's Geography*, ed. Stuart Elden and Eduardo Mendieta, 319–43.

[162]Höffe, *Kant's Cosmopolitan Theory of Law and Peace*, xv.

[163]Kant, *Perpetual Peace*, trans. Ted Humphrey, 126.

[164]For the phrase "Thinking with Kant against Kant," see Fine and Cohen, "Four Cosmopolitan Moments," in *Conceiving Cosmopolitanism: Theory, Context, and Practice*, 140.

[165]Emmanuel Levinas, *Otherwise than Being or Beyond Essence*, trans. Alphonso Lingis (1974; Pittsburgh: Duquesne University Press, 1998).

[166]Adriaan T. Peperzak, *Beyond: The Philosophy of Emmanuel Levinas* (Evanston, Ill.: Northwestern University Press, 1996), 74.

[167]United States Holocaust Memorial Museum. "The Holocaust." *Holocaust Encyclopedia.* http://www.ushmm.org/wlc/en/?ModuleId=10005143.

[168]United States Holocaust Memorial Museum. "Persecution of Homosexuals in the Third Reich." *Holocaust Encyclopedia.* http://www.ushmm.org/wlc/en/?ModuleId=10005143.

[169]Dan Stone, "Rafael Lemkin on the Holocaust," *Journal of Genocide Research*, 7.4 (December 2005): 539.

[170]Raphael Lemkin, *Axis Rule in Occupied Europe: Laws of Occupation, Analysis of Government, Proposals for Redress* (Washington, D.C.: Carnegie Endowment for International Peace, 1944), xi–xii. Quoted in Dan Stone, "Rafael Lemkin on the Holocaust," *Journal of Genocide Research*, 7.4 (December 2005): 540.

[171]Lemkin, *Axis Rule in Occupied Europe*, 79. Quoted in Dan Stone, "Rafael Lemkin on the Holocaust," 540.

[172]Ibid., 540.

[173]Emmanuel Levinas, *Totality and Infinity: An Essay on Exteriority*, trans. Alphonso Lingis (1961; Pittsburgh: Duquesne University Press, 1969), 43.

[174]Raphael Lemkin, as quoted in Henry T. King Jr., "Genocide and Nuremberg," in *The Criminal Law of Genocide: International, Comparative and Contextual Aspects*, ed. Ralph Henham and Paul Behrens (Burlington, Vt.: Ashgate, 2007), 30. For Lemkin's life and work, see Lemkin, *Axis Rule in Occupied Europe*.

[175]Michael R. Marrus, *The Nuremberg War Crimes Trial 1945–46: A Documentary History* (Boston: Bedford Books, 1997), 185.

[176]"Charter of the International Military Tribunal, August 8, 1945," quoted in Marrus, *The Nuremberg War Crimes Trial 1945–46*, 52.

[177]Marrus, *The Nuremberg War Crimes Trial 1945–46*, 5.

[178]The term "laws of humanity" was used after the First World War in the 1919 peace conference at Paris. Cf. Marrus, *The Nuremberg War Crimes Trial 1945–46*, 185.

[179]Karl Jaspers, *The Question of German Guilt*, trans. E. B. Ashton (1945; New York: Capricorn Books, 1961), 60. Italics added.

[180]Hannah Arendt and Karl Jaspers, *Hannah Arendt and Karl Jaspers Correspondence 1926–1969*, trans. Robert and Rita Kimber (1985; New York: A Harvest Book, 1992), 410–11.

[181]Ibid., 423.

[182]Ibid., 424.

[183]Cf. Giorgio Agamben, *Remnants of Auschwitz: The Witness and the Archive*, trans. Daniel Heller-Roazen (New York: Zone Books, 1999), 34–39.

[184]Giorgio Agamben, *Homo Sacer: Sovereign Power and Bare Life*, trans. Daniel Heller-Roazen (Stanford, Calif.: Stanford University Press, 1998), 166.

[185]Ibid., 168. Italics in original.

[186]Ibid., 8.

[187]Agamben, *Remnants of Auschwitz*, 121.

[188]Giorgio Agamben, *Potentialities* (Stanford: Stanford University Press, 1999), 267.

[189]Agamben, *Remnants of Auschwitz*, 161–62.

[190]Ibid., 13.

[191]Agamben, *Homo Sacer*, 166.

[192]Primo Levi, *Survival in Auschwitz: The Nazi Assault on Humanity*, trans. Stuart Woolf (1958; New York: Simon and Schuster, 1996), 90.

[193]Giorgio Agamben, "The Camp as the 'Nomos' of the Modern," in *Homo Sacer*, 166–80.

[194]United Nations, "Universal Declaration of Human Rights," in Geoffrey Robertson, *Crimes Against Humanity: The Struggle for Global Justice* (New York: The New Press, 1999), 486. It would be necessary to produce a revised version of the Declaration because it uses the masculine pronouns throughout the thirty articles, including such exclusive words as "brotherhood" in article 1.

[195]Ibid., 486.

[196]Seyla Benhabib argues that although Kant's cosmopolitan thought and his moral theory have influenced Arendt, she, as a "political existentialist," "remains committed to a civic republican vision of political self-determination." Seyla Benhabib, *Another Cosmopolitanism* (Oxford, U.K.: Oxford University Press, 2006), 15.

[197]Arendt, *The Origins of Totalitarianism,* 379. Italics added.

[198]Benhabib, *Another Cosmopolitanism,* 2.

[199]Heinrich Blücher letter in Arendt and Jaspers, *Hannah Arendt and Karl Jaspers Correspondence,* 400–401.

[200]United Nations, "Universal Declaration of Human Rights," 1948, articles 1 and 2.

[201]Jacques Derrida, *On Cosmopolitanism and Forgiveness,* trans. Mark Dooley and Michael Hughes (London and New York: Routeledge, 2001), 9.

[202]Ibid., 29.

[203]Ibid.

[204]Ibid.

[205]Jason E. Powell, *Jacques Derrida: A Biography* (London: Continuum, 2006), 218.

[206]Hannah Arendt, *Eichmann in Jerusalem: A Report on the Banality of Evil,* rev. ed. (1963; New York: Penguin Books, 1977), 244–55.

[207]Seyla Benhabib, "Arendt's *Eichmann in Jerusalem,*" in *The Cambridge Companion to Hannah Arendt,* ed. Dana Villa (Cambridge, U.K.: Cambridge University Press, 2000), 79.

[208]Adolf Eichmann, as quoted in Arendt, *Eichmann in Jerusalem,* 248.

[209]Ibid., 252.

[210]Mark W. Clark, "A Prophet without Honour: Karl Jaspers in Germany, 1945–48," *Journal of Contemporary History,* vol. 37, no. 2 (April 2002): 204.

[211]Jaspers, *The Question of German Guilt,* 61.

[212]Ibid., 61.

[213]Ibid., 63.

[214]Ibid.

[215]Ibid., 64.

[216]Ibid., 71, 72.

[217]Clark, "A Prophet without Honour," 208.

[218]Jaspers, *The Question of German Guilt,* 123.

[219]Ibid.

[220]Anson Rabinbach, *In the Shadow of Catastrophe: German Intellectuals Between Apocalypse and Enlightenment* (Weimar and Now: German Cultural Criticism) (1997; Berkeley, Calif.: University of California Press, 2001), 143–44.

[221]Adolf Hitler, as quoted in U.K. Foreign Office, *Documents on British Foreign Policy, 1919–1939,* 3rd series, 9 vols. (HMSO, 1949–55), vol. 7, 258. Quoted in Geoffrey Robertson, *Crime Against Humanity: The Struggle for Global Justice,* 3rd ed. (1999; New York: The New Press, 2006), ix. Italics added.

[222]Jaspers, *The Question of German Guilt,* 71.

[223]Hannah Arendt, *The Human Condition* (1958; Chicago: University of Chicago Press, 1998), 241.

Chapter 4

[1]Charles Taylor, *Sources of the Self: The Making of Modern Identity* (Cambridge, Mass.: Harvard University Press, 1989), 35.

[2]Luce Irigaray, *Key Writings* (London: Continuum, 2004), 172. Italics added.

[3]Cited in David Frum, *The Right Man: An Inside Account of the Bush White House* (New York: Random House, 2003), 283.

[4]Cf. Elizabeth H. Prodromou, "U.S. Foreign Policy and Global Religious Pluralism," in *Religious Pluralism: Globalization, and World Politics,* ed. Thomas Babchoff (Oxford, U.K.: Oxford University Press, 2008), 306.

[5]Ibid., 306.

[6]Bob Woodward, *Bush at War* (New York: Simon and Schuster, 2002), 46.

[7]Cf. Diana Eck, *A New Religious America: How a "Christian" Country Has Become the World's Most Religiously Diverse Nation* (San Francisco: HarperCollins, 1999).

[8]Hent de Vries, *Religion and Violence: Philosophical Perspectives from Kant to Derrida* (Baltimore and London: The Johns Hopkins University Press, 2002), 1. For the issue of religion and violence in contemporary world, also see Mark Juergensmeyer, *Terror in the Mind of God: The Global Rise of Religious Violence* (Berkeley, Calif.: University of California Press, 2003); and Bruce Lincoln, *Holy Terrors: Thinking about Religion after September 11th* (Chicago: University of Chicago Press, 2003).

[9]Hent de Vries, *Religion and Violence,* 1.

[10]Cf. George Herbert Mead, *Mind, Self, and Society* (Chicago: University of Chicago Press, 1934).

[11]Charles Taylor, "Politics of Recognition," in *Multiculturalism: A Critical Reader,* ed. David Theo Goldberg (Malden, Mass.: Blackwell, 1994).

[12]Ibid., 75.

[13]For a comprehensive discussion about multiculturalism and politics of recognition, see Amy Gutmann, ed., *Multiculturalism: Examining the Politics of Recognition* (Princeton, N.J.: Princeton University Press, 1994); for a wide range of multiculturalism including "critical multiculturalism," see David Theo Goldberg, ed., *Multiculturalism: A Critical Reader.*

[14]Peter McLaren, "White Terror and Oppositional Agency: Toward a Critical Multiculturalism," in Goldberg, ed., *Multiculturalism: A Critical Reader,* 45–74.

[15]Ibid., 48.

[16]Ibid.

[17]Ibid., 49.

[18]Ibid., 53.

[19]Taylor, "Politics of Recognition," 76.

[20]Ibid., 81.

[21]For example, see the following American Academy of Religion Web site for the sample syllabi for the courses on religions. http://www.aarweb.org/Programs/Syllabus_Project/browse.asp

[22]John Hick and Paul F. Knitter, eds., *The Myth of Christian Uniqueness: Toward a Pluralistic Theology of Religions* (Maryknoll, N.Y.: Orbis, 1987), 22.

[23]Ibid., 22.

[24]Jacques Dupius, *Toward a Christian Theology of Religious Pluralism* (Maryknoll, N.Y.: Orbis, 2004), 10. For an extensive discussion about various positions of theology of religion, see Veli-Matti Kärkkäinen, *An Introduction to the Theology of Religions: Biblical, Historical & Contemporary Perspectives* (Downers Grove, Ill.: InterVarsity Press, 2003); John Hick, *An Interpretation of Religion: Human Response to the Transcendent* (New Haven, Conn.: Yale University Press, 2004). There are scholars, including myself, who do not wish to identify themselves with any such category as inclusivist or pluralist, as this way of categorization itself has a rationalizing and totalizing tendency of modernism. Cf. Tom Driver, "The Case for Pluralism," in *The Myth of Christian Uniqueness,* ed. Hick and Knitter, 205–206.

[25]Owen C. Thomas, "Religious Plurality and Contemporary Philosophy: A Critical Survey," *The Harvard Theological Review,* vol. 87, no. 2 (April 1994): 200.

[26]Thomas Banchoff, ed., *Religious Pluralism: Globalization, and World Politics* (Oxford, U.K.: Oxford University Press, 2008), 5.

[27]John C. Murray, *Religious Liberty: Catholic Struggle with Pluralism,* ed. J. Leon Hooper (Louisville, Ky.: Westminster/John Knox, 1993), 150.

[28]Chandra T. Mohanty, "On Race and Voice: Challenges for Liberal Education in the 1990s," *Cultural Critique* No. 14 (Winter 1989): 207.

[29]Marnia Lazreg, "Feminism and Difference: The Perils of Writing as a Woman on Women in Algeria," *Feminist Studies* 14, no. 1 (Spring 1988): 98.

[30]Giovanna Borradori, "A Dialogue with Jacques Derrida," in *Philosophy in a Time of Terror: Dialogues with Jürgen Habermas and Jacques Derrida* (Chicago: The University of Chicago Press, 2003), 127.

[31]Ibid., 128.

[32]Russell T. McCutcheon, "'Category of "Religion' and the Politics of Tolerance," in *Defining Religion: Investigating the Boundaries Between the Sacred and Secular,* Religion and the Social Order, vol.

10, ed. Arthur L. Greil and David C. Bromley (Bingley, U.K.: Emerald Group Publishing Limited, 2003), 158.

Chapter 5

[1]Richard Rorty, "Anticlericalism and Atheism," in Richard Rorty and Gianni Vattimo, *Future of Religion,* ed. Santiago Zabala (New York: Columbia University Press, 2005), 40

[2]Achille Mbembe, *On the Postcolony* (Berkeley and Los Angeles: University of California Press, 2001), 174.

[3]Cited in Jacques Derrida, *On the Name,* ed. Thomas Dutoit, trans. David Wood, John P. Leavey Jr., and Ian McLeod (Stanford, Calif.: Stanford University Press, 1993), 75. Angelus Silesius, a German mystic, is one of Derrida's often-quoted figures.

[4]Hannah Arendt, *Love and Saint Augustine* (1929; Chicago: Chicago University Press, 1996), 96.

[5]Jacques Derrida, *The Gift of Death,* trans. David Willis (1992; Chicago: University of Chicago Press, 1995), 80.

[6]Yvonne Sherwood, ed., *Derrida's Bible (Reading a Page of Scripture with a Little Help from Derrida)* (New York: Palgrave Macmillan, 2004), 29.

[7]Cf. John 3:3–4. For the word "kindom," instead of "kingdom," see *The Inclusive New Testament* (Brentwood, Maryland: Priests for Equality, 1996).

[8]Jacques Derrida, "Force of Law," in *Acts of Religion,* ed. Gil Anidjar (New York: Routledge, 2002), 251.

[9]Hannah Arendt, *The Human Condition* (Chicago: University of Chicago Press, 1958), 177. Here Arendt introduces Augustine's distinction between *initium* and *principium.* Whereas the beginning of the world, *principium,* does not imply that nothing was created before, the beginning of human, *initium,* means "nobody was before" the person.

[10]Cf. ibid., 177, 247.

[11]Ibid., 9.

[12]Cf. Patricia Bowen-Moore, *Hannah Arendt's Philosophy of Natality* (New York: St. Martin's Press, 1989); Francoise Collin, "Birth as Praxis," in *The Judge and the Spectator: Arendt's Political Philosophy,* ed. J. Herman and D. Villa (Belgium: Peeters, 1999); Margarete Durst, "Birth and Natality in Hannah Arendt," *Analecta husserliana* 79 (2004): 777–97; and Patchen Markell, "The Rule of the People: Arendt, Arche, and Democracy," *The American Political Science Review* 100, 1 (2006): 1–14.

[13]Cf. "…das faktische Dasein existiert gebürtig und gebürtig stirbt es auch schon im Sinne des Seins zum Tode...(factical Dasein exists natively and natively it dies also already in the sense of being-towards-death). " Martin Heidegger, *Sein und Zeit* (Tübingen: Max Niemeyer, 1986), 374. Cited and translated in Miguel Vatter, "Natality and Biopolitics in Hannah Arendt, " *Revista De Ciencia Politica,* vol. 26, no. 2 (2006): 139.

[14]Hannah Arendt, *Denkentagebuch: 1950 bis 1973,* Erster Band (München: Piper, 2002), 461, 462. Here Arendt juxtaposes Natalität (natality) and Mortalität (mortality).

[15]Roberto Esposito, *Bios: Biopolitics and Philosophy* (Minnesota: University of Minnesota Press, 2008), 15.

[16]Cf. Arendt, *The Human Condition*, 8.

[17]Ibid., 247.

[18]Compare both texts that announce the birth of Messiah: The gospel according to Luke, 2:11, says, "To you is born this day in the city of David a Savior, who is the Messiah, the Lord," whereas Isaiah 9:6a says, "For a child has been born for us, / a son given to us."

[19]For a detailed discussion about Arendt's citation from the Christian Bible, see Frederick M. Dolan, "An Ambiguous Citation in Hannah Arendt's 'The Human Condition,'" *The Journal of Politics,* vol. 66, no. 2 (May 2004): 606–610.

[20]For a philosophical analysis of Arendt's notion of natality, see Bowen-Moore, *Hannah Arendt's Philosophy of Natality.*

[21]Arendt, *The Human Condition,* 247.

[22]Ibid., 9.

[23]Franz Rosenzweig, *The Star of Redemption,* trans. William W. Hallo (Norte Dame, Ind.: University of Norte Dame Press, 1985). Note that there are two translations that I use, as each translation has its limit and strength respectively.

[24]Ibid., 97.

[25]Ibid., 95.

[26]Rosenzweig, *The Star of Redemption,* trans. Barbara E. Galli (Madison, Wis.: University of Wisconsin, 2005), 231.

[27]Cf. Bowen-Moore, *Hannah Arendt's Philosophy of Natality,* 2.

[28]Michel Foucault, *Language, Counter-Memory, Practice: Selected Essays and Interviews* (1977; Ithaca, N.Y.: Cornell University Press, 1993), 162.

[29]Bruce James Smith, *Politics and Remembrance* (Princeton: Princeton University Press, 1985), 15–16.

[30]Michel Foucault, *The History of Sexuality, Vol. 1: An Introduction,* trans. Robert Hurley (New York: Vintage Books, 1990), 136.

[31]Michel Foucault, *"Society Must Be Defended": Lectures at the College de France, 1975–76,* trans. David Macey (1997; New York: Picador, 2003), 36.

[32]Foucault, *History of Sexuality,* 141.

[33]Ibid., 138.

[34]Primo Levi, *Survival in Auschwitz: The Nazi Assault on Humanity,* trans. Stuart Woolf (1958; New York: Simon and Schuster, 1996), 87.

[35]Ibid., 90.

[36]Ibid.

[37]Giorgio Agamben, *Homo Sacer: Sovereign Power and Bare Life,* trans. Daniel Heller-Roazen (Stanford: Stanford University Press, 1998), 8.

[38]Ibid., 9.

[39]Ibid.

[40]Ibid., 71.

[41]Ibid., 181.

[42]Ibid.

[43]Ibid., 73.

[44]The Greeks used to express the word "life" in two terms: *zoe* and *bios*. Whereas *zoe* denotes the simple fact of living common to all living beings—"bare life"—*bios* refers to "the form or way of living proper to an individual or a group." Agamben, *Homo Sacer,* 1.

[45]Ibid., 166.

[46]Ibid., 174.

[47]Cf. ibid., 122, and Peter Fitzpatrick, "These Mad Abandon's Times," *Economy and Society,* vol. 30, no. 2 (May 2001): 255–70.

[48]Hannah Arendt, *The Origins of Totalitarianism* (1951; New York: Schocken Books, 2004), 365.

[49]Ibid., 582, 585.

[50]Ibid., 577.

[51]Cf. Willem Schinkel, "Illegal Aliens and the State, or: Bare Bodies vs. the Zombie," *International Sociology,* vol. 24. No. 6 (Nov 2009): 779–806.

[52]Agamben, *Homo Sacer,* 166.

[53]Schinkel, "Illegal Aliens and the State," 780.

[54]Cf. http://www.iom.int/jahia/Jahia/about-migration/facts-and-figures/lang/en and http://esa.un.org/migration/p2k0data.asp.

[55]Schinkel, "Illegal Aliens and the State," 783.

[56]Agamben, *Homo Sacer,* 181.

[57]Section 1: Findings and Declaration, California Proposition 187. http://en.wikisource.org/wiki/California_Proposition_187_(1994).

[58]Glen Gendzel, "It Didn't Start with Proposition 187: One Hundred and Fifty Years of Nativist Legislation in California," *Journal of the West,* vol. 48, no. 2 (Spring 2009): 76–85. Here Gendzel starts his analysis of xenophobic anti-immigration law, beginning with the Foreign Miners' Tax of 1850 in California.

[59]Slavoj Zizek, "From Homo Sacer to the Neighbor," in *Welcome to the Desert of the Real* (London and New York: Verso, 2002), 113.

[60]Ibid. Italics added.

[61]Frantz Fanon, *Black Skin, White Masks,* trans. Charles Lam Markmann (1952; New York: Grove Press, 1967), 8.

[62]Dawn Rae Davis, "(Love Is) The Ability of Not Knowing: Feminist Experience of the Impossible in Ethical Singularity," *Hypatia,* vol. 17, no. 2 (Spring 2002): 147.

[63]Rosenzweig, *The Star of Redemption,* 240.

[64]Cf. Roberto Esposito, *Bios: Biopolitics and Philosophy* (Minnesota: University of Minnesota Press, 2008).

[65]Arendt, *The Human Condition,* 177–78.

[66]Ibid., 8–9.

[67]Søren Kierkegaard, *Works of Love,* trans. Howard Hong (New York: Harper, 1994), 75.

[68]Ibid., 74.

[69]Theodore Adorno, "On Kierkegaard's Doctrine of Love," *Studies in Philosophy and Social Science* 8 (1939–1940): 417.

[70]Adorno, "On Kierkegaard's Doctrine of Love," 419.

[71]Arendt, *The Human Condition,* 5.

[72]Bowen-Moore, *Hannah Arendt's Philosophy of Natality,* 36.

[73]St. Augustine, *Commentaries on the Psalms* 25, ii, 2, cited in Arendt, *Love and Saint Augustine,* 94.

[74]Rosenzweig, *The Star of Redemption,* trans. William W. Hallo, 236.

[75]Rosenzweig, *The Star of Redemption,* trans. Barbara E. Galli, 230.

[76]Ibid., 234.

[77]Cited in John Caputo, *The Prayers and Tears of Jacques Derrida: Religion without Religion* (Bloomington and Indianapolis: Indiana University Press, 1997), 49.

[78]Rosenzweig, *The Star of Redemption,* trans. Barbara E. Galli, 241. Italics added.

[79]Arendt, *The Human Condition,* 103–104.

[80]Augustine, *St. Augustine's Confessions: or, Praises of God,* trans. Richard Challoner, Bishop of Debra, Eighteenth Century Collections Online (Dublin: E. Bate, 1746), Book X, Chapter VII, 342.

[81]Paul Celan, cited in Emmanuel Levinas, *Otherwise than Being or Beyond Essence,* trans. Alphonso Lingis (1981; Pittsburgh: Duquesne University Press, 1998), 99. Author's translation .

[82]Friedrich Nietzsche, "On Love of the Neighbor," in *Thus Spoke Zarathustra: A Book for None or All,* trans. Walter Kaufmann (New York: Penguin, 1966), 60–61.

[83]Gayatri Chakravorty Spivak, *A Critique of Postcolonial Reason: Toward a History of the Vanishing Present* (Cambridge, Mass.: Harvard University Press, 1999), 383.

[84]http://www.goodasyou.org/good_as_you/2010/07/video-spriggs-suggested-both-jail-and-deportation——but-yea-its-probably-knowledge-thats-the-real-enemy-sigh-eye-ro.html.

[85]http://www.rightwingwatch.org/content/sprigg-nothing-we-have-done-can-reasonably-be-called-hate.

[86]Cf. http://www.frc.org.

Chapter 6

[1]Lao Tsu, *Tao Te Ching,* trans. Gia-fu Feng and Jane English (New York: Vintage Books, 1972), chap. 13.

[2]Emmanuel Levinas, *Otherwise than Being or Beyond Essence,* trans. Alphonso Lingis (1974; Pittsburgh: Duquesne University Press, 1998), 114.

[3]Jacques Derrida, *The Gift of Death,* trans. David Willis (1992; Chicago: University of Chicago Press, 1995), 2.

[4]Jean-Luc Nancy, *Being Singular Plural,* trans. Robert D. Richardson and Anne E. O'Byrne (1996; Stanford: Stanford University Press, 2000), xiii.

[5]MerckEngage advertisement, http://www.msnbc.msn.com/id/26315908/#44825241.

[6]Immanuel Kant, "Perpetual Peace: A Philosophical Sketch (1795)," in *Perpetual Peace and Other Essays on Politics, History, and Morals,* trans. Ted Humphrey (Indianapolis, Ind., and Cambridge, Mass.: Hackett Publishing Company, 1983), 126.

[7]Emmanuel Levinas, *Totality and Infinity: An Essay on Exteriority,* trans. Alphonso Lingis (1961; Pittsburgh, Pa.: Duquesne University Press, 1969), 43.

[8]Adriaan Theodoor Peperzak, *Beyond: The Philosophy of Emmanuel Levinas* (Evanston, Ill.: Northwestern University Press, 1997), 4.

[9]Nancy, *Being Singular Plural,* 1.

[10]Ibid., 2. Italics in original.

[11]Ibid., 5.

[12]Drucilla Cornell, *The Philosophy of the Limit* (New York: Routledge, 1992), 22.

[13]Levinas, *Totality and Infinity,* 51.

[14]Jacques Derrida, "Force of Law: The Mystical Foundation of Authority," in *Acts of Religion,* ed. Gil Anidjar (New York and London: Routledge, 2002), 404.

[15]Levinas, *Totality and Infinity,* 37.

[16]Ibid., 46–47.

[17]Gerald Robert Vizenor, *Fugitive Poses: Native American Indian Scenes of Absence and Presence* (Lincoln, Neb.: University of Nebraska Press, 1998), 14.

[18]Levinas, *Otherwise than Being or Beyond Essence,* 114. Italics in original.

[19]Ibid., 116.

[20]Ibid., 149.

[21]Alain Badiou, *Saint Paul: The Foundation of Universalism* (Stanford: Stanford University Press, 2003), 108.

[22]Douglas Harink, "Introduction: From Apocalypse to Philosophy—and Back," in *Paul, Philosophy, and the Theopolitical Vision: Critical Engagements with Agamben, Badiou, Zizek and Others,* ed. Douglas Harink (Eugene, Oreg.: Cascade Books, 2010), 1.

[23]Badiou, *Saint Paul,* 17.

[24]Ibid., 1, 2.

[25]Ibid., 108.

[26]Ibid.

[27]Justin D. Klassen, "Heidegger's Paul and Radical Orthodoxy on the Structure of Christian Hope," in *Paul, Philosophy, and the Theopolitical Vision,* ed. Douglas Harink, 65.

[28]Cf. Theodore W. Jennings, *Reading Derrida/Thinking Paul: On Justice* (Stanford, Calif.: Stanford University Press, 2006), 7. This book is a good example for viewing Paul as a philosopher by locating him in a conversation with philosopher Jacques Derrida.

[29]Slavoj Zizek, *The Puppet and the Dwarf: The Perverse Core of Christianity* (Cambridge, Mass.: MIT Press, 2003), 10.

[30]Ibid.

[31]Ibid.

[32]Giorgio Agamben, *The Time That Remains: A Commentary on the Letter to the Romans,* trans. Patricia Dailey (2000; Stanford, Calif.: Stanford University Press, 2005), 1.

[33]Friedrich Nietzsche, *Daybreak: Thoughts on the Prejudices of Morality,* ed. Maudemarie Clark and Brian Leiter, trans. R. J. Hollingdale (Cambridge, U.K.: Cambridge University Press, 1997), 39–40.

[34]Ibid., 40. Italics in original.

[35]Ibid. Italics in original.

[36]Elsa Tamez, *The Amnesty of Grace: Justification by Faith from a Latin American Perspective,* trans. Sharon H. Ringe (Nashville: Abingdon Press, 1993), 48.

[37]Ibid., 47–48.

[38]Levinas, *Totality and Infinity,* 43.

[39]Jacques Derrida, "Violence and Metaphysics: An Essay on the Thought of Emmanuel Levinas," in *Writing and Difference,* trans. Alan Bass (Chicago: The University of Chicago Press, 1978), 90.

[40]Nancy, *Being Singular Plural,* 5.

[41]Ibid., 4.

[42]Ibid., xiii.

[43]Ibid., xvi.

[44]Jean-Luc Nancy, *The Inoperative Community,* ed. Peter Connor, trans. Peter Connor, Lisa Garbus, Michael Holland, and Simona Sawhney (Minneapolis: University of Minnesota Press, 1991), 3.

[45]Nancy, *Being Singular Plural,* 6.

[46]Ibid., 66.

[47]Ibid., 154.

[48]Ibid., 39.

[49]Ibid.

[50]Nancy, *The Inoperative Community,* 77.

[51]Nancy, *Being Singular Plural,* 35.

[52]Cf. Jean-Luc Nancy, "Conloquium," in *Communitas: origine et destin de la communaute,* Roberto Esposito(Paris: Presses Universitaires de France, 2000), 10. Cited in Christopher Watkin, "A Different Alterity: Jean-Luc Nancy's 'Singular Plural,'" *Paragraph* 30: 2 (2007): 56.

[53]Emile Durkheim, *The Division of Labour in Society,* trans. W. D. Halls (1893; New York: Free Press, 1984), 162–63.

[54]Ibid., 333.

[55]Emile Durkheim, *Professional Ethics and Civic Morals,* trans. Cornelia Brookfield (1950; Glencoe, Ill.: The Free Press, 1958), 219.

[56]Derrida, "Force of Law," 244.

[57]Jodi Dean, *Solidarity of Strangers: Feminism after Identity Politics* (Berkeley, Calif.: University of California Press, 1996), 1.

[58]Ed Cohen, "Who are 'We'? Gay 'Identity' as Political (E)motion (A Theoretical Rumination)," in *Inside/Out: Lesbian Theories, Gay Theories,* ed. Diana Fuss (New York: Routledge, 1991), 71.

[59]Ibid., 72.

[60]Ibid.

[61]R. Radhakrishnan, *Diasporic Mediations: Between Home and Location* (Minneapolis: University of Minnesota Press, 1996), 75.

[62]Ibid.

[63]Ibid.

[64]Steven Epstein, "Gay Politics, Ethnic Identity: The Limits of Social Constructionism," in *Forms of Desire: Sexual Orientation and the Social Constructionist Controversy,* ed. Edward Stein (1990; New York: Routledge, 1992), 254.

[65]Giorgio Agamben, *The Coming Community,* trans. Michael Hardt (1990; Minneapolis: University of Minnesota Press, 1993), 18.

[66]United Nations Development Programme, *Sustainability and Equity: A Better Future for All,* Human Development Report 2011 (New York: Palgrave Macmillan, 2011), 127–130.

[67]Ibid., 162–65.

[68]United Nations Development Programme, *The Real Wealth of Nations: Pathways to Human Development,* Human Development Report 2010 (New York: Palgrave Macmillan, 2010), 8.

[69]Charles Beitz, "Does Global Inequality Matter?" in *Global Justice,* ed. Thomas W. Pogge (Oxford, U.K.: Blackwell, 2001), 106.

[70]Agamben, *The Coming Community,* 86, 87. Italics added.

[71]Ibid., 86.

[72]Ibid., 64.

[73]Karen Baker-Fletcher and Garth Kasimu Baker-Flecher, *My Sister, My Brother: Womanist and Xodus God-Talk* (Maryknoll, N.Y.: Orbis, 1997), 203–204.

[74]Agamben, *The Coming Community,* 18–19. Italics in original.

[75]John Caputo, *What Would Jesus Deconstruct?: The Good News of Postmodernism for the Church* (Grand Rapids, Mich.: Baker Academic, 2007), 31.

[76]Ibid., 32.

[77]Ernst Bloch, as quoted in Agamben, *The Coming Community*, 53.

[78]Agamben, *The Coming Community*, 53.

[79]Ibid., 1–2.

[80]Ibid., 2. Italics in original.

[81]Ibid., 73.

[82]Ibid., 90.

[83]Ibid., 92, 93.

[84]John D. Caputo, *The Prayers and Tears of Jacques Derrida: Religion without Religion* (Bloomington, Ind.: Indiana University Press, 1997), 49.

[85]Jacques Derrida, *On the Name,* ed. Thomas Dutoit, trans. David Wood, John P. Leavey Jr., and Ian McLeod (Stanford, Calif.: Stanford University Press, 1993), 74.

[86]Slavoj Zizek, Eric L. Santner, and Kenneth Reinhard, "Introduction," in *The Neighbor: Three Inquiries in Political Theology* (Chicago and London: The University of Chicago Press, 2005), 3.

[87]Jacques Derrida, "Hostipitality," *Angelaki: Journal of the Theoretical Humanities,* vol. 5, no. 3 (December 2000): 6, 14.

[88]Jacques Derrida, as quoted in Simon Critchley and Richard Kearney, "Introduction," in Jacques Derrida, *On Cosmopolitanism and Forgiveness,* trans. Mark Dooley and Michael Hughes (London and New York: Routledge, 2001), x.

[89]Derrida, *The Gift of Death,* 2, 3.

[90]Cf. Amy G. Oden, ed., *And You Welcomed Me: A Sourcebook on Hospitality in Early Christianity* (Nashville: Abingdon Press, 2001); Luke Bretherton, *Hospitality as Holiness: Christian Witness Amid Moral Diversity* (Burlington, Vt.: Ashgate, 2006); Thomas E. Reynolds, *Vulnerable Communion: A Theology of Disability and Hospitality* (Grand Rapids, Mich.: BrazosPress, 2008); Amos Yong,

Hospitality & the Other: Pentecost, Christian Practices, and the Neighbor (Maryknoll, N.Y.: Orbis Books, 2008); Thomas W. Ogletree, *Hospitality to the Stranger: Dimensions of Moral Understanding* (Philadelphia: Fortress, 1985); Elizabeth Rankin Geitz, *Entertaining Angels: Hospitality Programs for the Caring Church* (Harrisburg, Pa.: Morehouse, 1993); Delia Halverson, *The Gift of Hospitality in the Church, in the Home, and in All of Life* (St. Louis, Mo.: Chalice Press, 1999); Conrad Lashley and Alison J. Morrison, eds., *In Search of Hospitality: Theoretical Perspectives and Debates* (Oxford, U.K., and Boston, Mass.: Butterworth-Heinemann, 2000); Freddy James Clark, *Hospitality: An Ecclesiological Practice of Ministry* (Lanham, Md.: Hamilton Books, 2007); Elizabeth Newman, *Untamed Hospitality: Welcoming God and Other Strangers* (Grand Rapids, Mich.: BrazosPress, 2007); Letty M. Russell, *Just Hospitality: God's Welcome in a World of Difference,* ed. Shannon Clarkson and Kate M. Ott (Louisville, Ky.: Westminster John Knox Press, 2009); Tory K. Baucum, *Evangelical Hospitality: Catechetical Evangelism in the Early Church and Its Recovery for Today* (Lanham, Md.: The Scarecrow Press, 2008); Michele Hershberger, *A Christian View of Hospitality: Expecting Surprises* (Scottsdale, Pa.: Herald Press, 1999); Leslie A. May, *Hospitality: The Heart of Spiritual Direction* (Harrisburg, N.Y.: Morehouse Publishing, 2006); Arthur Sutherland, *I Was a Stranger: A Christian Theology of Hospitality* (Nashville: Abingdon Press, 2006); and Diane C. Kessler, ed., *Receive One Another: Hospitality in Ecumenical Perspective* (Geneva: WCC Publication, 2005).

[91]Sophie Wahnich, *L'impossible citoyen: L'étranger dans le discours de la révolution française* (Paris: Albin Michel, 1997), 23, cited in Mireille Rosello, *Postcolonial Hospitality: The Immigrant as Guest* (Stanford, Calif.: Stanford University Press, 2001), 4. Italics added.

[92]After French President Jacques Chirac made an extremely negative comment about African immigrants in 1991, the French parliament approved the "Pasqua Law" in 1993, which consisted of three components (the reform of the law on citizenship, the bill on identity checks, and the bill on the entry and stay of foreigners in France). The Pasqua law requires polygamous foreigners to keep only one wife and "de-cohabitate" the other wives in order to renew their legal residence card in France. The Pasqua law was named after Charles Pasqua, France's then interior minister of justice, who introduced the law. Cf. http://www.worldpress.org/europe/0402lemonde.htm and http://www.fecl.org/circular/1706.htm.

[93]Levinas, *Totality and Infinity,* 300.

[94]Cf. Rosello, *Postcolonial Hospitality: The Immigrant as Guest,* 2–3.

[95]Jacques Derrida, *Adieu to Emmanuel Levinas,* ed. Werner Hamacher and David E. Wellbery (Stanford, Calif.: Stanford University Press, 1999), 19.

[96]Ibid., 21.

[97]Levinas, *Totality and Infinity,* 299. Interestingly, the word *hospitality* is not even in the index of the book.

[98]Derrida, "Hostipitality," *Angelaki,* 3.

[99]Ibid., 5.

[100]Emile Benveniste, *Indo-European Language and Society,* Miami Linguistics Series No. 12, trans. Elizabeth Palmer (1969; Coral Gables, Florida: University of Miami Press, 1973) 71.

[101]Ibid., 72–73.

[102]Ibid., 75.

[103]Jacques Derrida, "Hostipitality," in *Acts of Religion,* ed. Gil Anidjar (New York: Routledge, 2002), 358–420. Also see, Derrida, "Hostipitality," *Angelaki,* 3–18.

[104]Gil Anidjar, "A Note on Hostipitality," in Jacques Derrida, *Acts of Religion,* 356.

[105]Derrida, "Hostipitality," in *Acts of Religion,* 372.

[106]Ibid., 360.

[107]Derrida, "Hostipitality," *Angelaki*: 6.

[108]Jacques Derrida, *Monolingualism of the Other; or, The Prosthesis of Origin,* trans. Patrick Mensah (1996; Stanford, Calif.: Stanford University Press, 1998), 14.

[109]For more detailed discussion about the issue of linguistic rankism, see Namsoon Kang, "Envisioning Postcolonial Theological Education: Dilemmas and Possibilities," in *Handbook of Theological Education in World Christianity,* ed. Dietrich Werner, David Esterline, Namsoon Kang, and Joshva Raja (Oxford, U.K.: Regnum Books International, 2010).

[110]Derrida, "Hostipitality," *Angelaki,* 14.

[111]Ibid.

[112]Ibid.

[113]Ibid., 8.

[114]Ibid.

[115]Ibid., 10

[116]Ibid., 8.

[117]Ibid., 11

[118]Jacques Derrida, *Of Hospitality* (Stanford, Calif.: Stanford University Press, 2000), 77.

[119]Ibid.

[120]Ibid., 83.

[121]Derrida, "Hostipitality," in *Acts of Religion,* 364.

[122]Derrida, "Force of Law," in *Acts of Religion,* 243.

[123]Lao Tsu, *Tao Te Ching,* chap. 34.

[124]Rene Backmann, "Ce que ni la gauche ni la droite n'ont voulu dire. Immigration: La grande hypocrisie," *Nouvel Observateur,* 1685, Feb. 20, 1997, 44. Cited in Rosello, *Postcolonial Hospitality: The Immigrant as Guest,* 36.

[125]E. J. Dionne, "Arizona's Shameful 'Immigration' Bill," *The Washington Post,* April 24, 2010. http://voices.washingtonpost.com/postpartisan/2010/04/arizonas_shameful_immigration.html?hpid=opinionsbox1.

[126]Anne E. Komblut and Spencer S. Hsu, "Arizona governor signs immigration bill, reopening national debate," *The Washington Post,* April 24, 2010. http://www.washingtonpost.com/wp-dyn/content/article/2010/04/23/AR2010042301441.html?sid=ST2010042304357.

[127]Michel Foucault, "Polemics, Politics, and Problematizations," in *The Foucault Reader,* ed. Paul Rabinow (New York: Random House, 1984), 385.

[128]Ibid.

[129]Dionne, "Arizona's Shameful 'Immigration' Bill."

[130]Michel Foucault, *The History of Sexuality, Vol. 1: An Introduction,* trans. Robert Hurley (1976; New York: Vintage Books, 1990), 140.

[131]Rosello, *Postcolonial Hospitality: The Immigrant as Guest,* 37.

[132]Ibid., 39.

[133]John D. Caputo and Michael J. Scanlon, eds., *Augustine and Postmodernism: Confessions and Circumfession* (Bloomington and Indianapolis, Ind.: Indiana University Press, 2005), 23.

[134]Ibid., 4.

[135]Cf. Jacques Derrida, "Foreigner Question: Coming from Abroad/ from the Foreigner," in *Of Hospitality* (Stanford, Calif.: Stanford University Press, 2000).

[136]http://www.universityofcalifornia.edu/senate/inmemoriam/JacquesDerrida.htm.

[137]Derrida, *Monolingualism of the Other,* 15.

[138]Ibid., 16.

[139]*World Refugee Survey 2008,* http://www.refugees.org/uploadedFiles/Investigate/Publications_&_Archives/WRS_Archives/2008/refugees%20and%20asylum%20seekers%20worldwide.pdf .

[140]Cf. Mark Jordan, *The Invention of Sodomy in Christian Theology* (Chicago: University of Chicago Press, 1997), 30.

[141]Phyllis Trible, *Texts of Terror: Literary-Feminist Readings of Biblical Narratives* (Philadelphia: Fortress Press, 1984), 75.

[142]Stephen D. Moore, "Situating Spivak," in *Planetary Loves: Spivak, Postcoloniality, and Theology,* ed. Stephen D. Moore and Mayra Rivera (New York: Fordham University Press, 2011), 20.

[143]Jacques Derrida, *Points…Interviews, 1974–1994,* ed. Elisabeth Weber, trans. Peggy Kamuf and Others (Stanford, Calif.: Stanford University Press, 1995), 389.

[144]Gayatri Chakravorty Spivak, "Can Subaltern Speak?" in *Marxism and the Interpretation of Culture,* ed. Cary Nelson and Lawrence Grossberg (Urbana and Chicago, Ill.: University of Illinois Press, 1988), 104.

[145]Gayatri Chakravorty Spivak, *The Postcolonial Critic: Interviews, Strategies, Dialogues,* ed. Sarah Harasym (New York and London: Routledge, 1990), 158.

[146]Moore and Rivera, eds., *Planetary Loves,* 144, 145.

[147]Derrida, "Hostipitality," in *Acts of Religion,* 359.

[148]Ibid., 417.

[149]Ibid., 409–410.

[150]Louis Massignon, as quoted in Cleo McNelly Kearns, "Mary, Maternity, and Abrahamic Hospitality in Derrida's Reading of Massignon," in *Derrida and Religion: Other Testaments*, ed. Yvonne Sherwood and Kevin Hart (New York: Routledge, 2005), 84.

[151]Cf. Derrida, *Of Hospitality,* 3–9.

[152]Ibid., 27.

[153]Levinas, *Totality and Infinity,* 202.

[154]Ibid., 197.

[155]Ibid., 198.

[156]Ibid., 201, 213. Italics in original.

[157]Emmanuel Levinas, *Collected Philosophical Papers,* trans. Alphonso Lingis (Pittsburgh: Duquesne University Press, 1998), 106.

[158]Derrida, "Hostipitality," in *Acts of Religion,* 365.

[159]Jacques Derrida, *Writing and Difference,* trans. Alan Bass (Chicago: The University of Chicago Press, 1978), 101.

[160]Derrida, "Hostipitality," in *Acts of Religion,* 360.

[161]Louis Massignon, in *L'hospitalité sacrée,* as cited in Derrida, "Hostipitality," in *Acts of Religion,* 373.

[162]Derrida, "Hostipitality," in *Acts of Religion,* 364.

[163]Levinas, *Otherwise than Being or Beyond Essence,* 158.

[164]Ibid.

[165]Frantz Fanon, *Black Skin, White Masks,* trans. Charles Lam Markmann (1952; New York: Grove Press, 1967), 231–32.

[166]Derrida, "Hostipitality," in *Acts of Religion,* 358.

[167]Ibid.

[168]Derrida, *Of Hospitality,* 27, 29. Italics in original.

[169]Ibid., 29.

[170]Jacques Derrida, *Aporias,* trans. Thosmas Dutoit (Stanford, Calif.: Stanford University Press, 1993), 34.

[171]Derrida, "Hostipitality," in *Acts of Religion,* 360.

[172]Jacques Derrida, "Il n'y a pas de culture ni de lien social sans un principe d'hospitalité," *Le Monde,* December 2, 1997. Cited in Michael Nass, "'Alors, qui êtes-vous?' Jacques Derrida and the Question of Hospitality," *SubStance,* vol. 34. no. 1, issue 106 (2005): 8–9.

[173]Derrida, *Aporias,* 33.

[174]Martin Luther, *Luther's Works,* vol. 3: *Lectures on Genesis, Chapter 15–20* (St. Louis: Concordia, 1961), 189.

[175]N. Lynne Westfield, *Dear Sisters: A Womanist Practice of Hospitality* (Cleveland: Pilgrim Press, 2001), 46.

[176]Agamben, *The Coming Community,* 1.

[177]Ibid.

[178]Ibid., 1–2. Italics in original.

[179]Gayatri Chakravorty Spivak, *Death of Discipline* (New York: Columbia University Press, 2005), 72.

[180]Ibid.

[181]Ibid., 73.

[182]Maurice Blanchot, *The Unavowable Community,* trans. Pierre Joris (Barrytown, N.Y.: Station Hill, 1988), 1.

[183]Geoffrey Bennington and Jacques Derrida, *Jacques Derrida,* trans. Geoffrey Bennington (Chicago and London: The University of Chicago Press, 1993), 352.

[184]Nass, "'Alors, qui êtes-vous?' Jacques Derrida and the Question of Hospitality," 10.

[185]Derrida, *Of Hospitality,* 77. Italics in original.

[186]Levinas, *Otherwise than Being or Beyond Essence,* 157.

[187]Derrida, "Hostipitality," 363.

[188]Caputo, *The Prayers and Tears of Jacques Derrida,* 26.

[189]Ibid.

[190]Jacques Derrida, *On Cosmopolitanism and Forgiveness* (Thinking in Action) (London: Routledge, 2001), viii.

[191]Gayatri Chakravorty Spivak, *A Critique of Postcolonial Reason: Toward a History of the Vanishing Present* (Cambridge, Mass.: Harvard University Press, 1999), 384.

[192]Agamben, *The Coming Community,* 43.

[193]Benedict Anderson, *Imagined Communities: Reflections on the Origin and Spread of Nationalism* (New York: Verso, 1983), 16.

[194]Jacques Derrida, "A 'Madness' Must Watch Over Thinking," in *Points…Interviews, 1974–1994,* ed. Elisabeth Weber, trans. Peggy Kamuf and others, 355.

[195]Jean-Luc Nancy, *The Inoperative Community,* ed. Peter Connor, trans. Peter Connor, Lisa Garbus, Michael Holland, and Simona Sawhney (Minneapolis: University of Minnesota Press, 1991), 71.

[196]Agamben, *The Coming Community,* 86.

[197]Nancy, *The Inoperative Community,* 33.

[198]Agamben, *The Coming Community,* 25.

Chapter 7

[1]Jean Baudrillard, "Viral Hospitality," *The Transparency of Evil: Essays on Extreme Phenomena,* trans. James Benedict (London and New York: Verso, 1993), 161.

[2]John D. Caputo, *The Prayers and Tears of Jacques Derrida: Religion without Religion* (Bloomington & Indianapolis, Ind.: Indiana University Press, 1997), 229.

[3]Richard Rorty, "Anticlericalism and Atheism," in *Future of Religion,* Richard Rorty and Gianni Vattimo, ed. Santiago Zabala (New York: Columbia University Press, 2005), 40.

[4]Thomas More, *Utopia* (1516; Cambridge, U.K.: Cambridge University Press, 1989).

[5]Cf. Bertrand de Jouvenel, "Utopia for Practical Purposes," in *Utopias and Utopian Thought,* ed. Frank E. Manuel (Boston: Houghton Mifflin Company, 1966), 219.

[6]Constance Penley, *The Future of Illusion: Film, Feminism and Psychoanalysis* (Minneapolis: University of Minnesota, 1989), 122.

[7]Karl Mannheim, *Ideology and Utopia: An Introduction to Sociology of Knowledge,* trans. Louis Wirth and Edward Shils (1927; New York: A Harvest/HBJ Book, 1985), 196.

[8]Ibid., 197.

[9]I put "black" in quotation marks because I believe categorizing Obama into "black" is itself a result of invention of race. He is "half-white" and "half-black," to be exact, having a white mother and a black father. Categorizing him as black—whether socially ascribed or self-claimed—is not a scientific but an inventive aspect of racial category based on the racial desire for white purity. Such a one-drop-rule that claims one drop of black blood makes one black has been a basis of white racism. Cf. David Hollenger, "The One Drop Rule and the One Hate Rule," in *Cosmopolitanism and Solidarity: Studies in Ethnoracial, Religious, and Professional Affiliation in the United States* (Madison, Wis.: University of Wisconsin Press, 2006), 39–56.

[10]Manheim, *Ideology and Utopia,* 262–63.

[11]Ibid., 195.

[12]Ibid., 193.

[13]Paul Tillich, "Critique and Justification of Utopia," in *Utopias and Utopian Thought,* ed. Frank E. Manuel (Boston: Houghton Mifflin, 1966), 297.

[14]Jacques Derrida, *On the Name,* ed. Thomas Dutoit, trans. David Wood, John P. Leavey Jr., and Ian McLeod (Stanford, Calif.: Stanford University Press, 1993), 75.

[15]R.A. Markus, *Saeculum: History and Society in the Theology of St. Augustine* (New York: Cambridge University Press, 1970), 169 and 170.

[16]Matthew Fox, *The Coming of the Cosmic Christ: The Healing of Mother Earth and the Birth of a Global Renaissance* (New York: HarperSanFrancisco, 1988).

[17]For the interview of Derrida, see "Intellectual Courage: An Interview," *Culture Machine,* 2 (2002): http://culturemachine.tees.ac.uk/frm_f1.htm.

[18]Jacques Derrida, *Le Figaro Magazine,* October 16, 1999, cited in Obrad Savic, "Introduction—Duty of Unconditional Hospitality," *Parallax* 11 (2005): 4.

[19]Paul Celan, cited in Emmanuel Levinas, *Otherwise than Being or Beyond Essence,* trans. Alphonso Lingis (Pittsburgh: Duquesne University Press, 1998), 99.

[20]John Caputo, edited with a commentary, *Deconstruction in a Nutshell: A Conversation with Jacques Derrida* (New York: Fordham University Press, 1997), 55–56.

[21]Ludwig Wittgenstein, *Culture and Value,* ed. G. H. von Wright and Heikki Nyman, trans. Peter Winch (Chicago: University of Chicago Press, 1980), 85.

[22]Catriona McKinnon, "Cosmopolitan Hope," in *The Political Philosophy of Cosmopolitanism,* ed. Gillian Brock and Harry Brighouse (2005; Cambridge, U.K.: Cambridge University Press, 2007), 235.

[23]Jacques Derrida, *Of Hospitality* (Stanford, Calif.: Stanford University Press, 2000), 77.

[24]Paul A. Bove, "Introduction," in *Edward Said and the Work of the Critic: Speaking Truth to Power*, ed. Paul A. Bove (Durham and London: Duke University Press, 2000), 4.

[25]Rorty, "Anticlericalism and Atheism," 40.

Bibliography

Ackerman, Bruce. "Rooted Cosmopolitanism," *Ethics*. Vol. 104. No.3 (April 1994): 516–35.

Agamben, Giorgio. *Homo Sacer: Sovereign Power and Bare Life*. Trans. Daniel Heller-Roazen. Stanford: Stanford University Press, 1998.

_____. *Remnants of Auschwitz: The Witness and the Archive*. Trans. Daniel Heller-Roazen. New York: Zone Books, 1999.

_____. *Potentialities*. Trans. Daniel Heller-Roazen. Stanford: Stanford University Press, 1999.

_____. *The Coming Community*. Trans. Michael Hardt. 1990; Minneapolis: University of Minnesota Press, 1993.

Akcan, Esra. "Toward a Cosmopolitan Ethics in Architecture: Bruno Taut's Translations out of Germany." *New German Critique*. No. 99. Modernism after Postmodernity (Fall, 2006): 7–39.

Alexander, M. Jacqui, and Chandra Talpade Mohanty, eds. *Feminist Genealogies, Colonial Legacies, Democratic Futures*. New York: Routledge, 1997.

Almond, Ian. "Doing Violence upon God: Nonviolent Alterities and Their Medieval Precedents." *The Harvard Theological Review*. Vol. 92. No. 3 (Jul. 1999): 325–47.

Amour, Ellen T. *Deconstruction, Feminist Theology, and the Problem of Difference: Subverting the Race/Gender Divide*. University of Chicago Press, 1999.

Anderson, Benedict. *Imagined Communities: Reflections on the Origin and Spread of Nationalism*. New York: Verso, 1983.

Anderson-Gold, Sharon. *Cosmopolitanism and Human Rights*. Cardiff: University of Wales Press, 2001.

Anthias, Floya. "Culture, Identity and Rights: Challenging Contemporary Discourses of Belonging," in *The Situated Politics of Belonging*. Ed. Nira Yuval-davis, Kalpana Kannabiran and Ulrike M. Vieten (London: Sage Publication, 2006).

Anzaldua, Gloria. *Borderlands/La Frontera: The New Mestiza*. San Francisco; Aunt Lute Books, 1987.

Appiah, Kwame Anthony. *Cosmopolitanism: Ethics in a World of Strangers*. New York: W.W. Norton & Company, 2006.

_____. *In My Father's House: Africa in the Philosophy of Culture.* Oxford, U.K.: Oxford University Press, 1992.

_____. "Rooted Cosmopolitanism." In *The Ethics of Identity*. Princeton: Princeton University Press, 2005.

Aquino, Maria Pilar and Roberto S. Goizueta, eds. *Theology: Expanding the Borders*. The Annual Publication of the College Theology Society. Vol. 43. Mystic, Ct.: Twenty-Third Publications, 1998.

Arendt, Hannah. *The Origins of Totalitarianism.* 1951; New York: Schocken Books, 2004.

_____. *The Human Condition*. 1958; Chicago: University of Chicago Press, 1998.

_____. *On Revolution*. 1963; London: Penguin Books, 1990.

_____. *Eichmann in Jerusalem: A Report on the Banality of Evil*, revised and enlarged edition. 1963; New York: Penguin Books, 1994.

_____. *Lectures on Kant's Political Philosophy*. Ed. Ronald Briner. 1982; Chicago: Chicago University Press, 1992.

_____. *Love and Saint Augustine*. Ed. Joanna Vecchiarelli Scott and Judith Chelius Stark. Chicago and London: University of Chicago Press, 1996.

_____. and Karl Jaspers. *Hannah Arendt and Karl Jaspers Correspondence 1926–1969*. Trans. Robert and Rita Kimber. 1985; New York: A Harvest Book, 1992.

Attridge, Derek, ed. *Acts of Literature*. London: Routledge Press, 1985.

Audinet, Jacques. *The Human Face of Globalization: From Multicultural to Mestizaje*. Rowman & Littlefield, 2004.

Badiou, Alain. *Saint Paul: The Foundation of Universalism*. Stanford: Stanford University Press, 2003.

Baker-Fletcher, Karen, and Garth Kasimu Baker-Flecher. *My Sister, My Brother: Womanist and Xodus God-Talk*. Maryknoll, NY: Orbis, 1997.

Banchoff, Thomas, ed. *Religious Pluralism: Globalization, and World Politics*. Oxford, U.K.: Oxford University Press, 2008.

Barthes, Roland. "The Death of the Author." In *Image, Music, Text*. Trans. Stephen Heath. New York: Hill and Wang, 1977.

Baudrillard, Jean. "Viral Hospitality." In *The Transparency of Evil: Essays on Extreme Phenomena* . Trans. James Benedict. London & New York: Verso, 1993.

Beck, Ulrich. *Cosmopolitan Vision*. Trans. Ciaran Cronin. 2004; Cambridge, U.K., and Malden, Mass.: Polity Press, 2006.

_____. "The Cosmopolitan Perspective: Sociology of the Second Age of Modernity." *British Journal of Sociology*. Vol. 51. No. 1 (January/March 2000): 79–105.

Beitz, Charles R. "Does Global Inequality Matter?" In *Global Justice*. Ed. Thomas Pogge. Oxford, U.K.: Blackwell Publisher, 2001.

Benhabib, Seyla. *Another Cosmopolitanism*. Oxford, U.K.: Oxford University Press, 2006.

_____. *The Rights of Others: Aliens, Residents and Citizens*. Cambridge, U.K.: Cambridge University Press, 2004.

_____. *The Claims of Culture: Equality and Diversity in the Global Era*. Princeton: Princeton University Press, 2002.

Bennington, Geoffrey and Jacques Derrida. *Jacques Derrida*. Trans. Geoffrey Bennington. Chicago: University of Chicago Press, 1993.

Bernstein, Richard. "Serious Play: The Ethical-Political Horizon of Jacques Derrida." *The Journal of Speculative Philosophy* 1 (1987): 93–116.

Bhabha, Homi. "The Vernacular Cosmopolitanism." In *Voices of the Crossing: The Impact of Britain on Writers from Asia, the Caribbean and Africa*. Ed. Ferdinand Dennis and Naseem Khan. London: Serpent's Tail, 2000.

_____. "Unsatisfied: Notes on Vernacular Cosmopolitanism." In *Postcolonial Discourses: An Anthology*. Ed. Gregory Castle (Oxford, U.K. and Malden, Mass.: Blackwell, 2001.

Blanchot, Maurice. *The Infinite Conversation*. Trans. Susan Hanson. Minneapolis: University of Minnesota Press, 1993.

Blanchot, Maurice. *The Unavowable Community*. Trans. Pierre Joris. Barrytown, NY: Station Hill, 1988.

Bohman, James and Matthias Lutz-Bachmann, eds. *Perpetual Peace: Essays on Kant's Cosmopolitan Ideal*. Cambridge, Mass.: The MIT Press, 1997.

Bolton, Linda. *Facing the Other: Ethical Disruption and the American Mind*. Baton Rouge, LA: Louisiana State University Press, 2004.

Bongie, Chris. *Islands and Exiles: The Creole Identities of Post/colonial Literature*. Stanford: Stanford University Press, 1998.

Borradori, Giovanna. *Philosophy in a Time of Terror: Dialogues with Jürgen Habermas and Jacque Derrida*. Chicago: The University of Chicago Press, 2003.

Bove, Paul A., ed. *Edward Said and the Work of the Critic: Speaking Truth to Power*. Durham and London: Duke University Press, 2000.

Bowen-Moore, Patricia. *Hannah Arendt's Philosophy of Natality*. New York: St. Martin's Press, 1989.

Branham, R. Bracht and Marie-Odile Goulet-Caze, eds. *The Cynics: The Cynic Movement in Antiquity and Its Legacy*. Berkeley: University of California Press, 1996.

Brennan, Tim. "Cosmopolitans and Celebrities." *Race & Class*. 31, No. 1 (1989): 1–19.

_____. "Rushdie, Islam, and Postcolonial Criticism." *Social Text*. No. 31/32. Third World and Post-Colonial Issues (1992): 271–76.

Brock, Gillian and Harry Brighouse, eds. *The Political Philosophy of Cosmopolitanism*. Cambridge, U.K.: Cambridge University Press, 2005.

Brown, Garrett Wallace and David Held, eds. *The Cosmopolitanism Reader*. Malden, Mass.: Polity Press, 2011.

Burggraeve, Roger, ed. *The Awakening to the Other: A Provocative Dialogue with Emmanuel Levinas*. Leuven-Dudley, MA: Peeters, 2008.

Butler, Judith. *Gender Trouble: Feminism and the Subversion of Identity*. New York: Routledge, 1990.

Butler, Judith and Joan W. Scott, eds. *Feminists Theorize the Political*. New York: Routledge, 1992.

Caputo, John D. *The Prayers and Tears of Jacques Derrida: Religion without Religion*. Bloomington: Indiana University Press, 1997.

_____. *What Would Jesus Deconstruct?: The Good News of Postmodernism for the Church*. Grand Rapids, MI: Baker Academic, 2007.

_____. *The Weakness of God: A Theology of the Event*. Bloomington: Indiana University Press, 2006.

_____. Edited with a Commentary. *Deconstruction in a Nutshell: A Conversation with Jacques Derrida*. New York: Fordham Univ. Press, 1997.

Caputo, John D., and Gianni Vattimo. *After the Death of God*. Ed. Jeffrey W. Robbinsons. New York: Columbia University Press, 2007.

Caputo, John D., and Michael J. Scanlon, eds. *Augustine and Postmodernism: Confessions and Circumfession*. Bloomington and Indianapolis: Indiana University Press, 2005.

Caputo, John D. and Michael J. Scanlon, eds. *God, the Gift, and Postmodernism*. Bloomington and Indianapolis: Indiana University Press, 1999.

Caputo, John, Mark Dooley, and Michael Scanlon, eds. Questioning God. Bloomington and Indianapolis: Indiana University Press, 2001.

Castles, Stephen and Alistair Davidson. *Citizenship and Migration: Globalization and the Politics of Belonging*. New York: Macmillan, 2000.

Chakrabarty, Dipesh. *Provincializing Europe: Postcolonial Thought and Historical Difference*. Princeton: Princeton University Press, 2000.

Cheah, Pheng. *Inhuman Conditions: On Cosmopolitanism and Human Rights*. Cambridge, Mass., and London, U.K.: Harvard University Press, 2006.

Cheah, Pheng and Bruce Robbins, eds. *Cosmopolitics: Thinking and Feeling Beyond Nation*. Minneapolis: University of Minnesota Press, 1998.

Ching, Leo. "Globalizing the Regional, Regionalizing the Global: Mass Culture and Asianism in the Age of Late Capital." *Public Culture*. Winter 2000; 12: 233–57.

Christiansen, Flemming and Ulf Hedetoft, eds. *The Politics of Multiple Belonging: Ethnicity and Nationalism in Europe and East Asia*. Research in Migration and Ethnic Relations Series. Burlington, VT: Ashgate Publishing, 2004.

Chopp, Rebecca S. and Sheila Greeve Davaney, eds. *Horizons in Feminist Theology: Identity, Tradition, and Norms.* Minneapolis: Fortress Press, 1997.

Chow, Rey. *Writing Diaspora: Tactics of Intervention in Contemporary Cultural Studies*. Bloomington and Indianapolis: Indiana University Press, 1993.

_____. "Postmodern Automatons." In *Feminists Theorize the Political.* Ed. Judith Butler and Joan W. Scott .New York: Routledge, 1992.

Clark, Mark W. "A Prophet without Honour: Karl Jaspers in Germany, 1945–48." *Journal of Contemporary History*. Vol. 37. No. 2 (April 2002): 197–222.

Clifford, James. "Traveling Cultures." In *Cultural Studies*. Ed. Lawrence Grossberg, Cary Nelson, and Paula Treichler. New York: Routledge, 1992.

Cocks, Joan. *Passion and Paradox: Intellectuals Confront the National Question.* Princeton: Princeton University Press, 2002.

Cohen, Ed. "Who are 'We'? Gay Identity as Political (E)motion (A Theoretical Rumination)." In *Inside/Out: Lesbian Theories, Gay Theories*. Ed. Diana Fuss. NewYork: Routledge, 1991.

Cornell, Drucilla. *The Philosophy of the Limit* (New York: Routledge, 1992).

Critchley, Simon and Robert Bernasconi, eds. *The Cambridge Companion to Levinas*. Cambridge, U.K.: Cambridge University Press, 2002.

Crosby, Christina. "Dealing with Differences." In *Feminists Theorize the Political*. Ed. Judith Butler and Joan W. Scott. New York: Routledge, 1992.

Cunningham, David S., ed. *To Teach, To Delight, and To Move: Theological Education in a Post-Christian World.* Eugene, OR: Cascade Books, 2004.

Cutting-Gray, Joanne. "Hannah Arendt, Feminist, and the Politics of Alterity: What Will We Lose if We Win?" *Hypatia*. Vol. 8. No. 1(Winter, 1993): 35–54.

Davis, Dawn Rae. "(Love Is) The Ability of Not Knowing: Feminist Experience of the Impossible in Ethical Singularity." *Hypatia*. Vol. 17. No. 2 (Spring 2002): 145–61.

De Bary, William Theodore. *Neo-Confucian Orthodoxy and the Learning of the Mind-and- Heart.* New York: Columbia University Press, 1981.

Dean, Jodi. *Solidarity of Strangers: Feminism after Identity Politics*. Berkeley, CA: University of California Press, 1996.

Derrida, Jacques. *Of Grammatology*. Corrected Edition. Trans. Gayatri Chakravorty Spivak. 1967; Baltimore: Johns Hopkins University Press, 1997.

_____. *Writing and Difference*. Trans. Alan Bass. Chicago: The University of Chicago Press, 1978.

_____. *The Margin of Philosophy*. Trans Alan Bass. Chicago: University of Chicago Press, 1982.

_____. *On the Name*. Ed. Thomas Dutoit. Trans. David Wood, John P. Leavey, JR., and Ian McLeod. Stanford, CA: Stanford University Press, 1993.

_____. *Circumfession: Fifty-nine Periods and Periphrases*. In *Jacques Derrida*. Geoffrey Bennington and Jacques Derrida. Chicago: University of Chicago Press, 1993.

_____. *Aporias*. Trans. Thosmas Dutoit. Stanford, CA: Stanford University Press, 1993.

_____. *The Gift of Death*. Trans. David Willis. 1992; Chicago: University of Chicago Press, 1995.

_____. *Points…Interviews, 1974–1994*. Ed. Elisabeth Weber. Trans. Peggy Kamuf & Others. Stanford, CA: Stanford University Press, 1995.

_____. *Monolingualism of the Other; or, The Prosthesis of Origin*. Trans. Patrick Mensah. 1996; Stanford, CA: Stanford University Press, 1998.

_____. *Adieu to Emmanuel Levinas*. Ed. Werner Hamacher & David E. Wellbery. Stanford, CA: Stanford University Press, 1999.

_____. and Anne Dufourmantelle. *Of Hospitality*. Stanford: Stanford University Press, 2000.

_____. *On Cosmopolitanism and Forgiveness*. Trans. Mark Dooley and Michael Hughes. London and New York: Routledge, 2001.

_____. *The Work of Mourning*. Ed. Pascale-Anne Brault and Michael Naas. Chicago and London: University of Chicago Press, 2001.

_____. *Acts of Religion*. Ed. Gil Anidjar. New York: Routledge, 2002.

_____. *The Politics of Friendship*. Trans. George Collins. 1994; London and New York: Verso, 2005 .

_____. *Learning to Live Finally*. Trans. Pascale-Anne Brault and Michael Nass. Hoboken, NJ: Melville House Publishing, 2007.

_____. "Deconstruction and the Other." In Richard Kearney. *Dialogues with Contemporary Continental Thinkers*. Manchester: University Press, 1984.

_____. "Hostipitality." *Angelaki: Journal of the Theoretical Humanities*. Vol. 5. No. 3 (December 2000): 3–18.

De Vries, Hent. *Religion and Violence: Philosophical Perspectives from Kant to Derrida*. Baltimore: Johns Hopkins University Press, 2002.

Diogenes Laertius, *Lives of Eminent Philosophers*. Vol. I & II. Trans. H.D. Hicks. Cambridge, Mass.: Harvard University Press, 1925.

Driver, Tom. "The Case for Pluralism." In *The Myth of Christian Uniqueness: Toward a Pluralistic Theology of Religions*. Ed. John Hick and Paul Knitter. 1987; Maryknoll, NY: Orbis, 1989.

duCille, Ann. "The Occult of True Black Womanhood: Critical Demeanor and Black Feminist Studies." *Signs: Journal of Women in Culture and Society* 9.3 (1994):591–628.

Dungey, Nicholas. "(Re)Turning Derrida to Heidegger: Being-With-Other as Primordial Politics." *Polity*. Vol. 32. Number 3(Spring 2001): 455–77.

Dupius, Jacques. *Toward a Christian Theology of Religious Pluralism*. Marynoll, NY: Orbis, 2004.

Durkheim, Emile. *The Division of Labour in Society*. 1893; New York: Free Press, 1997.

Dussel, Enrique. "Eurocentrism and Modernity." *Postmodernism in Latin America*. Ed. J. Beverley et al. Durham, NC: Duke University Press, 1995.

Eck, Diana. *A New Religious America: How a "Christian" Country Has Become the World's Most Religiously Diverse Nation*. San Francisco: HarperCollins, 1999.

Elden, Stuart and Eduardo Mendieta, eds. *Reading Kant's Geography*. Albany, NY: State University of New York Press, 2011.

Ellis, H. Marc. *Ending Auschwiz: The Future of Jewish and Christian Life*. Louisville: Westminster/John Knox Press, 1994.

Epstein, Steven. "Gay Politics, Ethnic Identity: The Limit of Social Constructionism." In *Forms of Desire: Sexual Orientation and the Social Constructionist Controversy*. Ed. Edward Stein (1990; New York: Routledge, 1992).

Esposito, Roberto. *Bios: Biopolitics and Philosophy*. Minnesota: University of Minnesota Press, 2008.

Eze, Emmanuel Chukwudi, ed. *Race and the Enlightenment: A Reader*. Malden, Mass.: Blackwell, 1997.

_____, "The Color of Reason: The Idea of 'Race' in Kant's Anthropology." In *Postcolonial African Philosophy: A Critical Reader*. Ed. Emmanuel Chukwudi Eze. Cambridge, Mass.: Blackwell, 1997.

Fanon, Frantz. *The Wretched of the Earth*. Preface by Jean-Paul Sartre. Trans. Constance Farrington. 1961; New York: Grove Weidenfeld, 1963.

_____. *Black Skin, White Masks*. Trans. Charles Lam Markmann. 1952; New York: Grove Press, 1967.

Ferguson, Russell, Martha Gever, Trinh T. Minh-ha, and Cornel West, eds. *Out There: Marginalization and Contemporary Culture.* New York, N.Y., and Cambridge, Mass.: The New Museum of Contemporary Art and MIT Press, 1990

Ferrara. Alessamdro. *Reflective Authenticity: Rethinking the Project of Modernity*. London and New York: Routledge, 1998.

Fine, Robert and Robin Cohen. "Four Cosmopolitan Moments." In *Conceiving Cosmopolitanism: Theory, Contextand Practice.* Ed. Vertovec, Steven and Robin Cohen. Oxford, U.K.: Oxford University Press, 2002.

Flax, Jane. "The End of Innocence." In *Feminists Theorize the Political*. Ed. Judith Butler and Joan W. Scott. New York: Routledge, 1992.

Fojas, Camilla. *Cosmopolitanism in the Americas*. West Lafayette, Indiana: Purdue University Press, 2005.

Foucault, Michel. *The Essential Foucault: Selections from Essential Works of Foucault1954–1984*. Ed. Paul Rabinow and Nikolas Rose. 1994; New York: The New Press, 2003.

_____. *Language, Counter-Memory, Practice: Selected Essays and Interviews*. 1977; Ithaca, N.Y.: Cornell University Press, 1993.

_____. *The Foucault Reader*. Ed. Paul Rabinow. New York: Random House, 1984.

_____. *Power/Knowledge: Selected Interviews and Other Writings 1972–1977*. Ed. Colin Gordon. Trans. Colin Gordon, Leo Marshall, John Mepham, Kate Soper. New York: Pantheon Books, 1980.

_____. *The Order of Things*. New York: Vintage Books, 1970.

_____. "Of Other Spaces." Michel Foucault. *Diacritics*. 16. No.1 (Spring 1986): 22–27.

_____. *The History of Sexuality, Vol. 1: An Introduction*. Trans. Robert Hurley. New York: Vintage Books, 1990.

_____. *"Society Must Be Defended": Lectures at the College de France, 1975–76*. Trans. David Macey. 1997; New York: Picador, 2003.

Frazer, Nancy. "The French Derrideans: Politicizing Deconstruction or Deconstructing the Political?" *New German Critique* 33 (1984): 127–54.

Friedman, Susan Stanford. *Mappings: Feminism and the Cultural Geographies of Encounter*. Princeton: Princeton University, 1998.

Frum, David. *The Right Man: An Inside Account of the Bush White House*. New York: Random House, 2003.

Fu, Hongchu. "Deconstruction and Taoism: Comparisons Reconsidered." *Comparative Literature Studies*. Vol. 29. No. 3 (1992): 296–321.

Fulkerson, Mary McClintock. *Changing the Subject: Women's Discourses and Feminist Theology.* Minneapolis: Fortress Press, 1994.

_____. "Feminist Theology." In *The Cambridge Companion to Postmodern Theology*. Ed. Kevin J. Vanhoozer. Cambridge, U.K.: Cambridge University Press, 2003.

Fung, Yu-Lan. *A History of Chinese Philosophy.* Princeton: Princeton University Press, 1952.

Giovanna, Borradori. *Philosophy in a Time of Terror: Dialogues with Jurgen Habermas and Jacques Derrida.* Chicago: University of Chicago Press, 2003.

Giroux, Henry. *The Giroux Reader*. Colorado: Paradigm Publishers, 2006.

_____. *Border Crossing: Cultural Workers and the Politics of Education*. New York and London: Routeledge, 1992.

Giroux, Henry and Peter McLaren, eds. *Between Borders: Pedagogy and the Politics of Cultural Studies.* New York: Routledge, 1994.

Goldberg, David Theo, ed. *Multiculturalism: A Critical Reader*. Oxford, U.K. and Cambridge, Mass.: Blackwell, 1994.

Gonzalez-Ruibal, Alfredo. "Vernacular Cosmopolitanism: An Archaeological Critique of Universalistic Readon." In *Cosmopolitan Archaeologies*. Ed. Lynn Meskell. Durham, NC: Duke University Press, 2009.

Gorden, Mordechai, ed. *Hannah Arendt and Education: Renewing our Common World*. Boulder, Colorado: Westview Press, 2001.

Gosepath, Stefan. "The Global Scope of Justice." In *Global Justice*. Ed. Thomas Pogge. Oxford, U.K.: Blackwell Publisher, 2001.

Graham, A. G. *Disputers of the Tao: Philosophical Argument in Ancient China*. Salle, Ill.: Open Court. 1999.

Gramsci, Antonio. *Selections from the Prison Notebooks*. Ed. and trans. Quintin Hoare and Geoffrey Nowell Smith. New York: International, 1971.

Grewal, Inderpal and Caren Kaplan, ed. *Scattered Hegemonies: Postmodernity and Transnational Feminist Practice*. Minnesota: University of Minnesota Press, 1994.

Grillo, Trina. "Anti-Essentialism and Intersectionality: Tools to Dismantle the Master's House." *Berkeley Women's Law Journal* 10.1 (1995): 16–30.

Gueye, Cheikh Mbacke. *Late Stoic Cosmopolitanism: Foundations and Relevance*. Heidelberg: Universitaetsverlag Winter, 2006.

Gutmann, Amy, ed. *Multiculturalism: Examining the Politics of Recognition*. Princeton, NJ: Princeton University Press, 1994

Habermas, Jürgen. *The Inclusion of the Other*. Trans. C. Cronin and P. De Greiff. Cambridge, Mass.: MIT Press, 1998.

Hand, Sean, ed. *Facing the Other: The Ethics of Emmanuel Levinas*. Richmond: Curzon Press, 1996.

_____, ed. *The Levinas Reader*. Oxford, U.K.: Blackwell, 1989.

Hannerz, Ulf. *Cultural Complexity: Studies in the Social Organisation of Meaning.* New York: Columbia University Press, 1992.

_____. "Cosmopolitans and Locals in World Culture," in *Theory, Culture & Society*, 7 (1990): 237–51.

Haraway, Donna. "Ecce Homo, Ain't (Ar'n't) I a Woman, and Inappropriate/d Others: The Human in a Post-Humanist Landscape." In *Feminists Theorize the Political*. Ed. Judith Butler and Joan W. Scott .New York: Routledge, 1992.

Harink, Douglas, ed. *Paul, Philosophy, and the Theopolitical Vision: Critical Engagements with Agamben, Badiou, Zizek and Others*. Eugene, Oregon: Cascade Books, 2010.

Harvey, David. *Cosmopolitanism and the Geographies of Freedom*. New York: Columbia University Press, 2009.

_____. *Spaces of Global Capitalism: Towards a Theory of Uneven Geographical Development*. New York: Verso, 2006.

_____. "Cosmopolitanism and the Banality of Geographical Evils." *Public Culture.* Vol. 12. No. 2 (2000): 529–64.

_____. *Justice, Nature & the Geography of Difference*. Cambridge, Mass.: Blackwell, 1996.

Heidegger, Martin. *Being and Time*. Trans. Joan Stambaugh. New York: State University of NY Press, 1996.

_____. *The Basic Problems of Phenomenology*. Trans. Albert Hofstadler. Bloomington: Indiana University Press, 1988.

_____. *History of the Concept of Time*. Trans. Theodore Kisiel. Bloomington: Indiana University Press, 1992.

Held, David. *Cosmopolitanism: Ideals and Realities*. Malden, Mass.: Polity Press, 2010.

_____. "Principles of Cosmopolitan Order." In *The Political Philosophy of Cosmopolitanism*. Ed. Gillian Brock and Harry Brighouse. Cambridge, U.K.: Cambridge University Press, 2005.

_____. "Cosmopolitanism: Globalisation Tamed?" *Review of International Studies*. Vol. 29. No. 4 (October 2003): 465–80

Hendrick, Todd. "Race, Difference and Anthropology in Kant's Cosmopolitanism." *Journal of the History of Philosophy*. Vol. 46. No 2 (April 2008): 245–68.

Heng, Geraldine. "A Great Way to Fly": Nationalism, the State, and the Varieties of Third-World Feminism." In *Feminist Genealogies, Colonial*

Legacies, Democratic Futures. Ed. M. Jacqui Alexander and Chandra Talpade Mohanty. New York: Routledge, 1997.

Henham, Ralph and Paul Behrens, eds. *The Criminal Law of Genocide: International, Comparative and Contextual Aspects*. Burlington, VT: Ashgate, 2007.

Hick, John. *An Interpretation of Religion: Human Response to the Transcendent.* New Haven, CT: Yale University Press, 2004.

Hick, John and Paul F. Knitter, eds., *The Myth of Christian Uniqueness: Toward a Pluralistic Theology of Religions.* Maryknoll, NY: Orbis, 1987.

Hoeffe, Otfried. *Kant's Cosmopolitan Theory of Law and Peace*. Trans. Alexandra Newton. 2001; Cambridge, U.K.: Cambridge University Press, 2006.

_____. *Immanuel Kant*. Trans. Marshall Farrier. 1992; Albany, NY: State University of New York, 1994.

Hollinger, David A. *Postethnic America: Beyond Multiculturalism*. New York: Basic Books, 1995.

_____. *Cosmopolitanism and Solidarity: Studies in Ethnoracial, Religious, and Professional Affiliation in the United States*. Madison, WI: University of Wisconsin Press, 2006.

hooks, bell. *Teaching to Transgress*. New York: Crossing, 1984.

Hoy, David Couzens. *Critical Resistance: From Poststructuralism to Post-Critique*. Cambridge, Mass.: The MIT Press, 2004.

Hutcheon, Linda, Homi K. Bhabha, Daniel Boyarin, and Sabine I. Goelz, "Four Views on Ethnicity," *PMLA*, Vol. 113, No.1, Special Topic: Ethnicity (Jan. 1998): 28–51.

Inwood, Brad and L. P. Gerson, trans. *Hellenistic Philosophy: Introductory Readings*. Second Edition. Indianapolis, and Cambridge, Mass.: Hackett Publishing Company, 1988.

Izutsu, Toshihiko. *Sufism and Taoism: A Comparative Study of Key Philosophical Concepts*. LA:University of California Press, 1983

JanMohamed, Abdul R. and David Lloyd, eds. *The Nature and Context of Minority Discourse*. New York, N.Y., and Oxford, U.K.: Oxford University Press, 1990.

Jaspers, Karl. *The Question of German Guilt*. Trans. E. B. Ashton. 1947; New York: Capricorn Books, 1961.

Jay, Martin. "The Political Existentialism of Hannah Arendt." *Permanent Exiles.* New York: Columbia University Press, 1986.

Jennings, Theodore. *Reading Derrida/Thinking Paul: On Justice*. Stanford, Calif.: Stanford University Press, 2006.

John, Mary E. *Discrepant Dislocations: Feminism, Theory, and Postcolonial Histories*. Berkeley: University of California Press, 1996.

Jones, Charles. *Global Justice: Defending Cosmopolitanism*. Oxford, U.K.: Oxford University Press, 1999.

Kaltenmark, Max. "The Ideology of the T'ai-p'ing ching." In *Facets of Taoism: Essays in Chinese Religion*. Ed. Holmes Welch and Anna Seidel. New Heaven: Yale University Press, 1979.

Kang, Namsoon. "Towards a Cosmopolitan Theology: Constructing Public Theology from the Future." In *Planetary Loves: Spivak, Postcoloniality, and Theology*. Ed. Stephen D. Moore and Mayra Rivera. New York: Fordham University Press, 2010.

_____. "Who/What Is Asian: A Postcolonial Theological Reading of Orientalism and Neo-Orientalism." In *Postcolonial Theologies: Divinity, Hybridity, and Empire*. Ed. Catherine Keller, Michael Nausner, and Mayra Rivera. St. Louis, MO: Chalice Press, 2004.

Kant, Immanuel. *Perpetual Peace and Other Essays on Politics, History, and Morals*. Trans. Ted Humphrey. Indianapolis, Ind., and Cambridge. Mass.: Hackett Publishing Company, 1983.

_____. *Anthropology from a Pragmatic Point of View*. Trans. Victor Lyle Dowdell. 1797; Carbondale: Southern Illinois University, 1996.

_____. *Anthropology, History, and Education*. Ed. Günter Zöller and Robert B. Louden. Trans. Mary Gregor, et al. Cambridge, U.K.: University of Cambridge Press, 2007.

_____. *Grounding for the Metaphysics of Morals: On a Supposed Right to Lie because of Philanthropic Concerns*. Trans. James W. Ellington. Indianapolis, Ind., and Cambridge, Mass.: Hackett Publishing, 1993.

Kaplan, Caren. *Questions of Travel: Postmodern Discourse of Displacement*. Durham: Duke University Press, 1996.

Kearney, Richard. *Dialogues with Contemporary Continental Thinkers*. Manchester: University Press, 1984.

Kearns, Cleo McNelly. "Mary, Maternity, and Abrahamic Hospitality in Derrida's Reading of Massignon." In *Derrida and Religion: Other Testaments*. Ed. Yvonne Sherwood and Kevin Hart. New York: Routledge, 2005.

Keller, Catherine, Michael Nausner, and Mayra Rivera, eds. *Postcolonial Theologies: Divinity and Empire*. St. Louis: Chalice Press, 2004.

Khader, Jamil. "Subaltern Cosmopolitanism: Community and Transnational Mobility in Caribbean Postcolonial Feminist Writings." *Feminist Studies*. Vol. 29. No. 1 (Spring 2003): 63–81.

Kierkegaard, Søren. *Works of Love: Some Christian Reflections in the Form of Discourses*. Trans. Howard and Edna Hong. New York: Harper & Row Publisher, 1964.

King, Henry T. Jr. "Genocide and Nuremberg." In *The Criminal Law of Genocide: International, Comparative and Contextual Aspects*. Ed. Ralph Henham and Paul Behrens (Burlington, VT: Ashgate, 2007.

Kleingeld, Pauline. "Kant's Second Thoughts on Race." *The Philosophical Quarterly*. Vol. 57. No. 229 (October 2007): 573–92.

Kleingeld, Pauline. "Six Varieties of Cosmopolitanism in Late Eighteenth-Century Germany." *Journal of the History of Ideas*. Vol. 60. No. 3 (July 1999): 505–24.

Kristiva, Julia. *Hannah Arendt: Life is a Narrative*. Trans. Frank Collins. Toronto: University of Toronto Press, 2001.

_____. *Strangers to Ourselves.* Trans. L. S. Roudiez. New York: Columbia University Press, 1991.

Kymlicka, Will, ed. *The Rights of Minority Cultures*. Oxford, U.K.: Oxford University Press, 1995.

Kymlicka, Will. *Multicultural Citizenship: A Liberal Theory of Minority Rights*. Oxford, U.K.: Oxford University Press, 1998.

_____. *Contemporary Political Philosophy*. Second Edition. Oxford, U.K.: Oxford University Press, 2002.

_____. *Politics in the Vernacular: Nationalism, Multiculturalism, Citizenship.* New York: Oxford Press, 2001.

______ and Wayne Norman, eds. *Citizenship in Diverse Societies.* New York: Oxford Press, 2000.

Lao Tsu, *Tao Te Ching*. Trans. Gia-fu Feng and Jane English. New York: Vintage Books, 1972.

Lazreg, Marnia, "Feminism and Difference: The Perils of Writing as a Woman on Womenin Algeria," *Feminist Studies.* Vol. 14, No. 1 (Spring 1988): 81–107.

Lee, Kay C. "Confucian Ethics, Judges, and Women: Divorce Under the Revised Korean Family Law," *Pacific Rim Law & Policy Journal*. Vol. 4, No. 2 (1995): 479–503.

Levinas, Emmanuel. *Totality and Infinity: An Essay on Exteriority*. Trans. Alphonso Lingis. 1961; Pittsburgh, PA : Duquesne University Press, 1969.

_____. *Otherwise than Being or Beyond Essence*. Trans. Alphonso Lingis. 1974; Pittsburgh: Duquesne University Press, 1998.

_____. *Entre Nous: On Thinking-of-the-Other*. Trans. Barbara Harshav and Michael B. Smith, New York, NY: Columbia University Press, 2000.

_____. *Difficult Freedom, Essays on Judaism*. Baltimore: The Johns Hopkins University Press, 1990.

_____. *Alterity and Transcendence*. Trans. Michael B. Smith. New York: Columbia University Press, 1999.

_____. *Ethics and Infinity: Conversation with Philippe Nemo*. Trans. R.A Cohen. Pittsburgh, PA: Duquesne University Press, 1985.

_____. *Collected Philosophical Papers*. Trans. Alphonso Lingis. Pittsburgh: Duquesne University Press, 1998.

Levi, Primo. *Survival in Auschwitz: The Nazi Assault on Humanity*. Trans. Stuart Woolf. 1958; New York: Simon & Schuster, 1996.

Llewelyn, John. *Appositions of Jacques Derrida and Emmanuel Levinas*. Bloomington: Indiana University Press, 2002.

Lilla, Mark. "The Politics of Jacques Derrida." *New York Review of Books* 45 (June 1998): 36–42.

Lincoln, Bruce. *Holy Terrors: Thinking about Religion after September 11th*. Chicago: University of Chicago Press, 2003.

Long, A. A. "The Concept of the Cosmopolitan in Greek & Roman Thought." *Daedalus* Summer 2008: 50–58.

_____, ed. *The Cambridge Companion to Early Greek Philosophy*. Cambridge, U.K.: Cambridge University Press, 1999.

Lyotard, Jean-Francois. *The Postmodern Condition: A Report on Knowledge*. Trans. G. Benington and B. Massumi . Minneapolis: University of Minnesota Press, 1984.

Mannheim, Karl. *Ideology and Utopia: An Introduction to Sociology of Knowledge*. Trans. Louis Wirth and Edward Shils. 1927; New York: A Harvest/ HBJ Book, 1985.

Malcomson, Scott, "The Varieties of Cosmopolitan Experience." In *Cosmopolitics: Thinking and Feeling BeyondNation*. Ed. Cheah, Pheng and Bruce Robbins. Minneapolis: University of Minnesota Press, 1998.

Marcus Aurelius, *Meditations*. Trans. Robin Hard. Introduction and Notes by Christopher Gill. London: Wordsworth Classics of World Literature, 1997.

Markus, R. A. *Saeculum: History and Society in the Theology of St. Augustine*. New York: Cambridge University Press, 1970.

Marrus, Michael. *The Nuremberg War Crimes Trial 1945–46: A Documentary History*. Boston: Bedford Books, 1997.

Marty, Martin and R. Scott Appleby, eds. *Religion, Ethnicity, and Self-Identity: Nations in Turmoil*. Salzburg Seminar. Hanover and London: University Press of New England, 1997.

May, J.A. *Kant's Concept of Geography and Its Relation to Recent Geographical Thought*. Toronto: University of Toronto Press, 1970.

Mbembe, Achille. "Necropolitics." *Public Culture*, Winter 2003; 15: 11–40.

_____. *On the Postcolony*. Berkeley and Los Angeles: University of California Press, 2001.

McCarthy, Thomas. "The Politics of the Ineffable." *The Philosophic Forum* 21 (Fall-Winter, 1989-90): 146–68.

McKinnon, Catriona. "Cosmopolitan Hope." In *The Political Philosophy of Cosmopolitanism*. Ed. Gillian Brock and Harry Brighouse. Cambridge, U.K.: Cambridge University Press, 2005.

McLaren, Peter. "White Terror and Oppositional Agency: Towards a Critical Multiculturalism, in *Multiculturalism: A Critical Reader.* Ed. David Theo Goldberg. Oxford, U.K., and Cambridge, Mass.: Blackwell, 1994.

McQuillan, Martin, ed. *Deconstruction: A Reader*. Edinburgh: Edinburgh University Press, 2000.

Mead, George Herbert. *Mind, Self, and Society*. Chicago: University of Chicago Press, 1934.

Mignolo, Walter. *Local Histories/Global Designs: Coloniality, Subaltern Knowledge and Border Thinking.* Princeton: Princeton University Press, 2000.

_____. *The Darker Side of the Renaissance: Literacy, Territoriality, and Colonization.* 2nd edition. 1995; Ann Arbor, MI: The University of Michigan Press, 2003.

_____. "The Many Faces of Cosmo-polis: Border Thinking and Critical Cosmopolitanism," *Public Culture*. Vol. 11. No 3 (Fall 2000): 721–48.

_____. "The Splendors and Miseries of 'Science': Coloniality, Geopolitics of Knowledge and Epistemic Pluriversality." In *Cognitive Justice in a Global World*. Ed. Boaventura de Sousa Santos. Lexington Books, 2007.

_____. "Editor's Introduction." *Poetics Today*. Vol. 15. No. 4. Loci of Enunciation and Imaginary Construction: The Case of (Latin) America. 1 (Winter 1994): 505–21.

Moeller, Hans-Georg . "The "Exotic" Nietzsche—East and West. *Journal of Nietzsche Studies*. No. 28 (AUTUMN 2004): 57–69.

Mohanty, Chandra Talpade. *Feminism Without Border: Decolonizing Theory, Practicing Solidarity*. Durham: Duke University Press, 2003.

_____. "Women Workers and Capitalist Scripts: Ideologies of Dominion, Common Interests, and the Politics of Solidarity." In *Feminist Genealogies, Colonial Legacies, Democratic Futures*. Ed. M. Jacqui Alexander and Chandra Talpade Mohanty. New York: Routledge, 1997.

_____. "On Race and Voice: Challenges for Liberal Education in the 1990s." *Cultural Critique* No. 14 (Winter 1989): 179–208.

Mohanty, Chandra Talpade, Ann Russo, and Lourdes Torres, eds. *Third World Women and the Politics of Feminism*. Bloomington and Indianapolis: Indiana University Press, 1991.

Moles, John. "Cynic Cosmopolitanism." In *The Cynics: The Cynic Movement in Antiquity and Its Legacy.* Ed. R. Bracht Branham and Marie-Odile Goulet-Caze, Berkeley: University of California Press, 1996.

Moltmann, Juergen. *God for a Secular Society.* London: SCM Press, 1999.

Moore, Stephen D. and Mayra Rivera, eds. *Planetary Loves: Spivak, Postcoloniality, and Theology.* New York: Fordham University Press, 2011.

Moraga, Cherrie and Gloria Anzaldua, eds. *This Bridge Called My Back: Writings by Radical Women of Color.* New York: Kitchen Table/ Women of Color Press, 1983.

Morgan, Michael L., ed. *A Holocaust Reader: Responses to the Nazi Extermination.* Oxford, U.K.: Oxford University Press, 2001.

Mouffe, Chantal. "Radical Democracy: Modern or Postmodern?" in *Universal Abandon?: The Politics of Postmodernism.* Ed. A. Ross. Minneapolis: University of Minnesota Press, 1988.

_____. "Feminism, Citizenship, and Radical Democratic Politics."In *Feminists Theorize the Political.* Ed. Judith Butler and Joan W. Scott .New York: Routledge, 1992.

Moya, Paula M. "Postmodernism, "Realism," and the Politics of Identity: Cherrie Moraga and Chicana Feminism." In *Feminist Genealogies, Colonial Legacies, Democratic Futures.* Ed. M. Jacqui Alexander and Chandra Talpade Mohanty. New York: Routledge, 1997.

Murray, John C. *Religious Liberty: Catholic Struggle with Pluralism.* Ed. J. Leon Hooper. Louisville, Kentucky: Westminster/John Knox, 1993.

Nancy, Jean-Luc. *Being Singular Plural.* Trans. Robert D. Richardson and Anne E. O'Byrne. 1996; Stanford: Stanford University Press, 2000.

_____. *The Inoperative Community.* Ed. Peter Connor. Trans. Peter Connor, Lisa Garbus, Michael Holland and Simona Sawhney. Minneapolis: University of Minnesota Press, 1991.

Narayan, Uma. *Dislocating Cultures: Identities, Traditions, and Third World Feminism.* New York: Routledge, 1997.

Nass, Michael. "'Alors, qui êtes-vous?' Jacques Derrida and the Question of Hospitality."*SubStance.* Vol. 34. No. 1, Issue 106 (2005): 6–17.

Nicholson, Linda and Steven Seidman, eds. *Social Postmodernism: Beyond IdentityPolitics.* Cambridge, U.K.: Cambridge University Press, 1995.

Nietzsche, Friedrich. *Ecce Homo.* In *Basic Writings of Nietzsche.* Trans. and ed. Walter Kaufmann. New York: The Modern Library, 1972.

_____. *The Anti-Christ.* Translated and with an Introduction by H. L. Mencken.Tucson, AZ: See Sharp Press, 1999.

_____. "On Love of the Neighbor." In *Thus Spoke Zarathustra: A Book for None or All.* Trans. Walter Kaufmann. New York: Penguin, 1966.

Novitz, David. "The Rage for Deconstruction." *The Monist* 69 (1986): 39–55.

Nowicka, Magdalena and Maria Rovisco, eds. *Cosmopolitanism in Practice*. Burlington, VT: Ashgate, 2009.

Nussbaum, Martha. *Frontiers of Justice: Disability, Nationality, Specific Membership*. The Tanner Lectures on Human Values. 2006; Cambridge, Mass.: The Belknap Press of Harvard University Press, 2007.

_____. "Beyond the Social Contract: Capabilities and Global Justice." In *The Political Philosophy of Cosmopolitanism*. Ed. Gillian Brock and Harry Brighouse. Cambridge, U.K.: Cambridge University Press, 2005.

_____. *Women and Human Development: The Capabilities Approach*. Cambridge, U.K.: Cambridge University Press, 2000.

_____. *Poetic Justice: The Literary Imagination and Public Life*. Boston: Beacon Press, 1995.

_____. Love's Knowledge: Essays on Philosophy and Literature. New York, N.Y., and Oxford, U.K.: Oxford University Press, 1990.

_____. "Kant and Cosmopolitanism." In *Perpetual Peace: Essays on Kant's Cosmopolitan Ideal*. Ed. James Bohman and Matthias Lutz-Backmann. Cambridge, Mass.: The MIT Press, 1997.

_____. "Patriotism and Cosmopolitanism." In Martha C. Nussbaum with Respondents. *For Love of Country: Debating the Limits of Patriotism*. Ed. Joshua Cohen. Cambridge, Mass.: Beacon Press, 1996.

_____. "Patriotism and Cosmopolitanism." *Boston Review*. 19. 5(1994): 3–34.

Nyers, Peter. "Abject Cosmopolitanism: The Politics of Protection in the Anti-Deportation Movement." *Third World Quarterly*. Vol. 24. No. 6 (December 2003): 1069–93.

Parekh, Bhikhu. *Rethinking Multiculturalism: Cultural Diversity and Political Theory*. Cambridge, Mass.: Harvard University Press, 2002.

Peperzak, Adriaan T. *Beyond: The Philosophy of Emmanuel Levinas*. Evanston, Ill.: Northwestern University Press, 1997.

_____. *To the Other: An Introduction to the Philosophy of Emmanuel Levinas*. West Lafayette, IN: Purdue University Press, 1993.

Pitte, Frederick P. Van De. *Kant as Philosophical Anthropologist*. Hague, Netherlands: Martinus Nijhoff, 1971.

Pogge, Thomas W. *World Poverty and Human Rights: Cosmopolitan Responsibilities and Reforms*. Cambridge, U.K.: Polity, 2002.

_____, ed. *Global Justice*. Oxford, U.K.: Blackwell Publisher, 2001.

Pollock, Sheldon, Homi K. Bhabha, Carol A. Breckenridge. "Cosmopolitanisms." *Public Culture*. Vol. 12. No 3 (Fall 2000): 577–90.

Powell, Jason E. *Jacques Derrida: A Biography* . London: Continuum, 2006.

Prodromou, Elizabeth H. "U.S Foreign Policy and Global Religious Pluralism," in *Religious Pluralism: Globalization, and World Politics*, ed. Thomas Babchoff. Oxford, U.K.: Oxford University Press, 2008.

Quaintance, Mary and Rosenfeld Calson, eds. *Deconstruction and the Possibility of Justice*. New York: Routledge, 1992.

Rabinow, Paul. "Representations Are Social Facts: Modernity and Post-Modernity in Anthropology." In *Writing Culture: The Poetics of Ethnography*. Ed. James Clifford and George E. Marcus. Berkeley: University of California Press, 1986.

Radhakrishnan, R. *Diasporic Mediations: Between Home and Location*. Minneapolis: University of Minnesota Press, 1996.

_____. *Theory in an Uneven World*. Malden, MA: Blackwell Publishing, 2003.

Razack, Sherene. *Looking White People in the Eye: Gender, Race, and Culture in Courtrooms and Classrooms*. Toronto: University of Toronto Press, 1998.

Ricoeur, Paul. *Lectures on Ideology and Utopia*. Ed. George H. Taylor. New York: Columbia University Press, 1986.

Robertson, Geoffrey. *Crime against Humanity: The Struggle for Global Justice*. 3rd Edition. 1999; New York: New Press, 2007.

Robbins, Bruce. "Introduction Part I: Actually Existing Cosmopolitanism." In Pheng Cheah and Bruce Robbins, eds. *Cosmopolitics: Thinking and Feeling Beyond Nation*. Minneapolis: University of Minnesota Press, 1998.

Roof, Clark W. The Local-Cosmopolitan Orientation and Traditional Religious Commitment. Sociological Analysis. Vol. 33. No. 1 (Spring 1972): 1–15.

Rorty, Richard. "Anticlericalism and Atheism." In Richard Rorty and Gianni Vattimo, *Future of Religion*. Ed. Santiago Zabala. New York: Columbia University Press, 2005.

Rosello, Mireille. *Postcolonial Hospitality: The Immigrant as Guest*. Stanford, Calif.: Stanford University Press, 2001.

Rosen, Stanley. *Hermeneutics as Politics*. New York: Oxford University Press, 1987.

Rosenzweig, Franz. *The Star of Redemption*. Trans. William W. Hallo. Notre Dame, Ind.: University of Notre Dame Press, 1985.

Rushdie, Salman. *Imaginary Homelands: Essays and Criticism, 1981–1991*. London: Granta Books, 1991.

Said, Edward W. *Culture and Imperialism*. 1993; New York: Vintage Books, 1994.

_____. *Orientalism*. 1978; New York: Vintage Books, 1994.

_____. *Out of Place: A Memoir*. New York: Knopf, 1999.

_____. *The World, The Text and the Critic.* Cambridge, Mass.: Harvard University Press, 1984.

Scheffler, Samuel. *Boundaries and Allegiances: Problems of Justice and Responsibility in Liberal Thought*. Oxford, U.K.: Oxford University Press, 2001.

_____. "Conceptions of Cosmopolitanism." *Utilitas.* Vol. 11. No. 3 (November 1999): 255–76.

_____. "Relationships and Responsibilities." *Philosophy and Public Affairs*. 26. 3 (Summer 1997): 189–209.

Shelby, Tommie and Paul Gilroy. "Cosmopolitanism, Blackness, and Utopia." *Transition*. No. 98 (2008):116–35.

Schinkel, Willem. "Illegal Aliens and the State, or: Bare Bodies vs the Zombie,". *International Sociology*. Vol. 24. No. 6 (Nov 2009): 779–806.

Schofield, Malcolm. *The Stoic Idea of the City*. Chicago: University of Chicago Press, 1999.

Sedwick, Peter R., ed. *Nietzsche: A Critical Reader*. Oxford, U.K.: Blackwell, 1995.

Sherwood, Yvonne, ed. *Derrida's Bible (Reading a Page of Scripture with a Little Help from Derrida)*. New York: Palgrave Macmillan, 2004.

Sherwood, Yvonne and Kevin Hart, eds. *Derrida and Religion: Other Testaments*. New York: Routledge, 2005.

Shohat, Ella. "Post-Third-Worldist Culture: Gender, Nation, and the Cinema. In *Feminist Genealogies, Colonial Legacies, Democratic Futures*. Ed. M. Jacqui Alexander and Chandra Talpade Mohanty. New York: Routledge, 1997.

Smith, James Bruce. *Politics and Remembrance*. Princeton: Princeton University Press,1985.

Smith, James K. A. *Jacques Derrida: Live Theory*. New York: Continuum, 2005.

Spelman, Elizabeth V. *Inessential Woman: Problems of Exclusion in Feminist Thought*. Boston: Beacon Press, 1988.

Spivak, Gayatri Chakravorty. *A Critique of Postcolonial Reason: Toward a History of the Vanishing Present.* Cambridge, Mass.: Harvard University Press, 1999.

_____. *The Spivak Reader*, Ed. Donna Landry and Gerald Maclean. New York and London: Routledge, 1996.

_____. *Outside in the Teaching Machine*. New York and London: Routledge, 1993.

_____. "French Feminism Revisited: Ethics and Politics." In *Feminists Theorize the Political.* Ed. Judith Butler and Joan W. Scott .New York: Routledge, 1992.

_____. *The Postcolonial Critic: Interviews, Strategies, Dialogues*. Ed. Sarah Harasym. New York & London: Routledge, 1990.

_____. *In Other Worlds: Essays in Cultural Politics*. New York: Routledge, 1988.

_____. "Can Subaltern Speak?" In *Marxism and the Interpretation of Culture*. Ed. Cary Nelson and Lawrence Grossberg (Urbana and Chicago: University of Illinois Press, 1988.

_____. *Death of Discipline*. New York: Columbia University Press, 2005.

Spurr, David. *The Rhetoric of Empire: Colonial Discourse in Journalism, Travel Writing, and Imperial Administration*. Durham & London: Duke University Press, 1993.

Stone, Dan. "Rafael Lemkin on the Holocaust." *Journal of Genocide Research*. 7.4 (December 2005): 539–50.

Storrar, William and Andrew Morton, eds. *Public Theology for the 21st Century*. London & New York: T & T Clark, 2004.

Sykes, Stephen. *Power and Christian Theology*. London: Continum, 2006.

Tan, Kok-Chor. *Justice without Borders: Cosmopolitanism, Nationalism, and Patriotism*. Cambridge, U.K.: Cambridge University Press, 2004.

_____. "The Demand of Justice and National Allegiances." In *The Political Philosophy of Cosmopolitanism*. Ed. Gillian Brock and Harry Brighouse. Cambridge, U.K.: Cambridge University Press, 2005.

Taylor, Charles, Amy Gutmann, Stephen Rockefeller, Michael Walzer, and Susan Wolf. *Multiculturalism and the 'Politics of Recognition.'* Edited and introduced by Amy Gutmann. Princeton, NJ: Princeton University Press, 1994.

Taylor, Charles, "Politics of Recognition." In *Multiculturalism: Examining the Politics of Recognition*. Ed. Charles Taylor and Amy Gutmann.

Theodossopoulos, Dimitrios and Elisabeth Kirtsoglou, eds. *United in Discontent: Local Responses to Cosmopolitanism and Globalization*. Berghahn Books, 2010.

Thiele, Leslie Paul. *Timely Meditations: Martin Heidegger and Postmodern Politics*. Princeton: Princeton University Press, 1995.

Thomas, Owen C. "Religious Plurality and Contemporary Philosophy: A Critical Survey."*The Harvard Theological Review*. Vol. 87. No. 2 (April 1994): 197–213.

Toulmin, Stephen. *Cosmopolis: The Hidden Agenda of Modernity*. New York: Free Press, 1990.

Touillot, Michel-Rolph. *Silencing the Past: Power and the Production of History*. Boston: Beacon Press, 1995.

Trinh T. Minh-ha. *Woman, Native, Other: Writing Postcoloniality and Feminism*. Bloomington: Indiana University Press, 1989.

United Nations Development Programme. *Human Development Report 2010, The Real Wealth of Nations: Pathways to Human Development.* 20th Anniversary Edition . New York: Palgrave Macmillan, 2010.

_____. *Sustainability and Equity: A Better Future for All.* Human Development Report 2011. New York: Palgrave Macmillan, 2011.

_____. *The Real Wealth of Nations: Pathways to Human Development.* Human Development Report 2010. 20th Anniversary Edition. New York: Palgrave Macmillan, 2010.

Vanhoozer, Kevin J, ed. *The Cambridge Companion to Postmodern Theology*. Cambridge, U.K.: Cambridge University Press, 2003.

Vattimo, Gianni. *After Christianity*. New York: Columbia University, 2002.

Vertovec, Steven and Robin Cohen, eds, *Conceiving Cosmopolitanism: Theory, Context, and Practice.* Oxford, U.K.: Oxford University Press, 2002.

Vila, Dana, ed. *The Cambridge Companion to Hannah Arendt.* Cambridge, U.K.: Cambridge University Press, 2000.

Waldron, Jeremy. "Minority Cultures and the Cosmopolitan Alternatives." *The Rights of Minority Cultures*. Ed. Will Kymlicka. Oxford, U.K.: Oxford University Press, 1995.

Waldenfels, Bernhard. "Levinas and the Face of the Other." In *The Cambridge Companion to Levinas*. Ed. Simon Critchley and Robert Bernasconi. Cambridge, U.K.: Cambridge University Press, 2002.

Weber, Samuel. "Toward a Politics of Singularity: Protection and Projection." in *Religion: Beyond a Concept*. Ed. Hent de Vries. New York: Fordham University Press, 2008.

Welch, Sharon. *After Empire: The Art and Ethos of Enduring Peace*. Minneapolis: Fortress Press, 2004.

Werbner, Pnina. "Global Pathways: Working Class Cosmopolitans and the Creation of Transnational Ethnic Worlds." *Social Anthropology*. Vol. 7. No. 1 (1999): 17–35.

West, Cornel. "The New Cultural Politics of Difference." *Out There: Marginalization and Contemporary Culture*. Ed. Russell Ferguson, Martha Gever, Trinh Minh–ha, and Cornel West. New York and Boston: New Museum of Contemporary Art and MIT Press, 1990.

Westmoreland, Mark W. "Interruptions: Derrida and Hospitality." *Kritike*. Vol. 2. No. 1 (June 2008): 1–10.

White, Stephen K. *Political Theory and Postmodernism*. Cambridge, U.K.: Cambridge University Press, 1991.

Wilson, Holly L. *Kant's Pragmatic Anthropology: Its Origin, Meaning, and Critical Significance*. Albany: SUNY Press, 2006.

Wittgenstein, Ludwig. *Culture and Value*. Ed. G. H. von Wright and Heikki

Nyman. Trans. Peter Winch. Chicago: University of Chicago Press, 1980.

Wood, David, ed. *Derrida: A Critical Reader.* Cambridge, U.K.: Blackwell, 1992.

Woodward, Bob. *Bush at War*. New York: Simon and Schuster, 2002.

Wurgaft, Benjamin Aldes. "Starbucks and Rootless Cosmopolitanism." *The Journal of Good and Culture*. Vol. 3. No. 4 (Fall 2003): 71–75.

Yang, Hyunah. "Vision of Postcolonial Feminist Jurisprudence in Korea: Seen from the 'Family-Head System' in Family Law," *Journal of Korean Law*, vol. 5, no. 2 (2006): 12–28.

Yegenoglu, Meyda. *Colonial Fantasies: Towards a Feminist Reading of Orientalism*. Cambridge, U.K.: Cambridge University Press, 1998.

Yeh, Michelle. "Deconstructive Way: A Comparative Study of Derrida and Chuang Tzu." *Journal of Chinese Philosophy*. 10 (1983): 95–126.

Young-Bruehl, Elizabeth. *Hannah Arendt: For the Love of the World*. New Haven and London: Yale University Press, 1982.

Zizek, Slavoj. *The Puppet and the Dwarf: The Perverse Core of Christianity*. Cambridge, Mass.: MIT Press, 2003.

_____. "Neighbors and Other Monsters: A Plea for Ethical Violence," In *The Neighbor: Three Inquiries in Political Theology*. Ed. Slavoj Zizek, Eric L. Santner, and Kenneth Reinhard. Chicago and London: The University of Chicago Press, 2005.

_____. "From Homo Sacer to the Neighbor," in *Welcome to the Desert of the Real*. London and New York: Verso, 2002.

Zuckert, Catherine. "The Politics of Derridean Deconstruction." *Polity* 23 (Spring 1991): 335–56.

Index

C

D

E

H

M

N

O

P

S

T

U